Global Security in
the Twenty-first Century

Global Security in the Twenty-first Century

The Quest for Power and the Search for Peace

Sean Kay

ROWMAN & LITTLEFIELD PUBLISHERS, INC.
Lanham • Boulder • New York • Toronto • Oxford

ROWMAN & LITTLEFIELD PUBLISHERS, INC.

Published in the United States of America
by Rowman & Littlefield Publishers, Inc.
A wholly owned subsidiary of The Rowman & Littlefield Publishing Group, Inc.
4501 Forbes Boulevard, Suite 200, Lanham, Maryland 20706
www.rowmanlittlefield.com

P.O. Box 317, Oxford OX2 9RU, UK

British Library Cataloguing in Publication Information Available

Library of Congress Cataloging-in-Publication Data

Kay, Sean, 1967–
    Global security in the twenty-first century : the quest for power and the search for
peace / Sean Kay.
        p. cm.
    Includes bibliographical references and index.
    ISBN-13: 978-0-7425-3766-8 (cloth : alk. paper)
    ISBN-10: 0-7425-3766-8 (cloth : alk. paper)
    ISBN-13: 978-0-7425-3767-5 (pbk. : alk. paper)
    ISBN-10: 0-7425-3767-6 (pbk. : alk. paper)
    1. Security, International.   2. Peace.   I. Title.
    JZ5588.K39 2006
    355'.033—dc22   2005030128

Printed in the United States of America

♾ ™ The paper used in this publication meets the minimum requirements of American
National Standard for Information Sciences—Permanence of Paper for Printed Library
Materials, ANSI/NISO Z39.48-1992.

Contents

Preface

Just after finishing a draft of this book in summer 2005, I traveled to Europe to give a number of presentations based on the research. Thinking back on the range of issues I had engaged in—from nuclear war to disease, from terrorism to nanotechnology, I sat in Ireland—per capita one of the most globalized economies in the world. In previous generations, the quest for security had sent Irish families scurrying around the globe in search of relief from famine and in a quest for a better future. Now, this country with so much rich history had been radically transformed as economic development had wiped away decades of economic and security challenges. Long an island associated with conflict and terrorism in its north, my family and I were able to witness announcements that the Irish Republican Army was abandoning violence, decommissioning, and pursuing a purely political future. Meanwhile, I could sit in Howth, near Dublin, and watch a live satellite feed of the Live 8 concerts held in London and other major cities of the world. People and musicians from around the world successfully raised awareness of the need for debt relief and economic assistance thus illustrating the core theme of this book—that power remains the defining variable in international security—but that the forms through which power is manifested have been radically transformed. At the same time, the leaders of the G-8 leading industrial powers began their meetings in Scotland to produce a package of economic engagement with the underdeveloped world—under the watchful eye and pressure of Bob Geldoff, Bono, and the millions of politically engaged people whom they represented.

On the 4th of July, my daughter and I traveled to the United Kingdom where I gave a speech at the British Royal Defence Academy on asymmetrical warfighting. Driving two days later to Oxford we delighted in the awarding of the 2012 Olympics to London. The joy on the faces of London, however, would turn within twenty-four hours to shock and horror at barbaric terrorist attacks. The morning of July 7 we set out by train into Piccadilly en route via the Tube to our hotel at Russell Square when bombs hit London—killing over fifty civilians in a barbaric terrorist attack. It took two years to write this book—but it seemed in those few days that the entire story was being played out in front of our eyes.

My daughter and I were never in any direct danger on the trains that morning. But, like thousands of others, a matter of a few minutes here or there, and we would have been in the thick of it. Being in the relative proximity of a major terrorist attack put the dynamics of this book into a new perspective, but still the basic strategic analysis remained. At times in the writing, and reading, of this book the issues could seem overwhelming. The continued danger of great power war, major regional conflicts, the role of new technologies, genocide and terrorism, human security, and the environment all combine to show that we are in for challenging days in the decades to come. Surprisingly, I finished this book with far more idealism and optimism than I would have imagined. All of these security threats have solutions if people are willing to engage them and seek creative approaches. As the final chapter shows, education is perhaps the central strategic asset in the twenty-first century. Education will help promote awareness as both the scope of threats and potential solutions can be better understood. It is my hope to make a small contribution through this book to promote a conceptual starting point for thinking about the nature of global security.

As a student of international security, I have been extremely fortunate to be influenced by a range of outstanding scholars. I owe a particular debt to Robert A. Pape who has served to both challenge and inspire me to persevere in the field and to make what best contributions I can either in the policy or the scholarly world. During my days as a student, I was heavily influenced by a number of world-class scholars whom I am proud to consider friends today including Boleslaw Bozcek, Robert W. Clawson, Georges Delcoigne, James Der Derian, Eric S. Einhorn, Peter M. Haas, Lawrence S. Kaplan, John Logue, Victor Papacosma, Bruce Parrott, M. J. Peterson, Mark Rubin, and Karl Ryavec. Many individuals over the years have served as crucial colleagues for exchanging policy and scholarly ideas that have challenged me to refine and sharpen my analysis. Some gave direct assistance with ideas in this book—though all responsibility for the content, of course, is mine. I owe a very special debt to my close friends and colleagues Lawrence Chalmer, Andrew Michta, Jeffrey Simon, and especially Joshua Spero. I am also very grateful to a range of colleagues, mentors, and security professionals who have helped out in some form over the years including Andres Mejia Acosta, Ron Asmus, Charles Barry, Hans Binnedijk, Ian Brzezinski, Richard Caplan, Derek Chollet, Wesley Clark,

Christopher Coker, Richard Combs, Andrew Cottey, Patrick Cronin, Peter Dauvergne, Chris Donnelly, Bill Drennan, Mark Dubois, Michael Dziedzic, Susan Eisenhower, Paul Evans, Stephen Flanagan, Robert Gilpin, James Goldgeier, Peter Hays, Richard Herrmann, Theresa Hitchens, Brian Job, Karl Kaltenthaler, David Kang, Stuart Kaufman, Robert O. Keohane, Charles Kupchan, Richard Ned Lebow, Charles Lipson, S. Neil MacFarlane, Andy Mack, John J. Mearsheimer, Michael McFaul, Jennifer Mitzen, Cameron Munter, Daniel Nelson, John Owen, Vernon Penner, Therese Raphael, Allen Sens, Simon Serfaty, Jamie Shea, Peter Singer, Stanley Sloan, James Sperling, Kristina Spohr-Readman, Jessica Stern, Jeremy Strozer, Elizabeth Sullivan, Strobe Talbott, Ron Tiersky, Alexander Vershbow, Stephen Walt, Alexander Wendt, Fred Williams, Jody Williams, Phil Williams, Donald Winkleman, Judith Yaphe, Mark Zacher, and Anthony Zinni.

As a professor, I am privileged to work at one of the nation's top liberal arts institutions—Ohio Wesleyan University. The greatest treasure at such institutions is the students from whom I learn as much as I teach. I am grateful to all I've engaged with in and out of the classroom and the following in particular were both helpful and supportive in shaping the thinking that went into this book: Scott Augenbaugh, Sarah Badgerow, Calina Bowman, Dana Bucin, Ahsan Butt, Donald Chambers, Anita Chandrasekhar, Ali Chaudry, Joey Cohen, Louise Cooley, Erin Donnally, Alison Drake, Janeane Fazio, Nathaniel Fick, Kemi George, James Glanville, Kristen Hajduk, Ben Hill, Daniel Hlavin, Tiffany Hrabusa, Marija Ignatovic, Mary Kinney, Harris Lali, Steele Means, Sam Moore, Emily Munoz, Farooq Nomani, Chris Ploszaj, Nadir Pracha, Alison Reikert, P.J. Roberts, Jill Schoenblum, Monika Serowka, Danish Shafi, Tim Stanos, Kristen Vasan, Annie Yea, and Sadaf Zahid.

At Ohio Wesleyan, I am particularly indebted to William Louthan and Richard Fusch who provided both time and support for primary research on this book. More than that, they have served as role models for me as a professor and person. I am also especially indebted to Corrine Lyman who founded the International Studies program at Ohio Wesleyan University and serves today as mentor and friend. Also in the Department of Politics and Government, I am very fortunate to have as colleagues and friends Craig Ramsay, Carl Pinkele, Joan McLean, Michael Esler, and James Franklin. Additional colleagues and friends at Ohio Wesleyan have also provided outstanding support and advice including Jeremy Baskes, John Boos, Scott Calef, David Caplan, Ted Cohen, John Delaney, Kay Ebel, Michael Flamm, Norm Gharrity, Mark Gingrich, Bob Gitter, Robert Harmon, Mary Howard, Helmut Kremling, Akbar Madhi, Louise Musser, Jim Peoples, Jon Powers, Jan Smith, Dale Swartzentruber, Dan Vogt, and George Wallace. I am also very fortunate to have benefited from administrative support from Pam Besel, Paul Burnam,

Karen McNeil, Mary Lou Shannon, and Alice Winters. My research assistant Sahar Khan played a crucial role in helping to see this project through to completion. Ms. Khan provided the crucial perspective of a student but also the keen eye of a professional who will play a major role in international relations in the years to come. Finally, words alone could not express how grateful I am to work with Pam Laucher—one could find no better administrative assistant and no better person. At Rowman and Littlefield, I am especially grateful for the encouragement, patience, and professionalism of Susan McEachern, Sarah Wood, Carol Bifulco, and Dawn Anderson. Closer to home, key friends Jim Breece, Damien Crim, Don Gliebe, Joanne Meyer, David Pengra, Heather Prindle, Tim Prindle, Michael Tucci, and Adam Vaughn helped keep me pleasantly engaged with life outside writing a book!

My family is the bedrock of my work and life. Earle B. Kay, James Grimes, Anne Grimes, Matt Madigan, and Anna Madigan all have stimulated a desire to learn and always strive for the best. My parents, David and Jenni Kay, have been more supportive and encouraging than words can say. I am very lucky to have a large extended family in Ireland who has welcomed me into their community. I am especially grateful to Des and Mary Mullan and Gerry and Orlagh Lyons and their wonderful families—both in-laws and great friends. Finally, my wife Anna-Marie and our three daughters Cria, Siobhan, and Alana are the true inspiration for this book. They have provided me with the love—and patience—necessary to get it done. I could not have done it without them. But more importantly it is for them, and their generations, that one most hopes to understand the quest for power and the search for peace. This book is thus dedicated with love and appreciation to my wife and children.

Sean Kay
Delaware, Ohio, December 2005

I hope our wisdom will grow with our power, and teach us, that the less we use our power the greater it will be.

—Thomas Jefferson (1743–1826), U.S. president, Letter, June 12, 1815

I like to believe that people in the long run are going to do more to promote peace than our governments. Indeed, I think that people want peace so much that one of these days governments had better get out of the way and let them have it.

—Dwight D. Eisenhower (1890–1969), U.S. president, August 31, 1959

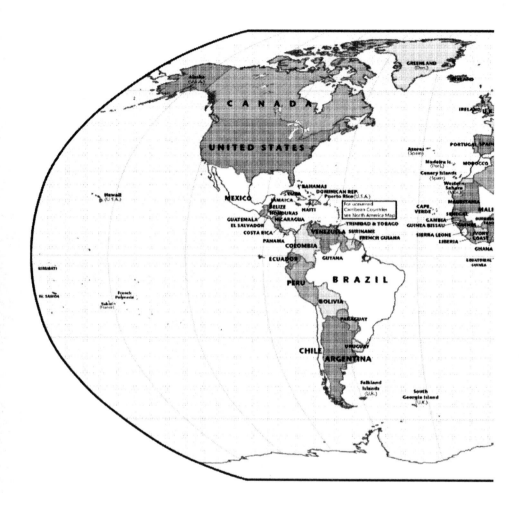

The World in the Early Twenty-first Century

RUSSIAN FEDERATION

KAZAKSTAN

MONGOLIA

PEOPLE'S REPUBLIC OF CHINA

JAPAN

D.P.R.K.
REP. of KOREA

TAIWAN
(Rep. of China)

INDIA

SAUDI ARABIA

EGYPT

IRAN

PAKISTAN

TURKEY

ALGERIA   LIBYA

NIGER   CHAD   SUDAN

NIGERIA

ETHIOPIA

DJIBOUTI

SRI LANKA

BANGLA-
DESH

MYANMAR

LAOS

VIETNAM

THAILAND

CAMBODIA

PHILIPPINES

MALAYSIA

BRUNEI

SINGAPORE

MICRONESIA

MARSHALL
ISLAND

NAURU

CENTRAL
AFRICAN
REPUBLIC

TOGO

CAMEROON

RWANDA   UGANDA

KENYA

DEM. REP.
OF THE
CONGO

TANZANIA

BURUNDI

ANGOLA

ZAMBIA

MALAWI

NAMIBIA

ZIMBABWE

BOTSWANA

MADAGASCAR

MOZAMBIQUE

SWAZILAND

SOUTH
AFRICA

LESOTHO

SEYCHELLES

COMOROS

MAURITIUS
(France)

INDONESIA

E. Timor

PAPUA
NEW GUINEA

SOLOMON
ISLANDS

TUVALU

AUSTRALIA

VANUATU

New
Caledonia
(France)

FIJI

NEW ZEALAND

Abbreviations:			
ALB.	Albania	LITH.	Lithuania
BELG.	Belgium	LUX.	Luxembourg
BOS.	Bosnia & Herzegovina	MAC.	Macedonia
CR.	Croatia	MOL.	Moldova
CZECH.	Czech Republic	NETH.	Netherlands
DEN.	Denmark	PORT.	Portugal
D.P.R.K.	Democratic People's	SER.	Serbia & Montenegro
	Republic of Korea	SL.	Slovenia
HUN.	Hungary	SLOV.	Slovakia
GER.	Germany	U.A.E.	United Arab Emirates
LAT.	Latvia	U.K.	United Kingdom

Chapter One

The Dynamics of Global Security

Post-Katrina relief: Search and rescue crew members from Helicopter Sea Combat Squadron 28 observe a rescue in progress along the Louisiana coast, August 2005. *Source*: U.S. Navy. Photo by Photographer's Mate Airman Jeremy L. Grisham.

S ecurity is the absence of a threat to the stability of the international system, to countries, or to individuals. Until recently, thinking about security has emphasized the nation-state and competition for power in the international system. In the twenty-first century, this traditional focus on the nation-state and power remains central. However, major transformations within the international system demand a broader understanding of the sources of both security and insecurity. The quest for power and the search for peace have become global as great power interests coexist uneasily with risks of major regional conflict. A multitude of new challenges are posed by technology and trade, asymmetrical threats such as genocide and terrorism, issues affecting human security, and environmental and energy concerns. This book examines the evolving global dimensions of security, surveys the major conceptual frameworks for understanding the quest for power and the search for peace, and provides detailed strategic assessments of major security challenges at the dawn of the twenty-first century. The book concludes with an assessment of the relationship between conceptual frameworks and policy practice to make the quest for power and the search for peace one and the same.

THE GLOBALIZATION OF SECURITY

Terrorist attacks on the United States on September 11, 2001, introduced many Americans to a new sense of danger. The nature of the attacks was particularly troubling because they illustrated three new elements of global security. First, the nation-state as a protective barrier to ward off threats was no longer as strong as many people had presumed. Second, modern technology that people rely on for global access—in this case, the airplane—was the weapon. Third, the attackers were linked through a network of global relationships stretching from the United States to Europe and the Middle East, commencing in Afghanistan. This attack was symbolic of a new kind of war in which the pathways of globalization were the means through which power was channeled. The expanded opportunity for power to serve both conflict and peace represents perhaps the most fundamental challenge for international relations in the twenty-first century. Will globalization provide new capacities for war, threats, and danger? Or, will globalization facilitate new and innovative paths to peace?

Globalization's central component is interdependence, which is accelerated by advanced technology, trade, political relationships, transboundary communication, and movement of people, goods, and services. Interdependence also implies interconnectedness; it is almost impossible for a state to be completely isolated from events occurring elsewhere in the world.[1] This process includes an enormous reduction of transportation costs and accelerated communication while breaking down artificial barriers to the flows of goods, services, capital, knowledge, and people across borders.[2] Globalization allows new forms of interactions that alter the nature of power in the international system and globalize security in four ways. First, major countries in the international system continue to reflect the relative distribution of global power. The United States, Russia, China, and the European Union reflect a hierarchy of military capabilities in the international system. Second, the expansion of trade, travel, communications, and other manifestations of the integrated global economy create new channels for exercising power outside the nation-state. Third, globalization can rapidly turn local problems into major international challenges which impact regional and global security. Fourth, the processes of globalization increase the complexity and the reach of international anarchy, creating fear in some cases, and stimulating demands for creative problem-solving. Because there is no global government, globalization remains an unregulated phenomenon.

International security experts have been pointing to the rise of global security challenges for some time. In 1952, Arnold Wolfers introduced debate over the larger meaning of national security beyond the defense of territory.[3] In 1977, Lester Brown introduced global assessments of environmental and energy challenges, arguing that national security included these dimensions as well as military issues.[4] In 1983, Barry Buzan framed the meaning of security as including military, social, economic, political, and environmental dimensions.[5] In 2000, Graham Allison identified the security consequences of globalization as: technology that helps with military targeting of weapons, advances in technologies of weapons of mass destruction, the erosion of the dominant role of the nation-state, "CNNization" which allows citizens to watch wars in their living rooms, global networks in communication and trade, global networks that create incentives among elites to coordinate policy to create predictability, and the prominent role of non-state actors that impact international outcomes. Crucially, globalization heightens new security priorities such as illegal drug trade, terrorism, disease, smuggling, and organized crime.[6]

Globalization dynamics have had a major impact on the security dilemma. The traditional security dilemma focused analytical attention onto the degree to which an effort by one state to increase its security might be perceived as a threat by another state. Globalization forces a more expansive understanding of the security dilemma because of the number of issues with security implications. For example, China would see globalization as a tool for increasing its national economic power—which reflects an increase in security. As China's strength grows, the standard of living for its citizens will grow. Subsequently, China's energy consumption will increase dramatically with local, regional, and global effects on the environment. Meanwhile, as China integrates into the global economic system, its leadership faces a significant dilemma. Global information flows can lead to increasing pressure on China's communist leadership to democratize or risk popular unrest and internal instability. Globalization also exposes historically isolated China to a range of transboundary phenomena such as diseases like HIV/AIDS. Thus, for a country like China, the dynamics of global security provide both challenges and opportunities.

THE NEW DISTRIBUTION OF POWER

Globalization has altered the meaning of power and the means through which power is channeled. Traditionally, power grew from military capabilities, economic strength, natural resources, and the capacity to transform these assets into influence. In this context, applied power is the ability to get someone to do something that they otherwise would not do.[7] Though its manifestations are transforming, power remains a constant. As David Baldwin writes: "Economic security, environmental security, identity security, social security, and military security are different forms of security, not fundamentally different concepts. . . . Voting power, military power, economic power, and persuasive power are different forms of the same social phenomenon, i.e. power."[8] Thus globalization is both a product and a tool of power in the international system. As Stanley Hoffman notes, globalization is a "sum of techniques (audio and videocassettes, the Internet, instantaneous communications) that are at the disposal of states or private actors."[9] In this sense, globalization dynamics and their continued advancement through technological innovations are not a cause or effect, but rather a means through which the key determining factor—power—is exercised. There are five particularly important kinds of power at the dawn of the twenty-first century: state power; soft power; asymmetric power; people, ideas, and information power; and the power of nature.

The Nation-State

The first major form of power reflects the classic function of the nation-state. State power is derived from the tradition of sovereignty in international relations. Sovereignty implies that states have the sole authority over what happens within their own borders. States have both a right to sovereignty and a duty to respect the sovereignty of other states. Sovereignty has often been threatened as state interests clash, leading to wars. Historically, states have sought to marshal resources necessary either to provide for their defense or to project state power. States with insufficient power have often fallen victim to external aggression, or had to make bargains with other states to garner protection. State power is thus generally measured in terms of hard military capabilities, natural resources, population, and economic capacity.

States remain the primary actors in the global security environment. However, the means of exercising and measuring state power are undergoing significant change. Globalization can erode state authority as interdependence breaks down national barriers. However, globalization can also be an important tool for enhancing state power. For example, during the 1990s, in considering warfighting options against the United States, the Chinese military studied a range of new kinds of attacks to achieve victory. These included terrorism, drug-trafficking, environmental degradation, and computer virus propagation. When China was confronted with possible conflict with the United States over Taiwan in 1996, military strategists indicated that "we would not be sufficient. . . . So we realized that China needs a new strategy to right the balance of power."[10] These planners saw complexity in warfare as a neutralizing factor against American conventional military dominance. Any war between China and the United States would thus be guided in Beijing as "unrestricted war," which takes "nonmilitary forms and military forms and creates a war on many fronts."[11]

The complexity of globalization can also show significant limits on the exercise of state power. When Yugoslavia began threatening Kosovar Albanians with ethnic cleansing in 1999, the members of the North Atlantic Treaty Organization (NATO) went to war against Yugoslavia. The war raised significant sovereignty questions because Kosovo was a territorial region within Yugoslavia. Moreover, the states in NATO were deeply divided over how to wage the war. Knowing this, Yugoslavia sought to influence NATO's consensus-based decision-making procedures by swaying public sentiment against the war, hoping to break the coalition of allied states. Yugoslavia had no hope of defeating the allied countries of North America and Western Europe that make up NATO. So, rather than fight conventionally, Yugoslavia sought to deter an attack by pointing its military not at NATO, but at the ethnic Albanians that NATO was trying to save. When NATO went to war in March 1999, Yugoslavia carried out its threat and 800,000 ethnic Albanians were forced to flee Kosovo. Unable to reach agreement on a ground invasion, NATO went to war only with air power—which was insufficient to achieve the objective of a quick victory and a negotiated settlement. Yugoslavia thus adopted a strategy of waiting out the NATO air campaign and hoping that the alliance would divide. Yet a key element of globalization unraveled this Yugoslav strategy. Televised images of mass deportations of ethnic Albanians were reminiscent of the World War II Holocaust. These images hardened European public opinion against Yugoslavia and bolstered NATO's resolve to win the war.[12]

The Kosovo war also showed the limits of conventional military power. The combined capabilities of nineteen of the most powerful countries in the world took three months to defeat Yugoslavia—a backward and isolated country at the time. This weakness was not because of a lack of military capability, but rather because of political division over waging war as an alliance for a humanitarian cause. Technology also showed significant limitations in the battlefield. America had become so militarily advanced that keeping communications with allied countries secret was problematic. American military advancement had its own vulnerabilities and limitations. American stealth bomber technology makes airplanes very hard to detect on radar; however, Yugoslav forces shot down one of these planes when it was flying slowly with the moon backlighting it. The United States has the greatest geospacial mapping capability in the world; yet the people working the technology had not updated the maps of Belgrade—leading American airplanes to bomb the Chinese embassy. The technology, in that case, was accurate with great precision, but the people working it had made serious errors. American airplanes were prepared to target antiaircraft batteries—but the Yugoslav forces opted not to fire them and risk exposing their locations; this decision forced American airplanes to fly above 15,000 feet, thereby limiting their accuracy. Ultimately, technology is not a substitute for sound state strategy. As Edward Luttwak writes: "New technologies are only relevant insofar as their potential is exploited, which in turn is only possible if resources are denied to old structures and old activities—perhaps to the point of extinction—in order to supply resources for new structures and new activities."[13]

Soft Power

Globalization places a high value on the ability of states to work within the realm of "soft" power. Soft power refers to the overall attractiveness of a state to others and its ability to accomplish goals without resorting to the threat or the use of force. Soft power gains are made not by imposing one's will on others, but by setting examples with one's actions that others might want to emulate. Key tools to soft power are credibility in relation to commitments, economic and educational capacity, and an ability to build effective multilateral coalitions for negotiating the networks of global security. States that are making these kinds of adjustments are likely to emerge as winners in conditions in which the exercise of effective soft power is necessary. Measuring soft power focuses attention on issues such as effective diplomacy and education, for example, because a strong understanding of and attention to the culture, traditions, and security concerns of others is essential to effective persuasion.[14]

In a global security dynamic that emphasizes soft power, economic capacity can become a crucial measurement of power. The traditional emphasis in studying globalization has been on the worldwide interconnectedness of economic activity. This economic interdependence creates both opportunity and vulnerability among nation-states. How well states adjust to emerging economic trends can be crucial to their capacity of soft power influence in international relations. China, for example, wields growing economic influence over the United States because it has been purchasing American treasury bonds which Washington sold in order to finance its spending deficits. China gained from this by promoting a strong dollar which helped it to export goods to the United States. However, if China and other Asian countries seek other currencies or commodities to invest in, the subsequent withdrawal of resources from the American economy could have a devastating impact on U.S. power. Indeed, by summer 2005, China was expressing interest in purchasing large American oil companies. Ultimately, economic power can also translate into hard military power. The relative rise of the economic capacity of countries like China and India thus serve as a fundamental challenge to American economic dominance in the twenty-first century.[15]

The effective exercise of soft power can create conundrums for states that have significant advantages in hard military power. A country with substantial military capabilities might find that, in wartime, it is more efficient to fight alone or with coalitions-of-the-willing, rather than adhere to cumbersome decision-making procedures of international organizations. By "going it alone," a state will not have other countries shaping its warfighting plans and strategies. On the other hand, without the diplomatic approval of the international community, a military intervention can lack legitimacy and set dangerous precedents for the future. More immediately, while independent warfighting might be more efficient, a state also will find itself alone in the aftermath of victory (or defeat) paying virtually all of the human and economic costs. Significantly, without allies to share the burden of winning the peace after a war, a state might find that fighting a war in the first place was not worth it. If isolated in costly unilateral military operations, a state can deplete both its hard and soft power.

Debates over the exercise of hard military power and effective use of soft power surrounded the American decision to invade Iraq in 2003. Soft power did play into some of America's strategy toward Iraq through fall 2002. The U.S. initially challenged the United Nations to enforce its own requirements for Iraqi disarmament. This effort eventually gained a new resolution that led to UN weapons inspectors returning to Iraq in fall 2002. The effort to build a case at the United Nations reflected a desire to shape international and domestic opinion in favor of American policy toward Iraq. This strategy appeared to work when Iraq agreed to readmit weapons inspectors. Nevertheless, during the winter, the Americans continued to build up their hard power capabilities in the Persian Gulf, thus signaling limits to its willingness to apply soft power tactics. Meanwhile, the U.S. sought to build an international coalition that would support the use of force. A coalition was achieved, though it was largely political with few additional countries supplying troops. The United States, by March 2003, opted not to allow another round of weapons inspections that would have gained additional diplomatic support. That diplomatic support could have translated into more cost sharing and additional troops to assist the U.S. long-term occupation in Iraq. However, the United States invaded without that support and consequently paid the high price of war largely alone. The United States also paid significant costs to its reputation when, after invading, little evidence to support its prewar intelligence claims on Iraqi weapons of mass destruction was discovered.

Countries that opposed the American invasion of Iraq were able to gain short-term concessions or raise the costs to the U.S. for its action by exercising their own soft power options. Germany, France, and Russia successfully insisted on the return of UN weapons inspectors to Iraq during fall 2002. Turkey refused to give basing access to American troops, thus forcing the United States to fight only a one-front war through Kuwait. With no invasion from the north, it became much harder to move troops into key strategic locations in Iraq. American offers of up to $30 billion in direct money and loan credits were not sufficient to persuade Turkey to support Washington's Iraq invasion. Tiny Belgium used procedures in NATO to halt a separate Turkish request for collective defense in the event of an Iraqi attack on Turkey following an American invasion. The Belgian view appeared to be that the best way to prevent an attack on Turkey was not to have a war in the first place. Authorizing defense of Turkey, the Belgians argued, only made a war more likely. The UN weapons inspectors also played an important role by putting information into the public debate which bolstered the diplomatic initiatives of those countries that opposed the war. Ultimately, however, the limits of soft power were exposed when additional inspections were rejected by the United States and the invasion of Iraq went forward.

Asymmetrical Power

How much hard or soft power a state possesses is no longer an absolute measure of security. Through channels of global trade, transportation, technology, and communication, even actors who have very little power can do serious damage to the national interests and security of powerful countries. Power is diffused so that the asymmetrical exercise of influence is possible. There are rarely symmetries of power—when everyone in a security dynamic has equal power. Military, economic, and political differences skew the balance of forces among international actors. However, conflicting parties can apply tactics that are asymmetrical in nature—those that are outside the legitimate realm of power projection—in other words, "not fight fair." While such activity is not new, the acceleration of globalization provides a range of means for non-state actors to apply asymmetrical power and increase its effects.

Asymmetrical tactics are used to overcome conventional military superiority with violence that humanity generally considers unacceptable. States and societies do not have the luxury of assuming chivalry in enemies. This challenge surfaced in a contemporary environment after, in late 1992, the United States deployed troops on a humanitarian mission to feed starving famine victims in Somalia. Local political dynamics eventually led to conflict between American troops and Somali warlords. Somali irregular militias used asymmetrical tactics to kill eighteen American soldiers in October 1993. These Somalis then took the bodies of American soldiers, abused them, and paraded them stripped of clothing on worldwide television. The American response was to withdraw from Somalia. The killing and barbaric desecration of these American soldiers was sufficient to send the United States, the world's most advanced military superpower, into retreat. The lesson was sent that the way to attack the United States was to inflict casualties and to create shock and horror through the networks of global communication. In fact, given that the United States had overwhelming conventional military power, the likelihood of anyone fighting it in a conventional sense seemed very unlikely.

The al Qaeda terrorist leader Osama bin Laden has said that he and his movement drew inspiration from the presumed weakness of the United States following the Somalia debacle. Subsequently, a gathering storm of terrorist threat culminated in the 2001 attacks by al Qaeda on the World Trade Center and the Pentagon in the United States. If the strategic objective of these attacks was to prompt a retrenchment of American power and expanded recruitment into the al Qaeda cause, they failed miserably. America's global engagement expanded dramatically after the September 11 attacks and the terrorists who claimed to act on behalf of Islam were widely condemned throughout the Muslim world. However, as tactics, these were spectacularly horrifying incidents—portrayed repeatedly on global television and seared into the memory of people around the world. The dilemma for powerful states is that their conventional power has little application in fighting such asymmetrical tactics.

The increasing appeal of asymmetrical tactics as a tool of warfare is due in part to globalization networks that facilitate the proliferation of technology that can allow for devastating asymmetrical attacks. Weapons of mass destruction in the hands of terrorists, for example, could prove particularly dangerous. Governments in some parts of the world might pursue limited nuclear weapons capabilities to have just enough power to raise the costs to any country that might attack. North Korea, for example, could not defeat the

United States conventionally. But the United States might have to think very hard about attacking North Korea if the cost of war could be losing Seattle or San Francisco in nuclear explosions. Considering the nexus of weapons of mass destruction, organized crime, and terrorism, the need for understanding and reducing asymmetrical threats to global security is pressing.

People, Ideas, and Media Power

The diffusion of power in the twenty-first century levels the playing field of international security in ways that nation-states can find difficult to constrain or adapt to. Popular movements and the ideas that they advocate through proliferating media networks place public demands on states as well as international institutions to react to security problems in ways that they might otherwise not. The powerless (as measured in traditional terms) can become powerful as control over information and access to knowledge become central to agenda-setting.[16] This new access to power has been reflected in major international social movements that demand significant international change. For example, during the 1990s nongovernmental organizations successfully lobbied the World Bank to alter its loan policy in the underdeveloped world so that development projects would first be given an environmental impact assessment. Public international interest groups advocating for the environment, human rights, and labor standards took to the streets with major demonstrations at the 1999 World Trade Organization (WTO) meetings in Seattle. While the legal mandate of the WTO was limited to trade issues, these protestors forced the WTO member-states to acknowledge the relationships between free trade and human rights, or free trade and the environment. In summer 2005, millions of people around the world united for simultaneous "Live 8" concerts by popular musicians to put pressure on the leaders of the leading industrial nations—the G-8—to respond to their agenda of assistance and debt relief in Africa.

The diffusion of power into the hands of activist citizens around the world means that states must account for both domestic and global public opinion. As interdependence unites national economies, changes in public attitudes ranging from purchasing choices to opinions on war and peace can have a significant impact on global security. Should international consumers opt, for example, to boycott American-made goods, stop sending students to American universities, or start buying environmentally friendly products for purchases like cars, the American economy would be seriously damaged. As with cigarette smoking, it is possible that at some point consumers will simply decide that driving fuel-inefficient SUVs is just not cool. If that happens, countries producing more environmentally friendly products will gain a competitive advantage. America confronts a unique dilemma because its productive economy is the engine that drives many of the processes of globalization. Yet, if globalization is seen as a primarily American phenomenon, then the United States will also be blamed for associated problems—even if that blame is not merited.

Illustrating America's dilemma, a 2002 opinion survey by the Pew Global Attitudes Project showed that 50 percent of the British and 54 percent of the Canadian public—America's two closest allies in the world—saw the expansion of American customs and values as a negative phenomenon. In Germany, the negative view toward American customs and values was 67 percent. Even across pro-American Eastern Europe the numbers on this question were negative including 61 percent in the Czech Republic and 55 percent in Poland.[17] Such public attitudes can make it very difficult for governments to pursue pro-American policies if they fear retribution at election time for supporting initiatives from Washington. China's growing economic investments have also contributed to public protest. For example, China's state-owned corporation Minimetals proposed buying Noranda, Canada's largest mining company. This effort prompted protests among Canada's miners who worried about what Chinese ownership would mean for their job security. In the shoe-producing town of Elche, Spain, 500 demonstrators set Chinese warehouses on fire to protest the cheap import of Chinese shoes while demanding that Spain restrict Chinese imports.[18]

Television and the Internet provide instant global images and communication that allow for ideas to be transmitted quickly across borders. The results can give real meaning to the idea that one person can change the world. For example, the 1997 Nobel Peace Prize was awarded to Jody Williams. Williams is a woman from Vermont who grew concerned about landmines, organized activists across borders, put her fax machine to work, and through tireless effort successfully promoted an international treaty that banned landmines, thus causing a direct increase in human security worldwide. Of course these channels of communication and action can be used for good and bad, and by strong and weak. By forcing serious security challenges onto the public agenda, hard questions can be asked and, perhaps, serious solutions achieved. Is, for example, the twenty-first century going to be one where a child lucky enough to be born in a developed country will have security but one born in an underdeveloped country will be insecure? Can the world be at peace when ten million children die every year from preventable and curable diseases, when 40 percent of the world's population cannot drink the water where they live, and when 2.7 billion people survive on less than $2.00 a day? Do the wealthy countries of the world, like the United States, want to live within a national gated community, keeping the dangerous outside world at bay? Is such a policy option even possible anymore? And, if it is not, then what proactive strategic engagement is necessary for resolving problems before they become unmanageable crises? Only when these hard questions are asked can solutions begin to be applied. The critical nexus of power in this condition of global security implies that any one individual can provide the answers.

The Power of Nature

Power must also be considered in terms of humanity's natural environment. "Don't mess with mother nature" is an oft repeated phrase. The natural world has a way of balancing itself. Yet the earth has never before witnessed the kind of activity that humans have engaged in during the past one hundred years. Human behavior is having significant environmental impact ranging from global warming to the destruction of forests and the diminishing availability of fresh water. Also catastrophic natural disasters—such as the December 2004 tsunami event in south Asia; Hurricane Katrina, which devastated much of the American Gulf Coast in August 2005; and the October 2005 earthquake in Pakistan—can cause their own security problems for states and their people. Meanwhile, the global demand for energy is growing exponentially with the rise of modern industrial powers such as China and India. In this sense, the question of environmental security is more than just achieving sustainable development or protecting endangered species. The central issue is whether humanity's own behavior is decreasing its own security in relation to the environment. Eventually, the power of nature might force a redefinition of the search for peace to include the need to live in harmony with the environment.

OVERVIEW OF THE BOOK

This text examines the conceptual and policy implications of global security. Chapter 2 surveys the role of realism in explaining power and security relationships, and shows how realism has been adapted for understanding new security challenges. Chapter 3 views the search for peace through the frameworks of liberalism and new security paradigms including constructivism, transnational civil society, pacifism and peace movements, postmodernism, feminism and gender, and revolutionary approaches to security. Chapter 4 reviews the distribution of power in the international system with detailed study of the grand strategies and military capabilities of the United States, Russia, China, and the European Union. Chapter 5 considers the strategic consequences of major regional flashpoints: India and Pakistan, the Korean peninsula, China and Taiwan, the Persian Gulf and the Middle East, and Eurasia. Chapter 6 outlines the security implications of technology and trade including revolutions in military affairs, the role of information and security, the military use of space, the business of security, security privatization, and the relationship between international sanctions and security. Chapter 7 examines asymmetrical conflict with a focus on genocide and ethnic cleansing, and terrorism and insurgency. Chapter 8 surveys challenges to human security with an emphasis on human rights and democracy, population and demographic change, food and health, and the human costs of war. Chapter 9 focuses on the meaning of environmental and energy security and assesses the security implications of global warming, deforestation and land use, water security, energy scarcity and safety, and the role of nuclear energy. Chapter 10 concludes with a reexamination of the major conceptual frameworks in light of these global security trends. The conclusion provides a perspective on strategic approaches to education and effective security planning as means to make the quest for power and the search for peace one and the same.

NOTES

1. These concepts were initially developed by Robert O. Keohane and Joseph S. Nye, *Power and Interdependence*, 3rd ed. (New York: Longman, 2001).

2. Joseph Stiglitz, *Globalization and Its Discontents* (New York: Norton, 2003), 1–10.

3. Arnold Wolfers, "National Security as an Ambiguous Symbol," *Political Science Quarterly* 67 (1952): 483.

4. Lester Brown, *Redefining National Security*, Worldwatch Paper no. 14 (Washington, D.C., 1977).

5. Barry Buzan, *People, States, and Fear: An Agenda for International Security Studies in the Post–Cold War Era*, 2nd ed. (New York: Lynne Rienner, 1991).

6. Graham Allison, "The Impact of Globalization on National and International Security," in *Governance in a Globalizing World*, ed. Joseph S. Nye and John D. Donahue (Washington, D.C.: Brookings Institute, 2000), 80–83.

7. Hans J. Morgenthau, *Politics among Nations*, 5th ed., rev. (New York: Knopf, 1978).

8. David A. Baldwin, "The Concept of Security," *Review of International Studies* 23, no. 1 (January 1997): 23.

9. Stanley Hoffmann, "The Clash of Globalizations," *Foreign Affairs* 81, no. 3 (July/August 2003): 106–7.

10. John Pomfret, "China Ponders New Rules of 'Unrestricted War,'" *Washington Post*, August 8, 1999.

11. Pomfret, "China Ponders New Rules."

12. Sean Kay, "NATO, the Kosovo War, and Neoliberal Theory," *Contemporary Security Policy* 25, no. 2 (August 2004): 252–78.

13. Edward N. Luttwak, "Power Relations in the New Economy," *Survival* 44, no. 2 (Summer 2002): 10.

14. These issues are elaborated in Joseph S. Nye, *The Paradox of American Power* (Oxford: Oxford University Press, 2002).

15. For further discussion see Clyde Prestowitz, *Three Billion New Capitalists: The Great Shift of Wealth and Power to the East* (New York: Basic Books, 2005).

16. Ernst B. Haas, *When Knowledge Is Power: Three Models of Change in International Organization* (Berkeley: University of California Press, 1991).

17. PEW Research Center for the People and the Press, *Global Attitudes Project* (Washington, D.C.: Pew Publications, 2002), 63.

18. Don Lee, "Global Cachet Comes with Chinese Deal for IBM Unit," *Los Angeles Times*, December 9, 2004.

SUGGESTED READING

Ersel Aydinli and James N. Rosenau, eds., *Globalization, Security and the Nation-State: Paradigms in Transition* (New York: SUNY Press, 2005).

Benjamin Barber, *Jihad vs. McWorld: How Globalism and Tribalism Are Reshaping the World* (New York: Ballantine Books, 1996).

Jagdish Bhagwati, *In Defense of Globalization* (Oxford: Oxford University Press, 2004).

Michael Brown, Steven E. Miller, Owen R. Côte, and Sean M. Lynn-Jones, eds., *New Global Dangers: Changing Dimensions of International Security* (Cambridge, Mass.: MIT Press, 2004).

Barry Buzan, *People, States, and Fear: An Agenda for Security Studies in the Post–Cold War Era*, 2nd ed. (New York: Lynne Rienner, 1991).

Ian Clark, *Globalization and International Relations Theory* (Oxford: Oxford University Press, 1999).

Thomas L. Friedman, *The Lexus and the Olive Tree: Understanding Globalization* (New York: Anchor, 2000).

Robert O. Keohane and Joseph S. Nye, *Power and Interdependence*, 3rd ed. (New York: Longman, 2001).

Richard L. Kugler and Ellen L. Frost, eds., *The Global Century: Globalization and National Security* (Washington, D.C.: National Defense University Press, 2001).

Hans J. Morgenthau, *Politics among Nations: The Struggle for Power and Peace* (New York: Knopf, 1985).

Chapter Two

The Quest for Power

Soldiers establish a security perimeter after exiting a U.S. Army CH-47 Chinook helicopter during an exercise near Bagram, Afghanistan, June 2005. *Source*: U.S. Department of Defense, photo by Spc. Harold Fields, U.S. Army.

The dominant approach to understanding the role power plays in international security has been realism. Realism reflects a set of assumptions about the way security relationships are ordered in the context of the international distribution of power. In the realist paradigm, the nation-state is traditionally the central actor in the international system and the quest for power is the key means to advancing security. Realists see international actors making cost-benefit assumptions to advance their national interest as defined in terms of power. Realists conclude that the key objective of states is survival, and power is the means to survival. States will, thus, calculate their interests in terms of power and the international situation that they face. Realists see the international system as reflecting a condition of anarchy where the nation-state is the highest source of legitimate political authority. Consequently, a state must rely on itself for safety. Realists generalize that all states are the same in their pursuit of national interests and that moral aspects of domestic laws and government are not relevant to determining international outcomes. Realists note, however, that there are various levels of power distribution among nation-states and that power must be understood in terms of both absolute and relative capabilities. Realists assume that states will ask not only "who will gain?" in a competitive situation but also "who will gain more?" Increasingly, realism has been adapted to move beyond the primary focus of the nation-state to apply its broader assumptions to the new dynamics of international security. Realists are generally pessimistic about human nature. Thus, while one might see oneself as peaceful, the same cannot be safely assumed about others. Humankind is power-maximizing, selfish, evil, and even sinful.[1] This chapter examines the core propositions of traditional realist approaches to international security. It then illustrates how key elements of realism have been adapted to meet the new circumstances of global security.

THE TRADITIONS OF REALISM

Many core assumptions of realism date to the work of the ancient Greek historian Thucydides. Through the *Melian Dialogue*, Thucydides illustrated that, when it comes to international security, the strong do what they can, and the weak do what they must. The Italian political philosopher Niccolo Machiavelli used his study *The Prince* to illustrate national interest in security and survival. As Machiavelli wrote, "A man striving in every way to be good will meet his ruin among the great number who are not good. Hence it is necessary for a prince, if he wishes to remain in power, to learn how not to be good and to use his knowledge or refrain from using it as he may need." In Machiavelli's view, a leader should "care nothing for the accusation of cruelty so long as he keeps his subjects united and loyal; by making a very few examples he can be more truly merciful than those who through too much tender-heartedness allow disorders to arise whence come killings and rapine."[2] Thomas Hobbes advanced the concept of power and anarchy. In *Leviathan*, Hobbes asserts, "Man has a perpetual and restless desire for power."[3] Hobbes noted that when two individuals desire the same thing—which in reality both together cannot enjoy—then they will become enemies. Over time, they will endeavor to destroy or subdue one another. Thus political actors have only themselves to rely upon for there is no government over the governments. In the anarchic world, incentives for war are built into the international system as men seek to become first "masters of other men's persons, wives, children and cattle." Hobbes separated the interests of survival from the moral imperatives of humankind, writing, "To this war of every man, against every man, this also is consequent; that nothing can be unjust. The notions of right and wrong, justice and injustice have there no place. Where there is no common power, there is no law: where no law, no injustice." To Hobbes, "covenants without the sword are but words and of no strength to secure man at all."

In the twentieth century, Hans J. Morgenthau characterized international politics as a struggle for power. Morgenthau stressed both the physical and psychological dimensions of power which he saw as the ability to control the minds and actions of others. Morgenthau believed that people seek the most power they can attain. How much power is needed for security is derived from the conditions a state faces and, thus, states could pursue power for maintaining a status quo (defensive), imperial expansion (offensive), or to gain prestige.[4] George Kennan critiqued efforts to create a moralistic and legalistic international order. Instead, states should set the best example at home so that other states will gravitate toward those values rather than recoil at having values foisted upon them. Kennan also was a firm believer in the defensive use of power to offset an enemy, as evidenced in his policy of containment toward the Soviet Union.[5] Henry Kissinger assessed the advantages of the balance of power for stability in international relations through detailed assessment of the strategies of great powers during the nineteenth century.[6] Kennan and Kissinger applied realism while serving in the U.S. government—Kennan as the author of the containment policy and Kissinger as the author of the doctrine of détente with the Soviet Union and China.

In the 1970s, some realists assessed how the structure of the international system shapes state behavior. Kenneth N. Waltz presented the structure of the international system as constant. He concluded that the system would only truly change if there were changes in its organizing principles or capabilities. As there is a finite amount of power in the international system, states will compete to gain access to advance self-help. To Waltz, the more states are exposed to vulnerabilities created by interdependence, the more likely they will come into conflict. Conflict is less likely when fewer interested actors compete for power.[7] Robert Gilpin focused attention on the relative distribution of power and systemic change. Territorial, political, and economic expansion will likely occur until the marginal costs of further change are equal to or greater than the marginal benefits. As states rise in terms of power and become overly invested in expansive military engagements, they can risk underinvesting in their domestic economic strength. Expansionistic foreign and military policies will promote reactions, such as external balancing forces, which limit the power of a rising state. Alternatively, they might lead to internal economic decline, forcing a retrenchment. Gilpin noted that when one actor's power is rising and another is declining, the international system is most likely to promote a transformational war.[8]

Realists have also been concerned with why and how power is exerted within the international system. Robert J. Art identified four kinds of military power. Defensive use of force is the deployment of military power so as to be able to do two things—to ward off an attack and to minimize danger if one is attacked. Deterrent use of force is the deployment of military power in order to prevent an adversary from doing something that one does not want him to do—that he might otherwise be tempted to do—by threatening him with unacceptable punishment if he does it. Compellant use of force is the deployment of military power so as to be able either to stop an adversary from doing something that he has already undertaken or to get him to do something that he has not yet undertaken. Finally, swaggering is the deployment of military power for purposes other than to defend, deter, or compel, usually with peaceful exercising or demonstrations of military capability.[9] The relative distribution of power is also a key determinant of how much security a state needs. At the core of concern over potential conflict lies the traditional concept of the security dilemma.

The Security Dilemma and Incentives for War

While two or more states in the international system might not want conflict with each other, the nature of the system can force them to assume the worst, thus creating a security dilemma. Latent power such as economic or technological gains in one state that can be transformed into military capabilities can cause a state to increase its defensive capacity. This defensive action can be perceived as threatening to other states. As John Herz writes: "Since none can ever feel entirely secure in such a world of competing units, power competition ensues, and the vicious circle of security and power accumulation is on."[10] There is danger in the belief that an increase in military strength always leads to an increase in security.[11] Robert Jervis places the relationship between offensive and defensive strategy within the context of the security dilemma. When offensive strategy has the advantage, one country's armed forces will find it easier to destroy those of another and to take the latter's territory rather than defend its own. When defensive strategy has the advantage, it is easier to protect and to hold than it is to move forward and destroy an adversary. Jervis notes that the security dilemma is most dangerous when the only good route to security for a state is perceived to be expansion. States which might prefer to maintain the status quo still might feel they have little choice but to prepare for an offensive strategy to ensure their safety. Even small gains made by another state can result in real or perceived vulnerabilities for another. As Jervis notes, a state might choose offensive weapons even if it prefers the status quo because: (1) if the offensive strategy has a great advantage over the defensive, protection through defensive forces will be too expensive; (2) status-quo states may need offensive weapons to regain territory lost in the opening stages of any war that might occur; and (3) a state might feel that it must be prepared to take the offensive either because the other side will make peace only if it loses territory or because the state has commitments to attack if the other makes war on a third party.[12]

Stephen Van Evera demonstrates several factors that create incentives for offensive doctrines: opportunistic expansionism appears easier; expansionism for defensive purposes or to resist expansion is attractive; rewards for moving first are higher; windows of opportunity for an enemy are larger if one is on the defensive; states tend (when conquest is easy) to adopt more dangerous diplomatic tactics that are more likely to cause war; states with offensive advantages will negotiate less when they can have their way with military power; states will become more secretive to protect their offensive edge; states will race harder and faster to develop arms when the offensive strategy dominates; and, finally, conquest becomes still easier as offensive dominance becomes self-reinforcing.[13] Van Evera concludes that "the prime threat to the security of modern great powers is . . . themselves. Their greatest menace lies in their own tendency to exaggerate the dangers they face, and to respond with counterproductive belligerence."[14]

The security dilemma is especially intense in a condition where nuclear weapons are involved. If there are only a handful of nuclear weapons between two adversarial parties, a state might risk launching a first-strike attack against the other to eliminate the latter's capability to retaliate. Conversely, a state that feels its retaliatory capability is threatened might opt to launch its weapons arsenal first—a "use it, or lose it" scenario. During the Cold War, this element of the security dilemma was ameliorated by the development by both adversaries of a full-scale "second-strike" capability. Had the Soviet Union launched a surprise attack against the United States, the U.S. still would have been able to retaliate because enough of its nuclear capability would have survived. For the United States, this meant developing a mix of nuclear capabilities via a triad including long-range intercontinental ballistic missiles (ICBM), mobile submarine-launched missiles, and heavy bombers ready to launch on moment's notice. The Soviet Union had similar forces, using mobile land forces via an extensive train system and submarines, long-range bombers, and ICBMs. The end result was that neither side could risk launching a surprise nuclear attack because it would have meant mutual suicide—or as it was called, MAD, mutual assured destruction.

Seeking to further ameliorate the security dilemma, the United States and the Soviet Union agreed in 1972 to ban the development and deployment of missile defense systems via the Anti-Ballistic Missile (ABM) treaty. The intent was to ensure that neither side might develop the capacity to eliminate the other's retaliatory capability and thereby create incentives for one or the other to launch a first-strike attack. If one side, for example, had a missile defense system able to shoot down incoming missiles, the other side would be extremely vulnerable because its retaliatory counterstrike would be insufficient to dissuade the former from starting a war. The missile defense dynamic reemerged during the 1980s with the Strategic Defense Initiative—derisively referred to by skeptics as "Star Wars"—proposed by the United States. By the 1990s, the United States opted initially to develop a limited system. By 2004, the United States had withdrawn from the ABM treaty and had begun deployment of a missile defense system. This new defensive system illustrates the dynamics behind the security dilemma. If the United States could shoot down a couple dozen incoming missiles from North Korea, that same capability would affect China, which in 2004 had two dozen harden-silo intercontinental ballistic missiles. If China felt that its limited nuclear deterrent was marginalized, it might build more missiles and make them mobile. If China did this, it would raise alarm in India, which might build more missiles and thus exacerbate fears in its long-time adversary Pakistan. Meanwhile, the United States might build a larger missile defense, alarming Russia. Though ostensibly a defensive technology, a missile defense capability would make it easier for the United States to wage first-strike wars against states with limited or nascent nuclear capabilities. Without a missile defense, the United States might not risk a war against North Korea or defend Taiwan against a Chinese invasion for fear of retaliation.

Misperception, Coercion, and Credibility

Threats can be real or perceived. For example, Poland still perceived Russia as a threat to its security after the Cold War. There was no material evidence that Russia posed a significant conventional threat, but Poland's historical experiences living under brutal totalitarian governments controlled by Moscow shaped how it viewed Russia. This perceived threat was a key factor that drove Poland to seek membership in the North Atlantic Treaty Organization. Conversely, NATO was seen by many Russians as a Cold War alliance led by its recent military adversaries, the United States and Germany. To many Russians, the expansion of this Cold War military alliance was a threat. National leaders might not always have perfect, or even near-perfect, information and thus often rely on existing perceptions when making cost-benefit assumptions. Additionally, states might impose their own standards of expected behavior on others by determining how they would behave in a given situation, rather than understanding how another actor might define its own interests. When two or more states look at a single phenomenon, some might see a threat and some might see nothing of consequence. Both reactions carry risks. Assuming a threat when there is none can create a self-fulfilling prophecy. Alternatively, seeing no threat when one looms can be catastrophic.

The personal characteristics of decision-makers also affect the way a particular state will perceive international events and thus shape policies. Existing or learned perceptions shape views of reality—even if those assumptions or learned patterns of cognition are wrong. Cognitive and psychological factors can exacerbate the security dilemma. Stress can lead decision-makers to respond with intellectual rigidity that limits their ability to cope with complexity. Also, when decision-time is short, the ability to examine a broad range of possibilities can be limited.[15] Domestic inputs also influence perceptions of threats. Bureaucratic interests can skew a full airing of factors pertaining to the national interest, or important information might be ignored in bureaucracies to satisfy cognitive worldviews of decision-makers. Also, when states undergo major changes in political culture, it affects how they perceive the international environment. Such internal changes also affect how these states are viewed by others. For example, Germany and Japan in 2004 were not the same war-prone states that they were in the first half of the twentieth century. Nevertheless, other states might view these countries as potential threats based both on their latent power capabilities and their historical patterns of behavior.

Realists also see states using their power capabilities, including military force, as a tool of coercion. Coercion can involve the threat of force designed to convince another actor or state to do something which they otherwise would not do. Coercion can take benign forms, like persuasion, or it can take more aggressive forms, as in intimidation and blackmail. Coercion might manifest in naked aggression to make strategic or tactical gains in an offensive campaign. However, coercion can also be a tool, as in the use of threat of force to back up diplomacy in order to avoid conflict. Alexander George notes that, in such a setting, decision-makers must choose: (1) what to demand of the opponent; (2) whether and how to create a sense of urgency for compliance; (3) whether and what kind of punishment to threaten for noncompliance; and (4) whether to rely solely on the threat of punishment or also to offer positive inducements to secure acceptance.[16] There are two operational dilemmas, however, associated with a solely diplomatic approach to coercion. First, it is hard to know how much threat is necessary to persuade an opponent to comply. Must a country mobilize divisions of its army, deploy aircraft carriers from around the world, put nuclear forces on alert? Or can small, limited air strikes send the necessary messages that diplomacy is intended to send? Second, coercive diplomacy only works if a state is prepared to actually use force. This creates a variation on the security dilemma that once having threatened force, a state might be compelled to use force to defend its credibility—even if the conflict was of relatively low national interest.

A credibility dilemma can pose two distinct problems for decision-makers. First, the target of coercion might not believe that a threat is serious and thus refuse to comply. Second, other major powers will be watching to see if a state conducting a coercive strategy will maintain the credibility of its diplomatic rhetoric. A state might thus find itself engaged in wars in the name of prestige and credibility rather than immediate vital interests. For example, in March 1998, U.S. Secretary of State Madeline K. Albright declared, "We are not going to stand by and watch the Serbian authorities do in Kosovo what they can no longer get away with doing in Bosnia."[17] In August 1998, Secretary Albright expressed her "strong view that the ongoing Serbian offensive and the unacceptable actions that have taken place in the context of that offensive only increase the chances of there being military action by NATO."[18] After a year of having American threats of military force ignored on the ground, the United States led its NATO allies into a major war. A crisis in which there was no vital interest emerged as a major challenge to American prestige and credibility, prompting the United States and its allies to launch an offensive war. As British Prime Minister Tony Blair said to his House of Commons at the onset of war, "To walk away now would destroy NATO's credibility."[19] After the war, the dilemma was exacerbated when President Clinton declared: "Whether you live in Africa or Central Europe, or any other place, if somebody comes after innocent civilians and tries to kill them en masse because of their race, their ethnic background or their religion, and it's within our power to stop it, we will stop it."[20]

Offensive Realism

The quest for material power can lead to aggressive, expansionist policy agendas, reflected historically in terms of colonial empire and hegemonic spheres of influence. John J. Mearsheimer assesses these tendencies via the concept of "offensive realism." Mearsheimer demonstrates that great powers are concerned mostly with survival and that this can only be achieved by attaining the maximum amount of military power and strategic influence. Mearsheimer sees the anarchical nature of the international system as requiring great powers to increase their capabilities at the expense of rivals and to take advantage of those situations when the benefits outweigh the costs.[21] Mearsheimer concludes that an ideal state of affairs for any great power would be to dominate the entire world. However, as that is impossible, states seek to become regional hegemonic powers where they can assert the maximum degree of control and influence. As great powers attain this status, they will inevitably run into other powers with similar geostrategic interests and conflict can result. This, Mearsheimer concludes, is the tragedy of great power politics—that states would likely prefer to sustain a status quo via defensive mechanisms but that the structure of the international system forces them into offensive postures which can provoke conflict as states seek domination through war.

The sources of conflict, according to offensive realism, come from the great powers' attempts to achieve four basic objectives: regional hegemony (which includes offensive action and actions designed to prevent other powers from infringing on that regional domination); maximization of wealth; dominance of power with large land armies; and nuclear superiority over rivals.[22] Strategies for attaining these objectives include war and blackmail. States might also pursue bloodletting, which snares other powers into intractable conflicts and forces them to drain resources and thus sap their strength. Mearsheimer finds evidence to support the case for offensive realism by looking at the historical examples of Japan, Germany, the Soviet Union, and Italy during the late 1800s through 1945. In these cases, evidence shows that each sought as much domination in the international system as it could get. When poor choices were made, overstretch occurred or they were confronted by defensive coalitions that forced them to retrench.

Mearsheimer also notes that, even during the Cold War period of mutual assured destruction, the United States and the Soviet Union did not willingly accept the status quo. Instead, each side sought, through arms races, to gain some form of nuclear advantage over the other. Mearsheimer observes that the United States would have been able to absorb a first strike by the Soviet Union and still retaliate with a level of destruction that would kill about 30 percent of the Soviet Union's population and destroy about 70 percent of its industry. This would be done by effective targeting of the 200 largest Soviet cities. This task could have been accomplished with a mix of nuclear weapons resulting in the equivalent of about 400 one-megaton weapons. However, the United States was not satisfied with this minimal level of deterrence and Washington's military plans far exceeded this estimate. In 1976, even after a period of détente and arms control treaties with the Soviets, U.S. military planning listed 25,000 potential targets in the USSR for nuclear attack. By 1983, this listing contained 50,000 potential targets.[23] While both sides did seek such advantages, the structure of mutual assured destruction was nevertheless a barrier to war.

THE REALIST PATH TO SECURITY

Realists believe that peace is possible as a product of the distribution of power. War might be prevented because a powerful state may be relatively satisfied with the status quo and act with restraint. Alternatively, several powers might share a common interest in an existing status quo and adjust their relations as necessary to maintain equilibrium. States might also find themselves, as during the Cold War, engaged with each other in a manner that reinforces a stable international system. States can also capitulate in the face of a threat to avoid war. States may choose balancing or bandwagoning strategies to preserve their sovereignty. Balancing can be done unilaterally, by increasing capabilities to create equilibrium, or gathering enough capabilities that will make any attack too costly to contemplate. Balancing also can include forming mutual defense agreements between two or more states. States might also bandwagon toward the state that is a threat or dominates a region.[24] In bandwagoning, smaller states align with the source of danger by cutting a deal with a more powerful state to ensure survival or even to share the gains of conquest.[25] Balancing and bandwagoning can contribute to a stable balance of power which is the primary source of security among states according to most realist analysis. An ideal balance of power system would be one in which defensive military postures were dominant and there was no power seeking to alter the status quo.

Deterrence

Deterrence is often seen as the most effective way to marshal the use of power to prevent war. Deterrence is a psychological relationship in a conflict situation in which one side convinces the other not to attack because of the threat of a damaging response. As Gordon A. Craig and Alexander L. George summarize, deterrence is an "effort by one actor to persuade an opponent not to take action of some kind against his interests by convincing the opponent that the costs and risk of doing so will outweigh what he hopes to gain thereby."[26] Craig and George stress that the key elements of deterrence rest on the assumption that an opponent is rational. States will weigh their interests and thus convey a commitment to defend those interests backed by threats that must be credible and sufficiently potent in the eyes of an opponent. Such threats must have will and resolution and thus adequate capabilities must exist to make such will credible.[27] Deterrence is built into a stable balance of power relationship. If adversaries have an equal amount of military capability, neither side will want to engage in direct conflict because the costs of war will be not worth any potential gains. When each side in a conflict has the ability to punish the other in the face of aggression, then war is not likely.

Deterrence works at two levels—conventional and nuclear. Conventional land deterrence is central to controlling territory and has, historically, been the most important measure of the balance of power. Naval power and, in the twentieth century, air power are critical tools of power projection, but land capabilities are key to stability even in a situation where nuclear deterrence is also important. Even under the nuclear umbrella of the Cold War, the United States and the Soviet Union each invested in massive ground troop deployments in Europe and Asia. Conventional deterrence is also important because not all wars involving nuclear powers will include the use of nuclear weapons.[28] States possessing nuclear weapons must be prepared to engage in land warfare as an insurance against preemptive attack. Conventional deterrence is also important because the level of destruction that can be made by nonnuclear weapons remains very high. As the conventional balance of power reached a stalemate during World War I, for example, hundreds of thousands of soldiers still died in months-long battles.

Nuclear weapons play a unique political and operational role in modern deterrence. As Robert Jervis notes, there are several political effects of nuclear weapons. First, the devastation of an all-out war would be unimaginably enormous. Second, both sides in a conflict would be exposed to this devastation—thus both being major losers in a conflict. Third, this devastation would occur extremely quickly and even the smallest of skirmishes could lead to a very dangerous escalation.[29] Nuclear deterrence theory has a built-in assumption of extreme risk. Should the theory ever be proven wrong, the consequences would be devastating. Deterrence posits that a state will not instigate conflict because the assumed benefits of aggression are not worth the associated costs. Also built into the theory is the assumption that, as with the Cold War, geographic separation would provide some warning time before a local conflict would escalate into nuclear war. The theory leaves unanswered the question of how much capability is needed to attain effective deterrence at either the conventional or the nuclear level. Alternatively, how little deterrence a state might have can also raise questions about the possibility of waging war. War would thus still be likely even if nuclear weapons are present—and their use might be more likely when too few nuclear weapons are present. The theory also raises unanswered questions about the threshold at which a state would risk introduction of nuclear weapons into a conflict. The United States would use its nuclear deterrent to defend its own territory but would it risk its territory to protect allies? War is more likely, as John Mearsheimer observes, when states under-estimate the relative power of an opposing state or coalition because they exaggerate their own capability or the number of allies that they can count on to fight on their side.[30]

The Cuban Missile Crisis illustrates both the effects and danger of deterrence. By the mid-1950s, the United States had established military and economic advantages over the Soviet Union. The Soviet Union embarked on a strategy to project its deterrent capacity, and perhaps also to increase its negotiating leverage on European issues, through coercion, by deploying nuclear capable missile systems and associated warheads 90 miles off the American coast in Cuba. The Soviet Union did not necessarily need to deploy nuclear missiles in Cuba in 1962. They could have granted political guarantees to Fidel Castro with potentially the same effect of deterring an American attack on Cuba. However, by 1962, the health of the Soviet system was in question. Some four million East Berliners had fled into West Berlin, prompting the Soviet Union to order construction of the Berlin Wall. The Soviets faced a credibility dilemma in Cuba. If Moscow failed to support its newfound ally in Castro, its other allies around the world might question the legitimacy of the Soviet commitment to their security. Prestige, strategy, and survival combined to provoke the Soviet Union to pursue an offensive strategy as a reflection of its perceived security needs. These weapons and missiles were basically useless as defensive weapons. Moscow gambled that its actions would yield an outcome favorable to Soviet objectives—successful deterrence and a possible negotiation.

United States aerial intelligence discovered the presence of missile delivery systems in Cuba in September 1962. The Americans did not know at the time that nuclear warheads were in Cuba. However, missiles and their launching systems could be seen in place. The United States ruled out an invasion of Cuba to remove the missiles as too risky. Thus, American options were limited by Soviet deterrence. On October 22, 1962, President John F. Kennedy addressed the American public on television and informed them of the presence of the missiles. President Kennedy declared a precise deterrent posture, stating that the United States would consider any attack from Cuba as an attack on America by the Soviet Union. Kennedy also declared that the United States would impose a naval "quarantine" to isolate Cuba from any further shipments of weapons. The American ambassador to the United Nations went before the Security Council and presented the evidence of the Soviet missiles in Cuba to the world.

The United States did not have good information about Moscow's intentions. For example, had there been a coup in Moscow that precipitated the crisis? How would the Soviets respond to the American deterrent posture especially regarding naval action on international waters? At what point might the Soviets back down? At what point might the Soviets challenge Kennedy on the credibility of his deterrent threat? Likewise, the Soviet Union could not know for sure if America was prepared to engage in global thermonuclear war. In the end, the Cuban Missile Crisis was managed by a combination of power and diplomacy. The United States agreed that, if Moscow withdrew the missiles from Cuba under United Nations inspection, Washington would promise not to invade Cuba. Washington also agreed to remove nuclear missiles it had based in Turkey. Both sides had stared into the depth of nuclear annihilation and both sides reacted as deterrence theory would have predicted. War was avoided through the exercise of power. Nonetheless, this was an extremely dangerous test of deterrence. The extent of the danger convinced each side to recognize a need for coexistence. The structure of nuclear deterrence would be sustained but with increased controls such as a hotline between Washington and Moscow and nuclear arms control treaties designed to prevent future crises.[31]

Another Cold War example of deterrence involved intermediate range nuclear forces (INFs) deployed in Europe by the Soviet Union and the United States. During the 1970s, détente gradually failed as Soviet economic stagnation and decline prompted them to challenge the international system with offensive strategies. The Soviet Union developed and deployed a new missile system—the SS-20—an intermediate range missile to be launched from within the Soviet Union and targeted at Western European targets. The SS-20 was a 2-stage land-mobile missile with a range between 4400 and 5000 kilometers. The intent of the deployment was to undermine the credibility of the American commitment to Western Europe and, perhaps, to coerce the Europeans into a negotiation with Moscow. The Soviet deployment upset the existing balance of power by giving Moscow an advantage in first-strike capabilities against Western European targets. The United States responded with a "dual track" approach, diplomacy backed with a threat of military power. The United States and its NATO allies declared that the Soviets could either withdraw their forces, or the United States would deploy a deterrent force to restore the balance of power. The Soviets did not respond affirmatively and in December 1979, the United States announced its decision to deploy 108 Pershing II and 464 ground-launched cruise missiles in Western Europe targeted at the Soviet Union. The United States offered not to deploy if the Soviets would withdraw their INFs, but this was rejected as Moscow insisted on linking British and French nuclear systems into the equation. Efforts to negotiate failed and the United States deployed its missiles, restoring the balance of nuclear power in

Europe. By 1987, however, the Soviet Union was in deep retrenchment under the policies of its new leader Mikhail Gorbachev, and a first order of business was to negotiate the INF treaty with the United States, entirely eliminating this class of nuclear weapons.

Deterrence is inherently dangerous because it must be credible to succeed. In 1939, both France and Britain made deterrence-based promises to defend Poland if it were attacked by Germany. But that promise was worth no more than the paper it was written on. The threat was not respected by Germany because the British and the French provided no guarantees to back up the deterrent promise. No forces were deployed to Poland in advance to signal the consequences of action. Similarly, in 1990, the United States failed to send an adequate deterrent message to Iraq about the consequences of any invasion of Kuwait. When, in the days before the invasion, the U.S. ambassador to Iraq was called in to meet with Saddam Hussein, he asked her what America's position was toward ongoing Iraqi-Kuwaiti oil and territorial disputes. Her official instructions were that the United States did not take a position on such inter-Arab issues. Saddam Hussein took this as a yellow, if not a green, light to invade Kuwait and gambled that the United States was not willing to defend Kuwait. After the invasion of Kuwait, the U.S. did deploy 300,000 troops to Saudi Arabia, which successfully deterred further aggression by Iraq.

Alliances and Concerts

An alliance is a grouping of two or more actors intended to accomplish a particular objective. Alliances can facilitate expansion and aggression or they can be defensive measures formed in response to a threat. Alliances are an important means to security for smaller states that can join forces to attain a balance of power against a threat that one state acting alone cannot accomplish. Alliances can thus be necessary for effective deterrence. However, the commitments that alliances entail can also be causes of war. Alliances are often short-term relationships established during wartime that typically do not last beyond the threat that initiated them. Permanent alliances can present significant management problems once they are entered into because smaller states might not contribute equally to providing collective benefits of safety that larger states guarantee. If a threat becomes too overriding or an alliance is not based on credible commitments, states might seek neutrality, negotiate a deal with the adversary, or pursue alternative means to their own defense.

The modern state system originated from an alliance formed as a key provision of the Peace of Westphalia, which ended the Thirty Years War in 1648. The treaty allowed that it was

Free perpetually to each of the states of the Empire, to make Alliances with strangers for their preservation and safety; Provided nevertheless such Alliances be not against the Emperor, and the Empire; nor against the Public Peace of this Treaty.[32]

The next several hundred years reflected patterns of shifting alliances as a means of averting or winning war. Alliances were not seen as permanent and the notions of "the enemy of my enemy is my friend" and "today's friend is tomorrow's enemy" were common. At the core of the shifting alliance pattern lasting up to World War I was the basic premise that alliances should shift depending on the balance of power. Fluctuating alliance commitments during the nineteenth century were seen as useful to maintaining the general health of the international system. In particular, states would make alliances to ensure that no single power would become strong enough to overturn the status quo.

Two significant alliances emerged in the early nineteenth century that reflected variations on balance of power as a means toward peace. The first, formed as the "Quadruple Alliance" between Britain, Prussia, Russia, and the Austrio-Hungarian Empire was formed in response to the rise in power and expansionistic war waged by Napoleonic France. The Quadruple Alliance was a strategic arrangement born of necessity to defeat France. Embedded within it was another alliance, the Holy Alliance, consisting of the three monarchic eastern powers of Prussia, Russia, and the Austrio-Hungarian Empire. Their objective was to prevent the system from being overturned but also to prevent the revolutionary ideas of France from disrupting their domestic rule. By the late 1800s, the international system witnessed a return to shifting alliances which eventually became a major cause of World War I when states mobilized their militaries to show support for alliance commitments, thus prompting fear among potential enemies. Alliance commitments also served to undermine the general peace after World War I as the international community sought to build the League of Nations. Rather than putting faith in such international commitments to alleviate its fear of Germany, France built a system of alliances designed to encircle Germany. The result, however, was that this sense of external threat was used to justify the rise in German nationalism which would impel Germany to pursue an expansionist and aggressive effort, leading to World War II.

During the Cold War, the United States led a global network of defensive alliances to contain the Soviet Union. In Europe, the United States worked with its allies to establish NATO which signaled in advance to the Soviet Union that an attack on any member of the organization would be considered an attack on all the members. In Asia, the United States used a combination of multilateral and bilateral frameworks. In the Anzus treaty, the United States established security pacts with Australia and New Zealand. The South East Asia Treaty Organization (SEATO) paralleled the NATO concept though was never as fully developed. SEATO included the United States, Australia, France, Britain, New Zealand, Pakistan, the Philippines, and Thailand. Unable to maintain cohesion during the Vietnam War, this alliance was disbanded in 1977. Meanwhile, the United States had bilateral alliances with Japan and South Korea. Taiwan was told by Washington that it would be defended if it was attacked, but not if that attack was provoked by actions taken by Taiwan.

The promise of collective defense creates a public good—a benefit that, once provided, is utilized by all recipients whether they contribute to the costs of service provision or not. If one nation has a greater demand for a public good than others, it will place a higher valuation on its provision. That state may provide a disproportionate level of the collective good, while the smaller members of an alliance tend to supply only suboptimal amounts. A small country that views defense costs as a burden could withdraw from (or not contribute to) an alliance but still receive defense benefits.[33] Disproportionate cost-sharing in NATO was demonstrated by comparing relative defense expenditures as a percentage of gross national product (GNP) among major alliance members.[34] In 1953, the United States spent 14.7 percent of its GNP on defense while France and Britain spent around 11 percent, and in the Federal Republic of Germany, the spending was less than 5 percent. As the U.S. level fell over time, so too did those of the European allies. By 1970, the American percentage had leveled off while European contributions continued to fall. By 1980, the U.S. figure fell to 5.5 percent, but only Britain raised its percentage. At the height of the 1980s Cold War tensions, U.S. defense spending rose to 6.5 percent while European spending remained unchanged. Over time, European contributions to the collective defense hovered just above or below 3.0 of GNP on average. While America was a global power with significant out-of-area responsibilities such as the Korean and Vietnam Wars, even adjusting for the non-NATO portion of national defense expenditures shows a significant disproportionate defense burden. As one study demonstrated, the United States, with 48 percent of the aggregated NATO gross domestic product, provided 66 percent of NATO defense costs when Vietnam was excluded from the assessment. For equity to have been attained, the United States would have to have spent $1.1 trillion less on defense between 1961 and 1988.[35]

The basic trade-off within NATO was that the United States gained significant influence over European defense priorities while the Europeans gained by cost-saving on defense spending, allowing them to invest in socioeconomic priorities. While this trade-off worked for both sides, the alliance would, nevertheless, be affected by ebbs and flows of the Cold War. Non-European conflicts, especially the Vietnam War, would strain the allies who took divergent views on the war. Most significantly, the nuclear equation raised doubts about the credibility of America's commitment to defend its European allies. To France, the answer was clearly no—America could not be relied on. In 1966, France thus withdrew from the military planning component of NATO. Nevertheless, for all of the associated costs and management difficulties, NATO remained cohesive throughout the Cold War and ultimately emerged as the victor without ever having to fire a shot. The credibility of the deterrent value of America's defensive grand strategy embodied in its alliance system was thus a key variable that prevented World War III.

An alternative to alliances is the more collective concept of great power systems management. During the 1800s the international system witnessed the rise of five relatively equal powers that dominated the international system. The form was referred to as a "concert" of powers which saw individual states acting on their interests in ways that reflected a harmony of interests. This multipolar order began with the Quadruple Alliance of Britain, Prussia, Russia, and Austria-Hungary but was expanded in 1815 to include the defeated power France after the Napoleonic Wars. During this period, states increased their communication with each other and incorporated other states' interests into their calculation of their own interests. The general health of the system was seen as good and thus a preference for the status quo was ingrained into the interests of the participating powers. War was seen as a legitimate tool of statecraft, but generally, the major powers coordinated efforts to manage change. States also negotiated for mutual gain as it might be worth sacrificing a momentary benefit for longer-term payoffs. Institutional mechanisms of communication were created to facilitate this approach to systems management via conference diplomacy.[36] The goal was, as Lord Castlereagh of Britain put it, "to adopt an open and direct mode of intercourse in the conduct of business and to repress on all sides, as much as possible, the spirit of local intrigue in which diplomatic policy is so falsely considered to consist and which so frequently creates the very evil which it is intended to avert."[37]

The nineteenth-century balance of power management model could not be sustained as the harmony of interests eventually diverged—culminating in World War I. However, the basic idea of great power systems management was enshrined in the architecture of the League of Nations which created a council for the major powers to act as an executive body to manage international security. After World War II, this model survived in the United Nations Security Council with its five permanent members—the United States, Britain, France, Russia, and China remaining as the core managers of global power into the twenty-first century. Less formal means of concert management have helped states to prevent conflict or to negotiate its end. The G-8 group of leading economic powers has coordinated economic priorities and helped to resolve disputes among the world's leading economic powers. In the 1990s, a "Contact Group" was created among the leading European powers to sponsor negotiations to end war in the former Yugoslavia. This model is attractive to many realists who see the results of international cooperation over anarchy while affirming the basic argument that the causal factor in those outcomes was the relative distribution of power.

Hegemonic Stability and Off-Shore Balancing

Hegemonic stability implies that peace is the by-product of great power dominance over a region. A particular region might be highly unstable, but if a major power dominates, it will maintain order based on its own interest. In this context, France and Germany reconciled their historic security dilemma after World War II because of the presence of American power in Western Europe. France felt secure that it could rely on a lasting peace because Germany had American troops on its soil and was divided. Hegemonic stability theory is consistent with the argument that the bipolar distribution of power during the Cold War ensured stability. As Kenneth N. Waltz wrote, "Although we would prefer that East Europeans freely choose their governors, we may nevertheless understand that the Soviet Union's managing a traditionally volatile part of the world has its good points."[38] The benefit of regional hegemony is that wars are not likely to occur when one country has dominance over a region. This condition exists when the embedded great power within a region will not tolerate instability in its sphere of influence for fear of outside interference. Efforts by an outside power to exert influence within a major regional power's area of interest is likely to provoke hard balancing behavior by the local hegemon—as in the Cuban Missile Crisis.

The overall benefit of hegemonic stability is the absence of regional war. The downside is that smaller states can be subjugated to the will of the larger power. This condition puts pressure on regional great powers to exercise dominance in a way that is acceptable to the smaller states who receive benefits from the collective good of stability. The United States appeared to understand this dilemma during the Cold War as it chose a form of hegemony that fostered multilateralism over total dominance. The United States did not exploit its smaller allies but engaged them in a system of regional security management. When France chose to depart from NATO's military planning organization in 1966, the United States permitted this. Conversely, when the Hungarians and Czechoslovaks pursued policies divergent from that of the Soviet Union during the Cold War, Moscow intervened with force. Thus hegemonic power can create management problems, especially given efforts by states to escape the influence of the dominant power. Hegemonic stability is, nevertheless, often beneficial if previously aggressive states are pacified as a result—as in the case of Germany and Japan after World War II.[39] Of course, the quality of that stability would depend greatly on the nature of the hegemonic power.

An alternative approach to exercising regional power is off-shore balancing. When a state pursues off-shore balancing, its presence is constantly felt but no direct footprint is left on the ground. An off-shore balancer—like Britain in the nineteenth century and the United States before World War I and World War II—must act with a careful mix of power and restraint.[40] An off-shore balancer holds its power in reserve and only intervenes when it is necessary to shift the balance of power or to restore order to a region. The end result can be military intervention and war. However, it is just as likely that war can be prevented by the careful exertion of power by an outside actor at precisely the right moment and with the right amount of power exercised. Off-shore balancing can be exercised by large and small powers. The ultimate effect of the strategy is for an external actor to gain power as it holds the capacity to shift alignments based on how it perceives its interests. Such powers are in an especially strong position to shape security outcomes because they often hold the key to consolidating, or opposing, whatever trends in regional security might be emerging.

REALISM REVISED

Realism remains central to explaining international security at the beginning of the twenty-first century because most of its bedrock assumptions remain valid. States remain the primary actors in the international system and they assess their security requirements in terms of power. New threats such as terrorism and weapons proliferation confirm the growing role of anarchy in international relations but also prompt citizens to look to their governments for protection. In this context, the caution and pessimism inherent in realism continues to be merited. Additionally, real or potential conflicts among states continue to exist. Realists rightly demonstrate that the relative distribution of power in the international system is still in a competitive flux in the twenty-first century. Great powers, grand strategy, and national competition continue as the United States dominates, but other powers—including Russia, China, and Europe and regional powers—contend for influence. Some core elements of realism are also challenged by the twenty-first-century security transformation. A conceptual framework that defined national and international security strictly in state and in military terms would not be dealing with the "reality" of international security in this century. Moreover, the way that actors respond to challenges might take new forms. Balancing behavior still exists, but it will not necessarily take the traditional forms realists might assume. Asymmetrical power also raises significant questions about the traditional function of deterrence. Additionally, the traditional realist, in placing an overemphasis on self-help, risks failing to recognize that states might choose to define their interests in cooperative terms. Indeed, a purely realist-driven security strategy might lead states to assert power in ways that can create significant costs in a condition of global interdependence.

Global Security

Realists do not ignore the impact of globalization on security. Rather, they find that power remains the dominant variable affecting systems structure and state behavior. Michael Mastanduno notes that there are at least three major realist approaches to explaining the emerging international system. First, realists who focus on international competition, not only actual military conflict, provide a geoeconomic framework for assessing global security. In this context, the lessening of military conflict among great powers does not mean that competitive forces are eliminated. Rather, they "evolve into different areas such as the competition for markets, raw materials, high value-added employment, and the mastery of advanced technology all becoming a surrogate for traditional military competition."[41] Such competition will likely continue until the point that a state opts for a more aggressive strategy to turn the distribution of power in the international system to its favorable advantage and thus spark more traditional security competition. This approach suggests that great powers will mobilize for international economic competition; states will therefore be sensitive to their relative position to other states' economic gains; and powerful states will likely organize relations with their neighbors in order to enhance their relative position in the global system, thus leading to new alliance structures. A second realist model sees the international system returning to a multipolar structure. A third model, unipolarity, views the international system as dominated by American primacy. Globalization thus takes on a predominantly American content. America would thus have to adopt a specific strategy of preponderance to ensure that no other major regional powers can rise to the level of peer competitor.[42]

In 1990, at a moment of general optimism about the prospects for peace with the end of the Cold War, John J. Mearsheimer laid out a realist scenario for a new era that would be defined by a return to anarchy, dangerous multipolarity, and resulting instability. The international system would likely see major crises in areas of the world that were stable during the Cold War. Mearsheimer argued that the United States could not sustain global primacy and that it would eventually withdraw from areas such as Germany where it placed high priority during the Cold War. The end result would be a multipolar system in which power imbalances and relative power competition would dominate and more actors would seek nuclear weapons. Mearsheimer predicted a rise in nationalism prompting states not benefiting from the status quo to seek a more aggressive foreign policy. Meanwhile, areas with close ethnic and national integration would experience intense conflict. Mearsheimer looked to Europe and saw several possible scenarios based on realist assumptions. Europe might emerge without any nuclear weapons—which would be the most dangerous prospect as it would in effect return Europe to a state of affairs similar to that between World War I and World War II. Alternatively, a "current ownership" scenario—where existing nuclear states retain weapons (Britain, France, and Russia) and nonnuclear states remain nuclear-free (e.g., Germany)—might persist in Central Europe. Such a scenario seemed unlikely as eventually Germany would be insecure if relying on conventional weapons in the absence of a permanent American security guarantee (which it may, or may not, want to sustain). The final scenario follows the logic that Germany would develop nuclear weapons. If such an outcome is likely, it would be better if it were well-managed by those powers who currently have nuclear weapons.[43]

A strong counterargument to Mearsheimer's assumptions, especially about Europe, was that international institutions would constrain states by promoting rules and norms of acceptable international behavior and thereby facilitate cooperation toward peace. Mearsheimer addressed this assumption by critiquing the role of international institutions and what he referred to as a "false promise of security" that they promote. Institutions such as the European Union or NATO are seen in this realist perspective as dependent on the distribution of power in the international system—not as having independent effects on state behavior. This realist view cautions that there is a risk that a state would put hopes in an international institution for security. As Mearsheimer writes, "Another state may be reliably benign, but it is impossible to be certain of that judgment because intentions are impossible to divine with 100 percent certainty."[44] Institutions might matter, but only as tools of state strategy.

Kenneth N. Waltz used realist assumptions to predict an emerging multipolarity in the international system based on an eventual rise of Germany (or Europe collectively), Japan, and China. Waltz saw the role of nuclear weapons remaining central to the structure of the international system—to which Germany and Japan would inevitably aspire:

Pride knows no nationality. How long can Japan and Germany live alongside
other nuclear states while denying themselves similar capabilities? Conflicts and
crises are certain to make them aware of the disadvantages of being without the
military instruments that other powers command. Japanese and German nuclear
inhibitions arising from World War II will not last indefinitely; one might expect
them to expire as generational memories fade.[45]

Christopher Layne offers a similar analysis, noting that the international system will move toward multipolarity because (1) unipolar systems contain the
seeds of their own demise because the hegemonic power's dominance creates
an environment conducive to the emergence of new great powers; and (2) the
entry of new great powers into the international system erodes the hegemon's
relative power and, ultimately, its preeminence.[46] To this, Peter Liberman
contests the assertion that war is inhibited by modernization and that conquest
does not pay. Liberman notes that modernization makes nations easy to
coerce. Modernization allows tyrants to monopolize coercive resources more
easily; rapid communication and mobility allow conquerors to use their coercive resources efficiently. Moreover, modern societies' wealth provides vulnerability to coercion, as wealth can be held hostage for compliance.[47]

To the extent that globalization reflects accelerated interdependence, neorealism has considerable ground on which to expand the assumption that
interdependence breeds conflict. As Waltz wrote in 1979, interdependence
raises a core problem as self-help implies that "states that feel insecure must
ask how the gain will be divided. They are compelled to ask not 'Will both of
us gain?' but 'Who will gain more?'"[48] This situation is heightened in a condition of interdependence for, as Waltz writes: "States that are heavily
dependent or closely interdependent worry about securing that which they
depend on. The high interdependence of states means that the states in question experience, or are subject to, the common vulnerability that high interdependence entails."[49] Waltz notes that rather than overcoming inequality,
globalization has reinforced disparity in the international system, which continues to be dominated not by economic integration, but rather the continued
role of the state. Waltz uses data to show that, as a percentage of gross national
product, the world is only about as interdependent in 2000 as it was in 1910 if
measured by trade and capital flows. Significantly, Waltz notes that the core of
the global system remains power—and that globalization is a phenomenon
that reflects the dominance of American power in the international system.[50]

While acknowledging that new security challenges have emerged, John
Mearsheimer concludes that they are not sufficient a threat to alter the basic
dynamics of power among the states in the international system. Dangers such
as AIDS, environmental degradation, unbounded population growth, and

global warming are, Mearsheimer writes, a cause for concern, but "there is little evidence that any of them is serious enough to threaten the survival of a great power."[51] Also, as Randall Schweller has shown, actors in international politics can find themselves having to compete over positional goods in a climate of social scarcity. Positional goods are either scarce in some imposed sense or they are subject to congestion and crowding through more extensive use. Scarcities include physical scarcity such as raw materials, but they can also include social scarcity, which has to do with pride of place and the quest for goods that maintain a certain level of existence. Such scarcity can include, for example, "the increased demand for oil due to the emergence of newly industrialized states; or, more generally, the destruction of the global commons due to over-utilization of dwindling resources for the dumping of industrial waste products into common water supplies."[52] Given these conditions of high interdependence and mutual vulnerability, economic growth and social mobility can be a direct cause of competition and conflict.

Primacy and the New Balancing

From a structural perspective, globalization reflects an outward push of American dominance in the international system. As Waltz posits,

> what appears to us as globalization appears to much of the world, no doubt to most of the world, very simply as Americanization. In other words, the world is no longer bipolar. It's now unipolar. There is one great power and one only. This condition has not existed since Rome. That is, no country has dominated the relevant part of the globe since Rome, to the extent that we do. And of course Rome's realm was a part of the world. Our realm is the entire globe.[53]

The frustration that some states and cultures feel at being on the receiving end of creeping globalization might subsequently work against this trend toward interdependence. As such, American unipolarity might be seen as a threat against which to balance. Alternatively, the unipolar moment is heralded as a positive force that spreads peace and harmony in international politics because of the unique role that the United States plays as a benign hegemon and as a stabilizing force in world politics. The phrase "unipolar moment" was introduced into the international security lexicon in 1990 by the journalist Charles Krauthammer, who argued that: "The true geopolitical structure of the post–Cold War world . . . [is] a single pole of world power that consists of the United States at the apex of the industrial West. Perhaps it is more accurate to say the United States and behind it the West."[54] Krauthammer argues against multipolarity and asserts that realists should not "want to forfeit unipolarity for the familiarity of traditional multipolarity" as "multipolarity is inherently fluid and unpredictable."[55] Krauthammer argues for a "new unilateralism" which is "clear in its determination to self-consciously and confidently deploy American power in pursuit of global ends."[56]

American primacy might be seen as healthy for the international system because, were it not there, the system could collapse into traditional patterns of international competition. As Michael Mastanduno has shown, the United States has, since the end of the Cold War, pursued a grand strategy designed to sustain American primacy.[57] These dynamics are likely to persist because, as Stephen Brooks and William Wolforth have shown, there are virtually no major constraints on the exercise of American power.[58] Yet, America's rise to power has been based on norms of both restraint and multilateralism—historically making its power less threatening to other states.[59] States will compete for primacy because its value lies not only in the ability to win wars, but also to achieve a state's goals without military force. Samuel Huntington asserts that "primacy is thus an alternative to war. . . . A state such as the United States that has achieved international primacy has every reason to attempt to maintain that primacy through peaceful means so as to preclude the need of having to fight a war to maintain it."[60]

Huntington argues that, while primacy is an important component of world order, the international system at the dawn of the twenty-first century was, in fact, not unipolar. To be purely unipolar would mean that there was one superpower, no significant major powers, and many minor powers. Huntington saw the distribution of power as being "uni-multipolar" with one superpower and several major powers. This situation creates a dilemma for both the United States and other major powers as Washington often acts as if it were a unipolar power and provokes resentment and a desire for change among other significant states. Huntington asserts that there was a brief unipolar moment at the end of the Cold War, but that this moment had passed by the end of the century. These conditions create a serious problem for the United States because, as Huntington writes, "On issue after issue, the United States has found itself increasingly alone, with one or a few partners, opposing most of the rest of the world's states and peoples."[61] Huntington notes that the United States was increasingly viewed internationally—and well before the invasion of Iraq in 2003—as a "rogue superpower." Responses to American primacy at the international level could include the formation of an anti-hegemonic coalition involving several major powers. Huntington observes that this has yet to occur, however, because it is too early and also because many states benefit from America's world position. Huntington notes that "the international relations theory that predicts balancing under the current circumstances is a theory developed in the context of the European Westphalian system established in

1648."[62] Instead, Huntington sees global politics as "multicivilational" so that balancing might occur in ways that not only cross the traditional boundaries of nation-states, but also include cultural cleavages that might prevent states from forming anti-balancing coalitions (e.g., between Russia and China).

States and non-state actors have new tools provided by globalization which impact the means to pursuing balancing strategies. Steven Walt notes that in some cases, states might bandwagon toward the United States from fear of American power or a desire to reap rewards for cooperation. States might also engage in regional balancing to make it more difficult for Washington to exert influence into a particular region; this may be done directly or, simply by frustrating the use of American power, indirectly. States and their associated non-state advocates might penetrate into the American political system. As an open democracy, the United States is particularly vulnerable to this new form of balancing. A variety of actors are able to gain access to internal political processes—via direct lobbying or by expatriates or citizens of their country—to influence U.S. foreign policy. States might also align with the United States to influence and constrain American policy by acting as part of the American-led coalitions. States might use international institutions and international public opinion to constrain the exertion of American power. Other options include passive resistance where international actors effectually ignore the United States. States also might blackmail the United States—for example, by attaining weapons of mass destruction. Additionally, states and other international actors might incorporate asymmetric tools such as terrorism. Finally, large popular movements might seek to delegitimize the United States in an effort to win hearts and minds across borders.[63]

An emerging tool for states that wish to redistribute power in the modern international system is "soft-power balancing." "Soft power" has been described primarily by neoliberal scholars drawing from the traditions of idealism. However, on the role of soft power there is a convergence of analysis between realists and contemporary liberals who see soft power as essential to the legitimacy of the United States as a sole superpower in the international system. To sustain that legitimacy, the United States has historically used calculated policy mechanisms and choices to avoid soft-power balancing by both allies and enemies. A country's relative soft power is derived from the ability to attract others through the appeal of one's values by co-opting people rather than coercing them. To Joseph S. Nye, soft power "rests on the ability to set the political agenda in a way that shapes the preferences of others."[64] Nye shows that "the universality of a country's culture and its ability to establish a set of favorable rules and institutions that govern areas of international activity are critical sources of power."[65] Though realists maintain that hard military and economic power are still the predominant variables shaping international security, soft power is increasingly seen as an important component of contemporary grand strategy, especially for balancing options. This is an ironic development because the mechanisms through which the United States rose to power—multilateral institutions such as the United Nations, NATO, and global economic institutions—are now the tools through which other states can conduct soft-power balancing.

The dynamics of soft-power balancing have been detailed by Robert A. Pape who notes that the unilateral tendencies of the United States at the turn of the century have provoked balancing behavior—but of a nonmilitary nature. Pape explains the lack of hard balancing against the United States as being initially based on its "unparalleled reputation for non-aggressive intentions."[66] Pape argues that, in fact, major powers are in early stages of creating balancing mechanisms against the United States and that if the United States continues to pursue an aggressive unilateralist tendency, such forces will intensify. Pape notes that in addition to the historical fear of a possible attack by a larger power, states also worry about the "possibility that one major power will rise to the position of a global hegemon." In such a case, "a state could do many harmful acts, from re-writing the rules of international conduct to its long-term advantage to exploiting world economic resources for relative gain, to imposing imperial rule on second ranked powers, and, potentially, to conquer any state in the system."[67] To Pape, soft-power balancing behavior includes

> actions that do not directly challenge unipolar leader's military preponderance, but that do delay, complicate, and increase the costs of using that extraordinary power. Non-military tools, such as international institutions, economic statecraft, and strict interpretations of neutrality, can have a real, if indirect, effect on the military prospects of a superior state. More important, soft balancing can also establish a basis of cooperation for more forceful, hard balancing measures in the future.[68]

Pape notes that traditional realists should not dismiss soft balancing because there do exist concrete options which can constrain and frustrate the exercise of primacy. Such policy options include: territorial denial for staging areas or air and naval transit; economic strengthening via regional trade blocs and other restrictive trade actions; entangling diplomacy via the use of rules and procedures in important international organizations; and the signaling capacity of states to coordinate expectations of mutual balancing behavior. While soft balancing might not stop the United States from making near-term gains, it can impose real military and economic costs on the ability of the U.S., or any other large state, to exert power.

Alliances, Dissuasion, and Strategic Partnerships

Modern realism is challenged to explain the role of deterrence and alliances in the context of new security challenges. Realists do assert that deterrence remains effective against states in the traditional sense. Also, some realists posit that the demands for emerging threats like nuclear proliferation are logical and, in fact, will produce peace. Realists also view the role of alliances in the contemporary environment with some skepticism. Alliances are possible as a response to new security threats but, to be effective, they must be organized around a common threat perception and an agreed response. Realists do note, however, that new forms of cooperation at the strategic level are possible among great and medium powers as shifts in global power place a high premium on temporary alignments such as strategic partnerships and coalitions of the willing.

Realists have struggled with the survival of NATO after the Cold War. Realist theory of alliances generally predicts that, in the absence of a threat, alliances collapse. Some analysts suggest that NATO might have been sustained as a reserve "insurance" policy to hedge against a hypothetical new Russian threat. However, few would have predicted NATO's expansion to include new members in Central and Eastern Europe and that it would wage an offensive war against Yugoslavia in 1999. As a pillar of American dominance in Europe, NATO has served as a tool for Washington to manage the rise of the European Union as a security alternative and to constrain both Germany and Russia as peer competitors. Nevertheless, by 2004, the United States was beginning a process of removing major troop deployments from Germany. While NATO's survival seemed assured, the relevance of its survival was largely in doubt.

Many pro-NATO advocates and bureaucratic interests advocated a change for NATO to meet new threats. However, identifying a common threat and aligning shared means is not the same thing. On September 12, 2001, after the terrorist attacks by al Qaeda on New York and Washington, D.C., the NATO allies declared the attacks an "Article 5" matter, meaning it was an attack on all NATO members. However, when the United States went to retaliate, it circumvented NATO and excluded all the allies except for Britain. Rajan Menon notes that alliances like NATO might be useful for the promotion of values and democracy—but there is no reason why a military alliance per se is necessary to accomplish this objective.[69] As Bruno Tertrais observes, the assertion by U.S. President George Bush that in the war on terrorism you are "either with us, or against us" harkens to a broad coalition of those who are on the inside of a grand coalition of as many as 136 countries aligned to fight terrorism.[70] Nevertheless, if "alignment" replaces formal "alliances" and if "temporary and bilateral" replaces "permanent and multilateral," then there is also risk in such relationships over time. States that align with a major power might find themselves attacked by terrorists for their affiliation. Large powers might put undue pressure on those states that support it to engage in circumstances that are either counter to their own national interests or unsustainable in terms of domestic public support.

Variations on realism also address the challenges to the traditional notion of deterrence and its application to nonconventional threats. Richard Kugler offers "dissuasion" as a complement to traditional deterrence. Dissuasion is an effort by a state to convince a country or coalition to refrain from courses of action that would menace its interests and goals or otherwise endanger world peace.[71] Dissuasion implies an international relationship that is not confrontational, but one that could become so if not carefully handled. Dissuasion is intended to discourage an adversary from engaging in foreign policies and military behavior that could produce political confrontation, military competition, and war. At a tactical level, sufficient defensive measures for homeland security can dissuade terrorist groups that the risk of detection and failure of terrorist plots is not worth the expenditure of scarce resources. At a strategic level, dissuasion can send a signal from one country to another (e.g., from the United States to China) that it is not worth even considering a military build-up that might in the future rival another power as that build-up will be met with true military capabilities. If, however, dissuasion is "pursued in heavy-handed ways, it can be counterproductive, it can help intensify regional polarization and militarization, motivate countries to pursue asymmetric strategies aimed at negating U.S. strengths, alienate allies, and trigger the formation of coalitions against the United States."[72]

Another emerging strategy consistent with realism is the "strategic partnership" concept. A strategic partnership is used by states to enhance or justify a close relationship with others who seek mutual gains.[73] The concept is purposefully vague and has been applied to define a variety of international security relationships. For offensive realism, a strategic partnership can be a tool used by a powerful state, or states, to maximize political, economic, and military dominance in the international system. Consistent with defensive realism, strategic partnerships can reflect balancing behavior as states use them to constrain other powers. Strategic partnerships are sometimes part of a grand scheme for systemic change, but they may also be a rhetorical device used by diplomats to help them around the rough edges of shifting global politics. The term can also be a contemporary spin on traditional balance of power politics. Or, it may be a window dressing to justify bilateral alliances arising out of pragmatic necessity.

A survey of strategic partnerships shows that the term has been used in five specific kinds of state-to-state relationships. First, the United States and Turkey used the term to describe their bilateral relationship during the 1990s. Turkey, in turn, also set out to build its own strategic partnership with Israel. In this case, the term was used to bolster the relationship between traditional allies (U.S.-Turkey) and to signal a desire for a new relationship (Turkey-Israel). However, if the term could be used to define a relationship between hard military allies, what did the term do to the overall concept of alliance? In the second case, the term was used to project reassurance—for example, the United States built a strategic partnership with Romania after Romania was excluded from NATO membership in 1997. Meanwhile, the United States also offered a third form of strategic partnership to Russia as a means of engaging Moscow as a tool to manage Russia's great power decline. But if Romania and Turkey had the same relationship as Russia, what did that entail? The term was applied, fourth, by the United States to its relationship with China as a justification for engagement with a potential adversary. In a fifth example, balancing, Russia and China developed their own strategic partnership, explicitly intending to promote their cooperation as a tool for complicating American primacy.

Asymmetric Threats, Ethnic Conflict, and Identity Realism

Realism has shown adaptability as scholars apply traditional realist concepts to new threats such as terrorism and ethnic conflict. Additionally, the notion that states are all, in effect, "the same" has been adapted to better reflect the relationship between a state "identity" and variations in how states define their interests. Core concepts of realism, including rational actor models and balance of power stability still apply to these cases. These new security threats do challenge the traditional realist focus on the primacy of the nation-state. However, the fact that there are security challenges beyond the nation-state does not necessarily mean that other core assumptions that drive realist thinking are outdated.

Assessing the asymmetrical threat of terrorism, Robert Pape surveyed suicide terrorist attacks from 1980 through 2001. The data shows that there is a strategic, and rational, logic behind them—rather than being driven solely by "crazy" fanatics.[74] Religion is a relevant factor, but mainly as a recruitment tool. Pape's evidence illustrates four key conclusions about suicide terrorism: suicide terrorism is strategic, designed to coerce modern democracies to make concessions; suicide terrorism is rising in numbers of incidents because terrorists are learning that it pays; in spite of some gains, more ambitious suicide terrorist campaigns are not going to achieve major gains; and, finally, the most promising way to contain suicide terrorism is to reduce terrorists' confidence in their ability to carry out such attacks on the target society.[75] These conclusions are supported by three key findings: (1) timing—nearly all suicide attacks occur in organized, coherent campaigns, not as isolated or randomly timed incidents; (2) nationalist goals—suicide terrorists' campaigns are directed at gaining control of what the terrorists see as their national homeland territory, specifically at ejecting foreign forces from that territory; and (3) target selection—all suicide terrorist campaigns in the last two decades have been aimed at democracies, which make more suitable targets from the terrorists' point of view.[76] Pape also shows that overly ambitious terrorist goals are not likely to be achieved. Overly dramatic attacks can backfire for terrorist groups as such acts will not likely impact the interests of states that have significant wealth or security issues at stake.

Ethnic conflict, because it occurs within states or can transcend state borders, is an important challenge for realist approaches to contemporary security. Nevertheless, application of realist assumptions to this growing security challenge has helped to better explain the origins of, and possible solutions to, ethnic conflict. For example, Chaim Kaufmann notes that, in ethnic wars, the extreme forces and passions that drive ethnic identities to the point of war are unlikely to yield to appeals to cease fire and negotiate a settlement. Intermingled population settlement patterns can thus create a new variation on the security dilemma which serves to intensify violence, motivate ethnic cleansing, and prevent de-escalation unless warring parties are separated. Kaufmann shows that stable resolutions of ethnic conflict can only occur when opposing groups are separated into defensible enclaves. The result is that the international community should abandon idealistic hopes of restoring multiethnic states and integrating populations and instead facilitate and protect population movements to create national homelands. The only other alternative is to let the warring parties battle it out via ethnic cleansing until one side emerges victorious.[77]

Another variation on realism, "identity realism" combines realist assumptions with the study of culture. This approach seeks to explain how states come to perceive their interests and why states might not always behave in ways that traditional realism would predict. Alastair Iain Johnston argues that the balance of power and balance-of-threat aspects of neorealism do not adequately explain contemporary Chinese security choices. Realist focus on the offensive desire to expand power and compete for primacy does help to describe some of China's behavior. However, it fails to provide a complete explanation because China does not appear to be especially unsatisfied with the status-quo of American primacy and indeed is making some important gains from political and economic cooperation with the United States. Johnston concludes that Chinese security policy is best explained by "identity realism"—which explains why status is as important to Chinese leaders as is security—and that the major threats to China are those that serve to constrain the achievement of higher status.[78] Identity realism suggests that if there is an increase in the intensity of identity or efforts to intensify identification, one would expect to see more competitive behavior directed at external forces.[79] Such an approach, Johnston maintains, helps to address a shortcoming in more traditional realist assessments of state strategies because it accounts for variations in the intensity of strategic choices and in the responses of different groups to similar changes in relative capabilities.[80] In this context, self-help is shaped by internal identity formation which then devalues external forces, turning them into threats to the legitimacy of a group's concept of itself inside the nation-state.

Clash of Civilizations

A "clash of civilizations" blends realist assessments of interdependence with the impact of culture to explain the sources of conflict. The idea of cultural conflict is not new in international security. However, the idea of a clash of civilizations posits that international security trends are increasingly reflecting a repositioning of global conflict away from states and toward alignment among civilizational kinship. Samuel Huntington advanced this position in 1993 with his assessment of the rise of civilizations and impending conflict along new fault lines that transcend the traditional nation-state.[81] Huntington assumes that international relations in the twenty-first century will not be driven by ideological or economic incentives, but instead will be cultural. A civilization is defined as the broadest level of community with which individuals affiliate—to which Huntington identified eight major world civilizations: Western, Confucian, Japanese, Islamic, Hindu, Slavic-Orthodox, Latin American, and possibly African.

Huntington offered six reasons for a pending clash of civilizations. First, the kinds of differences that emerge between civilizational groups are real and basic. Such identities are the most difficult for people to abandon. Second, the interactions between different civilizations are increasing. This enhances people's consciousness of their own identity, which heightens differences and animosities when contrasted against others. Third, economic modernization and subsequent social change separates people from their basic identities and weakens nation-states as a source of identification. This process has been replaced by religion, which often manifests in the form of fundamentalist movements designed to advance and protect the boundaries of civilizations. Fourth, civilization-consciousness is enhanced by the "dual role of the West"—which is at its peak of power, but which also prompts a backlash against it. Fifth, culture is a less-mutable force and thus less easily compromised and resolved than political or economic differences. Finally, economic regionalism is growing along cultural lines, which will further enhance the global dynamics of civilizational conflict.

Huntington points to regional fault lines in the world where civilizations meet and conflict is likely. As civilizations transcend traditional state boundaries, groups or states are likely to rally around states that most closely approximate their civilizational interests. Huntington notes that the "West" faces a particularly difficult challenge because other civilizations have a common cause in challenging the dominant civilization. Facing likely conflict, civilizations have three possible reactions: (1) to isolate themselves to avoid penetration by the West; (2) to bandwagon and join with the West; and (3) to balance the West by developing economic and military capabilities and forging alliances with other non-Western societies. States that are torn internally by competing civilizational preferences are likely to face a particularly high amount of stress in this kind of conflict.

Huntington asserts he was not endorsing a clash. Rather, he sought to set forth a descriptive hypothesis as to what the future might be like. Nevertheless, traditional realists might resist the temptation to move beyond the interest of states, noting also that there have been a number of state-to-state and civil conflicts within the civilizations identified by Huntington—for example, between Iran and Iraq in the 1980s. By 2005 the largest numbers of Iraqis killed in Iraq were dying in attacks undertaken by fellow Iraqis. Subsequently, Huntington's approach has been criticized for assuming cohesion within civilizations that are in fact quite diverse and in some cases divided—for example, among the Shiite and Sunni Muslims. Furthermore, if strictly applied as policy, Huntington's assumptions might generate self-fulfilling prophecies. For example, if one looks at Russia and assumes that there are certain civilizational traits that will lead Moscow toward conquest and authoritarianism, expanding NATO as an anti-Russian alliance would seem important. Russia's authoritarian and expansionist past, however, does not predispose its future. Indeed, expansion of NATO risked creating a self-fulfilling prophecy in Russia—exacerbating the clash of civilizations should Russia abandon the West in favor of its own perceived security needs. Nonetheless, Huntington's analysis, while controversial, has been one of the most important conceptual arguments, and significant modifications of the realist paradigm, at the onset of the twenty-first century.

Economic Realism

Economic realism is a state-centric approach to political economy which focuses on the role of the state in maximizing economic power to attain strategic objectives. To economic realists, the purpose of the state is to develop economic strengths and protect against vulnerabilities to advance the national interest. Economic realists view the international economic system as competitive and economic relationships as based on zero-sum gains in which there are always winners and losers. States might thus work within the emerging global security dynamics to use their economic power via the channels of globalization to expand their economic wealth and power. In this sense, globalization is a power tool used by states seeking to consolidate and expand their relative international position. Alternatively, economic realists might see a particular economic order as providing stability to the world economy and thus justifying hegemony, which prevents future conflict. Or, it could also have a defensive component in which states seek to adjust domestic economic policy to resist the encroachment of global challenges to sovereignty.

As Richard Rosecrance has shown, the modern trading system was embedded in world politics on the basis of the strength of the alliance arrangements that were pursued during the Cold War.[82] As such, this system reflected the dominant preferences exercised by the primacy of the United States with a close relationship to its strategic and security objectives. As Barry Buzan shows, three specific paths can lead to the extension of the relationship between economic strategy and security. The first is a direct argument: when the threat of war is high, an entire economy is geared towards enhancing military strength. The second extends military logic but adds to it by analogy other areas in which the legitimate responsibilities of governments can be defined in national security terms. For example, in a situation in which economic threats have the highest profile for many citizens, a conflation of social and national security logic can be highly appealing for political actors. In the third path, states might attack the nature of global free-market logic and the dangers of surrendering economic control to outside forces.[83] Investment into military capabilities can significantly increase the power of a state and thus create a perception of threat to other states. This, in turn, can lead them to adapt their strategies consistent with the security dilemma. Alternatively, an overinvestment into military capabilities can lead to an overstretch and force a state to retrench and reform, or even collapse. The end of the Cold War reflected key aspects of this dynamic as the United States significantly increased its economic investment in the military to the point that the Soviet Union either had to choose to match it, or negotiate. Meanwhile, the costs of the external occupation of Eastern Europe also domestically drained the economic power of the Soviet Union.

Within the global security environment, it is possible that economic warfare will serve as a surrogate for traditional means of conflict. States might employ international sanctions on enemy states to induce change or punish them for their behavior. States might, alternatively, offer economic rewards to those states that do cooperate with strategic objectives. Ethan Kapstein offers eight specific ways in which economic warfare can be employed:

export embargo, or a prohibition on exports to the enemy and its allies; boy-cott, or a prohibition against buying goods from the enemy and its allies; blacklist of domestic or third-country firms that trade with the enemy; strate-gic purchasing, or the buying of defense-related commodities on world mar-kets; dumping, or the sale of stockpiled goods at lower prices; impounding, confiscating, or nationalizing enemy-owned assets; strategic bombing, sabo-tage, or other military operations against enemy economic targets; and propa-ganda, or the deliberate use of economic misinformation to create panic, hoarding, and confusion in enemy territory.[84] Kapstein also notes the impact of the de-escalation from warfare or conflict as states have a high incentive to switch "from guns to butter." Such moves can be destabilizing because loss of demand for military goods and services can occur and thus the resource base for military capabilities might be redirected. While military conversion can be an economic gain, it can also lead states to be underprepared should new threats emerge on the horizon. Attaining the right balance between guns and butter remains one of the most significant challenges confronting states as they pursue their national interests.

Economic realists see a strong role for the state within the domestic econ-omy as a defensive response to external forces—such as the market pressures of economic globalization. The creation by the state of protective barriers can include the imposition of tariffs on foreign imported goods and services; non-tariff barriers such as health regulations, safety, and other standards; pricing limits to restrain trade; technological restrictions; and dumping of surplus goods into foreign markets at lower than competitive prices. States might also pursue protectionist policies to give infant industries an advantage via direct investment. The historical track record of such actions has not been good. However, it is a realist-based response to the perceived threat of globalization given the role of the state and its desire to sustain or maximize power.

The structural role of power distribution also can help explain the increased role in international relations played by multinational corporations. As Robert Gilpin has shown, the 1980s and 1990s saw an extraordinary amount of expansion of corporate power in the developed parts of the world combined with increasing concentration of power among media, entertainment, and telecommunications firms.[85] Such a development is a challenge both to the traditional dominance of nation-states and also to the ability of lesser devel-oped states and their own firms to expand their economic capabilities. The result is a tendency to pursue protectionist policies or to regulate multinational firms. However, if too many states pursued such a policy, the results would be costly for the global economy. Gilpin's analysis of international political economy strikes a balance in the conclusion that, "Although for many, globalization is a threat, it is also part of the solution to underdevelopment."[86] Gilpin's approach reflects pragmatism in economic realism, which often historically viewed underdeveloped economies as only being of value to the wealthy states to the extent that their resources could be exploited.

A central question for realists is whether the economic interdependence that drives globalization increases the likelihood of war. Realists have generally answered this question by noting that much of the same competitive logic of security competition can apply to economic models because relative power shifts are also important factors in assessing security needs of states. As John Mearsheimer writes, "once relative gains considerations are factored into the equation, it becomes impossible to maintain the neat dividing line between economic and military issues, mainly because military might is significantly dependent on economic might. . . . The relative size of a state's economy has profound consequences for its standing in the international balance of military power."[87] Realists see the interdependence of economic ties as creating vulnerability, and thus provide incentives for states to deny an enemy any economic advantage. Additionally, great powers are going to conflict with each other as they seek ever-expanding access to resources as a means of growing their economy. In sum, there is no reason, in the realist view, to assume that economic interdependence and globalization inherently create peace.

Realists as Optimists

Robert Gilpin notes that realists maintain a particular worldview grounded in core propositions—but that does not necessarily mean that they like it. Gilpin writes:

> Although realists recognize the central role of the state, security, and power in international affairs, they do not necessarily approve of this situation. The teacher who first introduced me to realism as an analytic perspective, Professor George Little of the University of Vermont, was a Quaker pacifist; yet, when I was an undergraduate, Little once chided me for my naïve and unrealistic views on a particular development in international politics. Martin Wight, the author of one of the most important tracts on realism in this century, *Power Politics* (1986), was also a Christian pacifist. Even Hans Morgenthau in his influential *Politics Among Nations*, having Adolf Hitler in mind, condemned "universal nationalism," that is, imperialistic behavior, as immoral. One of his basic messages was that states should try to respect the interests of other states.[88]

Indeed, a variety of factors that are related to perceptions of self-interest can modify many of the impulses that realists worry about. Dale C. Copeland has shown that expectations of future trade gains can lead states to avoid risks that would sever the benefits of future trade. "When expectations for trade are positive, leaders expect to realize the benefits of trade into the future and therefore have less reason for war now; trade will indeed 'constrain.' . . . If, however, leaders are pessimistic about future trade, fearing to be cut off from vital goods or believing that current restrictions will not be relaxed, then the negative expected value of peace may make war the rational strategic choice."[89] In that sense, the political economy of the global security environment can lead states to forgo conflict in expectation of future strategic gains. Charles Glaser uses realist concepts to show how states will work to organize their military-policy options during peacetime to coordinate policies designed to avoid arms races. Glaser proposes the use of "contingent realism" which asserts that cooperative policies are an important type of self-help in that "states seeking security should see benefits in cooperative policies that can communicate benign motives." Thus states will have a self-help motive in promoting policies that emphasize nonthreatening military capabilities and that signal their benign intentions via arms control, unilateral defense, and unilateral restraint (the later two implying the unilateral decision to prioritize defensive capabilities). Glaser concludes that: "Instead of a strong propensity toward security competition, we find that states' choices between cooperation and competition are highly conditional, with no general preference for competition."[90]

SUMMARY

Historically, realism has been the dominant approach to understanding the quest for power in international security. A long tradition in the form of anarchy, interest, power, and war gives strong evidence of the salience of realist traditions. Realism's primary focus on power continues to give it considerable relevance in the era of global security because, while its manifestations have expanded, power continues to be central to understanding security behavior. Realism has proven to be a flexible and adaptive approach to the emerging security environment. Perhaps the most important legacy of realism is that it can serve as a methodological tool with which to test and challenge ongoing efforts in the more idealistic search for peace. As a methodological tool, realism can serve as a means through which to test alternative approaches; this will only serve to make them more attainable if they are first challenged with the hard critiques made available by the traditions of realism. As E. H. Carr surmised, human nature seeks to build a better world, but if not challenged by realism, such approaches risk crashing on the rocks of reality.[91]

NOTES

1. This summary is derived from John J. Mearsheimer, "The False Promise of International Institutions," *International Security* 19, no. 3 (Winter 1994/1995): 5–49; and Charles W. Kegley Jr., ed., *Controversies in International Relations Theory: Realism and the Neoliberal Challenge* (New York: St. Martin's Press, 1995).

2. From Niccolo Machiavelli, *The Prince and the Discourses* (New York: Random House, 1940).

3. These quotes come from Thomas Hobbes, *Leviathan*, introduction by Richard S. Peters (New York: Macmillan, 1962).

4. Hans J. Morgenthau, *Politics among Nations, Brief Edition* (New York: McGraw-Hill, 1992).

5. George F. Kennan, *American Diplomacy, 1900–1950* (Chicago: University of Chicago Press, 1951).

6. Henry Kissinger, *A World Restored*, new ed. (London: Weidenfeld and Nicholson History, 2000).

7. Kenneth N. Waltz, *Theory of International Politics* (Reading, Mass.: Addison-Wesley, 1979).

8. Robert Gilpin, *War and Change in World Politics* (Cambridge: Cambridge University Press, 1983).

9. Robert J. Art, "To What Ends Military Power?" *International Security* 4, no. 4 (Spring 1980): 3–14.

10. John Herz, *The Nation-State and the Crisis of World Politics* (New York: David McKay, 1976), 157.

11. Robert Jervis, "Cooperation under the Security Dilemma," *World Politics* 30, no. 2 (January 1978): 186–214.

12. Jervis, "Cooperation under the Security Dilemma," 190.

13. Stephen Van Evera, "Offense, Defense, and the Causes of War," *International Security* 22, no. 4 (Spring 1998): 5–43.

14. Van Evera, "Offense, Defense," 43.

15. Ole R. Holsti, "Crisis Decision Making," in *Diplomacy: New Approaches in History, Theory and Policy*, ed. Paul Gorden Lauren (New York: Free Press, 1979).

16. Alexander George, "Coercive Diplomacy," in *The Use of Force: Military Power and International Politics*, 6th ed., ed. Robert J. Art and Kenneth N. Waltz (Lanham, Md.: Rowman and Littlefield, 2004), 70–76.

17. Barton Gellman, "The Path to Crisis: How the United States and Its Allies Went to War," *Washington Post*, April 18, 1999.

18. Mark Heinrich, "Is Kosovo Intervention More Bark Than Bite?" *Reuters*, August 7, 1998.

19. William Drozdiak, "Analysis: New Challenges Facing 50-Year-Old NATO," *Washington Post*, March 24, 1999.

20. Jim Hoagland, "Kosovos to Come," *Washington Post*, June 27, 1999.

21. John J. Mearsheimer, *The Tragedy of Great Power Politics* (New York: W. W. Norton, 2001), 29–54.

22. Mearsheimer, *Tragedy*, 141–47.

23. Mearsheimer, *Tragedy*, 227.

24. Stephen Walt, *The Origins of Alliances* (Ithaca, N.Y.: Cornell University Press, 1987).

25. Randall L. Schweller, "Bandwagoning for Profit: Bringing the Revisionist State Back In," *International Security* 19, no. 1 (Summer 1994): 72–107.

26. Gordon A. Craig and Alexander L. George, *Force and Statecraft: Diplomatic Problems of Our Time*, 2nd ed. (Oxford: Oxford University Press, 1990), 179.

27. Craig and George, *Force and Statecraft*, 179.

28. See John J. Mearsheimer, *Conventional Deterrence* (Ithaca, N.Y.: Cornell University Press, 1985).

29. Robert Jervis, "The Utility of Nuclear Deterrence," *International Security* 13, no. 2 (Fall 1988): 80–90.

30. John Mearsheimer, "Back to the Future: Instability in Europe After the Cold War," *International Security* 15, no. 1 (Summer 1990): 35–50.

31. See Graham T. Allison and Philip Zelikow, *Essence of a Decision: Explaining the Cuban Missile Crisis*, 2nd ed. (New York: Longman, 1999).

32. Treaty of Westphalia, Avalon Project of Yale Law School, November 2004.

33. Mancur Olson and Richard Zechkauser, "An Economic Theory of Alliances," *The Review of Economics and Statistics* 47, no. 3 (August 1966): 266–79; Mancur Olson, *The Logic of Collective Action: Public Goods and the Theory of Groups* (Cambridge, Mass.: Harvard University Press, 1965).

34. These figures on European and American defense expenditures as a percentage of GNP were compiled from the International Institute for Strategic Studies, *The Military Balance* (London: Brassey's, 1960–98).

35. Leonard Sullivan Jr. and Jack LeCuyer, *Comprehensive Security and Western Prosperity* (Washington, D.C.: The Atlantic Council of the United States, 1988), 48.

36. See Robert Jervis, "Security Regimes," in *International Regimes*, ed. Stephen D. Krasner, (Ithaca, N.Y.: Cornell University Press, 1983), 173–194; and Paul Schroeder, "The Transformation of Political Thinking in the International System," in *Coping with Complexity in the International System*, ed. Jack Snyder and Robert Jervis (Boulder, Colo.: Westview Press, 1993), 47–70.

37. Charles K. Webster, *The Foreign Policy of Castlereagh: Britain and the European Alliance, 1815–1822*, 2nd ed. (London: G. Bell, 1934), 2.

38. Waltz, *Theory of International Politics*, 208–9.

39. Lisa Martin, "The Rational State Choice of Multilateralism," in *Multilateralism Matters: The Theory and Praxis of an Institutional Form*, ed. John Gerard Ruggie (New York: Columbia University Press, 1993), 91–121.

40. Christopher Layne, "From Preponderance to Offshore Balancing: America's Future Grand Strategy," *International Security* 22, no. 1 (Summer 1997): 86–124.

41. Michael Mastanduno, "A Realist View: Three Images of the Coming International Order," in *International Order and the Future of World Politics*, ed. T. V. Paul and John A. Hall (Cambridge: Cambridge University Press, 1999), 23.

42. Mastanduno, "A Realist View," 28–36.

43. Mearsheimer, "Back to the Future," 35–50.

44. John J. Mearsheimer, "The False Promise of International Institutions," in *The Perils of Anarchy: Contemporary Realism and International Security*, ed. Michael E. Brown, Sean M. Lynn-Jones, and Steven E. Miller (Cambridge, Mass.: MIT Press, 1995), 337.

45. Kenneth N. Waltz, "The Emerging Structure of International Politics," *International Security* 18, no. 2 (Fall 1993): 44–79.

46. Christopher Layne, "The Unipolar Illusion: Why New Great Powers Will Rise," *International Security* 17, no. 4 (Spring 1993): 5–51.

47. Peter Liberman, "The Spoils of Conquest," *International Security* 18, no. 2 (Fall 1993): 125–54.

48. Kenneth N. Waltz, "The Anarchic Structure of World Politics," in *International Politics: Enduring Concepts and Contemporary Issues*, 5th ed., ed. Robert J. Art and Robert Jervis (New York: Longman, 2000), 61.

49. Waltz, "Anarchic Structure," 62.

50. Kenneth N. Waltz, "Globalization and Governance," *PS: Political Science and Politics* 32, no. 4 (December 2001): 693–700.

51. Mearsheimer, *Tragedy*, 372.

52. Randall L. Schweller, "Realism and the Present Great Power System: Growth and Positional Conflict Over Scarce Resources," in *Unipolar Politics: Realism and State Strategies After the Cold War*, ed. Ethan B. Kapstein and Michael Mastanduno (New York: Columbia University Press, 1999), 28–68.

53. "Theory and International Politics: Conversation with Kenneth N. Waltz," Institute of International Studies, University of California at Berkeley, February 2003.

54. Charles Krauthammer, "The Unipolar Moment," *Foreign Affairs: America and the World* 70, no. 1(1990/1991): 23–33.

55. Charles Krauthammer, "The Unipolar Moment Revisited," *The National Interest*, no. 70 (Winter 2002/2003): 13.

56. Krauthammer, "Unipolar Moment Revisited," 14.

57. Michael Mastanduno, "Preserving the Unipolar Moment: Realist Theories and U.S. Grand Strategy after the Cold War," *International Security* 21, no. 4 (Spring 1997): 49–88.

58. Stephen Brooks and William Wolforth, "American Primacy in Perspective," *Foreign Affairs* 81, no. 4 (July/August 2002): 20–33.

59. John Gerard Ruggie, "The Past as Prologue? Interests, Identity, and American Foreign Policy," *International Security* 21, no. 4 (Spring 1997): 89–125.

60. Samuel P. Huntington, "Why International Primacy Matters," *International Security* 17, no. 4 (Spring 1993): 68–83.

61. Samuel P. Huntington, "The Lonely Superpower," *Foreign Affairs* 78, no. 2 (March/April 1999): 41.

62. Huntington, "Lonely Superpower," 45.

63. Stephen Walt, "Living with the 800 lb. Gorilla: Global Responses to American Power," Lyman Lecture, Ohio Wesleyan University, April 2004.

64. Joseph S. Nye, *The Paradox of American Power: Why the World's Only Superpower Can't Go It Alone* (Oxford: Oxford University Press, 2002), 8–9.

65. Nye, *Paradox of American Power*, 10–11.

66. Robert A. Pape, "Preventing 'Soft Balancing' against the United States," draft, Fall 2004, presented as "Soft Balancing: How States Pursue Security in a Unipolar World," paper prepared for the annual meeting of the American Political Science Association, Chicago, Ill., September 2–5, 2004; also see Robert A. Pape, "Soft Balancing against the United States," *International Security* 30, no. 1 (Summer 2005), 7–45.

67. Pape, "Preventing 'Soft Balancing.'"

68. Pape, "Preventing 'Soft Balancing.'"

69. Rajan Menon, "The End of Alliances," *World Policy Journal* 20, no. 2 (Summer 2003): 1–20.

70. Bruno Tertrais, "The Changing Nature of Military Alliances," *The Washington Quarterly* 27, no. 2 (Spring 2004): 145–50.

71. Richard L. Kugler, "Dissuasion as a Strategic Concept," *Strategic Forum*, no. 196 (December 2002): 1–8.

72. Kugler, "Dissuasion," 4.

73. Sean Kay, "What Is a Strategic Partnership," *Problems of Post-Communism* 47, no. 3 (May/June 2000): 15–24.

74. Robert A. Pape, "The Strategic Logic of Suicide Terrorism," *American Political Science Review* 97, no. 3 (August 2003): 344.

75. Pape, "Strategic Logic," 345.

76. Pape, "Strategic Logic," 347.

77. Chaim Kaufmann, "Possible and Impossible Solutions to Ethnic Civil Wars," *International Security* 20, no. 4 (Spring 1996): 136–75.

78. Alastair Iain Johnston, "Realism(s) and Chinese Security Policy in the Post–Cold War Period," in *Unipolar Politics: Realism and State Strategies after the Cold War*, ed. Michael Mastanduno and Ethan Kapstein (New York: Columbia University Press, 1999), 261–318.

79. Johnston, "Realism(s) and Chinese Security Policy," 289.

80. Johnston, "Realism(s) and Chinese Security Policy," 290.

81. Samuel P. Huntington, *Foreign Affairs* 72, no. 3 (Summer 1993): 22–49.

82. Richard N. Rosecrance, *The Rise of the Trading State: Commerce and Conquest in the Modern World* (New York: Basic Books, 1986); Richard N. Rosecrance, *The Rise of the Virtual State: Wealth and Power in the Coming Century* (New York: Basic Books, 1999).

83. Barry Buzan, *People, States, and Fear*, 2nd ed. (Boulder, Colo.: Lynne Rienner, 1991), 244–46.

84. Ethan B. Kapstein, *The Political Economy of National Security: A Global Perspective* (New York: McGraw-Hill, 1992), 80.

85. Robert Gilpin, *Global Political Economy: Understanding the International Economic Order* (Princeton, N.J.: Princeton University Press, 2001), 302.

86. Gilpin, *Global Political Economy*, 304.

87. John J. Mearsheimer, "The False Promise of International Institutions," 347.

88. Gilpin, *Global Political Economy*, 16.

89. Dale C. Copeland, "Economic Interdependence and War: A Theory of Trade Expectations," *International Security* 20, no. 4 (Spring 1996): 5–41.

90. Charles L. Glaser, "Realists as Optimists," *International Security* 19, no. 3 (Winter 1994/95): 50–90.

91. E. H. Carr, *The Twenty Years' Crisis: 1919–1939* (New York: St. Martin's, 1939).

SUGGESTED READING

Michael Brown, Sean Lynn-Jones, and Steven E. Miller, eds., *Contemporary Realism and International Security* (Cambridge, Mass.: MIT Press, 1995).

E. H. Carr, *The Twenty Years' Crisis, 1919–1939* (London: Perennial, 1964).

Gordon A. Craig and Alexander L. George, *Force and Statecraft: Diplomatic Problems of Our Time*, 3rd ed. (Oxford: Oxford University Press, 1995).

Jack Donnelly, *Realism and International Relations* (Cambridge: Cambridge University Press, 2000).

Robert Gilpin, *Global Political Economy: Understanding the International Economic Order* (Princeton, N.J.: Princeton University Press, 2001).

Samuel J. Huntington, *The Clash of Civilizations and the Remaking of World Order* (New York: Simon and Schuster, 1998).

Ethan B. Kapstein and Michael Mastanduno, eds., *Unipolar Politics: Realism and State Strategies after the Cold War* (New York: Columbia University Press, 1999).

Robert O. Keohane, ed., *Neorealism and Its Critics* (New York: Columbia University Press, 1985).

John J. Mearsheimer, *The Tragedy of Great Power Politics* (New York: W. W. Norton, 2003).

Joseph S. Nye, *Soft Power: The Means to Success in World Politics* (New York: Public Affairs, 2004).

Chapter Three

The Search for Peace

Mrs. Eleanor Roosevelt, wife of the president of the United States, holding the Universal Declaration of Human Rights as a poster in English, November 1949. *Source*: UN Photo.

The counterpoint to realism is idealism—which asserts that human nature is inherently good and that power can be used for positive outcomes in the search for peace. While reflecting popular sentiment, traditional manifestations of idealism have shown significant limits in terms of guaranteeing peace. Broadly, idealism is made problematic by the basic question of whose ideals should dominate. Functionally, the approach has often had counterproductive results. The idea, for example, that diplomatic accommodation promotes peace was shattered at the beginning of World War II when Germany broke various international commitments. The effort to build a hierarchical security governance system based on collective security in the League of Nations, where all states in a community identify and punish an aggressor, failed to prevent the rise of Germany and the outbreak of World War II. International law has fared somewhat better as some general rules governing international conflicts have been broadly accepted by governments—as with the Geneva Conventions which govern the conduct of war, define war crimes, and protect prisoners of war and civilians in conflict. Arms control and disarmament have also had a mixed record in terms of limiting or reducing armaments as a path to peace. Some general moral rules, such as human rights, have become embedded as universal norms. Despite inherent dilemmas, idealism remains an international constant as states and citizens work to build a world that is both secure and peaceful. This chapter surveys contemporary idealist frameworks associated with liberalism and examines modern approaches to security studies including social theory, civil-society, pacifism, postmodernism, gender studies, and revolutionary approaches to international change.

LIBERALISM

Liberalism is grounded primarily in idealism and seeks to identify the conditions under which a more peaceful international society is attainable. As Michael Doyle notes, "the peaceful intent and restraint that liberalism does manifest in limited aspects of its foreign affairs announces the possibility of a world peace this side of the grave or of world conquest. . . . It has strengthened the prospects for a world peace established by the steady expansion of a separate peace among liberal societies."[1] Doyle focuses analytical attention on the moral commitment to three sets of rights: (1) freedom from arbitrary authority; (2) rights necessary to protect and promote the capacity for freedom—which include social and economic rights such as equal opportunity in education and rights to health care and employment; and (3) democratic participation or representation.[2] Some liberals fault realists for being intellectually incapable of adequately explaining the "reality" of the new international system. Seyom Brown, for example, asserts that the "narrowly focused 'realist' lens fails to illuminate many of the momentous developments occurring within, above, and across the jurisdictions of the nation-states that are creating dangerous incongruities in world politics and society."[3] Brown argues that realism has become largely irrelevant to policy analysis because of its failure to comprehend some of the world's most serious predicaments. Brown challenges the meaning of "interests" which should evolve from "national" to "world" levels including: (1) survival of the human species; (2) reduction in the amount of killing and other extremely brutal treatment of human beings; (3) provision of conditions for healthy subsistence to all people; (4) protection of citizens' rights; (5) preservation of cultural diversity; (6) preservation of the planet's basic natural ecologies and environment; and (7) enhancement of accountability.[4]

Stephen Krasner summarizes liberal theory as having three core assumptions. First, there are many different kinds of actors including state-owned enterprises, multinational corporations, public international organizations, nongovernmental organizations, private foundations, and terrorists, as well as states. Second, these actors are all rational and calculating but they pursue different objectives: corporate executives want profits or sales; the rulers of states want security and higher levels of well-being for their populations; environmental groups want to preserve the ecosphere. Furthermore, various actors have different power capabilities in different areas; specific actors influence outcomes in some arenas but not in others. Third, international relations, and especially international political economy, offer opportunities for everyone to gain at the same time. Actors are more concerned with their absolute well-being than with their relative position vis-à-vis others.[5] Andrew Moravcsik asserts that liberalism is at least as methodologically sound as realist traditions. He argues that liberalism, like realism, focuses on the primacy of societal actors. Liberalism also assumes that states represent a subset of domestic society and that it is via these interests that a state establishes preferences in world politics. Furthermore, liberals believe that the situation of interdependence is a key determinant of state behavior.[6] Robert O. Keohane identifies three kinds of modern liberalism: republican liberalism, commercial liberalism, and regulatory liberalism. Republican liberalism views democratic republics as more peaceful than dictatorships, thus placing domestic systems as a key determinant of state behavior. Commercial liberalism focuses on the natural harmony of interests that lead to cooperation derived from trade and mutual dependency. Regulatory liberalism stresses the role that the establishment of international rules can play in facilitating peace.[7]

Contemporary liberalism offers no procedural guarantees of peace—a departure from more utopian forms of collective security or international law.

Liberalism does offer a basic belief that peace is possible—but inducements and facilitation might be necessary. Keohane notes that liberalism may reduce the likelihood of the use of force. However, the opposite is possible as moral causes have motivated wars such as with U.S. intervention in Vietnam. Keohane points to the desire to protect American direct foreign investment in underdeveloped countries as a reason for intervention; a need to protect access to raw materials that fuel economic power such as oil in the Persian Gulf; and a need to punish those who use asymmetric power to threaten the liberal state—such as terrorists who would seek to disrupt the freedom of movement of goods and services or citizens' travel.[8]

One of the more ambitious statements of contemporary liberalism was heralded by Francis Fukuyama who argued in 1989 that the world had witnessed the "end of history." Fukuyama argued that the end of the Cold War meant not only the triumph of the West—but of the Western idea of liberalism. Moving away from Marxism and nationalism, Fukuyama saw Western liberal democracy as representing the final form of human government. Fukuyama asserted that the end of history will be a difficult time: "The struggle for recognition, the willingness to risk one's life for a purely abstract goal, the worldwide ideological struggle that called forth daring, courage, imagination, and idealism, will be replaced by economic calculation, the endless solving of technical problems, environmental concerns, and the satisfaction of sophisticated consumer demand."[9] Nonetheless, the kinds of traditional behavior patterns that had brought nations into conflict would be overcome by new dominant patterns in the international system. Ten years later, however, Fukuyama retreated significantly from this position, after witnessing ten years of rising nationalism and ongoing conflict around the world.[10]

Neoliberal Institutionalism

As a theory of international relations, neoliberalism was first explained by Robert Keohane and Joseph Nye in 1974. Neoliberal institutionalism explains the conditions that complex interdependence presents to states and posits that anarchy creates an interest among states to achieve cooperation. The focus on the role of the state, anarchy in the international system, and the advancement of the national interest is consistent with realist traditions. However, unlike realists, neoliberals are optimistic that cooperation and mutual gains are possible. Neoliberals seek to show how informal international institutions and formal international organizations can facilitate such cooperation—leading to a higher prospect of a more peaceful world. Neoliberal institutionalism focuses analytical attention on the study of international regimes and the norms, principles, rules, and decision-making procedures that they embody through formal or informal processes.[11] Neoliberal theory places international institutions and their embodiment in international organizations at the core of state-driven efforts to facilitate cooperation. So long as the benefits of cooperation outpace the costs, states will sacrifice short-term interests for long-term mutual gains.[12] The fact that states invest prestige and resources into international institutions is seen as important evidence of the demand for formalized multilateral cooperation. Neoliberal institutionalism does not, however, assert that all institutions will matter at all times. Also, the theory does not suggest that institutions act independent of the distribution of power among states. Moreover, neoliberal scholarship does not intrinsically assume successful outcomes of cooperation. As Robert Keohane writes, "neoliberal approaches can backfire as policy prescriptions."[13]

The neoliberal approach to international institutions traditionally focused analytical attention on economic and environmental cooperation where the dangers of defection from cooperation are low, rather than classical security cooperation, where the dangers of defection are high.[14] Nevertheless, in a global security environment, neoliberals have advanced important arguments about the relationship between international institutions and security. International institutions—through established headquarters, staff, planning, rules, and procedures—are thought to help states manage coordination and collaboration problems of collective action and make cooperation on security provision easier to achieve. Such interaction, proximity, and transparency are thought to foster reassurance and trust, thereby reducing the sense of vulnerability and fear that results from international anarchy. As Robert Keohane and Joseph Nye demonstrate, security institutions can aid the exercise of influence, constrain bargaining strategies, balance or replace other institutions, signal governments' intentions by providing others with information and making policies more predictable, specify obligations, and impact both the interests and preferences of states.[15]

Contemporary liberalism also emphasizes the role of institutions—reflecting and advancing principles and norms of community standards, working in conjunction with information sharing, rules, and decision-making procedures—as mechanisms for lowering the transaction costs of multilateral enforcement strategies against states that violate global or regional community standards of acceptable state behavior. Neoliberal theory posits that states share an interest in establishing principles and norms to facilitate cooperation and provide clarity from international anarchy. Principles and rules of institutions help states to address the uncertainty of the future and to avoid establishing counterproductive precedents.[16] From this interaction, institutions are thought to, as Charles Kupchan notes, raise the costs of defection and define what constitutes defection while at the same time advancing interstate socialization by promoting the concept of an international community.[17] In this sense, security institutions can become important promoters of community values and also tools for channeling enforcement against violators of community principles and norms.

Some neoliberal scholars note that the theory has insufficiently accounted for the content of principles, norms, and institutional activity.[18] Judith Goldstein and Robert Keohane assess the role of ideas shaping interests in terms of world views, principled beliefs, and causal beliefs. Goldstein and Keohane write that, as regarding ideas embedded in institutions, "once a policy choice leads to the creation of reinforcing organizational and normative structures, that policy idea can affect the incentives of political entrepreneurs long after the interests of its initial proponents have changed."[19] There are limits, however, to the power of ideas and institutions in a world governed by interest-maximizing states. For example, as Keohane notes, just because democracies come together to cooperate does not by nature mean that they will work together to export democracy. He writes: "Democracies may act to stop starvation or extreme abuses of human rights, as in Somalia, but they are unlikely to sacrifice significant welfare for the sake of democracy—especially when people realize how hard it is to create democracy and how ineffective intervention often is in doing so."[20] Some neoliberal assumptions also appear to be founded on normative assumptions, rather than on hard evidence. Keohane acknowledges a normative assumption in modern liberal theory stating that "the strength of liberalism as a moral theory lies in its attention to how governmental arrangements will operate in practice, and in particular, how institutions can protect human rights against the malign inclinations of power holders."[21] The ability of an institution to promote such outcomes might thus be higher when institutions reflect what Katja Weber calls a heterogeneity of states based on religious, linguistic, cultural, and political backgrounds of countries.[22] From this basis, formal institutions can act as a "community representative" and as "managers of enforcement" of international principles and norms.[23]

Neoliberal institutional theory proposes that, as states seek to coordinate policy, institutions will lower the transaction costs of cooperation in ways that would not be possible were there no institution available. This conclusion about transaction costs draws from the assumption that states will assess the costs of bargaining relative to the costs of alternative policy choices. Information sharing is seen as helping states overcome various obstacles to cooperation while the rules and procedures of international institutions produce efficiency gains in security cooperation.[24] As Keohane demonstrates, international institutions and their functions are best understood as "information-providing and transaction cost-reducing entities."[25] Celeste Wallander maintains international institutions can facilitate security cooperation by reducing transaction costs and making it possible for states to cooperate. To

Wallander, rules and procedures are "institutional assets" that "enable states to cooperate by providing resources, such as information on intentions or compliance; by establishing rules for negotiations, decision-making, and implementation; and by creating incentives to conform to international standards necessary for multilateral action."[26] Such transaction cost models assume that states will seek and maintain institutions to increase the efficiency of providing for a common good.

Cooperative Security

Cooperative security is an effort to build inclusive mechanisms for security management, without rigid hierarchical architectures. Cooperative security views the organized use of military power on behalf of the international community as necessary and acceptable, while at the same time looking favorably at the role of international institutions to coordinate such efforts. The idea became popular in the 1990s as a way to emphasize the ideals that drive multinational security cooperation but without the historical weaknesses of collective security. Cooperative security accepts the basic premise that global security conditions require a complex approach that places a high demand on the management of risk. Underlying cooperative security is a principle of "cooperative engagement" which is a "strategic principle that seeks to accomplish its purposes through institutionalized consent rather than through threats of material or physical coercion. It presupposes fundamentally compatible security objectives and promotes collaborative rather than confrontational relationships among national military establishments."[27] Such a strategic approach emphasizes reassurance over traditional deterrence and containment. The end goal is not a normative world order, but rather a division of labor designed to enforce agreed upon means of preventing war and managing crises.

The concept of cooperative security emerged from a Brookings Institution study in the mid-1990s which stressed five major elements: (1) the establishment of strict controls and security measures for nuclear forces; (2) a regime for the conversion of defense industries whose excess capacity could lead to unwarranted global weapons proliferation and thus exacerbate international instability; (3) cooperative arrangements regulating the size and composition of forces to emphasize defensive configurations and also to restrict the flow of dangerous technologies; (4) articulation of an internationally supported concept of effective and legitimate intervention, in which the use of force is always multilateral and elected only as a last resort; and (5) the promotion of transparency and mutual interest as the basis for monitoring agreed upon constraints, including those on the diffusion of advanced technologies.[28] Antonia Handler Chayes and Abram Chayes built on the role of reassurance to show

how an ideal type of cooperative security architecture would function. First, Chayes and Chayes maintain that a strong normative base is necessary for those who participate so they will have an expectation of fairness and equally applicable procedures. The second core element is a combination of inclusiveness and nondiscrimination. Transparency, the critical third ingredient, is the availability and accessibility of information about the security arrangement itself and the activities of those working within it. Regime management, the fourth component, requires the collection and analysis of information; review assessment, and response to information; capacity building based on known security requirements; interpretation of agreements and settlement of dispute capacity; and the ability to maintain adaptability and flexibility to changed security requirements. Finally, a cooperative security order requires the capacity of its members to engage, when necessary, in effective sanction of those who violate agreed norms.[29]

Allen Sens explains cooperative security as a conceptual bridge between the realist and neoliberal frameworks. Cooperative security organizations are based on reassurance and engagement, rather than deterrence and containment. As such, they are inclusive in nature, rather than exclusive, and aim to engage members and nonmembers and like-minded and non-like-minded actors into a larger framework. The primary activities of cooperative security organizations are not directed against a specific external threat but exist for the achievement of shared security objectives. Cooperative security is built on a broadened conception of security in order to promote military and nonmilitary security objectives. Cooperative security is also aimed at the transformation and/or adaptation of existing security institutions. Cooperative security envisions a cautious, gradual approach to institutionalization, preferring to establish the conditions under which improvised, informal, and flexible patterns of cooperation can develop that are consistent with existing modalities and sensibilities. Finally, cooperative security recognizes the value of other bilateral or multilateral security arrangements in the maintenance of regional security.[30] Sens notes that there are significant challenges to this model. For example, the temptation to free-ride. Smaller states may provide suboptimal investments into shared security management, leading to a divergence in capabilities and a willingness to take security risks. In this sense, it may prove difficult to sustain cooperative security architectures if there is not high agreement on the nature of the challenges being faced.

The divergence of opinion in the international community during the crisis of 2002–2003 over Iraq's assumed weapons-of-mass-destruction programs illustrates some of the dilemmas of cooperative security. At one level, cooperative security was challenged between 1998 and 2002 because United Nations weapons inspectors had been kicked out of Iraq and there had been no penalty for this action. From this perspective, cooperative security was shown to be ineffective as Iraq had violated the norms of the cooperative system on weapons of mass destruction but there was no serious consequence. The power dynamics of cooperative security did appear to work through early 2003 when the UN was able to return weapons inspectors to Iraq aided by the threat of American military intervention. By March 2003, the UN weapons inspectors were close to being able to declare Iraq in compliance with UN resolutions. However, rather than wait for additional information from the UN, the United States opted instead for preemptive war, throwing the existing foundations of cooperative security into disarray. In the eyes of some critics, including some of America's closest allies, by resorting to unilateral actions, the United States violated the principles of reassurance and restraint.

Peace through Commerce

Commercial liberalism is based on the perceived benefits of the liberal free-market trading system, regional economic integration, efforts to promote economic development in poorer areas of the world, and a presumed positive impact of multinational corporations. Overall, there is a belief that the "spirit of commerce" can promote harmonious international relations through mutual economic gains. This approach differs from neoliberalism in that the truest form of commercial liberalism would seek to limit state involvement in the international economic system. However, commercial liberalism is also pragmatic on the role of the nation-states as actors working within the international economic system to manage inefficiencies that might lead to economic and security instability.

A core objective of commercial liberalism is to promote the maximum amount of economic development for as many people as possible. The more people have access to markets and the more competition is fostered, the more innovation can lead to increased employment and economic development. In addition to fostering international cooperation, liberal approaches to economic development see the expansion of incomes and wealth as a strong deterrent to nationalism and other sources of national, regional, or even global instability. Economic development is the combined process for a country or peoples of capital accumulation, rising per capita income (with corresponding falling birthrate), an increasingly skilled workforce, the adoption of new technical styles, and other related socioeconomic changes.[31] The key means of measuring economic development is the accumulation of capital and growth in both gross domestic product (GDP) and gross national product (GNP) as accumulated over time. Commercial liberals see general gains being made by the expansion of trade, which helps underdeveloped countries grow their economies and integrate into the international trading system. Where necessary, developed states should thus help the less-developed grow their economic capacity. Since World War II, this approach has been manifested in terms of foreign economic assistance—significantly, the developmental assistance granted to Western Europe via the Marshall Plan in the late 1940s. Commercial liberalism sees strong prospects for international economic organizations to help states organize themselves for conducting effective trading, managing trade conflicts, and helping to make up for inefficiencies. Some organizations like the European Union have become models for deeply embedded trade, political, and security cooperation at the regional level.

Commercial liberalism posits that corporations that transcend borders—multinational corporations (MNCs)—help to break down the barrier of the nation-state and bring societies closer via economic globalization. MNCs are enterprises that control and manage production establishments located in at least two countries.[32] This relationship reflects more than trading and is in fact direct ownership of manufacturing plants and/or resource extraction and processing operations in a variety of countries. MNCs transcend sovereignty and thus while commercial liberals see them as beneficial, many others see them as a threat or a function of one large state's exploitative economic hegemony. Some MNCs are massive and maintain spheres of economic influence that historically were the domain of states. General Motors, for example, has gross sales that exceed those of many governments in the world. Two thousand of the largest MNCs are based in six of the wealthiest countries in the world and, by the turn of the century, the top 500 MNCs had combined assets of about $32 trillion.[33]

Commercial liberals nevertheless assert that there is an inherent idealism in the expansion of foreign direct investment by MNCs. Such advocates argue that the benefits are split between MNCs and the countries that host them. MNCs often build roads, schools, and other infrastructure that might help a country's productivity and thus further meet the needs of its people. Some commercial liberals see MNCs as the principal agents for the exchange of ideas and technology across borders that will lead to a more united world order.[34] MNCs, however, have not always been benign actors and some states have undermined the sovereignty of others to protect their own home-based MNCs. In Guatemala in 1954 and in Chile in 1972 the United States supported covert action to destabilize governments that were hostile to American business interests in those countries. For many on the receiving end of their activity, MNCs are seen as the harbingers of neocolonialism. Moreover, underdeveloped countries that have their people educated and employed by MNCs are at risk of having their best and brightest members of society attracted outside their homelands seeking better economic opportunities. Nonetheless, there is clearly a trend in globalization toward commercial liberalism. Even the most underdeveloped of countries testify that what they most want is not a handout, but rather fair access to compete in developed economies and an opportunity to join the processes of economic globalization.

Democratic Peace and Security Communities

At the core of liberalism lies a normative assumption that republican democracies are inherently peaceful. Emmanuel Kant promulgated the notion that democratic government is an important condition for peace. Kant reasoned that "if the consent of the citizens is required in order to decide that war should be declared . . . nothing is more natural than that they would be very cautious in commencing such a poor game, decreeing for themselves all the calamities of war."[35] Such calamities include paying the costs of war from society's resources, paying the costs of war from their own resources, repairing the painful devastation war leaves behind, and incurring national debt. In modern liberal theory, the "democratic peace" assumes that there is a civilizing function in democracies—where conflicts are dealt with under the rule of law and peacefully rather than via the brute use of force. Democracies are transparent—political, economic, and military activity is done with a degree of openness and accountability within the political system. This transparency can alleviate relative gains concerns among democracies and worries about offensive military capacity as other states can take advantage of this transparency to increase their own levels of reassurance. Nevertheless, some analytical confusion emerges over the question of what defines a "democracy" within the democratic peace theory. After all, Adolf Hitler rose to power in the midst of a young German democracy. Postrevolutionary Iran has incorporated elements of democracy but is seen by many adversaries as a threat. The Palestinian Authority has elections for its leadership and yet many Israelis still fear the Palestinian political movement. In Turkey, the military intervenes to prevent religious representation in government. Thus John M. Owen points to the content of democracy and the embedded nature of liberal ideas, not just the institutional mechanisms of democratic processes, as key to the democratic peace.[36]

Democratic peace theory generates skepticism because there are a number of cases where democracies have gone to war with each other. Also, there are a number of cases where democracies have rushed into or started wars including the Spanish-American War, the U.S.-Serbia conflict in 1998, and the 2003 invasion of Iraq by the United States.[37] Nevertheless, it is true that democracies rarely fight wars with each other. Charles Lipson argues that this is because of "contracting advantages" among democratic governments, which allow them to negotiate a separate peace. Lipson demonstrates that "constitutional democracies have a special capacity to make and sustain promises with each other, including those about war and peace."[38] Democratic systems increase the confidence that negotiating partners will uphold promises, as accountability is built into the system. The continuity of governance in democracies promotes stability and predictable behavior. Moreover, high audience costs mean that leaders will be held accountable by their electorates and legislators if they violate contracts such as treaties. Constitutional governance limits the powers of public officials and thus makes it harder for them to move quickly into external conflicts.[39]

There is an important policy implication behind the democratic peace theory. If it is true that there is more peace among democracies—then, there should be more democracies. Yet, there are several dilemmas created by this assumption. First, democracies might opt to overthrow nondemocracies via war in favor of spreading this strategic logic to other parts of the world—as advocated by some people who argued for regime change in Iraq before the U.S. invasion. There is, however, no necessary reason to believe that democracy can be imposed—especially via external military force. Second, there is no guarantee that, once begun, the democratization process breeds peace and stability. The opposite can be true if the institutions of democracy and the structural economic and political foundations are not present. Finally, democracies are vulnerable to asymmetric attacks by terrorism because of their openness, which could then prompt a warlike response, and even lead to a reduction in democracy if the state trumps rights in the name of security.

A more evolutionary variation on the democratic peace school is the idea of a security community. The security community concept was devised by Karl Deutsch in 1957. Deutsch sought to explain why there appeared to be certain regions where the prospect for interstate war seemed improbable. In areas with high amounts of cross-border communication and similar political identities (such as between the United States and Canada and in Scandinavia) it seemed as though the prospect for expanding peace based on areas of embedded security communities might be possible. Deutsch defined a security community as a region where there is no prospect for war among a group of states.[40] Deutsch focused on "pluralistic security communities" in which states retain their legal independence within a region defined by a group of people who have become integrated. Integration promotes a "sense of community" and institutions and practices thought to assure dependable expectations of peaceful change.

Deutsch argued that NATO might, over time, contribute to the evolution of a transatlantic security community by developing its economic and social potential to make it "more than a military alliance."[41] With the end of the Cold War, Stephen Weber asserted that NATO reflected a peculiar mix of alliance and security community. Weber suggested that a security community can be institutionalized as equivalence is favored over hierarchy, with decisions requiring unanimity and the formal organization existing primarily to enhance transparency and to facilitate the transfer of information among states.[42] The logic of both the democratic peace and security community was a key argument for advocates of NATO expansion during the 1990s. United States Secretary of State Madeline K. Albright argued in 1997 that "by adding Poland, Hungary, and the Czech Republic to the alliance, we will expand the area within Europe where wars simply do not happen" and that

> NATO defines a community of interest among the free nations of North America and Europe that both preceded and outlasted the Cold War. America has long stood for the proposition that the Atlantic community should not be artificially divided and that its nations should be free to shape their destiny. We have long argued that the nations of Central and Eastern Europe belong to the same democratic family as our allies in Western Europe.[43]

Yet, as Emanuel Adler has shown, a more likely geographic basis for a well-defined security community is to be found in the European Union rather than NATO.[44] Empirically, while NATO has constrained hostility between Greece and Turkey, so long as the institution has these two members among whom war is a real possibility, it cannot meet the basic criteria of a security community. The agenda of research into the security community concept is highly ambitious and as yet it is more a goal than a guaranteed outcome. As Deutsch put it, "We undertook this inquiry as a contribution to the study of possible ways in which men some day might abolish war."[45]

EMERGING SECURITY PARADIGMS

The study of international security is often divided into the broad paradigms of realism and idealism and variations associated with each. However, both approaches leave unanswered key methodological questions and each is open to significant challenges by alternative conceptual approaches. As the process of globalization accelerates, new approaches derived from structural power dynamics outside the nation-state and broader utopian concepts have emerged. Some aspects of both realism and, especially, idealism can be found in some of these approaches. However, they are also unique in their characteristics as fundamentally new approaches to understanding international security. Among these new schools are constructivism, transnational civil society, postmodernism, and feminism.

Constructivism

Neither realists nor idealists offer a core explanation on how interests and perceptions of security requirements emerge. Do all states share the same basic needs and concerns? Or, are interests relative, shaped by both the domestic and international environment? To what extent does the "identity" of the nation-state shape perceptions of security and insecurity? Sociological approaches to identity formation provide a means to understanding the relationship between the domestic and international sphere of identity and interest formation. As Ronald Jepperson, Alexander Wendt, and Peter Katzenstein note, there are at least three layers to the international environment in which national security policies are made. First, formal institutions play an important role in reflecting and reinforcing specific norms. A second aspect is the sphere of world politics which includes basic rules such as sovereignty. Third, international patterns of friendship or enmity also have important functions as the product of social interactions and perceptions. For example, Canada and Cuba are each states which should, by nature of relative power distribution, significantly fear the United States. However, as Jepperson, Wendt, and Katzenstein write, "while one is a threat, the other is an ally, a result, we believe, of ideational factors operating at the international level."[46] Thus, the core question in this sociological approach to security: Are the manifold uses and forms of power explained by material factors alone, or are ideational and cultural factors necessary to account for how states decide what is, and is not, important to their security?[47]

Social theory has been central to the work of Alexander Wendt who pioneered the school of constructivism. Constructivism addresses the relationship between the international environment and the domestic identity of nation-states. Constructivists accept the idea of anarchy in the international system, but assert that how states react to anarchy will be affected by their own internal identity. Constructivists see international politics as a dynamic process in which states are both simultaneously shaping, and shaped by, the international environment. Anarchy, or at least the degree to which states see anarchy as threatening or as benign, is a socially constructed phenomenon. Wendt notes that "people act toward objects, including other actors, on the basis of the meanings that the objects have for them. . . . States act differently toward enemies than they do toward friends because enemies are threatening and friends are not." Moreover, to Wendt, it is "collective meanings that constitute the structures which organize our actions."[48]

In constructivist theory, concepts such as self-help, formal institutions like international organizations and regimes, order, and power exist to the degree that they are consciously chosen to serve the interests of states. Consequently, the international order is constructed by state action and simultaneously constitutive of it. However, the content of that order is dependent upon the nature of the actors who are interacting and shaping the international system. To understand whether anarchy is a threat to security, one has to understand the nature of the actors as defined by their identity and the ideas they hold important. That identity is defined by the social interaction of the domestic actors within society. What makes this dynamic especially unique is that, while ideas are cultivated within a state and then expressed within the international system, the nature of the international system is simultaneously feeding into the domestic sphere of the state.

The role of the nation-state as a protective barrier against international anarchy and as a unitary actor advancing self-interest is thus challenged by ongoing social interactions that transcend the domestic and international sphere of international security. In this constructivist perspective, states exist as a consequence both of their relationship to the structure of the international system and of their individual characteristics. As such, the configuration of international structures serves to define what is possible among the existing agents that interact with each other. To Wendt, the international system represents a hierarchy of activity in which the existence of some actors makes possible the existence of others. Wendt provides a framework for understanding the conceptual application of personality to states. States are seen as representing the collective sum of the interactions of society within them—which helps to explain why certain states take on the attributes of "people" as such.[49] This approach makes a major contribution toward explaining why certain kinds of outcomes occur in international security relationships. For example, as Wendt observes, the United States would not be overly concerned with Britain or Israel having nuclear weapons. However, the United States would perceive the Soviet Union or Iran as a threat. In this sense, the security dilemma is relative, and therefore a constructed phenomenon.

While constructivism is more theoretical than policy oriented, the approach does have significant practical implications. For example, it allows for the possibility that states can change over time. In this sense, evolving ideas become important shapers of what defines and gives value to power. Consequently, the international system can be an agent of transformation as ideas transcend borders and shape change within a state. If that is the case, then constructivism can explain why the Cold War ended without war—because the ideas of human rights and freedom were ultimately more powerful than tyranny and military force. If enough states were exposed to and inculcated in particular ideas, such as in the democratic peace, then powerful dynamics of change could become deeply embedded in the international system. Such embedded norms can expand and transform nation-states. Just over a half a century ago Japan and Germany were expansionistic, chauvinistic, and war prone. Now, neither state chooses war as a preferred policy. In a constructivist world, states have the capacity to change how they perceive and pursue their interests and that change can be derived either from external and internal forces.

Transnational Civil Society

The idea of an international society is not new. Hedley Bull, for example, examined the social dynamics of anarchy and society to challenge the notion that the two are not compatible. Bull noted that the lack of a universal government or the dominance of the nation-state in providing for security has not limited nation-states' willingness to participate in economic interdependence. War is also not seen as an essential part of anarchy, but rather a regulative mechanism of international society for settling political disputes or enforcing commonly agreed on international principles and norms. Bull saw international society and anarchy as not essentially in conflict. Through balance of power systems and other forms of regulative behavior, some degree of regulation in the international system was a natural occurrence.[50] Bull's focus, however, was on the role of the nation-state. New approaches to international society address the role of the state and transnational phenomenon.

Contemporary approaches to international society look to the networks of globalization as the basis for the expansion of domestic civil society into the international sphere. The expansion of a transnational civil society implies that rules which help provide for a peaceful and legitimate maintenance of order (usually associated with a combination of sovereignty and democracy) at the domestic level of politics can be extended internationally. As Jessica Tuchman Mathews writes, in the new security environment "national governments are not simply losing autonomy in a globalizing economy. . . . They are sharing powers—including political, social, and security roles at the core of sovereignty—with businesses, with international organizations, and with a multitude of citizens groups, known as nongovernmental organizations (NGOs)."[51] At the core of this concept, argues Mathews, is the notion that an individual's security may no longer reliably be guaranteed by the nation's security. Rather, the emerging dynamic of "human security" is competing with national security as a dominant concept that has more to do with the conditions of daily life than the traditional conflicts between states.

The idea of a transnational civil society looks to globalization as facilitating a world shaped by norms that transcend the role of the state as delivering primary goods for individuals. Mathews looks at the rising role of transnational interest groups lobbying on behalf of particular causes as shaping the new civil society. There were an estimated 35,000 NGOs operating in developing countries by the mid-1990s. By the turn of the century, NGOs were delivering more official development assistance than the United Nations.[52] Related to the rise of NGOs is the expansion of their ability to breed new ideas; advocate, protest, and mobilize public support; do legal, scientific, technical, and policy analysis; provide services; shape, implement, monitor, and enforce national and international commitments; and change institutions and norms.[53] To this extent knowledge, science and associated truths become tools to power and influence via global transmission.[54] As Peter Haas shows, a new basis for transnational change is possible when transnational networks emerge that are comprised of private experts with scientific or other factual consensual knowledge. This knowledge can then be transferred to bureaucracies within international organizations and then be shared with counterparts inside national governments. Such a basis of information exchange can lead to outcomes that otherwise would not have been possible—such as advancing common interests in international environmental protection.[55]

The growth of transnational civil society creates new demands for international law. The codification of principles and norms can reflect the emergence of transnational civil society—for example, the global rejection of genocide.[56] One of the key elements of civil society is the agreed consent to a particular form of governance. The desire among international actors to facilitate cooperation and punish violators of rules is considerably higher in the era of accelerating interdependence. Rather than seeking hard and fast traditional international law, states are increasingly open to a new legal principle of "soft law" in addressing new security concerns. Soft laws are, according to Steven Ratner, "precepts emanating from international bodies that conform in some sense to expectations of required behavior but that are not binding on states."[57] The effectiveness of soft law lies in the ability of states to gradually conform to emerging international norms and rules in ways that are more quickly evolved than traditional legal codification processes, but that do not carry the immediate threat of punishment.

Hard international law still is practiced and transnational enforcement procedures are expanding. For example, domestic courts are increasingly utilized for transnational trials. Some governments have granted their domestic courts the power of "universal jurisdiction," which allows for criminal indictment of citizens from other countries. Ratner notes that new sources of international law include private lawmakers, private codes, private right-holders, and private armies. The expansion of transnational civil society also reflects the complexity of new issues requiring regulatory rules such as trade policy, business, the environment, and human rights.[58] The legal process of building norms can be as important as the development of treaty-based law. "Legalization" is the overall process of establishing binding obligations, precision as to rules, and delegation to third parties for interpretation, enforcement, or the creation of new rules as necessary.[59] Such activity helps to form the basis for the effective role of soft law. Ultimately, soft law provides more flexibility in dealing with the uncertainty of the global security environment. Such outcomes might move states toward compromises necessary for consolidating an effective transnational civil society.[60]

Pacifism and Peace Movements

To many individuals, scholars, and some policymakers, war is an immoral and unethical act. Therefore, they prioritize peace above all else. As John Dewey declared, "The only way to abolish war [is] to make peace heroic." Pacifism is the rejection of violence as a means of conflict resolution; it stresses belief in the power of nonviolence. From this perspective, moral authority is gained by promoting a peaceful world order. St. Augustine wrote, "The purpose of all war is ultimately peace." What differentiates pacifism from other approaches toward peace is the means through which peace is to be achieved—via a steadfast commitment to the principle of nonviolence. As Martin Luther King Jr. stated, "Peace is not merely a distant goal that we seek, but a means by which we arrive at that goal."

The idea of pacifism begins with the notion that if one individual acts with the moral courage to reject violence, this concept will thrive and spread. Thomas Merton wrote, "If you yourself are at peace, then there is at least some peace in the world." If the idea of peace grows from one to many, it might also grow at the international level. President Franklin D. Roosevelt, though not a pacifist, enshrined this idea in his statement, "Peace, like charity, begins at home." Those who best understood the ravages of war often set the template for the goal of peace. Roosevelt's contemporary Winston Churchill declared, "If the human race wishes to have a prolonged and indefinite period of material prosperity, they have only got to behave in a peaceful and helpful way toward one another."

The major religions of the world have, at their core, the ideal of everlasting peace—be it a peace with a deity or peace among humankind. Many religions emphasize that salvation comes through peace. As the Bible teaches, "Blessed are the peacemakers: for they shall be called the children of God" (Matthew 5:9). In personifying wisdom, the Bible states that "Her ways are ways of pleasantness, and all her paths are peace" (Proverbs 3:17). Isaiah 2:4 declares that "They shall beat their swords into plowshares, and their spears into pruning hooks; nation shall not lift up sword against nation, neither shall they learn war any more." In the Catholic Mass is the greeting among parishioners— "Peace be with you"—which comes from Genesis 43:23. Such views transcend religious doctrine—as a Chinese proverb declares, "When my heart is at peace, the world is at peace." Buddha declared that "Better than a thousand hollow words is one word that brings peace." The Dalai Lama states: "I believe all suffering is caused by ignorance. People inflict pain on others in the selfish pursuit of their happiness or satisfaction. Yet true happiness comes from a sense of peace and contentment which in turn must be achieved through the cultivation of altruism, of love and compassion and elimination of ignorance, selfishness, and greed." The Muslim faith aspires to achieve peace as, according to the Quran, "The believers are but a single Brotherhood: So make peace and reconciliation and be careful of (your duty to) Allah that mercy may be had on you." An American Indian (Shenandoah) proverb states, "It is no longer good enough to cry peace, we must act peace, live peace, and live in peace."

Artists and musicians have also long advanced the cause of peace. Pablo Picasso used his painting *La Guernica*, to provide a graphic description of the horrors of battle. Filmmakers also have used their medium to illustrate some of the horrors and ironies that come with warfare. As the Cold War arms race grew in the 1960s, Stanley Kubrik produced *Dr. Strangelove* which, among many ironies, had a famous fisticuffs between an American general and a Russian diplomat who are interrupted by the American president who, noting their location states: "Hey! You can't fight in here! This is the war room!" Francis Ford Coppolla's *Apocalypse Now* showed the deep psychological impact that the Vietnam War took on its participants. In the 1980s, films such as *The Day After* illustrated the devastating impact that any nuclear exchange between the superpowers would have. During the 1960s and 1970s, musicians such as Peter, Paul, and Mary and Bob Dylan sang in protest of war. The Beatles declared that "All You Need Is Love" and Jimi Hendrix asserted in his lyrics that "When the power of love overcomes the love of power the world will know peace." John Lennon sounded a call to the masses to "Give Peace a Chance," noted that "War Is Over! (If You Want It)" and appealed, "Imagine all the people living life in peace. You may say I'm a dreamer, but I'm not the only one. Someday you'll join us, and the world will live as one." In 2003, the Black Eyed Peas and Justin Timberlake combined to sing: "What's wrong with the world mama—people livin' like they ain't got no mamas. I think the whole world addicted to drama—only attracted to things that'll bring you trauma. Overseas, yeah, we try to stop terrorism, but we still got terrorists here living in the USA, the big CIA, the Bloods and The Crips and the KKK."

Grassroots pacifist movements are not a new phenomenon in international security. As Ben Lowe has shown, there was a nascent, and evolving, interest both in the justification for war and the way war should be fought dating back at least to 1340 in medieval England.[61] Some religious movements such as the Christian Quakers and Mennonites hold peace and nonviolence as core elements of their religious faith, and many practitioners have claimed "conscientious objector" status and some have avoided military service during a draft. Modern peace movements can be dated to 1815 with the New York and Massachusetts Peace Societies and to 1816 with the founding of the Society of a Permanent and Universal Peace. Also in the 1800s, Henry David Thoreau proclaimed the necessity of civil disobedience in situations where one was forced into doing something immoral or unjust. Thoreau refused to pay a tax that he thought contributed to the funding of the Mexican-American War, which he considered unjust. Through the 1800s a number of private conferences were sponsored by peace activists. Prior to World War I and World War II, protests were relatively limited—and some might have actually contributed to war. Many advocates who opposed war—especially in the United States—did so out of traditions of isolation and disengagement from global affairs.

Well-intentioned movements to avoid war have been challenged by critics as actually contributing to the outbreak of conflict. In the Oxford Peace Union Pledge taken during the 1930s, many British students declared they would not fight in a war. Critics of that movement accused them of emboldening Hitler by suggesting that his aggressive designs might not be resisted.[62] Pacifism thus confronts a dilemma. Would, for example, an absolutist doctrine of nonviolence have defeated Hitler's tanks? In the twenty-first century, the question is pertinent as to whether pacifism could stop suicide terrorism. Alternatively, what if a military intervention is taken for humanitarian reasons that could save hundreds of thousands of lives? Would a pacifist then oppose military force? Ironically, many American and European peace activists who opposed the role of the military during the Cold War became strong supporters of humanitarian military intervention in Bosnia and Kosovo in the 1990s. Yet, many individuals from this same movement also opposed the invasion of Iraq in 2003.

The proof of the power of nonviolence was demonstrated by Mohandas K. Gandhi. Over several decades, Gandhi developed a philosophy of nonviolent struggle against tyranny and power that became known as the *satyagraha* movement. In her study of Gandhi's philosophy of conflict, Joan V. Bondurant summarizes the core elements of *satyagraha*. First, truth is essential and seeking truth is fundamental to understanding one's limitations and also exposing violations of honesty and integrity. Second, nonviolence underpins the legitimacy behind the quest for truth and the risk that all versions of truth might be relative to the eye of the beholder. By committing oneself to the philosophy of nonviolence one is willing to take the ultimate risk on behalf of "truth" and thus is forced to identify one's own self-limitations first and foremost. This approach thus forces one into a fuller self-awareness of one's own honesty and integrity. Closely related to the faith in nonviolence is the commitment to love—to love even that person who abuses you at least to the point where one refuses to harm them in spite of their evil actions. Third, self-suffering in public and private actions is seen as a test of one's commitment to love and truth. Gandhi undertook long, painstaking marches and endured extended and personally devastating fasts to expose truth by way of his own suffering. Finally *satyagraha* places considerable emphasis on the role of the individual in integrating the first three approaches in a quest for inner truth, self-awareness, love, and peace.[63]

Gandhi's pacifism was guided by a path to peace that began with the individual and sought to expand a general consciousness of truth. Gandhi was, however, also very publicity-conscious in his application of nonviolent tactics to remove the British Empire from India. He organized large protests, distributed pamphlets, and used fasts and other forms of peaceful action to expose the truths of colonial rule. "Non-violence cannot be preached. It has to be practiced," Gandhi concluded.[64] Such practice included duties based on a "common honesty" among those who practiced it. These duties included: they must "render heart discipline to their commander; there should be no mental reservation; they must be prepared to lose all, not merely their personal liberty, not merely their possessions, land, cash, etc., but also the liberty and possessions of their families, and they must be ready cheerfully to face bullets, bayonets, or even slow death by torture; they must not be violent in thought, word or deed toward the 'enemy' or among themselves."[65] In the face of massive nonviolent resistance, many of Britain's own actions undermined its colonial legitimacy in the eyes of the world. For example, in 1919 British troops fired into a crowd of unarmed Indians (including women and children) protesting in Amritsar. The troops killed some 400 peacefully assembled people.

Other movements have been even more specifically targeted at stopping a war through public protest and civil disobedience. In the 1960s and 1970s, large segments of the American public protested the Vietnam War. Many protesters were convinced that their actions helped to end the war. Critics, however, challenged this assessment, and argued that the protestors had prolonged the war by emboldening the enemy to fight on for a better settlement. During the 1980s, large antinuclear movements in Britain and Germany brought to public attention the dangers of nuclear weapon deployments in Europe. However, these movements were also infiltrated by Soviet intelligence agents who sought to use public opinion to disrupt the governments from their Cold War nuclear strategies.

One of history's most important moments of nonviolent change was the end of the Cold War. One major explanation for the Cold War's end was that, over many decades, the peoples of Eastern Europe and the Soviet Union were gradually exposed to western ideals of liberty, human rights, and free markets, while also being exposed to western goods and culture such as clothing and music. Over time, these ideas transcended the artificial barrier of the Cold War and became ingrained in the beliefs of political dissidents. By the time Mikhail Gorbachev consolidated power after 1986, the Soviet leadership had adopted at least some of these western political, economic, and cultural concepts. Throughout the Soviet Union and Eastern Europe, many dissidents had peacefully resisted oppressive governments and challenged the brutality of Soviet dictatorship. Early efforts to quell these pressures for internal change in the Soviet bloc were met with violence—as in the 1968 Soviet invasion of Czechoslovakia that ended the "Prague Spring" of democratic reform. However, the ideas of freedom and democracy could not be destroyed. Either imprisoned or in internal exile, individuals like Lech Walesa and Vaclev Havel maintained their efforts to bring about a peaceful change within the Soviet system. The importance of such individuals was made especially evident by Mikhail Gorbachev who, as the last Soviet leader, sought to modernize and reform the system. Whereas Stalin had accelerated Soviet economic growth with terror and mass murder, Gorbachev tried to reform and improve the Soviet political and economic situation through expanding freedoms and a more peaceful international security policy. Inadvertently, Gorbachev released forces, particularly nationalism, which the Soviet leadership could not control. While considerable nationalist and ethnic violence did occur in the former Soviet space, the overall exit of the Soviet Union from the Cold War military stalemate was peaceful. Another major internal transformation that led to a more peaceful international environment was the fall of Apartheid in South Africa. Once the white minority government collapsed, the new leadership in South Africa abandoned its ambitions to develop nuclear weapons. The limits of using popular pressure to change state behavior were evident in Tiananmen Square in China in 1989. Students who were peacefully protesting for basic liberties were violently dispersed, many killed or imprisoned, by the Chinese military.

An important variation on pacifism is found in those who have actually seen war. While some pacifists are quick to accuse the military of being warmongers, the opposite is more often the case. Military personnel and veterans who have served in combat are often reluctant to wage war because of their previous experiences. As a rule, they generally will insist that military force be used solely as a last resort. The military are often the most reluctant to go to war because they have to kill, or be killed, in battle. Those who have to plan and implement wartime decisions are shaped by their experiences. Retired U.S. general Lee Butler, who commanded the American strategic air command during the Cold War, called in 1996 for the United States to "make unequivocal its commitment to the elimination of nuclear arsenals, and take the lead in setting an agenda for moving forthrightly toward that objective."[66]

Butler's call for nuclear disarmament coincided with a letter signed in late 1996 by nearly sixty retired admirals and generals from the United States and the former Soviet Union calling for a cutback in existing nuclear stockpiles, a gradual removal of remaining nuclear weapons from alert status, and a goal of a "continuous, complete and irrevocable elimination" of nuclear weapons.

Postmodernism

Postmodernism seeks to expose the core meaning of various texts and discourses. A postmodern approach to realism would explain the meaning of "reality" by asserting that there is no single, objective reality, but rather a wide range of experiences and perspectives. As such, humans are conditioned to understand the meaning of the content of objects or interests based on their interactions.[67] The postmodernist looks at the state and views it as a construct of human interaction. A "state" only exists so long as it is given meaning by dominant actors and is reinforced through social interactions over time. If, for example, a man walks across the border between two countries and there is no man-made signpost, how will he know he is in another state? A dollar bill only has value because humans give its meaning value. In reality, it is a green piece of paper. Because humans give its meaning value, the dollar has power. [68]

Postmodernism seeks to "deconstruct" the nature of objects and interactions by exposing hidden meanings or subtexts. For example, anarchy is explained not by objective factors, but by difference. Individuals define themselves by what they are "not" and thus they create a sense of the "outside" or the "other" from themselves so they can learn more about what they are. Such "outside" forces or groups can be seen as threatening to one's own group or identity and thus anarchy can come to appear threatening because its nature poses challenges to one's sense of self. Postmodernists look at international security relationships and often see a reinforcing hierarchy of power. As governments retain the power of action and diplomacy, and as scholars teach the dominance of realism, neoliberalism, and other state-centric models, they are passing on a structure which reinforces preexisting paradigms. If a professor tells students that realism is the dominant approach to security studies, then he or she is creating a cognitive predisposition toward the state and the content or meaning of anarchy. As Richard K. Ashley writes, "the state as actor assumption is a metaphysical commitment prior to science and exempted from scientific criticism. . . . Despite neorealism's much ballyhooed emphasis on the role of hard falsifying tests as the measure of theoretical progress, neorealism immunizes its statist commitments from any form of falsification."[69]

William E. Connolly provides an example of the effort to expose the hierarchy of power embedded within language. Connolly references the "discovery" of America by Christopher Columbus in 1492. The word *discover* was important because Columbus did not invent the new world—he came upon it. But did he actually "discover" it? What actually had Columbus discovered? The land certainly had been there before and was, in fact, inhabited by natives who considered it their home. By pure definition, America had already been discovered by its existing inhabitants. Connolly notes that what Columbus truly discovered was a sense of newness and otherness—something entirely different from the European experience. The "discovery" that mattered was actually the beginning of a new text with new contextual meaning. The explorers who came upon America had to adjust their own assessments and predispositions to a new way of life. Thus the "new" world had been discovered because the Europeans had discovered a new sense of otherness to which they had to adapt. This adaptation would have lasting impact on the rhetoric and study of international relations as studied in western traditions.[70]

Another example is the act of placing a topic within the context of "security" and "war." As Ole Waever has shown, the process of "securitization" is an act which elevates a certain concept to the security realm or the realm of war as a rhetorical tool to raise the level of importance of an issue.[71] This act can increase a domestic actor's power by implying a threat that citizens need protection from. With the end of the Cold War, the "text" of security expanded to a variety of new areas as war rhetoric was advanced to include a "war on drugs" and a "war on terrorism." Whether or not a "war," implying a military response and social mobilization was the best way to manage these problems was highly debatable. By labeling them as war issues, it would ultimately be easier for one side in that debate to dominate and increase power.

Postmodern theory provides an important tool for understanding a global security order and its implications for the dominance of the nation-state. First, as David Campbell has shown, the concept of contingency implies that varying perspectives embodied in international anarchy are now permeating the traditional boundary of the state. Campbell writes:

> Danger, in short, is no longer capable of just being written as "out there." Security is not to be found "within." This is more than just a result of interdependence, the proliferation of threats, or the overflowing of domestic issues onto the world stage (the conventional response). This is an irruption of contingencies which renders all established containers problematic. It makes little sense to speak of politics occurring in terms of a distinct "inside" or "outside" (such as a "Third World" which is spatially beyond our borders and temporally backward) when, for example, US economic policies encourage "Third World export processing zones" in Los Angeles where manufacturers stamp their auto parts "made in Brazil" and the clothing goods "made in Taiwan" to attract lower tariffs; when the demographic changes that have made non-white children majori-

ties in the California and New York school systems, and will make whites a minority in the United States by the year 2056; and when the poverty and poor health care in Harlem makes the area a "zone of excess mortality" with a death rate for black males higher than their counterparts in Bangladesh.[72]

Second, postmodernism provides important insights into the foundational nature of a technologically conditioned global security network. If the modern era was shaped by large industry and massive armies, the postmodern era is defined largely by the new networks of power—particularly regarding the role of information technology and the power of ideas. By exposing the meaning of power and its origins, postmodernists hope to expose a more basic structure of reality embedded within the way the question of the meaning of security is both asked and answered.

Feminism and Gender

Feminist scholarship, or more broadly, gender studies, also provides unique perspectives toward international security. Feminist approaches note the traditionally male composition of the major actors in international security. The basic assumption behind this approach is that gender matters in understanding international security. The task of understanding the dynamics of international security must also expose overt or hidden assumptions about gender. As a policy issue, gender studies look at some of the unique challenges that women face in terms of the new security environment. Feminist scholarship challenges premises of "universal assumptions" in major approaches to international security such as realism. A critical approach would note that the realist focus on power and interest are derived from the fact that nearly all major realist scholars are men. As such, scholars and students are challenged by gender-based approaches to international security to determine how their gender affects their analysis and how this is passed on to others. Feminist scholars seek to break down what was often seen as a political barrier between the "public sphere" of politics versus the "domestic or private sphere" symbolic of the home where traditional women's roles were dominant.[73]

J. Ann Tickner shows that realists, in particular, have tended to view power as domination. Feminist scholars, however, view power as a relationship of mutual enabling requiring a reconceptualization of power to include realist notions and a more multidimensional approach that sees power in cooperative terms. Tickner notes, unlike realist claims, most of the population of the world views security in terms of the need to satisfy basic human needs rather than, or in addition to, traditional military concerns. Tickner sees economic development and basic human needs satisfaction, as well as environmental concerns, as security dynamics consistent with feminist approaches to security. By reassessing security along such perspectives, a more comprehensive means of alleviating the security dilemma might be accomplished. As Tickner writes, "Thinking about military, economic and environmental security in interdependent terms suggests the need for new methods of conflict resolution that seek to achieve mutually beneficial, rather than zero sum, outcomes."[74]

Tickner offers six elements of a feminist approach to international security. First, a feminist perspective believes that objectivity, as it is culturally defined, is associated with masculinity and thus "objective" assumptions claimed by realism only represent a partial, masculine view of human nature. Second, the national interest is multidimensional and contextually contingent. Third, power cannot be infused with meaning that is universally valid and thus must consider the possibility of collective empowerment. Fourth, it is impossible to separate moral issues from political action. Fifth, a feminist perspective hopes to find common moral elements in the aspirations of humanity. Sixth, a feminist perspective denies the autonomy of politics from the international sphere, and thus any effort to build a worldview which does not rest on a pluralistic conception of human nature is both incomplete and masculine.[75]

Feminist approaches to security issues are not monolithic, and in fact there are various schools of thought all derived from basic approaches that emphasize the gender dynamics of security. "Essentialist feminism" focuses primarily on the values that women bring to international security dynamics and stresses the unique contribution of women as women. There is a normative content to this school which asserts that women are, by nature, more effective in conflict resolution and in group decision-making dynamics. Essentialist feminists see real and positive differences between the potential contributions of women versus the male-dominated world of international security. "Liberal feminism" sees gender differences as not very important but instead stresses the political agenda of equality in politics. This school especially deplores the traditional exclusion of women as actors in international security. However, there is no fundamentally normative element to this approach as liberal feminists do not necessarily believe that the inclusion of women in international security will change basic outcomes. Nevertheless, as an issue of fairness, the lack of full representation of women in the security realm is seen as a basic inequity given that women make up more than one-half of the world's population. A third school, postmodern feminism, looks at the structure of power and the social activity that reinforces it. Postmodern feminists see the language of security discourse as reinforcing a hierarchy of power reflective of the persistent dominance of masculinity in international society.[76] Postmodern analysis explains why some of the most war-prone leaders in world politics have been women including Margaret Thatcher, Indira Gandhi, Golda Meir, and Benazir

Bhutto. The United States' first woman secretary of state Madeleine K. Albright was one of the toughest realists in the Clinton administration who led the charge for U.S. war against Serbia in 1999. At one point in her position as U.S. ambassador to the United Nations, Albright challenged the masculinity of Cubans who shot down a civilian airplane—arguing that they had no "cajones." Postmodernists would assert that, even if women hold positions of authority, the dominant structure of world politics reflects a text and discourse of a power hierarchy which reinforces the power position of men.

Revolutionary Approaches

If one takes the postmodern assumptions about power to their fullest logic, then the only prospect for change toward a more peaceful order is through a radical and fundamental reconceptualization of the distribution of power toward a new paradigm of human existence. Global security dynamics have produced a reservoir of popular discontent thus provoking radical movements including anarchists and terrorists but also including faithful and idealistic pacifists. Some schools draw from Marxism, advocating the radical redistribution of wealth as the best means of ending economic disparity and conflict. Other schools advance the idea of world government and the abolition of the state. The idea of revolutionary Marxism has receded with the end of the Cold War, though its proponents see merit in the tool of Marxist explanation for explaining economic and social injustice, if not clearly providing a realistic way forward.

SUMMARY

Liberalism offers a range of concepts and policy frameworks while recognizing areas where realism still has an important role to play. Other approaches seek less direct policy applications and instead try to expose the essential foundations of particular international security trends. While often maligned, the broader idealist search for peace is a constant in international security. Even leaders who most strongly have advocated the assertion of military power have also spoken on behalf of the ideal of peace. As the American president and war hero Dwight D. Eisenhower stated in 1953:

> Every gun that is made, every warship launched, every rocket fired signifies, in the final sense, a theft from those who hunger and are not fed, those who are cold and are not clothed. This world in arms is not spending money alone. It is spending the sweat of its laborers, the genius of its scientists, the hopes of its children.

The cost of one modern heavy bomber is this: a modern brick school in more than 30 cities. It is two electric power plants, each serving a town of 60,000 population. It is two fine, fully equipped hospitals. It is some 50 miles of concrete highway. We pay for a single fighter with a half million bushels of wheat. We pay for a single destroyer with new homes that could have housed more than 8000 people. This, I repeat, is the best way of life to be found on the road the world has been taking. This is not a way of life at all, in any true sense. Under the cloud of threatening war, it is humanity hanging from a cross of iron.[77]

Idealists are often criticized as naive and thus dangerously prioritizing peace over the capabilities and strategies that are necessary for true security. History is riddled with failed efforts to build a peace that reflected the goals and principles of idealism. Nevertheless, humankind continues to aspire to the goals articulated by idealists. The most intense analytical and strategic disputes lie over how exactly to get to the goal of more peaceful and just international relations.

NOTES

1. Michael Doyle, "Kant, Liberal Legacies, and Foreign Affairs, Part 2," *Philosophy and Public Affairs* 12, no. 4 (Fall 1983): 205.

2. Doyle, "Kant, Liberal Legacies," 206.

3. Seyom Brown, "World Interests and the Changing Dimensions of Security," in *World Security: Challenges for a New Century*, 3rd ed., ed. Michael Klare and Yogesh Chandrani (New York: St. Martin's Press, 1998), 1–17.

4. Brown, "World Interests," 11–14.

5. Stephen Krasner, "The Accomplishments of International Political Economy," in *International Theory: Positivism and Beyond*, ed. Steve Smith, Ken Booth, and Marvisia Zalewski (Cambridge: Cambridge University Press, 1996), 108–27.

6. Andrew Moravcsik, "Taking Preferences Seriously: A Positive Liberal Theory of International Politics," *International Organization* 51, no. 4 (Autumn 1997): 513–53.

7. Robert O. Keohane, *Power and Governance in a Partially Globalized World* (New York: Routledge, 2002), 44–63.

8. Keohane, *Power and Governance*, 54–55.

9. Francis Fukuyama, "The End of History?" *The National Interest*, no. 15 (Summer 1989): 3–18.

10. Francis Fukuyama, "Second Thoughts: The Last Man in a Bottle," *The National Interest*, no. 56 (Summer 1999): 16–33.

11. Robert O. Keohane and Joseph S. Nye, *Power and Interdependence*, 3rd ed. (New York: Longman, 2001), 7.

12. Robert Powell, "Absolute and Relative Gains in International Relations Theory," in *Neorealism and Neoliberalism: The Contemporary Debate*, ed. David Baldwin (New York: Columbia University Press, 1993), 213.

13. Keohane, *Power and Governance*, 54.

14. See Lisa L. Martin and Beth A. Simmons, eds., *International Institutions* (Cambridge: MIT Press, 2001).

15. Robert O. Keohane and Joseph S. Nye, "Introduction," in *After the Cold War: International Institutions and State Strategies in Europe, 1989–1991*, ed. Robert O. Keohane, Joseph S. Nye, and Stanley Hoffmann (Cambridge: Harvard University Press, 1994), 2–3.

16. Robert Axelrod and Robert O. Keohane, "Achieving Cooperation under Anarchy: Strategies and Institutions," in *Neorealism and Neoliberalism: The Contemporary Debate*, ed. David Baldwin (New York: Columbia University Press, 1993), 94.

17. Charles A. Kupchan, "The Case for Collective Security," in *Collective Security After the Cold War*, ed. George W. Downs (Ann Arbor: University of Michigan Press, 1994), 50–51.

18. Keohane, *Power and Governance*, 1.

19. Judith Goldstein and Robert O. Keohane, "Ideas and Foreign Policy: An Analytical Framework," in *Ideas and Foreign Policy: Beliefs, Institutions, and Political Change*, ed. Judith Goldstein and Robert O. Keohane (Ithaca, N.Y.: Cornell University Press, 1993), 13.

20. Keohane, *Power and Governance*, 75.

21. Keohane, *Power and Governance*, 59.

22. Katja Weber, "Hierarchy Amidst Anarchy: A Transaction Cost Approach to International Security Cooperation," *International Studies Quarterly* 41, no. 2 (June 1997): 334.

23. Kenneth W. Abbott and Duncan Snidal, "Why States Act through Formal International Organizations," *Journal of Conflict Resolution* 42, no. 1 (February 1998): 3–32.

24. See Lisa L. Martin, "Interests, Power, and Multilateralism," *International Organization* 46, no. 4 (1992): 765–92.

25. Robert O. Keohane, *After Hegemony: Cooperation and Discord in the World Political Economy* (Princeton, N.J.: Princeton University Press, 1984), 101.

26. Celeste Wallander, "Institutional Assets and Adaptability: NATO after the Cold War," *International Organization* 54, no. 4 (Autumn 2000): 709.

27. Janne E. Nolan et al., "The Concept of Cooperative Security," in *Global Engagement: Cooperation and Security in the 21st Century*, ed. Janne E. Nolan (Washington, D.C.: Brookings, 1994), 4–5.

28. Nolan, "Concept of Cooperative Security," 10.

29. Antonia Handler Chayes and Abram Chayes, "Regime Architecture: Elements and Principles," in *Global Engagement: Cooperation and Security in the 21st Century*, ed. Janne E. Nolan (Washington, D.C.: Brookings, 1994), 65–130.

30. Allen Sens, "From Collective Defense to Cooperative Security?" in *NATO after Fifty Years*, ed. S. Victor Papacosma, Sean Kay, and Mark Rubin (New York: Scholarly Resources, 2001), 169–70.

31. Robert Gilpin, *The Political Economy of International Relations* (Princeton, N.J.: Princeton University Press, 1987), 263–305.

32. Robert G. Gilpin, *Global Political Economy: Understanding the International Economic Order* (Princeton, N.J.: Princeton University Press, 2001), 278.

33. International Labor Organization, Bureau for Worker's Activities, "Multinational Corporations," at www.itcilo.it/english/actrav/telearn/global/ilo/multinat/multinat.htm (accessed Summer 2004).

34. Karen Mingst, *Essentials of International Relations*, 2nd ed. (New York: W. W. Norton, 2003), 209–12.

35. Emmanuel Kant, *Perpetual Peace*. Excerpted in Richard K. Betts, ed., *Conflict after the Cold War: Arguments on Causes of War and Peace*, 2nd ed. (New York: Longman, 2002), 103.

36. John M. Owen, "How Liberalism Produces Democratic Peace," *International Security* 19, no. 2 (Fall 1994): 87–125.

37. For a full critique, see Christopher Layne, "Kant or Cant: The Myth of the Democratic Peace," *International Security*, 19, no. 2 (Fall 1994): 5–49.

38. Charles Lipson, *Reliable Partners: How Democracies Have Made a Separate Peace* (Princeton, N.J.: Princeton University Press, 2003), 4. See pages 77–111 for his full argument.

39. Lipson, *Reliable Partners*, 14.

40. Karl Deutsch et al., *Political Community in the North Atlantic Area* (Princeton, N.J.: Princeton University Press, 1957), 5–6.

41. Deutsch et al., *Political Community*, 203.

42. Stephen Weber, "Does NATO Have a Future?" in *The Future of European Security*, ed. Beverly Crawford (Berkeley: Center for German and European Studies, University of California, 1992), 369–72.

43. Secretary of State Madeleine K. Albright, *Statement before the Senate Foreign Relations Committee*, Washington, D.C. (October 7, 1997).

44. Emanuel Adler, *European Union: A Pluralistic Security Community* (Berkeley: University of California Press, 1991).

45. Deutsch et al., *Political Community*, 3.

46. Ronald L. Jepperson, Alexander Wendt, and Peter J. Katzenstein, "Norms, Identity, and Culture in National Security," in *The Culture of National Security: Norms and Identity in World Politics*, ed. Peter Katzenstein (New York: Columbia University Press, 1996), 34.

47. Jepperson, Wendt, and Katzenstein, "Norms, Identity, and Culture," 40.

48. Alexander Wendt, "Anarchy Is What States Make of It: The Social Construction of Power Politics," *International Organization* 46, no. 2 (Spring 1992): 397.

49. Alexander Wendt, "The State as a Person in International Theory," *Review of International Studies* 30, no. 2 (2004): 289–316.

50. Hedley Bull, *The Anarchical Society: A Study of Order in World Politics*, 3rd ed. (New York: Pallgrave, 2002).

51. Jessica T. Mathews, "Power Shift," *Foreign Affairs* 76, no. 1 (January/February 1997): 50.

52. Mathews, "Power Shift," 50–66.

53. Mathews, "Power Shift," 50–66.

54. Ernst B. Haas, *When Knowledge Is Power: Three Models of Change in International Organizations* (Berkeley: University of California Press, 1990).

55. Peter Haas, "Introduction: Epistemic Communities and International Policy Coordination," *International Organization* 46, no. 1 (1992): 1–35.

56. Jennifer Mitzen, "Toward a Visible Hand: The International Public Sphere in Theory and Practice," Ph.D. Dissertation, University of Chicago, 2001.

57. Steven R. Ratner, "International Law: The Trials of Global Norms," *Foreign Policy*, no. 110 (Spring 1998): 67.

58. Ratner, "International Law," 72–77.

59. Robert O. Keohane et al., "The Concept of Legalization" *International Organization* 54, no. 3 (Summer 2000): 401–19.

60. Kenneth W. Abbott and Duncan Snidal, "Hard and Soft Law in International Governance" in *International Law: Classic and Contemporary Readings*, ed. Charlotte Ku and Paul F. Diehl (Boulder: Lynne Rienner, 2003), 51–79.

61. Ben Lowe, *Imagining Peace: A History of Early English Pacifist Ideas* (University Park: Pennsylvania State University Press, 1997).

62. David P. Barsh and Charles P. Webel, *Peace and Conflict Studies* (London: SAGE, 2002), 50.

63. Joan V. Bondurant, *Conquest of Violence: The Gandhian Philosophy of Conflict* (Princeton, N.J.: Princeton University Press, 1958).

64. Mary King, *Mahatma Gandhi and Martin Luther King Jr.: The Power of Non-Violent Action* (Paris: UNESCO Publishing, 1999), 272.

65. King, *Mahatma Gandhi*, 272.

66. General Lee Butler, USAF (Retired), "National Press Club Remarks," December 4, 1996, Washington D.C.

67. Paul R. Viotti and Mark V. Kioppi, *International Relations Theory: Realism, Pluralism, Globalism, and Beyond*, 3rd ed. (Boston: Allyn and Bacon, 1999), 18–21; and Pauline Marie Rosenau, *Post-modernism and Social Sciences* (Princeton, N.J.: Princeton University Press, 1992).

68. The author is grateful to Kemi George for advancing this analogy.

69. Richard K. Ashley, "The Poverty of Neorealism," in *Neorealism and Its Critics*, ed. Robert O. Keohane (New York: Columbia University Press, 1986), 270.

70. William E. Connolly, "Identity and Difference in Global Politics," in *International/Intertextual Relations: Postmodern Readings of World Politics*, ed. James Der Derian and Michael J. Shapiro (Lexington, Mass.: Lexington Books, 1989), 323–26.

71. Ole Waever, "Securitization and Desecuritization," in *On Security*, ed. Ronnie Lipschutz (New York: Columbia University Press, 1995), 46–86.

72. David Campbell, *Writing Security: United States Foreign Policy and the Politics of Identity* (Minneapolis: University of Minnesota Press, 1992), 19–20.

73. Cristine Sylvester, *Feminist Theory and International Relations in a Postmodern Era* (Cambridge: Cambridge University Press, 1994).

74. J. Ann Tickner, "A Critique of Morgenthau's Principles of Political Realism," in *Gender in International Relations*, ed. Rebecca Grant and Kathleen Newland (Bloomington: Indiana University Press, 1991), 17–29.

75. Tickner, "Critique of Morgnenthau's Principles," 17–29.

76. See Joshua Goldstein, *War and Gender: How Gender Shapes the War System and Vice-Versa* (Cambridge: Cambridge University Press, 2003); and Joshua Goldstein, *International Relations*, 6th ed. (New York: Longman, 2004).

77. Dwight D. Eisenhower, "Chance for Peace Speech," address to the American Society of Newspaper Editors, April 16, 1953.

SUGGESTED READING

David Baldwin, ed., *Neorealism and Neoliberalism: The Contemporary Debate* (New York: Columbia University Press, 1993).

James Der Derian and Michael J. Shapiro, *International/Intertextual Relations: Postmodern Readings of World Politics* (Lanham, Md.: Lexington Books, 1989).

Michael Doyle and G. John Ikenberry, eds., *New Thinking in International Relations Theory* (Boulder, Colo.: Westview Press, 1997).

Francis Fukuyama, *The End of History and the Last Man* (New York: Free Press, 1992).

Robert O. Keohane, *Power and Governance in a Partially Globalized World* (New York: Routledge, 2002).

Mary King, *Mahatma Gandhi and Martin Luther King Jr.: The Power of Non-Violent Action* (United Nations: UNESCO, 1999).

Charles Lipson, *Reliable Partners: How Democracies Have Made a Separate Peace* (Princeton, N.J.: Princeton University Press, 2003).

Anne-Marie Slaughter, *A New World Order* (Princeton, N.J.: Princeton University Press, 2004).

J. Ann Tickner, *Gendering World Politics* (New York: Columbia University Press, 2001).

Alexander Wendt, *Social Theory of International Politics* (Cambridge: Cambridge University Press, 1999).

Chapter Four

Great Powers and Grand Strategy

The Pentagon. *Source*: U.S. Department of Defense

The distribution of power among the major states in the modern international system reflects general stability and peaceful relations at the dawn of the twenty-first century. Only the United States has the capacity to project military power on a global basis. Nevertheless, Russia, China, and the European Union all have relative power capabilities which will make them major actors in shaping the twenty-first century security environment. While there is growing resentment of the reach of American power around the world, there has been little evidence that other powers are willing to overtly balance against the United States. There are, however, limits on the reach of American power. The possession of nuclear weapons, in particular, by the other major powers still makes direct great power war a losing proposition. America's financial capacity for international intervention is also not limitless. There is also no guarantee that the current international system will remain stable. American power can recede and new powers can rise. Or, America might overreach its capabilities to the point where effective balancing can occur or economic decline forces retrenchment. Finally, while the threat of great power conflict seems low, there are a number of regional conflicts which could draw great powers into war. This chapter provides a survey of the strategic trends and military capabilities of the major powers in the early twenty-first century—the United States, Russia, China, and the European Union.

THE UNITED STATES

The United States is the only state with the military, political, and economic capacity to influence events on a truly worldwide basis. Though its history was one of isolation from world events, since World War II the United States has grown to a position of global primacy. American power is derived both as a measure of its capabilities and, historically, on the attractiveness of its political system and strategic restraint. During the Cold War, the United States cultivated an extensive network of regional alliances and created institutional mechanisms to involve allies in decision making. Much of the legitimacy of American power in the world was generated by its commitment to a defensive strategic doctrine. After the Cold War, the United States found itself facing few external and internal constraints on its ability to shape the international environment should it choose to exercise its power. Much of the question for the United States is not whether to exercise its power, but rather how to exercise it.

During the 1990s, the United States pursued a grand strategy of "enlargement and engagement" under President Bill Clinton. The idea was to consolidate global alliances, enlarging the zone of countries favorable to U.S. interests, engage states that could challenge the United States, and deter states which lay outside the norms of the international system. Where possible, the United States would also engage in peace and humanitarian operations. The United States found itself in an awkward position as it sought to promote a normative agenda of democratic values and free markets. However, its interests also compelled it to stay out of major humanitarian crises. The major strategic challenge was to foster positive relationships with potential adversaries such as Russia and China. On the other hand, the United States also would want to ensure that no other state could become so strong that it could challenge America's primacy. Meanwhile, the United States found itself confronting the dangers of nuclear weapons proliferation among possibly threatening states such as Iraq, Iran, and North Korea. The United States did eventually deploy significant military forces in dangerous humanitarian conflicts in Somalia, Haiti, Bosnia-Herzegovina, and Kosovo in the 1990s. By 2003, the United States was occupying Iraq in the largest nation-building project since World War II.

The United States is well-equipped to address conventional challenges posed by any peer competitor or regional challenger. The kinds of threats such as the September 11th, 2001 terrorist attacks on New York and Washington D.C., however, showed that the United States was ill-prepared for a new dimension of security challenges. Suddenly, the United States faced a new enemy in al Qaeda and one which American power was not aligned to manage. Rather than retreat into a new isolationism as the terrorists appear to have hoped, the United States engaged proactively in Afghanistan and then in Iraq to overthrow unfriendly governments. America adopted a new strategic doctrine that any state which harbors or supports international terrorists would themselves be considered as supporting terrorists. "Either you are with us, or you are against us" was the rallying cry to the world. This perspective would also expand to incorporate an offensive doctrine of preemptive war. America has committed itself to eliminate possible threats before they emerge.

America's offensive doctrine rejects deterrence and is a major departure from the historical traditions of defensive American posture. The United States has demonstrated a willingness and ability to carry out offensive military actions and it has opted to do so outside existing norms of the international community. In the case of Iraq, the United States went to war over the strong opposition of much of the world, including its historically closest European allies. American credibility was particularly challenged when much of the intelligence evidence it presented to justify the Iraq invasion proved to be wrong. The military mission of toppling the government of Saddam Hussein was easier than many observers expected. However, it became clear that there were limits and costs to this new strategic action as postwar rebuilding efforts would be carried out by 90 percent of American troops and that the United States would pay 90 percent of the costs. Other rationales for war were thus left open to speculation ranging from a desire to control oil flows to a political-sociological grand experiment to spread democracy in the Middle East.

The international campaign against terrorists also prompted the United States to review international defense relationships. Cold War alliances like the North Atlantic Treaty Organization, while still of political value, were not initially engaged in the American-led coalition military operations in Afghanistan and Iraq. In August 2004, the United States announced that it would begin a phased reduction of troops which had been permanently based in Europe and Asia—a total of about 70,000 troops. Meanwhile, new strategic priorities emerged as the United States engaged new allies such as Pakistan in its efforts to destroy international terrorist networks. By 2004, however, America's ability to engage in war against terrorists with primarily military power had reached its limits. A leaked memo from U.S. Secretary of Defense Donald Rumsfeld suggested that the United States could not kill terrorists as fast as they were being created and it was not clear that the Department of Defense was the agency best suited for the lead role in the campaign against terrorists. Nevertheless, America's defense budget was projected to reach nearly $500 billion a year by 2010. America thus entered the twenty-first century under a growing sense of external threat, occupying Iraq, its international prestige in decline, and its economy increasingly invested in supporting international commitments and burdened by extensive domestic and trade deficits.

During the 1990s, America's military doctrine was based on fighting and winning two simultaneous major regional conflicts. The United States would maintain forward deployed equipment and force projection capabilities to fight a major war in the Persian Gulf region and on the Korean peninsula at the same time. As forces would be deployed in substantial numbers for other conflicts such as in the Balkans, this policy took on a posture more attuned to a win-hold strategy. In a crisis, a war in one region could be fought and won while a crisis in another region would be contained. This approach was put in place in the 2003 Iraq war when the United States deployed an array of troops and equipment to the Persian Gulf by taking assets from other key parts of the world. However, in a public show of deterrence, the United States also sent long-range bombers with nuclear capability to Guam as a signal to North Korea that it should not take advantage of the war in the Middle East. The degree to which forces were stretched thin had actually already become clear in the 1999 Kosovo war in which the United States European command had a very difficult time getting resources reallocated from other theaters of operation. When an aircraft carrier was moved from the Pacific Fleet, the Pacific Ocean was left unguarded by an American aircraft carrier for the first time since World War II. This commitment to a relatively rigid two-war doctrine thus required a significant realigning of strategy and resource commitments even before the commencement of the war against terrorism.

In 2001, the United States published its *Quadrennial Defense Review*, which established four main strategic objectives: assuring friends and allies; dissuading future military competition; deterring threats and coercion against U.S. interests; and decisively defeating any adversary should deterrence fail.[1] By 2006, the United States continued to maintain unchallenged military capability in relation to these objectives but also added to them the mission of combating international terrorism and occupying Iraq. Active duty U.S. forces totaled 1,473,966 with 1,290,988 reserves. The American strategic command included 432 submarine-launched ballistic missiles in 16 submarines plus 16 *Poseidon* C-3 launchers in one submarine, 550 intercontinental ballistic missiles, and 64 B-52 *Stratofortress* bombers and 21 B-2A *Spirit* long-range bombers. Active duty army forces included 502,000 troops; 376,750, naval forces; 175,350 marines; 379,500 air force personnel; and 31,496 special forces. The United States is able to exert a regular global presence with substantial airlift capability for troops including 927 planes in the civil reserve air fleet, 12 aircraft carrier battle groups, long-range ballistic and tactical submarines, and 1,577 combat capable aircraft including 191 with long-range strike capability.[2] The U.S. Navy has also proposed increasing the size of its total fleet to 313 ships by the year 2020, with a total expenditure of $13 billion a year. The focus on the naval expansion would be targeted toward rapid deployment on a global basis including 55 small combat vessels that operate in shallow coastal areas and an additional 31 amphibious assault ships while maintaining 11 aircraft carriers in the 2020 plan.[3]

With the end of the Cold War, the United States made major force reductions, and cut its overall defense spending to as low as $240 billion annually during the mid-1990s. However, by 2010 defense spending will approach $500 billion annually and new troop deployment arrangements are to be in place, absent some dramatic change in the conventional or nuclear environment. The United States will base the bulk of its armed forces in the continental United States. Overseas deployments such as those in Germany and South Korea will gradually be reduced. In their place, smaller forward operating bases will be built in allied countries bordering areas of potential conflict. These forward basing areas will not have many troops deployed in peacetime. Rather, they will be able to accommodate reinforcements on short notice in the event of a crisis and will use predeployed equipment. Between 2004 and 2014, the United States plans to bring 60,000–70,000 uniformed personnel and 100,000 family members and civilian employees back to the United States from overseas positions. As troops are redeployed or reduced, four new elements of strategy will guide future deployments: (1) expand U.S. defense relationships with allies and build new partnerships; (2) develop flexibility to contend with uncertainty; (3) enable rapid power projection; and (4) focus on capabilities instead of numbers. Washington intends to consolidate significant

American advantages in technological capabilities focused on reach, stealth, precision, knowledge, and combat power rather than the size of forces. Small, highly trained and networked units, platforms, and individual troops, it is believed, will have a major impact on strategic outcomes. One high-tech ship or tank or aircraft would have the same effect that was once only attainable by ten ships or tanks or aircraft.[4]

Instead of having large forward deployed concentrations of forces, the United States appears to envision a network of small operations spread around the world that will be able to accommodate a range of military operations on short notice. These plans include building an air field in Dakar, Senegal, for landing and fueling long-range aircraft. Singapore has built a deep draft pier at its Changi naval station that will accommodate berthing a U.S. aircraft carrier and has opened its Paya Lebar air base for American planes. The United States is operating units alongside Ecuadoran troops in counter-drug operations and running counter-drug surveillance flights from Aruba and Curacao in the Caribbean. Other likely locations include use of the island nation of Sao Tome and Principe off of West Africa, as a forward operating site for monitoring the movement of oil tankers and protecting oil platforms; use of Sarafovo and Graf Ignatievo air fields in Bulgaria; and the Mihail Kogalniceaunu air base and Babadag training range in the Black Sea military port of Mangalia in Romania. Joint training would also be conducted in Australia, though without creating permanent bases there. Overall, the United States will maintain about 550 overseas sites by 2010.[5] The United States is also increasingly relying on small groups of special operations forces dispatched to sensitive regions of the world to train local forces to carry out antiterrorist missions. The United States plans to devote over $130 million to training in western Africa via the Pan-Sahel Initiative, which will train forces in Mali, Mauritania, Niger, Chad, and Senegal.[6] This program is likely to have a budget of $660 million between 2004 and 2009 and be designed to train, equip, and provide logistical support for nations willing to participate in peace operations in Africa.[7]

The United States has also reviewed its nuclear weapons posture and plans a sharp reduction in nuclear missile capabilities. At the same time, it is beginning a process of developing a new nuclear doctrine and capabilities. The United States has, since 1991 dramatically reduced its nuclear arsenal. Through the 1990s it kept nuclear capabilities as a reserve component of military doctrine based on continued application of deterrence and mutual assured destruction—though at much lower levels. In 1991 the United States took its strategic bombers off alert from the Cold War status of having 30 percent on strip alert ready to fly. During the 1990s, the United States also removed nuclear weapons from its ground forces. Overall, the United States reduced its nuclear weapons by 90 percent from Cold War levels of deployments while also negotiating with Russia and China to no longer target nuclear missiles at each other. The United States also announced that it was no longer developing new nuclear weapons and would not be testing nuclear weapons. The United States signed, but did not ratify, an international treaty that would have banned nuclear weapons testing among those states that signed the treaty. However, it has abided by the spirit of the goal of restraint, by not actually testing nuclear weapons.

In 2002, the United States and Russia negotiated deep cuts in their total numbers of nuclear weapons. By December 2012, the United States and Russia agreed to achieve an aggregate number of nuclear weapons that will not exceed 1,700–2,200 for each party.[8] This was an easy treaty for both sides to negotiate as the Russians wanted deep cuts to save money and the United States was moving toward unilateral cuts. For Washington, this treaty also served to soften Russian opposition to America's plans for building a national missile defense. The United States had, in 2002, completed a review of its nuclear posture recognizing that the Russian nuclear arsenal was no longer a major strategic threat. Thus the United States could afford to cut its arsenal significantly without making itself vulnerable. By 2007, the United States intends to maintain 3,800 nuclear weapons en route to deeper reductions under the U.S.-Russian treaty. This force will include 14 *Trident* ballistic-missile submarines, 500 *Minuteman* III intercontinental ballistic missiles, 76 B-F2H bombers armed with cruise missiles and gravity bombs, and 21 B-2s armed with gravity bombs. While cutting programs, the United States has also begun enhancing nuclear-test readiness, revived nuclear warhead advanced concepts efforts at the national laboratories, and accelerated planning and design for a modern weapons-grade-plutonium production facility.[9]

A controversial addition to the updated nuclear posture was a program advanced in 2002 to begin research, but not deployment, of a new nuclear weapons system for conventional targeting such as deep-burrowing into the ground to destroy underground facilities.[10] Building a concept for use of nuclear weapons in battle was controversial because it changes the threshold in which nuclear weapons would be introduced into combat. Critics assert that this move provides a new sense of utility and legitimacy to these weapons, perhaps contributing to additional proliferation. Overall, while the number of weapons is significantly reduced, the strategic logic of the American nuclear posture continues to be to prepare for large-scale nuclear war with Russia and China.[11] Critics note that the basics of America's nuclear posture have not changed, but only continue at a lower, but still very dangerous level. Also, its approximately 1,600 tactical nuclear warheads are not part of any treaty structure. Alternatively, some critics assert that American strategic thinking has not done enough to support new uses of nuclear capabilities. According to a study and recommendations from the Pentagon's Defense Science Board, current plans for nuclear weapons use does not sufficiently consider greater precision, reduced radioactivity, and the ability to dig deep into the ground to get at hard targets (a capacity that is not currently technologically feasible). Rather than eliminate large intercontinental ballistic missiles, the Defense Science Board recommended developing special purpose nonnuclear weapons—long-range heavy conventional bombs for hitting precise targets within minutes; submarine-launched nonnuclear missiles; and a new sensor system for finding small, moving, and hidden targets.[12] This approach could have drawbacks as other countries, Russia and China, in particular, might not be able to recognize the difference between a conventional and a nuclear intercontinental ballistic missile. If that were the case, they could mistake a conventional attack, even on another country, as a nuclear attack, thus risking an accidental nuclear war.[13] Also, in September 2005, press reports indicated that the U.S. Defense Department was expanding its guidance for the use of nuclear weapons in combat to include preemptive strikes against terrorist organizations or nations which were in planning stages of using unconventional weapons against the United States.[14]

RUSSIA

Since it emerged from the Soviet Union as a sovereign state in 1992, Russia has undergone a dramatic transformation from feared global superpower to a country whose major threat is its weakness. Russia no longer sits at the top of many assessments of international security trends because it no longer carries the political, economic, or conventional military capacity to exert power within the international system. The primary capability that places Russia at the top of major powers in the world is its nuclear arsenal—though that is also the least useable of its power capabilities. As Russia's conventional capabilities have declined, Russia increasingly relies on its nuclear weapons for deterrence. In 2004, Russia announced that it was reinvigorating its nuclear arsenal with planned deployment of a new intercontinental ballistic missile (ICBM) that could change speed in flight as a means of avoiding missile defense systems. This missile would carry as many as 10 warheads with a range of 6,000 miles. This reliance on nuclear weapons has potentially destabilizing consequences as its nuclear arsenal suffers serious maintenance and security problems combined with a declining early warning system. Command and control issues have also raised concerns about accidental launch or a possible nexus between nuclear smuggling, organized crime, and international terrorism.

Russia continues to play a significant diplomatic role in international security affairs. However, Russia has suffered from a general tension over where it sees itself sitting geopolitically. Russia is caught between West and East while seeking to leverage influence within its area of influence in the former Soviet Union. Generally, when forced to choose, Russia has aligned itself with the West and sought good relations with Europe. Russia has often turned a weak power position into a successful negotiating tool of diplomacy by staking out hard-line opposition to some international policies and seeking payoffs for accommodation. For example, Russia strongly opposed NATO's enlargement during the 1990s. There was nothing functional Russia could do to halt NATO expansion. However, by staking out a strong diplomatic position in opposition to NATO's enlargement, Russia was able to negotiate favors as an exchange for not stopping what it really had no power to stop in any event. Moscow made gains as the West turned an eye away from the redeployment of Russian conventional forces toward the Caucuses region. Russia also gained promises from NATO not to deploy troops on new NATO members' territory, not to build nuclear weapons infrastructure or deploy nuclear weapons in these new members, and to create a NATO-Russia council that would give Russia limited say in NATO activities. Though not formerly related to NATO's enlargement, Russia also gained membership into an expanded G-7, the grouping of leading global economic powers, transforming it into a G-8—though Moscow's participation was limited to political discussions.

Much of Russia's diplomatic posture in the 1990s was, however, generated out of lost prestige and shaped by domestic politics. Russia's leaders initially had to tread carefully in order to keep the military reasonably satisfied and out of politics—in other words, to avoid coups. In 1993, Russian tanks intervened in domestic politics and opened fire on the Soviet-era parliament which was challenging the elected president, Boris Yeltsin, for power. More broadly, the deep decline in military prestige from the days of Soviet world power was a significant aspect of political frustration that could be manipulated by nationalist and former communist leaders. In Russia's first parliamentary election following its independence, in 1993, the public voted in favor of a majority party government by a nationalist-fascist, Vladimir Zhirinovsky. Failing to build a grassroots political network, Boris Yeltsin stood down on New Year's in 2000, handing power to his chosen successor Vladimir Putin. Putin was a former KGB agent who promised stability while centralizing power over Russia's regions and asserting heavy influence over the Russian media and business leaders. While communism was dead in Russia, traditions of a strong central government persisted under Putin, raising concerns in the West of a drift toward authoritarian government in Russia.

During the 1990s, Russia debated versions of a new strategic doctrine with an updated edition approved in 2003. The military is accorded a significant place in Russian society even though investment into defense has declined precipitously. Consequently, Russia's ability to actually meet its strategic objectives is substantially limited. Russia sees its general strategic interests in building a multipolar world order and working against the idea of one country having sole primacy in international affairs. Russia also asserts regional freedom of movement in neighboring states to include a right of preemptive intervention without approval of the United Nations. The military was also given a role within the borders of Russia to protect the territorial integrity of the country from breakaway areas such as Chechnya. A sustained war against the independent-minded Chechen region of Russia has preoccupied the Russian army since the early 1990s. While the rest of the world looked the other way, out of deference to Russian sovereignty and their larger interests in a cooperative relationship with Moscow, the Russian army leveled major Chechen cities such as Grozny. Russian official doctrine defines major threats as including: territorial claims to the Russian Federation from other post-Soviet states; local wars and armed conflicts near Russia's borders; proliferation of weapons of mass destruction and their means of delivery; the rights of Russians living in other former Soviet republics; and the enlargement of external military blocks such as NATO.[15]

Overall, Russia seeks a stable global situation so that it can focus on rebuilding and modernizing its economy while gaining international support and investment for that goal. Russia's security policy has thus focused primarily on developing stable relationships with the other major powers while at the same time exerting Russian influence within its periphery—or its so-called "near abroad" area of former Soviet republics. After the Soviet collapse, Russia initially made substantial overtures to the West under Foreign Minister Andrei Kosyrev in the early 1990s. However, as domestic political and economic crises led to a more nationalist perspective at home, domestic pressures placed constraints on Moscow's relationship with the West. Moscow and the West do have a common threat assessment in transnational terrorism. Moscow also requires heavy investment from the West to grow its economy while seeking entry into international economic institutions. Meanwhile, the West requires Russia's assistance in controlling nuclear proliferation and in managing the rise of China's power. Russia's assistance to and partnership with the United States in the international war on terrorism has enhanced Russia's bargaining power. At a crucial moment in fall 2001, Moscow acceded to American overflight of Russian territory and did not raise strong objections to basing U.S. military personnel in several former Soviet republics. In the long term, Russia's massive untapped oil and natural gas reserves could make it a major supplier of energy in the twenty-first century, thus significantly growing its relative power capabilities.

Russia is an ethnically and religiously diverse country covering a massive geopolitical space and with varying levels of economic development. Russian national security policy has historically been heavily influenced by a suspicion of the outside and a fear of external encirclement. Russia never went through the Western periods of enlightenment and modernization that Europe went through centuries ago. The Serfs were only freed in 1867, electricity only came to Russia after the Bolshevik revolution in 1917, and the large urbanization and industrial growth occurred under the terrorist rule of Joseph Stalin. Russia and the larger Soviet Union were attacked twice by Germany during the twentieth century—which took the fight right to the borders of Moscow during World War II. Russia has also had a long-standing tension on its border with China. From the Russian security perspective, their country lost the Cold War and their military returned home with very little to show for their efforts. Then, little of the promised Western aid of $22 billion for assistance in economic reform and democratization materialized. The United States led the expansion of NATO right to Moscow's borders and, in 2003, took former Soviet republics of Lithuania, Latvia, and Estonia into the alliance. Meanwhile, Russia acquiesced to the presence of American forces to its south during the war in Afghanistan. Moscow initially saw that as a temporary presence whereas the deployments of American troops in Uzbekistan and Kyrgyzstan had, in Russia's perspective, taken on a much more permanent appearance by 2004. Meanwhile, American forces remain in Japan and South Korea, while China is rising to Russia's south. Russia is strategically boxed-in with little room to maneuver. At the same time, Moscow has had to manage a number of separatist movements and advocate for over twenty million ethnic Russians left in neighboring republics after the collapse.

The Russian military was largely left to decay for lack of funding during the 1990s. The severity of the problem was highlighted by the accidental sinking of a Russian nuclear submarine, and the death of its 118 crewmen, in the North Atlantic in 2000. In August 2005, a Russian submarine became entangled in fishing nets near Japan—and rescue only became possible when American and British equipment and experts arrived at the scene. Within the ranks, 25 percent of all deaths in the Russian army are the result of suicide.[16] Army officers and their families returning from Eastern Europe (and then the former Soviet republics) were cramped into barracks and there was a high rate of no-shows from Russia's conscription. Russian air force pilots trained on average about 30 to 50 hours a year versus the NATO standard of between 180 and 260. In 1994, the air force received only 50 new aircraft and by 1995, less than 25.[17] Russia also began selling off equipment, becoming a major weapons exporter. However, Russia has not been able to afford its own weapons modernization programs. Russia's early warning system, which would help it to know whether or not it was under a nuclear attack, has weakened considerably. Russia has gone for considerable periods with no satellite coverage of its own territory and during the Y2K computer date turnover in 2000, Russia sent military personnel to the U.S. air surveillance command at NORAD to better monitor their own air space. Russia's weak economy often made it appear that Moscow could not see far past the sale of its equipment. For example, Russia sold technology to Iran that could be used to build nuclear weapons, which could ultimately be targeted at Russia. Indeed, Russia was reported in December 2005 to be preparing to deliver over $1 billion worth of tactical surface-to-air missiles and additional military equipment to Iran.[18]

While sympathetic to Russia's democratization and market reform efforts, the West has seen the country run an inconsistent foreign policy. Boris Yeltsin even raised the specter of nuclear weapons use when NATO intervened in Bosnia-Herzegovina in 1995. Skeptics of Russia's benign intentions point to its history of authoritarian government and expansionist foreign policy. Meanwhile, Russia has opened up a proactive relationship with China that Moscow says is designed to facilitate the promotion of a multipolar order at the expense of American power. Skeptics also point to gross violations of human rights carried out by the Russian military in Chechnya and the significant interference by the Russian military and intelligence operations in the independent countries of the former Soviet Union. In this view, Russia will eventually reemerge as a major force in world politics as its economy is revitalized. Some outside observers argue it is better to act now to constrain Russia while it is weak, as with the expansion of NATO, than to encounter it later when it is strong again. Countering this view is the belief that moves which isolate Russia will promote a self-fulfilling prophecy of Russian nationalism as it seeks to overturn any externally imposed constraints.

In the first four years of the presidency of Vladimir Putin, the Russian economy improved. Russia's gross domestic product grew by 7.2 percent in 2003, its budget surplus grew by over $30 billion, and its trade surplus increased by 32 percent between 2003 and 2004.[19] During the 2004 presidential election, Vladimir Putin observed a number of military exercises—though some produced embarrassing public failures of missile technology. Putin promised further efforts to restore prestige and capabilities to the Russian armed forces. Russia also conducted nuclear exercises and developed a new base near an American base in Kyrgyzstan while refusing to withdraw troops based in Georgia despite considerable Western pressure.[20] Overall, the Russian defense budget has grown by 84 percent since 1999, and it was set to increase by another 17 percent in 2005—but only to a real figure of $22 billion a year in total expenditure. Without a major—and politically and economically painful—reform of the military, Russia's ability to act as a major military power remains limited to its internal security operations, some engagement in nearby countries, and its nuclear deterrent.

The Russian military hopes to reduce its troop numbers to 1.1 million and to begin to professionalize its troops by building on targeted and specialized training programs. Between 2002 and 2003, Russia accelerated the training of its soldiers with ground forces tactical training time at the company level increased by 50 percent, air force flying time increased by 11 percent, and naval sea training increased by 25 percent. In 2006, Russia had total active armed forces numbering 1,037,000 based on conscription service of 18 to 24 months. Total reserves, an obligation to age 50, were about 20 million people—2 million of which had served within the previous five years. Russia's strategic deterrent forces include 129,000 troops that service 216 missiles in 15 operational nuclear submarines and 30,000 strategic missile force troops which service 570 ICBMs. The Russian army has 359,000 troops including 190,000 conscripts. The navy has 142,000 in service; the air force, 170,000. Russia also has about 415,000 active duty paramilitary forces including the border guard service that numbers 160,000.[21]

Russia's international deployments have dropped dramatically from the hundreds of thousands deployed outside the USSR during the Cold War to include, by 2006, some 3,500 troops in Armenia, about 3,000 in Georgia, about 500 in Kyrgyzstan, about 1,400 in Moldova, 7,800 in Tajikistan, 1,100 naval infantry in Ukraine, 100 in Africa, and 150 in Syria. Russia also has sent token troops to United Nations operations in Burundi; the Democratic Republic of Congo; Côte D'Ivoire; East Timor; Ethiopia/Eritrea; Georgia; the Middle East; Sierra Leone; and Western Sahara.[22] Russia's incapacity to project power significantly reduces its ability to commit troops far from home territory. For example, in 1999 about 200 Russian soldiers moved from Bosnia to Kosovo to establish an area of control near the Pristina airport—apparently to give Russia some leverage in further negotiations over a postwar phase in Kosovo. However, once the troops arrived, there were no reinforcements available. Any efforts to reinforce from Russia would have meant violating airspace of NATO-member Hungary.

The Russian armed forces maintain a heavy land component with large numbers of tanks, including about 22,800 main battle tanks which have not been updated significantly since the early 1990s. Russia has stockpiles of artillery pieces numbering 30,045 but much is in storage and is mostly of use for a Cold War scenario that no longer exists. Russia has 15 strategic submarines and 46 tactical submarines. Russia has 66 principal surface combatant naval vessels including 1 aircraft carrier and 15 destroyers. Russia maintains significant long-range aviation and tactical aviation but with minimal new equipment and very little training time for pilots—about 25 hours for long-range and 20 to 25 hours for tactical training. Transport air command includes 293 planes with additional planes available from its civilian fleet.[23]

Overall, however, airlift capabilities are severely limited and remaining Russian air power is largely medium-range bombers and operational-tactical missiles.[24] If Russia found it necessary to deter attacks on forward-deployed forces, it might have little choice but to resort to the use of tactical nuclear weapons. Indeed, Russia has reversed its prior political commitment to not be the first to introduce nuclear weapons in conflict.

The rise of organized crime in Russia combines with the decline of the role of the military to create a significant black market of illegal arms trafficking. By one account, some 27,000 firearms have been stolen from military units in Russia, and 53,900 crimes involving illegal trading in weapons were recorded in Russia in 2001.[25] Some 200 of the largest criminal gangs in Russia are global networks. These groups are pervasive in the economy and have a heavy influence on politics, contributing to a significant international investment chill. There is a risk that such groups would engage in trafficking of nuclear materials by exploiting corruption and what are often subhuman living conditions in the Russian military and at its nuclear facilities. Less likely, but possible, is a theft of an actual nuclear weapon or components via military transport vehicles that are not searched. Some short- and medium-range conventional missiles have been smuggled successfully out of Russia.[26] While it was not confirmed, a former Russian general claimed in 1996 that there were about 100 so-called "suitcase" tactical nuclear weapons missing from the Russian arsenal. These small nuclear devices had apparently been intended for paramilitary activity behind enemy lines during the Cold War.

During the 1990s, there were some incidents of nuclear smuggling out of Russia though the materiel was below weapons grade and undertaken by petty criminals. One case of 5.6 kilograms of Russian-produced plutonium 239 (enriched to 99.75 percent purity) was discovered unprotected in a garage in Tengen, Germany, and a large quantity of berylium was found in a vault in a bank in Vilnius, Lithuania.[27] Between 1993 and 2002, eighteen cases of seizure of small quantities of weapons-grade nuclear materiel were confirmed by the International Atomic Energy Agency.[28] A major irony of the nuclear decommissioning that accompanied the end of the Cold War is that many of the warheads being dismantled from missiles are still awaiting destruction and are both risky and expensive to store. These nuclear materials, or more likely their components, in some cases are highly vulnerable to theft or illegal sale. The United Nations estimates that "dangerous" levels for making a fissionable nuclear device are 17.6 pounds of plutonium or 55 pounds of uranium— though more likely 2.2 pounds of uranium would probably be enough to cause severe blast damage. The U.S. Department of Energy estimates that there is about 600 tons of weapons-grade separated plutonium and highly enriched uranium outside of nuclear weapons in Russia. This material is located at fifty-three locations across eleven time zones.[29] This weapons-grade material can be reprocessed or locked away, but it cannot be destroyed. In total, Russia has about 7,800 operational nuclear warheads divided between 4,400 strategic warheads and 3,400 tactical nuclear weapons and an additional 9,000 in storage or awaiting dismantling. The combined land- and sea-launched nuclear capacity in Russia comprises explosive power equal to 120,000 of the kind of bomb that was dropped on Hiroshima in World War II.[30]

Russian nuclear workers earn as little as $100.00 a month and military and nuclear personnel have on occasion gone months with no pay. Pride and patriotism keep the vast majority of Russian military and scientific experts working to keep nuclear material safe and secure.[31] According to the Nuclear Threat Reduction Initiative, there are, nevertheless, six key problems with management of nuclear weapons and material in the former Soviet Union: (1) the stockpiles are insecure and poorly accounted for; (2) once stolen, the measures in place to find and recover them, or stop their smuggle across borders, are inadequate; (3) stockpiles' custodians face lower pay and the prospect of mass layoffs, and are in an underfunded and oversized nuclear complex; (4) management of these stockpiles remains shrouded in secrecy, making clear understanding of the problems and effective implementation of solutions far more difficult; (5) more weapons-usable material continues to be produced; and (6) the stockpiles of nuclear weapons and materials that now exist are far larger than needed, and only slow progress is being made (or planned) in reducing them.[32] In 2001–2002, two nuclear warhead storage sites and two transport trains were found to have been under surveillance by terrorist groups and one group made plans, not carried out, to seize a reactor at the Kurchatov Institute in Moscow.[33]

Russia also has serious challenges with the declining command and control and early warning infrastructure for its strategic nuclear arsenal. While the risk is low, and the implications far less dangerous than during the Cold War, the risk still exists that there could be an accidental or unauthorized attack by Russia launched at the United States. While both Russia and the United States (and China) agreed to de-target their nuclear missiles during the 1990s, these missiles could be retargeted within a matter of minutes. Moreover, it is not 100 percent safe to assume that all nuclear weapons are always in completely competent hands. Even in the United States some 4,000 military personnel were removed from nuclear weapons responsibility from 1975–1990 for drug, alcohol, or psychological problems. In both 1979 and 1989 a computer malfunction in American missile alert systems led to false indications that massive Soviet nuclear attacks were inbound toward the United States.[34] If these kinds of conditions occurred in the United States, one can reasonably assume similar problems exist in the far weaker Russian system. In January 1995, Norway launched a satellite into space which Russian early warning systems falsely identified as an inbound nuclear attack from NATO. Russia's top political leadership had eight minutes to conclude that this was not a preemptive NATO attack on Russia—and less than four minutes remained before they had to decide whether or not to launch a retaliatory attack. Despite lower numbers of nuclear weapons, the United States and Russia continue to maintain the basics of mutual assured destruction and launch-on-warning nuclear response strategies. Poor early warning systems make this an especially dangerous condition.

While extremely unlikely, it is not impossible that a Russian nuclear missile could be accidentally, or purposely, launched by a nuclear submarine. Theoretically, terrorists could convince Russia it was under a nuclear attack from the United States, thus prompting Russia to launch a supposed retaliatory response. Russia maintains Delta IV ballistic missile submarines as the major component of its submarine fleet—each with 16 MIRV (multiple independent reentry vehicles) missiles on board. Either as a result of a breakdown in communication or the rogue actions of a ship, there is a slim possibility of an isolated launch of weapons. Even one such incident would be devastating. According to one study, if 4 missiles failed for technical reasons, but 12 missiles (a total of 48 warheads) were launched they would reach their primary targets—American cities. The immediate blast would kill everyone in a three-mile radius. It would then create—within hours depending on wind direction—a forty-mile by three-mile area laced with lethal radiation. If such an event occurred in New York City there would be an estimated three million killed; in San Francisco, 739,000 killed; and in Washington, D.C., 728,000 killed. The study concluded that a conservative estimate would produce a result of 6,838,000 Americans killed in hours, accompanied by a national breakdown of systems for food, water, electricity, and medicinal delivery with millions more deaths in the aftermath.[35]

Russia has yet to affirm its own place in the general scheme of major power relations. When pushed, Moscow has aligned with the West, though it has used the threat of breaking that cooperation as a tool to achieve diplomatic gains. Russia and the West share common threats from terrorism. Each shares a strong interest in nuclear safety and preventing proliferation. Yet Russia itself is one of the most likely sources of any eventual proliferation of nuclear weapons material to terrorists. Russia's greatest risk to the world is not the marching columns of soldiers and their tanks at Red Square. Rather, the most significant threat from Russia comes from its relative weakness at home and abroad. Russia does have a significant strategic role because while it cannot control international outcomes, Russia can serve as a balancing state between the United States and China or between Europe and the United States. Russia can threaten an alliance with China to extract gains from the United States. Or, Russia can align with the United States if its fear of China becomes too great.

Alternatively, Russia can work more closely with Europe than it does the United States, further promoting a vision of a world in which one power does not dominate.

CHINA

The People's Republic of China is often seen as the one country that, in the span of the next fifteen to twenty years, could emerge as a significant geopolitical challenger to the United States. A population of over a billion people, coupled with rapid economic development, has made China a significant emerging power. At the same time, China has historically been inward-looking and has a predominantly peasant-agrarian society lacking economic modernization. China has begun to open its economy and has entered the international trading system. As it enters the globalized international economy, China confronts a period of generational change which puts pressure on the government for reform and respect for human rights. Nevertheless, China continues to be governed by the Communist Party, which holds onto power with support of the military and which increasingly appeals to nationalism for popular support. While the rise of China appears inevitable, the question of what kind of China will emerge is open. Would, for example, population pressures push China toward aggression as a tool of gaining access to vital resources? Or, would China's entry into the global economic system facilitate economic growth and foster internal change toward democracy and a peaceful security policy?

China's dominant historical trend has focused on internal stability and isolation from global politics. At the core of Chinese tradition lies a desire to ensure national unity, stability, and sovereignty. Consequently, China has focused on defensive measures to prevent invasion and secure its periphery. China's recent historical memories include being invaded by Japan in World War II. China did venture into a variety of Cold War engagements, supporting some like-minded communist countries in the underdeveloped world. However, China and the Soviet Union competed both over leadership of the communist world and over territorial disputes on their common border. These differences were successfully exploited by the United States during the 1970s as U.S.-Chinese relations were normalized following overtures to China by President Richard Nixon. During the 1980s and 1990s, China gradually sought to engage the international community, though it faced serious external criticism caused by its internal disregard for human rights.

While much of the analytical focus on China's rise to power stresses its role as a potential challenger to the United States, the major countries most immediately affected by China's growth are Russia, Japan, and India. Russia and

China share a 4,000-mile border. As a result of sporadic conflict over several centuries, by the 1960s, China claimed over 500,000 miles of Soviet territory. In 1969, competing territorial claims provoked a small shooting conflict at the border. Chinese officials have looked at Russia as a model to avoid when implementing internal political and economic reforms. Moscow's model of combining market reform with political reform in the 1980s was rejected by China, which has preferred gradual market-liberalization, carefully managed by the Communist Party. Russia has become an important supplier of arms, for example, selling China fighter planes and associated equipment. China has, in turn, been modernizing this older Russian equipment for their use and for further export. The Russia-China relationship is complicated in that while Moscow would like to advance a multipolar world order, an unchecked rise in Chinese power could be as much a threat to Russia as to anyone. In the post–Cold War era, Russia has leveraged its relationship with China as a hedge against American power. At the same time, Russia is vulnerable to movements of Chinese populations into eastern Siberia, and a growing Chinese interest in diverting Caspian Sea energy supplies toward China. In 2004, some Chinese officials publicly considered the idea of purchasing Russia's largest oil company, *Yukos*, as it appeared Russia might favor a deal with Japan over construction of a pipeline to fuel east Asian energy needs.[36]

So long as the United States has maintained a troop presence in Japan (by 2005 at about 50,000), Tokyo has relied on its alliance with the United States for protection—including America's shield of nuclear deterrence. During the 1990s, however, the United States began developing a "strategic partnership" with China which raised concern in Japan about American priorities in Asia. When President Bill Clinton traveled to China in the late 1990s, he did not make a first stop in Japan to consult with what had been one of America's closest allies. While China's economy has been growing, in large part as a major exporter to the United States, the Japanese economy was in deep decline for most of the 1990s. Japan has remained committed to its alliance with the United States. However, the relative rise in China's power, combined with questions about the American security guarantee, could eventually lead Japan to rebuild its military capability and, in theory, even pursue its own nuclear deterrent.

Geography historically kept India and China from conflict and each have had other strategic priorities. Separated by the Himalayan mountains, direct conventional conflict between China and India has been a difficult proposition. Nevertheless, India has developed nuclear weapons with ranges that can hit targets in China. India has been concerned with China's support for Pakistan and its alleged role in facilitating the development of Pakistan's nuclear weapons. China and India also share a border near the areas of key dispute between India and Pakistan. Should China ever overtly side with Pakistan, this would significantly elevate security concerns in India. Conversely, China has to pay careful attention to India's expanding naval power, and missile and space technology. India's economy has considerable potential for development and its population now rivals China in size. How China and India define their relationships in the coming decades will thus be a key element in the overall dynamics of regional security in south Asia.

China's rise in power is generally associated with the potential to translate economic power into military capabilities. Between 1980 and 2000, China's economy grew by a factor of five annually, average incomes quadrupled, and 270 million people emerged out of absolute poverty. Nevertheless, China remains a predominantly agrarian society and annual incomes average around $1,000. If, however, China's growth rates continue, even at a slower pace, it will emerge as the second largest economy in the world after the United States by about 2020. Between 1996 and 2001, China's economy grew at an annual rate of 7.8 percent and in 2002 at 8 percent annual growth. By one estimate, in 2020, China could have a ten trillion-dollar economy which is about the equivalent of where the United States was in 2000.[37] Meanwhile, China has reformed its economy to facilitate future growth by cutting trade barriers and opening large sectors of the economy to external competition. China's economic development objectives were to double the gross national product between 2000 and 2010; further develop and improve the structure of the national economy by 2020; and achieve the level of development of an intermediate developed country with roughly $3,400 gross domestic product per capita by 2049.[38] Meanwhile, China has been establishing strong trade relationships with Australia, South Korea, and Japan—traditionally the United States' strongest allies in the Asia-Pacific region. In 2004, Chinese Prime Minister Wen Jiabao predicted that China's trade with southeast Asia would reach $100 billion by 2005—growing close to the $120 billion that the United States does each year in the region.[39]

The potential for China to transfer economic gains into military power is generated by China's size, location, and population, which could prompt China to adopt a more outward-looking national security policy. Already, China has implemented significant increases in defense spending with annual increases of about 17.5 percent in both 2001 and 2002 and 11 percent in 2003. In 2004, China announced an additional 11.6 percent increase in defense spending. In terms of contemporary capabilities, China has not developed a large capacity to project power on anything other than a regional basis. However, China does have the capacity to shape events in the South China Sea, south and southeast Asia, and on the Korean peninsula. China has decommissioned or moved large-scale deployments of troops away from the border with what was the Soviet Union. Redeployments or new capabilities have mainly focused on enhancing China's military means of influencing events in Taiwan, over which China claims territorial sovereignty. However, even by 2010, China is not expected to have developed a large-scale military capability that would allow it to exert significantly greater influence.

A key question affecting the future development of China's military potential will be its perceived interests vis-à-vis its relationship with the United States. The U.S.-China relationship is often disrupted by momentary tension. However, both states share an interest in a healthy economic relationship and in combating international terrorism. China has been concerned about America's building a national missile defense and over American support for Taiwan. At the same time, China appears to preference the stabilizing role that the United States has played in South Korea and especially in Japan. Some analysts in the Chinese military tend to view the United States as the principal obstacle to a rise in Chinese power and also as a potential threat to China's regional interests. China views American interventionism within other countries—as in the Kosovo and Iraq wars—with concern that new precedents regarding sovereignty are being set that have possible implications for Taiwan, Tibet, and the Xinjiang province. The 1999 Kosovo war unleashed significant, albeit momentary, expressions of Chinese nationalism manifested by popular protests, the burning of a U.S. consulate in Chengdu, defacing of British and American embassies in Beijing, and informal boycotts of *Kentucky Fried Chicken* and other American fast food outlets.[40] Within ten years, China had gone from protesters in Tiananmen Square emulating the American Statue of Liberty to large-scale public anger at the United States.[41]

A lack of transparency in defense planning makes it difficult to get precise measures of Chinese military power. When China releases defense budget information, the detail does not include the amount of money spent on weapons purchases, research, and a variety of additional costs. This missing information could make defense spending as much as four times greater than published figures suggest.[42] China emphasizes four areas for military reform to make its armed forces more professional and efficient including a ban on army engagement in private business activities; introduction of regular auditing and accounting procedures; market-based procurement bidding; and zero-based budgeting. Salaries for officers and regular soldiers have been increased by 84 percent and 92 percent respectively. Spending has been increased both on social benefits for servicemen and for training and equipment enhancements.[43] Equipment purchases have focused on adding fighter aircraft via Russian purchases, but China is also moving to produce its own aircraft and naval destroyers. While China's investments in naval power could serve as the foundation for a blue water navy, more immediate trends would appear to be designed to challenge American naval power near Taiwan.

China also appears to be embarking on a modernization and expansion of its nuclear deterrent in response to American plans to deploy a national missile defense system. China's intercontinental nuclear deterrence has historically been based on a limited deployment—historically about 24 hardened-silo nuclear missiles. However, to overcome American missile defense systems, China might expand its nuclear arsenal significantly and make it mobile with multiple independent reentry systems. A priority for Chinese espionage in the United States has been the successful theft or purchase of high technology nuclear missile and warhead technology. In 2004, China also launched its first new class of submarine, designed to fire an ICBM known as the "Type 094." This deployment was likely to be outfitted with a new missile known as the JL-2 which would have a range of over 4,600 miles and would be a significant upgrade from China's existing submarine capability, which in 2005 was comprised of one submarine carrying missiles that could only range 600 miles. Overall, China's intercontinental ballistic missile capability was likely to increase to over 100 by 2010.[44]

By 2006, China had 2,225,000 active duty armed forces and about 800,000 reserves making it the world's largest military. China had 100,000 personnel working on strategic missiles located at 30 intercontinental ballistic missile sites. China also had about 35 intermediate-range missile launch sites, and one submarine-based nuclear missile system. The army numbered about 1,600,000, though its number of conscripts—about 800,000—was being reduced. China's navy had about 215,000 personnel, in addition to 69 submarines and 63 principal surface combatant ships including 21 destroyers and 42 frigates. An important element of any Chinese military engagement involving Taiwan would be amphibious landing forces, though China only has 50 amphibious vehicles, China's capacity to project naval power far beyond its nearby seas remains limited. The Chinese air force included 400,000 troops, though the ability to project power via the air was limited as training ranges from 80 to 130 hours. China also has 1,500,000 active duty paramilitary forces, most of which are devoted to internal security functions. China maintains a limited number of overseas forces including small deployments in Burundi, Côte d'Ivoire, the Democratic Republic of Congo, Ethiopia/Eritrea, Liberia, the Middle East, Serbia and Montenegro, Sierra Leone, Sudan, and Western Sahara.[45] However, in terms of defense-ties or defense-industry relations, China had, by 2006, developed military relations with over 140 countries.

China's nuclear strategy has traditionally focused on maintaining a minimal deterrent capability via a limited array of missiles that could hit territory anywhere within the United States. China has kept its missile numbers low, but has also been willing to use its nuclear capabilities for political ends. In 1996, senior Chinese military officials interviewed in American newspapers pressed the rhetorical question of what major cities the American public was prepared to lose to defend Taiwan. Two dozen *Dong Feng* 5/5A ICBMs were the traditional core of China's nuclear forces. These were relatively aging, liquid-fueled, silo-based, single-warhead systems.[46] China also likely had by 2006 about 725 short-range ballistic missiles in range of Taiwan and could deploy land-attack cruise missiles targeted at Taiwan.[47] Hardened silo nuclear positions would make missiles vulnerable to a preemptive attack by the United States and an American missile-defense shield could neutralize China's nuclear deterrent posture. China has had the capacity to build a larger force, has attained MIRV technology and, according to one American government study, could deploy "upwards of 1,000 thermonuclear warheads on ICBMs by 2015."[48]

Chinese military planners became acutely aware of the challenges of modern warfare and the need for military modernization following the American-led NATO war in Kosovo in 1999. While public attention focused on the accidental NATO bombing of the Chinese embassy, the Chinese military focused on the means of modern warfare. Chinese military planners noted the application by NATO of laser-guided precision munitions employing active homing and direction-finding devices as well as satellite-guided bombs which could deliver 1,000- to 2,500-pound warheads with accuracy of a few meters. Chinese analysts also took note of microwave bombs that could sabotage electronic equipment, missile target seekers, computer networks, and data transmission lines.[49] While the 2003 U.S. invasion of Iraq confirmed Chinese suspicions about precision weapons and air power, they also took note of the new rapid movement role of ground forces which accompanied the invasion as well as the integrated role of psychological operations with air and rapid ground operations.

Of unique concern to Chinese defense planners was the reality that wars could now be waged by the United States from significant distances with great precision. The Chinese military had focused mostly on planning for large land battles on their soil or in a nearby territory. China's naval reach extends only as far as about 200 nautical miles off-shore and even then, it would only be able to disrupt, not defeat, an American presence.[50] Some weapons purchases such as surface destroyers with long-range anti-ship missiles might have been purchased by China for the purpose of preventing U.S. aircraft carrier battle groups from intervening in any conflict between mainland China and Taiwan. China also appeared to be enhancing its missile capacity to include an attack on American military bases in Japan, thus making it more difficult for Japan to support American military activity in the region.[51] A range of new capabilities and doctrines were being studied in China including mobile systems, solid fuel propellants, advanced guidance systems, warhead miniaturization, space-based capabilities, enhanced radiation and directed energy weapons, antisatellite munitions, and ballistic missile defense countermeasures.[52] Such programs appear to fall under the rubric of what China refers to as an "assassin's mace" that it would apply to any conflict involving Taiwan.

China appears uncertain as to how to approach relations with the United States given its economic need to engage America and its apparent strategic desire to reduce American influence in Asia. China has made gains from cooperation with the United States in the global campaign against international terrorism.[53] Also, while China had reservations about America's invasion of Iraq in 2003, it did not campaign actively against it. Chinese strategic doctrine tends to draw on a cultural-historical experience that emphasizes patience and thinking in terms of decades, not years or months. If the United States succeeded in Iraq, it would owe China a debt for not actively opposing the invasion; conversely, if America became bogged down in Iraq and had to devote large elements of its active military to the Middle East, this could erode America's general military and economic power and create a long-term relative gain for China.

Even if China's rise to power does not eventually create new military threats, its consumption of energy could prove to be just as destabilizing. As recently as the early 1990s, China was a net oil exporter. By 2004, it was the third largest importer after the United States and Japan. China will need to import up to 600 million tons of oil a year by 2020, which is three times its expected domestic productive capacity.[54] The use of energy and the resulting impact on international prices, as well as the environmental consequences, could have reverberating effects on the global economy. Alternatively, China's abuse of its own environment could have as much negative impact on its growth trends as anything. If China's economic potential goes unfulfilled or many citizens are left behind, nationalism could impact China's strategic thinking. Indeed, China's growth is not a win for all Chinese. As China adjusted its economy to join the World Trade Organization, some ten million farming jobs and one million jobs in the automobile and machine manufacturing sectors were expected to be lost.[55]

The geopolitical question posed by China's current trend-lines is a classic illustration of the security dilemma. If the United States believes that China is going to challenge America's primacy, Washington will likely adopt policies to forestall that outcome. China might see such gestures as dangerous, and thus America's posture could provoke the actual threat Washington fears. Meanwhile, China might misperceive U.S. intentions, and embark on dangerous military policies that do damage to its long-term interests. Both countries have much to gain from cooperation and stable relations—but there is no guarantee that these gains will not be subsumed by competition. Ultimately, China's patience and long view toward economic development and international objectives might be its greatest asset—drawing on the advice of Deng

Xiaoping who laid out general principles of Chinese strategy: "keep cool-headed to observe, be composed to make reactions, stand firmly, hide our capabilities and bide our time, never try to take the lead, and be able to accomplish something."[56]

THE EUROPEAN UNION

The major European states—Britain, Germany, and France, are individually no longer the world powers that they once were. Also, within the European area, traditional security dilemmas have largely been resolved. Some areas of Europe have faced significant instability, as in the Balkans. Overall, however, the European continent knows a degree of peace unlike any it has experienced in history. At the core of the general peace in Europe has been Franco-German reconciliation, deeply embedded within international institutions including NATO and the European Union. Nevertheless, Europe does face critical strategic and operational questions about its future security. The central issue is whether or not the European Union will have enough integrative pull to establish Europe as a collective military power. This question is crucial because of accelerating U.S. military disengagement from European security. Further complicating these dynamics is a general public perception that Europe need not overly invest in military capabilities and might be best served by staying out of military engagements promulgated by the United States. While Europe could rise to become a significant global actor, it equally could remain unable to coalesce and develop common strategies that would advance the shared interests of EU members. The danger in this scenario is that, at the very moment that America is disengaging from Europe, there is no strong institutional mechanism to fill that void. This would leave Europe confronting significant external challenges but with no effective means of organizing to meet them.

Individually, Europe's countries are not significant military actors. Only Britain and France have high-end military capabilities that allow them to project significant power at far ranges. Most European armies are large conscript forces, which were well-suited for the Cold War but lack the professionalism, efficiency, and deployment capabilities necessary for modern combat operations. Collectively, Europe spends about two-thirds of what the United States does on defense, but only has one-third of America's capability. Since the 1950s, European powers have expanded the foundations of economic integration into a European defense capability. However, such efforts were often stymied by a lack of cohesion among the Europeans, or opposition from the United States. Contemporary trends show, however, that the United States is reorienting its forces away from Europe and that it no longer sees European security as a primary concern. The transatlantic relationship remains vital to both Europe and the United States and the political and economic ties between the two are strong. Nevertheless, public opinion across Europe opposed America's invasion of Iraq in 2003. Europeans tend to prioritize diplomacy and engagement over the use of force in international affairs and threats such as international terrorism are widely viewed as solved with intelligence and police rather than military power. Europe is also undergoing significant demographic changes with large immigration movements coming from North Africa and the Middle East, which will likely have an impact on European strategic priorities.

Since 1992, EU members have committed to achieve a Common Foreign and Security Policy and to build an independent military capability. The European Union began by appointing a senior official to manage foreign affairs—the first being former NATO secretary general, Dr. Javier Solana. However, EU members quickly saw that diverging national security priorities would make it difficult to achieve common foreign and defense policies. France, for example, declared its intent to lead the European Union in opposition to the United States invasion of Iraq in 2003, only to find that many EU countries refused to follow its lead. The United Kingdom, Italy, and Spain as well as most countries about to join the European Union from central and eastern Europe all initially supported the United States. Germany, however, had already embarked on an unprecedented unilateral opposition to the American policy.

The incentives to pool military resources for the European countries are strong. A common EU defense capability can provide these states with a measure of influence in global security that, alone, none would have. The European Union includes twenty-five countries, which, combined, spend over $150 billion a year on defense. The combined EU population makes it the world's third largest after China and India. The European Union represents one of the world's largest economies. EU membership includes two nuclear powers and over two million troops among the member states. If it could coalesce, the European Union is well-perched to become a major global actor. In December 1999, the European Union agreed on an ambitious plan to create a rapid deployment force of 50,000 to 60,000 troops for use in humanitarian and rescue tasks, peacekeeping, and crisis management.

Politically, the European Union faces decision-making problems. Each member wishes to protect its freedom of movement on vital national-security issues. Making collective decisions among twenty-five members is a problematic proposition in the best of times, let alone if confronting a military crisis. Additionally, increasing European defense capabilities will require substantial investment of resources and money. Establishing a workable industrial base for

European defense is a significant challenge as nations tend to want to protect their own defense industries. One of the European Union's signature projects, the *Eurofighter Jet*, was only just procured in 2003, ten years later than it was first projected for completion. The European Union has only several long-range transport planes while the United States has several hundred. Consequently, Europe finds itself tempted to free-ride on American power capabilities while at the same time wanting to have more autonomy.

European defense investment, when compared with that of the United States, is clearly weak. Assessing just the United Kingdom, France, Germany, Italy, and Spain (which account for 80 percent of all defense spending in Europe) the U.S. naval tonnage is three times greater than these five EU members for nuclear-fuelled ballistic-missile-bearing submarines and surface combatants, and four times greater for operational transport and support ships. The United States has 66 nuclear-fuelled submarines, and these five EU countries have 18. The U.S. navy has 12 catapult-launch aircraft carriers and 29 cruisers; the EU leading five collectively, one cruiser and one catapult-launch aircraft carrier. Against America's 400 frigates, the main five EU members have about 100. American ships are produced as one single type and displace 2,800 tons; the European frigates are of various makes and a third of them displace only 1,300 tons or less. In terms of modern aircraft, the U.S. advantage over the main five EU members is 3.5:1 in numbers, and two-thirds of the EU member planes are C-160 Transalls (a third smaller than the C-130, the smallest U.S. transport aircraft). The ratio for tanker aircraft is around 30:1. The U.S. has 7,600 main battle tanks, all variants of the MA *Abrams*; the five main EU members have 4,800 main battle tanks comprised of six highly different brands. The U.S. Air Force has 366 A-10 ground-attack aircraft, for which the Europeans have no equivalent at all. Similar disparities exist in command control and intelligence capabilities.[57]

The European Union has agreed to establish a modest military planning center which will coordinate national contributions to a future European military force. The objective is to harmonize contributions with an eighty-person planning operation to be coordinated by the EU high representative for foreign and security policy. The European Union will have a political and security committee, and a military committee including military staff. While formally intended to be a complement, not a competitor, to NATO, it would nevertheless be able to plan for and control military operations not involving NATO.[58] Since fall 2003, the European Union has moved forward with three principal activities: (1) deploying a small group of operational planners to NATO headquarters in Mons, Belgium; (2) those states most ambitious about European defense cooperation would, if they chose, work to accelerate cooperation on military capabilities; and (3) the European Union has agreed to a renewed collective defense commitment while reaffirming that NATO is the primary tool for collective defense in Europe.[59] The EU members have agreed to a "headline goal" of capability commitments that governments aim to achieve by 2010.[60] The planned projected force contributions to the Helsinki force goals include: Germany—13,500; the United Kingdom—12,500; France—12,000; Italy and Spain—6,000 each; the Netherlands—5,000; Greece—3,500; Austria and Finland—2,000 each; Sweden, 1,500; Belgium, Ireland, and Portugal—1,000 each; and Luxembourg—100.[61] Subsequently, the European Union has undertaken small but important missions in Macedonia. The deployment in Macedonia included 320 troops and 80 civilians. In fall 2004, the European Union took over command responsibility for all forces in Bosnia-Herzegovina.

The European Union has developed strategic partnerships with Russia and opened a working relationship with China. European missions to the Middle East, Iran, and North Korea have also enhanced the diplomatic profile of the European Union. Meanwhile, Europe is also developing a niche capability in post-conflict civilian police missions. In 1997, the European Union took lead responsibility for organizing a multinational police training mission in Albania and in 2003 organized the European Union Police Mission in Bosnia-Herzegovina which included 900 personnel with 500 active police officers. The European Union also undertook *Operation Artemis* in Eastern Congo with control over 1,800 (mostly French) forces deployed to Bunia. Overall, the European Union has coordinated sustained deployment of 50,000 to 60,000 troops in and around the European areas including more than twenty countries in southeast Europe, Afghanistan, central Asia, Iraq and the Persian Gulf, and Africa. The total numbers deployed just in 2003–2004 averaged around 70,000 and if British deployments in the Iraq war are counted the number rises to 90,000. An additional 10,000 troops from ten countries that were joining the European Union in 2004 also contributed to these missions. These deployments were not without significant risk. By January 2004, European countries had sustained ninety fatalities in post-conflict Iraq. Germany had lost fourteen soldiers and Denmark lost three in Afghanistan by the end of 2003. Germany's first combat fatality from hostile fire since World War II occurred in Georgia in 2001.[62]

Of the major European powers, there are significant variations in military capabilities—though all share an overall trend of declining defense investment. By 2006, France had 254,895 forces and 21,650 reserves. France devotes 4,000 personnel to its strategic nuclear forces, which maintain 64 submarine-launched ballistic missiles on 4 submarines; 28 nuclear capable naval aircraft; and 3 air force squadrons with 60 *Mirage 2000* planes with nuclear capability. France's nuclear force is minimal and designed largely to establish French independence and pride-of-place among the larger nations of the

world. In 2006, France had 133,500 army personnel including 7,700 in its foreign legion and about 2,700 special operations forces; 104,275 paramilitary
troops; 2,050 marines; 43,995 serving in the French navy; and 63,600 in its air
force. France's primary means of power projection include its nuclear force,
submarines, and an aircraft carrier battle group. France has forces abroad
including 2,800 based in Germany in a Franco-German joint brigade, 1,300 in
French Guiana; 1,000 in the Indian Ocean; 2,030 in New Caledonia; 950 in
Chad; 3,800 in Côte d'Ivoire; 2,850 in Djibouti; 700 in Gabon; and 610 in
Senegal. France also has United Nations and other peacekeeping forces
deployed (at levels ranging from several observers to several thousand) in
Afghanistan, Bosnia-Herzegovina, Croatia, Democratic Republic of Congo,
Egypt, Ethiopia, Eritrea, Macedonia, Georgia, Italy, Lebanon, Middle East,
Tajikistan, Western Sahara, and Serbia and Montenegro.[63]

As of 2006, Germany maintained an active force of 284,500 with 94,500
conscripts and an additional 358,650 reserves. Its army had 117,900, its navy
20,700, and its air force 51,400. Since Germany was rearmed in the early
1950s, its military's primary function had been to deter aggression against the
inter-German border by the Soviet Union. With the unification of Germany and
the end of the Cold War, this mission became obsolete. Germany maintains a
very large land army but also has self-imposed constraints on the external use
of force, and training and equipment reflect these restraints. Meanwhile, the
conscription component of the German military has historically been seen as
an important function for civil-society, national service, and the maintenance
of civilian-controlled armed forces. Germany's history of aggression and the
legacy of the Holocaust have shaped this strategic culture to the extent that the
German public remains wary of external force projection. Germany has
engaged in lower-end military deployments by 2006 including 209 forces
based in France and 67 in Poland.[64] Germans have been increasingly enthusiastic about international peacekeeping operations which included assuming
command responsibility of NATO forces in Afghanistan for a period of time.
Germany deployed, by 2006, 1,909 troops in Afghanistan, 1,000 in Bosnia, and
more limited numbers in Djibouti, Ethiopia/Eritrea, Georgia, Italy (for operations in the Balkans), Sierra Leone, and Serbia and Montenegro. Meanwhile,
despite the end of the Cold War, Germany continues to host international forces
on its territory from Belgium, France, Italy, the Netherlands, the United Kingdom, and the United States.[65]

Of the European countries, the United Kingdom had the most modern and
capable forces in 2006. British armed forces total 205,890 and 272,550
reserves. There were 1,000 troops assigned to strategic forces including 58
nuclear missiles in 4 submarines—though with less than 200 operationally
available warheads. The British army includes 112,010, the navy 26,430, and

the air force 48,140 personnel. As an example of British fighting capabilities, a British pilot will receive anywhere from 188 to 218 flight training hours per year—compared to 150 for Germany, and between 10 and 60 for Russia. Britain is equipped to project power on a limited global basis. Britain is the primary European country that can accompany the United States in global military actions. Britain is able to project power though its nuclear force's 4 submarines and 11 additional conventional submarines, 3 aircraft carrier battle groups, 11 surface destroyers, and 415 combat tactical aircraft. Britain maintains ongoing overseas deployments in Germany and bases troops in Northern Ireland. By 2006, Britain also had troops deployed in varying numbers in Afghanistan, Antarctica, Ascension Island, Belgium, Belize, Brunei, Canada, Cyprus, Falkland Islands, Germany, Gibraltar, the Indian Ocean, Diego Garcia, Kenya, Nepal, the Netherlands, Oman, Sierra Leone, the United States, West Indies, and West Africa, as well as peacekeeping operations in Afghanistan, Bosnia-Herzegovina, Cyprus, Democratic Republic of Congo, Georgia, Italy, Sierra Leone, and Serbia and Montenegro. Britain also deployed 458 military advisers in twenty-six countries.[66] Britain contributed significant forces to the 2003 Iraq conflict and its aftermath—by 2005 maintaining 9,200 army personnel in Iraq. Britain also provides bases on its territory for American armed forces.

In summer 2004, Britain announced that it would be cutting 20,000 military (and civilian defense) personnel by eliminating four infantry battalions, three Royal Air Force squadrons, and twelve surface warships. Some key additions will, however, eventually include deployment of two new aircraft carriers. With the cuts, Britain will still be able to extend its reach, but for far shorter periods and with far less impact. While Britain will be able to apply modern, highly sophisticated technology, it will not be able to provide the same high-level ground-troop deployments. Such ground deployments have made Britain's role in places like post-invasion Iraq a crucial element of peace support operations, giving Britain some influence over American tactics, if not strategic choices. Britain's current doctrine is to plan for three concurrent military operations—of which one would be an ongoing peace support operation in addition to large-scale operations alongside the U.S. and other allies. Realistically, the Iraq operations had already made such a multitask commitment unlikely by 2006 and any additional pressures on the British military would likely place major strains on the army.

SUMMARY

While the risk of great power conflict leading to war appears to be very low, it is not nil. The major powers still maintain significant military capabilities, which serve as a deterrent, but which also makes any hypothetical confrontation scenarios appear very dangerous. The world still exists in a condition in which two major nuclear powers, the United States and Russia, base their structural security relationship on the concept of mutual assured destruction. While this architecture has worked historically, the declining state of Russia's military and, in particular, its nuclear arsenal and early warning systems, offers reason for serious concern about the stability of mutual assured destruction. Meanwhile, the United States is shifting policy away from classical deterrence to incorporate a doctrine of preemptive war. China's power is growing and already has altered the general balance of power in Asia and is on a trajectory toward being a global power by 2020. Should the United States enter into a period of overstretch and eventual retrenchment, China is positioned to fill any void left by American leadership in the international system if Beijing so chooses. Nonetheless, whether China's power will be defined by economic attractiveness or military threat remains to be determined. Finally, Europe is poised to emerge as an important actor in global security though it faces military deficiencies that can make it difficult to translate its political and economic power into diplomatic leverage. The international campaign against international terrorism serves to unite the interests of all the major powers and might play a role in easing tensions over issues that would otherwise divide them. Yet at the same time, significant regional "hot spots" carry the risk that these major powers might find themselves engaging in major international conflicts.

NOTES

1. *Quadrennial Defense Review 2001*, United States Department of Defense, September 30, 2001.

2. International Institute for Strategic Studies, *The Military Balance: 2005–2006* (Oxford: Oxford University Press, 2005), 20–35.

3. David S. Cloud, "Navy to Expand Fleet with New Enemies in Mind," *New York Times*, December 5, 2005.

4. These are the proposed plans announced by the White House on August 16, 2004, at www.whitehouse.gov.

5. Robert Burns, "Pentagon Expands Outposts in Middle East," *Associated Press*, September 23, 2004.

6. Craig S. Smith, "U.S. Training North Africans to Uproot Terrorists," *New York Times*, May 11, 2004.

7. Bradley Graham, "Bush Plans Aid to Build Foreign Peace Forces," *Washington Post*, April 19, 2004.

8. Text of Strategic Offensive Reductions Treaty, May 24, 2002, at www.whitehouse.gov/news/releases/2002/05/20020524–3.html (accessed Spring 2004).

9. International Institute of Strategic Studies, *Strategic Survey 2003–2004: An Evaluation and Forecast of World Affairs* (Oxford: Oxford University Press, 2003), 20–21.

10. Michael R. Gordon, "Nuclear Arms: For Deterring or Fighting?" *New York Times*, March 11, 2002.

11. Bruce Blair, "U.S. Nuclear Posture and Alert Status Post Sept. 11," September 10, 2002, *Center for Defense Information*, at www.cdi.org/nuclear/post911.cfm (accessed Summer 2004).

12. Walter Pincus, "Defense Panel Faults Nuclear Plans," *Washington Post*, March 28, 2004.

13. Richard Sokolsky, "Demystifying the US Nuclear Posture Review," *Survival* 44, no. 3 (Autumn 2002): 138.

14. David S. Cloud, "Pentagon Studies Pre-Emptive Nuclear Strikes," *New York Times*, September 11, 2005.

15. Christopher Bluth, "Russian Military Forces: Ambitions, Capabilities, and Constraints," in *Security Dilemmas in Russia and Eurasia*, ed. Roy Allison and Christopher Bluth (London: Royal Institute of International Affairs, 1998), 69.

16. "Russian Army Off-Duty Deaths Rise," *BBC News*, November 17, 2004.

17. Hans-Henning Schroder, "The Russian Army in Politics," in *Security Dilemmas in Russia and Eurasia*, ed. Roy Allison and Christopher Bluth (London: Royal Institute of International Affairs, 1998), 53.

18. Meg Clothier, "Iran and Russia Sign $1 bln Defense Deal: Reports," *Reuters*, December 2, 2005.

19. International Institute of Strategic Studies, *Strategic Survey 2003–2004: An Evaluation and Forecast of World Affairs* (Oxford: Oxford University Press, 2004), 121.

20. International Institute of Strategic Studies, *Strategic Survey 2003–2004*, 121.

21. International Institute for Strategic Studies, *Military Balance: 2005–2006*, 158–68.

22. International Institute for Strategic Studies, *Military Balance: 2005–2006*, 166–68.

23. International Institute for Strategic Studies, *Military Balance: 2005–2006*, 158–64.

24. Dmitri Trenin, "Central Asia's Stability and Russia's Security," *PONARS*, no. 168 (November 2000).

25. "The Threat in Russia and the Newly Independent States," Matthew Bunn at www.nunnturnerinitiative.org/eresearch/cnwm/threat/russia.asp (accessed Fall 2004).

26. William Webster, *Russian Organized Crime* (Washington, D.C.: Center for International and Strategic Studies, 1997 and 2000), October 28, 2002.

27. Webster, *Russian Organized Crime*, available from www.csis.org (accessed Fall 1998 and Summer 2000).

28. International Atomic Energy Agency, "Radioactive Sources: Facts and Figures," June 2002.

29. Bunn, "Threat in Russia."

30. David Holley, "Russia Seeks Safety in Nuclear Arms," *Los Angeles Times*, December 6, 2004.

31. Bunn, "The Threat in Russia and the Newly Independent States," October 28, 2002, at http://www.nunnturner.org/e_research/cnwm/threat/russia.asp (accessed Fall 2004).

32. Bunn, "Threat in Russia."

33. Bunn, "Threat in Russia."

34. Blair, "US Nuclear Posture."

35. Lachlan Forrow et al., "Accidental Nuclear War," *New England Journal of Medicine* 338, no. 18 (1998): 1328–29.

36. James Brooke, "The Asian Battle for Russia's Oil and Gas," *New York Times*, January 3, 2004.

37. "How Poor Is China?" *The Economist*, October 12, 1996, 35–36.

38. FY04 Report to Congress on PRC Military Power, *Annual Report on the Military Power of the People's Republic of China* (Washington, D.C.: U.S. Department of Defense, 2004).

39. Jane Perlez, "Across Asia, Beijing's Star Is in Ascendance," *Washington Post*, August 28, 2004.

40. James Miles, "Chinese Nationalism, US Policy and Asian Security," *Survival* 42, no. 4 (Winter 2000/2001): 51.

41. Miles, "Chinese Nationalism," 53.

42. Audra Ang, "China Boosts Military Spending in Budget," *Associated Press*, March 6, 2004.

43. International Institute of Strategic Studies, *The Military Balance: 2003–2004* (Oxford: Oxford University Press, 2003), 295.

44. John J. Lumpkin, "China Launches New Class of Nuclear Sub," *Associated Press*, December 4, 2004.

45. International Institute of Strategic Studies, *Military Balance: 2005–2006*, 270–75.

46. Jason D. Ellis and Todd M. Koca, "China Rising: New Challenges to the U.S. Security Posture," *Strategic Forum*, no. 175 (October 2000): 1.

47. International Institute of Strategic Studies, *Military Balance: 2005–2006*, 270.

48. Ellis and Koca, "China Rising," 2.

49. David Shambaugh, "China's Military Views the World: Ambivalent Security," *International Security* 24, no. 3 (Winter 1999/2000): 58.

50. FY04 Report to Congress, *Annual Report*, 58–60.

51. Denny Roy, "China's Reaction to American Predominance," *Survival* 45, no. 3 (Autumn 2003): 62.

52. Ellis and Koca, "China Rising," 2.

53. Roy, "China's Reaction," 69.

54. Peter S. Goodman, "1,500-Mile Oil Pipeline Fading Fast for China," *Washington Post*, April 5, 2004.

55. Miles, "Chinese Nationalism," 59.

56. Quoted in FY04 Report to Congress, *Annual Report*.

57. David S. Yost, "The NATO Capabilities Gap and the European Union," *Survival* 42, no. 4 (Winter 2000/2001): 101.

58. "European Defense 'Deal' Reached," *BBC News*, November 28, 2003.

59. Charles Grant, "Big Three Join Forces on Defence," Center for European Reform, March 2004.

60. Daniel Keohane, "EU on the Offensive about Defense," Center for European Reform, July 2004.

61. Kori N. Schake, "Do European Union Defense Initiatives Threaten NATO?" *Institute for National Strategic Studies: Strategic Forum*, no. 184 (August 2001): 6.

62. Bastian Giegerich and William Wallace, "Not Such a Soft Power: The External Deployment of European Forces," *Survival* 46, no. 2 (Summer 2004): 164–68.

63. International Institute of Strategic Studies, *Military Balance: 2005–2006*, 61–67.

64. International Institute of Strategic Studies, *Military Balance: 2005–2006*, 67–70.

65. International Institute of Strategic Studies, *Military Balance: 2005–2006*, 67–70.

66. International Institute of Strategic Studies, *Military Balance: 2005–2006*, 101–6.

SUGGESTED READING

Richard Bernstein and H. Ross Munro, *The Coming Conflict with China* (New York: Vintage, 1998).

Michael Brown, Owen R. Côte Jr., Sean Lynn-Jones, and Steven E. Miller, eds., *America's Strategic Choices* (Cambridge: MIT Press, 2000).

James M. Goldgeier and Michael McFaul, *Power and Purpose: U.S. Policy toward Russia after the Cold War* (Washington, D.C.: Brookings Institution Press, 2003).

Dale R. Herspring, *Putin's Russia: Past Imperfect, Future Uncertain*, 2nd ed. (Lanham, Md.: Rowman and Littlefield, 2004).

Charles Kupchan, *The End of the American Era: U.S. Foreign Policy and the Geopolitics of the Twenty-first Century* (New York: Vintage, 2003).

Dana Priest, *The Mission: Waging War and Keeping Peace with America's Military* (New York: W. W. Norton, 2004).

T. R. Reid, *The United States of Europe: The New European Superpower and the End of American Supremacy* (New York: Penguin Press, 2004).

David Shambaugh, *Modernizing China's Military: Progress, Problems, and Prospects* (Berkeley: University of California Press, 2004).

Michael D. Swaine and Ashley J. Tellis, *Interpreting China's Grand Strategy: Past, Present, and Future* (Santa Monica, Calif.: Rand Corporation, 2000).

Thomas Szayna. Daniel L. Byman, Steven C. Bankes, Derek Eaton, Seth G. Jones, Robert E. Mullins, Ian O. Lesser, and William Rosenau, *The Emergence of Peer Competitors: A Framework for Analysis* (Santa Monica, Calif.: Rand Corporation, 2001).

Chapter Five

Regional Flashpoints

American army searches a shed on a farm in Samarra, Iraq, July 2005. *Source*: U.S. Department of Defense, photo by Tech. Sgt. Russell E. Cooley IV.

Various global flashpoints present complex challenges for the quest for power and the search for peace in the twenty-first century. These areas include India-Pakistan, the Korean peninsula, Taiwan, the Middle East, and Eurasia. These potential regional conflicts each have the capacity to directly impact the interests of the great powers. War in these cases is not inevitable. Indeed, some events which can appear destabilizing, such as the attainment of nuclear weapons by India and Pakistan, could instead deter conflict in a crisis and provide the basis for negotiation. The purpose of this chapter is therefore not to predict that these specific conflicts are likely to occur. Rather, it is to illustrate why these areas were the world's key flashpoints for potentially major conflict by 2006, and to illustrate how serious the consequences would be.

INDIA AND PAKISTAN

India and Pakistan represented the most dangerous potential for interstate war at the beginning of the twenty-first century. These two countries are the area in the world where nuclear weapons are most likely to be used in anger. These two major regional powers have demonstrated a willingness to fight, primarily over the disputed territory of Kashmir. Kashmir is an Indian controlled area at the border of northern India and Pakistan over which Pakistan also makes a territorial claim. As India broke from British colonial rule in 1947, a major population movement of Muslims out of the Hindu-dominated India left for what became the new state of Pakistan. Some twelve million refugees fled their homes and, over time, one million were killed in related hostilities. The differences that developed between these two neighbors with common histories, but religious and cultural differences, grew over time. The two went to war in 1947, 1965, and 1971 and came very close to war in 1987 and 1990. History shapes the environment in which they assess their security needs and, while both sides have a deep interest in peace, both prepare for war.

The global security environment has also shaped perceptions of security requirements for India and Pakistan. India positioned itself outside the Cold War distribution of power. India sought to lead the "neutral and nonaligned" countries of the world, though it looked toward the Soviet Union for military and economic assistance. By the 1980s, India shifted its strategic focus more toward the West. However, India found itself largely ignored as the United States and Europe looked to China for economic engagement. Pakistan has had less ambitious goals, driven mainly by fear of its large Indian neighbor. During the 1980s, Pakistan sought strong ties both to the United States and to China for military and economic support. Pakistan became an important country for the United States, which needed assistance in containing Soviet aggression in Afghanistan. The United States provided economic and military

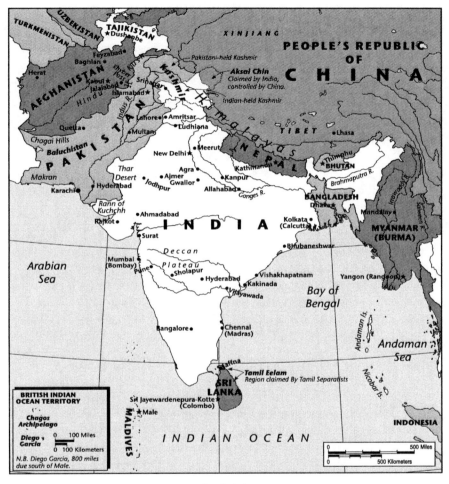

South Asia

assistance to Pakistan—on the condition that Pakistan would verify that it was a nonnuclear country.

India and Pakistan have been engaged in a classic security dilemma that neither can afford. Both countries have exceptionally high poverty rates and severe challenges to economic development. By the time each country became a declared nuclear power in 1998, each was devoting a high percentage of its economies to military spending. India spent at the time about 17 percent and Pakistan about 33 percent of their overall budgets on defense. While India has civilian control over the military, Pakistan has shifted to-and-from military governments that have occasionally seized power in extra-constitutional coups.

Both of these countries have had political leadership that utilized the appeal of nationalism to generate popular support for their governments and both have been willing to exacerbate tensions over Kashmir if it suited near-term political calculations. Conversely, by 2006, both India and Pakistan were also engaged in high-level and grassroots diplomatic efforts to lessen the risk of war.

The Balance of Power and Nuclear Weapons

India has significant military advantages over Pakistan. India maintained active duty armed forces numbering 1,325,000 with 1,155,000 in reserve by 2006. Largest among the services is the Indian army which numbers 1,100,000. The Indian navy is relatively small with 55,000 personnel and includes 16 submarines, 1 aircraft carrier, 8 destroyers, and 17 frigates. The Indian air force numbers 170,000 and includes 852 combat aircraft. The Indian air force is well-trained, averaging about 180 flying hours per year. India also maintains 1,293,229 active duty paramilitary forces, including 208,422 border security forces.[1] Pakistan has a smaller armed forces structure including 619,000 active duty forces and 513,000 reserves. The army has 550,000 troops. The navy has 24,000 and includes 11 submarines and 7 frigates as its main surface fleet. The Pakistani air force numbers 45,000 with 331 combat aircraft. Like India, the Pakistani air force is highly trained with about 210 annual flying hours per pilot. Pakistan also has large numbers of paramilitary forces ranging up to 302,000 on active duty with a national guard of 185,000.[2]

The conventional balance of power has always favored India. It has four times the territory and seven times the population of Pakistan in addition to a greater degree of political and economic stability.[3] However, India does not keep all of its forces positioned just toward Pakistan. Generally there has been a relative conventional balance of power near the India-Pakistan border. Since the 1960s, both sides sought advantage over the other via nuclear weapons development. For several decades, both India and Pakistan existed as *de facto* nuclear powers—each knew the other had the capacity to produce nuclear weapons, but none were tested or deployed. Both sides had been constrained in their nuclear efforts by lack of materials and financial obstacles. However, both sides also made their positions clear by not signing the Nuclear Non-Proliferation Treaty and later by refusing to sign the Comprehensive Test-Ban Treaty. India began to develop its nuclear weapons program in 1964 and by the 1970s was able to yield domestically-produced plutonium. In 1974, India conducted what it called a "peaceful" nuclear test which, while not formally a weapon, illustrated the technological advances that had been made. India also developed a variety of missile systems that had delivery capacity either to target Pakistan or China. The Indian air force also is an available tool of weapons delivery. India has also developed a space program which, if pushed forward, could lead to intercontinental ballistic missile capability.

Pakistan began its nuclear program in 1971—and accelerated it after India's 1974 tests. Pakistan does not have a domestic plutonium production capacity; instead, it embarked on a clandestine effort to procure uranium and then became self-sufficient in its ability to upgrade it. Pakistan likely received assistance from China in the 1980s; however, the extent of China's involvement in the Pakistani nuclear program is not publicly known. Pakistan's primary means of delivering weapons has been short-range missiles and aircraft purchased from China, the United States, and France. Both India and Pakistan developed fission-based nuclear weapons similar to those which were deployed by the United States against Japan at the end of World War II. Explosive yields are likely 5 to 25 kilotons (the equivalent of 500 to 25,000 tons of TNT).

In spring 1998, tension between these two countries reached a peak as each tested nuclear weapons. The result was the most serious nuclear standoff since the Cuban Missile Crisis standoff in 1962 between the United States and the Soviet Union. India was the first to test its nuclear weapons. While these nuclear tests caught the international community by surprise, they should not have. India's newly elected political party, the BJP, ascended to power on a nationalist agenda and one of its primary campaign promises was to test nuclear weapons. However, India had kept the tests hidden from outside surveillance and when it conducted a series of underground nuclear tests, the world was caught off guard. Pakistan, in turn, faced extraordinary domestic pressure to respond to India's tests. While a parade of Western officials offered Pakistan economic and political incentives not to test weapons, nationalist passions and a desire to rebalance the strategic equation pushed Pakistan into its own nuclear tests.

Limited Deterrence

The Cold War notion of nuclear deterrence rested on pillars that are largely missing from the India-Pakistan equation. Neither India nor Pakistan has a second-strike capability and the relative numbers of weapons for each was low (a dozen or more for Pakistan and 50 to 100 for India). In this situation, either side would have a strong incentive to strike first and hope to eliminate the other's nuclear retaliatory capability. The low numbers of nuclear weapons remove the possibility of mutual assured destruction and thus make the use of nuclear weapons an option in battle. The proximity of India and Pakistan to each other—they share a 1,500-kilometer border—means that any small crisis could escalate with very little warning. Both of the countries' capital cities are within 400 kilometers of the other's territory. Lahore, Pakistan, is only 30 kilometers from the Indian border.[4] This circumstance was very different from the U.S.-Soviet nuclear stalemate, where two large oceans separated one from the other. Also, neither India nor Pakistan had developed sufficient early warning capabilities or civil-response plans to help provide warning and preparation for any incoming attack. Moreover, both sides have strong strategic rationales for using nuclear weapons first. If India massed troops near the Pakistan border, perhaps to isolate Kashmir, Pakistan would have a strong incentive to use nuclear weapons on those forces. India would have a strong incentive, therefore, to attack first to eliminate Pakistan's nuclear weapons.

The U.S. government has conducted simulations of potential conflict between India and Pakistan. These war games consistently predict eventual escalation into a nuclear war once conventional conflict breaks out. Most scenarios begin with a conflict involving Kashmir. If it was concerned that Pakistan might move forces and equipment to the east of Lahore to isolate Kashmir, India might launch preemptive attacks to secure its access to the region. To do so, they would have to push deep into Pakistani territory—prompting Pakistan to use nuclear weapons against advancing Indian troops to make up for conventional disparity. Pakistan could even wait and drop nuclear weapons on Indian troops concentrated inside Pakistan's territory following an Indian invasion. Pakistan might then claim an upper hand politically, having only attacked invading troops on its own territory. Variations on that scenario have India launching preemptive attacks on areas where they believe Pakistan's nuclear weapons are located. While they might not be able to accomplish this, India might be convinced that this would prevent nuclear escalation. However, fear of such attacks could as easily prompt Pakistan to launch their weapons first in a "use-it-or-lose-it" scenario.

In one simulation, the United States would intervene to prevent a conflict by deploying a peacekeeping force between India and Pakistan. Set in the year 2010, this scenario would see the United States bring a temporary peace to Kashmir which is interpreted by Pakistan as reinforcing the existing status quo favoring India. Pakistan could move to isolate U.S. peacekeepers, putting long-range artillery pieces parallel to the Indian corridor to Kashmir, thus cutting off that access. Then, according to the scenario, Pakistan would place guerrilla fighters with *Stinger* antiaircraft missiles near Kashmiri airports. In the simulation, a U.S. cargo jet is shot down by the Pakistani guerrillas operating in the area. War begins when an Indian force chases the guerrillas and engages with the Pakistani military. Indian and Pakistani air strikes on each other's troops and facilities would follow, leading to an Indian attack against Lahore and then a Pakistani decision to launch its nuclear weapons. Eventually perceiving that the United States is aligning with India, Pakistan invites Iran to come to its aid, which responds by crossing Pakistan and attacking

Indian troops in the Thar Desert to block their advance. Follow-on forces, including American troops landing on the western Pakistani shore, would seek to cut off the Iranian force's supplies—leading Iran to attack that force and thus escalating the conflict dramatically.[5]

On several occasions since they tested nuclear weapons, India and Pakistan have come to the brink of war. India has complained about what it sees as Pakistan's support for cross-border terrorism into Kashmir, and even into India proper, targeting Indian troops and citizens. India moved large numbers of troops toward Pakistan's borders in early 2002 with the two sides deploying a combined one million armed personnel to the India-Pakistan border. This crisis was de-escalated, though each took different lessons from it. Pakistan appeared to conclude that it was their credible threat of nuclear deterrence—manifested by missile tests and public statements—which convinced India that it could not risk an escalation. India, meanwhile, appeared to conclude that it was the overwhelming nuclear and conventional balances of forces favoring it which compelled Pakistan to settle the crisis favorable to India's demands.[6] India played a high stakes game by elevating the crisis into a "global drama" which appeared to pay off with Pakistan promising to end support of groups using violence in Kashmir.[7]

Both India and Pakistan appear to recognize the dangers of war, thus giving some credence to the role of deterrence. By 2004, India and Pakistan restored diplomatic relations and instituted a number of confidence-building measures. Nevertheless, while neither side might want a war, they continue to remain perilously close to conflict. For Pakistan, there appeared to be four major "thresholds" under which it would introduce nuclear weapons: (1) conquest of large parts of its territory; (2) destruction of a large part of land or air forces; (3) economic strangulation; and (4) domestic political destabilization or large-scale internal subversion. India maintains a formal "no-first-use" policy, however, its language has left open options of using nuclear weapons in retaliation to attacks on Indian troops "anywhere"—including those which could be inside Pakistani territory. India appears to rely on its ability to contain any escalation, its numerical advantage in nuclear and conventional weapons, and its geographic size as a decisive advantage in any possible conflict with Pakistan. Meanwhile, both sides continue to develop a range of nuclear-capable ballistic missiles with India testing 150- to 250-kilometer-range missiles and longer range multistage rockets that can hit between 700 and 3,000 kilometers. In summer 2004, India tested a new missile system able to carry a one-ton warhead with guided capability. Pakistan has tested a 2,000-kilometer-range solid-fuelled two-stage nuclear-capable ballistic missile as well as shorter range missiles reaching 180, 300, and 700 kilometers. In August 2005, Pakistan tested its first cruise missile. Both states remain in a missile-delivery arms race though both are also constrained by how much they can spend.[8]

Nuclear Dangers

Any exchange of nuclear weapons between India and Pakistan would have devastating repercussions. An assessment of a possible nuclear exchange, done by the Natural Resources Defense Council, reviewed two scenarios— one with ten Hiroshima-sized explosions with no fallout and another with twenty-four nuclear explosions with significant radioactive fallout (findings are based on comparative population data with the impact of the Hiroshima weapon's effects in Japan). In the first scenario, a minimal nuclear exchange, ten bombs over ten cities in India and Pakistan—assuming five in India and five in Pakistan—would produce the outcomes shown in table 5.1. In this scenario, the nuclear weapons would be exploded above ground where the explosion would destroy much of the radioactive fallout.

In the assessment of twenty-four nuclear bombs exploded on the ground, more explosion and more fallout would result. In this scenario, radioactive fallout would be dispersed into the air. Depending on the amount of radioactivity and the prevailing winds, this scenario estimates that 22.1 million people in India and Pakistan would be exposed to lethal radiation doses of 600

Table 5.1.   Scenario involving nuclear weapons exchange between India and Pakistan: 10 bombs over 10 cities.

	Dead	Severely injured	Slightly injured
India			
Bangalore	314,978	175,136	411,336
Bombay	477,713	228,648	476,633
Calcutta	357,202	198,218	466,336
Madras	364,291	196,226	448,948
New Delhi	176,518	94,231	217,853
Subtotals	1,690,702	892,459	2,021,106
Pakistan			
Faisalabad	336,239	174,351	373,967
Islamabad	154,067	66,744	129,935
Karachi	239,643	126,810	283,290
Lahore	258,139	149,649	354,095
Rawalpindi	183,791	96,846	220,585
Subtotals	1,171,879	614,400	1,361,872
Totals	2,862,581	1,506,859	3,382,978

Source of data: Natural Resources Defense Council

rem or more in the first two days after the nuclear exchange. Another 8 million would receive additional doses between 100 and 600 rem causing severe radiation sickness and possibly death. A total of 30 million people would be at risk of exposure to radioactive fallout.[9]

Pakistan's acquisition of nuclear weapons raises serious question of command and control over its nuclear arsenal and related materials. While Pakistan's army insists its nuclear weapons are secure, security is heavily dependent on armed guards and gates rather than high-technology capabilities. Three specific scenarios most threaten the Pakistani nuclear arsenal and can have significant international repercussions. First, there are insider threats in Pakistan in which those working with the weapons could transfer, or assist the transfer, of weapons or nuclear materials to Islamists or terrorists who oppose the government of Pakistan. Second, an outside group could attempt to steal nuclear weapons or material. Third, it is possible that the secular government could fall and be replaced by an Islamic regime which would then be in control of Pakistan's nuclear weapons, materials, and expertise, all of which could then be proliferated purposefully.[10] In such an event, other countries, including India but also the United States, might launch preemptive attacks against Pakistan's known nuclear weapons facilities. Even a nuclear accident at a Pakistani nuclear facility could be interpreted as a preemptive attack by India—thus prompting Pakistan to launch a retaliatory response to a supposed attack.

THE KOREAN PENINSULA

The Korean peninsula includes two hostile and very well-armed countries facing each other across a common border. The situation also involved vital interests of the United States, and the regional influence of China, Japan, and, to a lesser degree, Russia. By 2006, North Korea was one of the few remaining totalitarian governments in the world and was a deeply isolated regime with very little experience in the nuances of world politics and international diplomacy. During the early 1950s, as Communists consolidated power in North Korea, the country divided between North and South. The United States and its allies intervened on behalf of the South Koreans. After several years of war, the North Koreans were driven to the 38th parallel, which eventually became the legal dividing line between the two Koreas. The two countries never signed a peace treaty and remained in a legal state of war. South Korea has been a strong ally of the United States, which stationed troops at the demilitarized zone between the two countries to deter a North Korean invasion. These forces stand opposite North Korean forces that are poised to attack and are within close range of the South Korean capital of Seoul. North Korea has elevated this already dangerous situation to a new level by striving to become a nuclear power with long-range missile capability.

The North Korean Threat

North Korea's leadership has generated a cult of personality around Kim Jong Il and his father, Kim Il Sung. The country entered the twenty-first century as an economic disaster, largely due to mismanagement of resources by the government, which had a general disregard for the welfare of its 22.6 million people. As many as 2 million people died as a result of food shortages in the 1990s. Human rights abuses, torture, public executions, slave labor, and forced abortions and infanticides in prison camps were regularly reported. There may be as many as 200,000 political prisoners in North Korea.[11] Meanwhile, North Korea spends about one-third of its gross domestic product on the military.[12] The North Korean leadership depends heavily on support from the military and thus it gets significant rewards. The military serves as the largest employer, purchaser, and consumer in the country.[13] The heavy investment in the military has seriously weakened North Korea's civilian infrastructure, leading to major energy and food shortages. Declining human and economic conditions could lead to large-scale social unrest prompting massive internal disruption or even civil war. Alternatively, this could prompt North Korea into a desperate invasion of the South to achieve the forceful reunification of the Korean peninsula.

Over several decades, North Korea amassed military capabilities to achieve strategic and operational surprise in wartime to sustain breakthrough operations in the South. North Korea appeared to see massive firepower with artillery barrages, multiple rocket launchers, and surface-to-surface missiles as central to this strategy. In war, North Korea apparently would seek to isolate the South Korean capital of Seoul and capture all air and naval facilities supporting lines of reinforcement into South Korea. North Korea also would likely seek to neutralize enemy air power. Finally, North Korea would attempt to instill confusion, panic, and fear as a means of imposing reunification of the Korean peninsula on its terms.[14] By 2006, North Korea had the world's fifth largest military. Its active duty military totaled 1,106,000 forces and about 4,700,000 reserves. Of these, 950,000 are active in the army. In the army, there are about 3,500 main battle tanks, 2,500 armored personnel carriers, and a total of 17,900 artillery pieces. Naval and air forces are much smaller with 88 submarines, 3 frigates, and 301 coastal combatants and an air force of 110,000 troops. The air force has limited equipment and between 10 and 20 hours average for annual training. There is a 189,000-strong active duty paramilitary force as well as a 3,500,000 worker and peasant guard.[15]

South Korea, with a population of 47.7 million, had in 2006 some 687,700 active duty forces, of which 159,000 are conscripts. South Korea had 4,500,000 reserves. The army numbered 560,000 and included 2,330 main battle tanks, 2,480 armored personnel carriers, and 10,774 towed artillery pieces. The South Korean navy numbered 63,000 personnel including 28,000 marines, 20 submarines, and 43 surface combatants. The air force personnel numbered 64,000 including 540 combat aircraft. South Korea also had 4,500 active duty paramilitary forces and a civilian defense force of 3,500,000 including qualified men up to age 50. The United States had 34,500 troops based in South Korea including 25,000 army, 420 navy, 8,900 air force and 180 marines.[16] Working together with the South Korean forces, both in command structures and regular training exercises, the U.S. forces provided important capabilities in the areas of airlift and sealift; prepositioning of heavy equipment and supplies; battlefield command, control, and communications; advanced munitions; aerial refueling; intelligence, surveillance, and reconnaissance; and counterfire against artillery attacks. Joint U.S.–South Korean military cooperation included major live-fire exercises, combined defense planning, intelligence integration and sharing, logistical interfacing, educational exchanges, and defense industry cooperation.[17]

North Korea has maintained an offensive troop posture, designed to act with surprise to quickly seize large parts of South Korean territory. The objective would appear to be to make an American reinforcement of South Korea's forward deployed troops impossible. The general parameters of a major conflict would commence according to several realistic scenarios. North Korea could use a peace initiative or other diplomatic overture as a ruse to launch a surprise attack.[18] Another scenario would be for the United States to launch a preemptive attack on North Korean nuclear facilities. In response, North Korea might attack into South Korea. In either scenario, the United States and South Korean forces would seek to slow a North Korean invasion and to protect Seoul. This goal could be hampered by lack of early warning, the narrowness of the Korean peninsula, mountain terrain well-known to the North Korean forces, and the possibility that the North would launch a two-front invasion into the South. North Korea could seek to terrorize South Korea by using mass artillery fire against Seoul, incorporating chemical, biological, and nuclear weapons. If enough ground could be seized, the North Korean military would likely hand over victory to their political leaders in the North who could then negotiate a settlement favorable to them.[19]

If the United States and South Korean forces could frustrate the North Koreans for long enough, they would eventually be reinforced by American troops based in Japan and from the United States. Medium- and long-range air power could also be employed against North Korean artillery and troop concentrations if they could be located. Then, the United States would likely counterattack by seizing key territory. In a final phase, a major counteroffensive would be engaged to destroy the North Korean military. In most estimates, eventually the United States forces would reverse a North Korean invasion of South Korea. However, the costs of combat would be extraordinary. U.S. forces pushing into North Korean territory would find the countryside a virtual fortress with hardened bunkers and massive tunnel complexes. Meanwhile, North Korean forces would have quickly dispersed into South Korean territory, perhaps mixing in with the civilian population. As much as 70 percent of North Korean troops is deployed within 150 kilometers of their border with South Korea, so North Korea would be able to concentrate forces quickly and make their supply lines less vulnerable to air power attack. Several thousand artillery pieces and 300 missiles are within target range (about 50 miles) of Seoul from North Korea and would be employed, likely with chemical and biological weapons. North Korea is believed to have stockpiled about 5,000 metric tons of nerve gas, choking, blister, and blood agents. North Korea likely has the capacity to weaponize some biological threats including anthrax, smallpox, and the bacteria that cause the plague and cholera.[20]

Without any movement of its artillery, North Korea could likely sustain fire of up to 500,000 rounds an hour against South Korean and American defense forces over a period of several hours.[21] As many as one million people could be killed in the early stages of a surprise attack against Seoul.[22] In 1993, the United States made tentative military plans for a possible attack on North Korean nuclear facilities. The U.S. Department of Defense estimated that, for victory, four months of high-intensity combat would be necessary and would require over 600,000 South Korean troops and 500,000 American reinforcements. Within the first ninety days of combat, U.S. casualties were predicted to run as high as 52,000. In addition to massive casualties, the economic and war-related costs were projected to range into the trillions of dollars.[23]

In another scenario, North Korea might take advantage of American deployments during a conflict elsewhere. In such a circumstance, America's ability to send massive numbers of reinforcement troops to South Korea would be severely limited. The United States has introduced plans to redeploy large numbers of forces away from forward areas and rely instead on prepositioned equipment and rapid deployment capacity. The United States can project power from the U.S. mainland to Korea combined with bases in Guam and Japan. If, however, the United States was deeply engaged in another major troop deployment, its military options against North Korean artillery might be limited. The United States might then have to introduce nuclear weapons if this was the only available means of stopping North Korean advances or artillery bombardment. The United States has run simulated bombing missions for precisely this scenario using a squadron of F15E fighter jets conducting mock bombing runs between North Carolina and Florida with simulated B61 nuclear bombs.[24]

The Nuclear Environment

In late 2002, North Korea indicated that it was processing materials that could be used to make nuclear weapons. This announcement ended a promise made in 1993 by North Korea to stop processing nuclear fuel if the United States provided it with economic assistance and light-water nuclear reactors for energy. During this time, the International Atomic Energy Agency monitored North Korea's adherence to the Nuclear Non-Proliferation Treaty. However, North Korea eventually indicated that it would no longer respect its commitments under this treaty and nuclear inspectors departed. North Korea seemed to elevate regime survival over unification and argued it sought nuclear weapons for defensive purposes of preventing a preemptive American attack. North Korea did offer to give up its nuclear arsenal, or large parts of it, if the United States would commit to a nonaggression treaty with North Korea. Nuclear weapons also help North Korea separate South Korea from the United States. In the late 1990s, South Korean leaders embarked on an overture toward the North known as the "sunshine" policy. A new generation of South Koreans had emerged, wanting to end tensions, and if North Korea could make its nuclear issue a bilateral question between it and the United States, then Washington might be blamed for a failure of diplomacy among the South Korean population. Nuclear weapons could also be useful to North Korea as a tool of blackmail, perhaps only giving some of them up in exchange for economic aid. Or, in a dangerous circumstance, North Korea could purposefully proliferate nuclear weapons for profit. Finally, they might be considered a tool of warfare against transportation locations in South Korea, transit points and American troop deployments in Japan, or even on the U.S. homeland.

By 2006, North Korea had likely developed at least several nuclear weapons and had rudimentary capacity to hit targets near-or-on American territory. During April–June 2003, North Korea announced it had begun reprocessing nuclear fuel rods which contained enough plutonium for 2 to 5 nuclear weapons, though it did not declare that it had actually created a nuclear weapon. If North Korea continued its program, it would have been able to develop 4 to 8 nuclear weapons by 2005 and to produce enough material to build 5 to 13 weapons per year depending on conditions within its production facilities. Meanwhile, North Korea also deployed about 120 short-range Scud-B/C missiles, which can reach most of South Korea, and 40 medium-range *No-dong* missiles, which can hit targets in Japan. North Korea's missile inventory totaled around 300 missiles in 2005. North Korea also developed the *Taepo-dong*-1 rocket, which has three stages. This missile was tested successfully for flight, but not for deployment of payload or accuracy at long ranges. However, if it proceeds to develop a second generation of this missile, North Korea would eventually be able to deliver nuclear weapons onto American cities.[25]

The North Korean acquisition of nuclear weapons significantly alters the strategic framework in northeast Asia. Washington preferred not to engage in direct negotiations with the North Korean government and thus encouraged a multilateral diplomatic framework (including South Korea, China, Japan, Russia, North Korea, and the United States). This approach appeared to force North Korea to constrain some of its more virulent rhetoric so long as it hoped to enhance its relations with China and South Korea. However, it also frustrated North Korea's efforts to isolate the United States and to extract a nonaggression promise. The United States has a military option and could eliminate, or at least dramatically set back the North Korean program with precision air strikes. Another alternative, explored by Pentagon planners, would be to conduct preconflict maneuvers that would strain the North Korean military with the hope of prompting a coup. For example, one U.S. plan (OPLAN 5030) would be to fly RC-135 surveillance aircraft very close to North Korean airspace. This action might force North Korea to deploy interceptor aircraft and thus use up their jet fuel prompting North Korean forces to disperse from their bunkers and deploy troops, which would expose positions and deplete supplies. Other elements of this alternative would be to disrupt the North Korean financial system and engage in strategic disinformation actions to play off of paranoia among North Korean leaders.[26] The danger in such a program is that it could also provoke North Korea into a false belief it was actually under attack, prompting it to launch its own attack.

There were, therefore, no good military options for addressing this explosive region. Diplomacy and deterrence combined with incentives for cooperation was thus the preferred path. By 2006, it appeared that outlines of a diplomatic agreement to end North Korea's nuclear production would include: (1) North Korea gives up its nuclear program and opens itself again to international inspections; (2) the United States provides a written security guarantee that it would not launch preemptive attacks against North Korea or attempt regime change; and (3) the international community, including the United States, would give financial assistance to aid the emergency economic situation in North Korea and gradually engage North Korea in international transactions which would hopefully reduce its own sense of insecurity.[27] The United States and North Korea were engaged in a high stakes relationship complicated by a lack of effective communication and understanding.

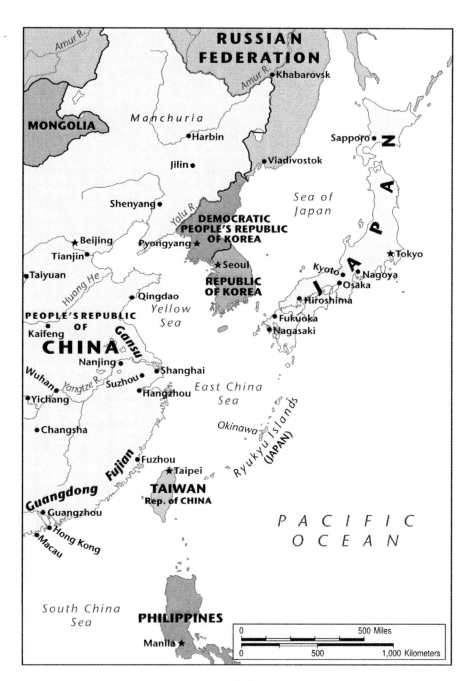

East Asia

Nuances such as language translations have led to confusion over what North Korea reveals about its nuclear weapons programs. Ideological blinders in the North that assume a hostile international environment are enhanced by American rhetoric labeling North Korea as an "evil" state governed by a madman. Washington also appeared to assume the North Korean leaders were crazy, whereas much of their desire for nuclear weapons might be explained with basic deterrence theory. Washington also appears not to see how its own behavior might be seen as threatening by other international actors—even if it is not intended to be. In that sense, American beliefs that North Korea is using its nuclear weapons merely as a bargaining chip might be misguided. Once attained, nuclear weapons might be kept for deterrent purposes.[28] On the other hand, North Korea might just be unpredictable enough to use their weapons.

Averting Conflict—or a Nuclear Chain Reaction?

Several longer-range questions could also impact the potential for conflict on the Korean peninsula. A new generation of South Koreans, for example, does not have the same sense of fear of North Korea as their forefathers. This generation is increasingly more likely to challenge their historical alliance with the United States—and some view the United States as the source of their security problems. Alternatively, if South Korea finds that the American commitment to their security becomes ambivalent or hollow, South Korea might develop its own nuclear deterrent. In summer 2004, the South Korean government disclosed that some of its scientists had experimented with enrichment capacity for nuclear fuel which could be made into weapons-grade material. South Korea had explored a nuclear option in the 1970s, but dropped those efforts and instead joined the Nuclear Non-Proliferation Treaty. However, the South Korean message during summer 2004 implied that the capacity existed to obtain a nuclear deterrent. Another consequence of a declining American commitment to northeast Asia could be a decision by Japan to nationalize its military and to develop its own nuclear deterrent. Any decision by Japan to go nuclear could raise significant security concerns in China, setting off either a regional arms race, a new balance of power, or in a worst case scenario—a nuclear chain reaction.

TAIWAN

Tensions between mainland China and the island of Taiwan date to the communist revolution when the pro-American and British leader Chiang Kai-shek was defeated by communist rebels led by Mao Tse-tung. In 1949, Chiang and his political allies fled to Taiwan and claimed to be the true representatives of China. Taiwan is treated by the government of mainland China as part of its territorial integrity. Taiwan's status is contested as many of its citizens and international backers see it as potentially being a sovereign state, though it has never claimed to be. Taiwan has some attributes of independence including its own constitution, representative government, and military. Taiwan has not declared formal independence for two reasons. First, for mainland China, sovereignty over Taiwan is seen as a justified reason for which it will use military force against the island. Second, the United States supports Taiwan's autonomy and has a defensive commitment to it—but only in the event that it does not provoke China by declaring independence.

One China or Two?

The United States, like most of the international community, has an official "one China" policy. However, Washington is pressured by a strong pro-Taiwan domestic lobby and wants to expand arms sales and other exports to Taiwan. This relationship makes it more difficult for the United States to balance its position on Taiwan with its significant economic and strategic interests in a good relationship with China. Meanwhile, Taiwan has transitioned from an authoritarian government to representative democracy, and some political leaders have advanced a more independence-minded agenda. A failure by the United States to defend Taiwan would risk ceding American primacy in Asia, perhaps causing Japan to doubt its own alliance with the United States. Japan might thus prefer a nationalized military strategy including the development of nuclear weapons. If mainland China had full access to Taiwan, Beijing would have a key anchor from which to project power throughout east Asia. China could expand its maritime position via an extended defense perimeter that would run from north to south Asia. China would also gain major influence over the South China Sea through which about 50 percent of the world's shipping passes.[29]

Taiwan has a population of 22.9 million and total armed forces of 290,000 active duty personnel and 1,653,500 reserves. Its main forces are assigned to the army with 200,000 troops in defensive positions utilizing 926 main battle tanks, 950 armored personnel carriers, and 1,815 artillery pieces, as an example of some of its major capabilities. Taiwan's navy numbers 45,000 and includes 4 submarines, 11 destroyers, and 21 frigates. The navy also includes 59 missile craft for patrol and coastal defense and 12 mine-laying vessels and 18 amphibious landing craft. The air force numbers 45,000 including 479 combat air craft with average annual flying hours for pilot training at 180. Taiwan also has 26,500 paramilitary forces.[30] The quality of Taiwan's equipment is mixed. Some of it is very good, and some is second or third generation.

American-built F-16 fighters and French-made Mirage jets are very capable and their Taiwanese pilots well-trained. However, Taiwan's submarines are aging and its coastal defense radar and interceptor forces are vulnerable. Budgetary pressures have also led to cuts in the Taiwanese navy and air force.

The military balance across the Taiwan Strait favors China. Though China's military capabilities for external power projection are limited, it has focused most of its military planning, modernization, and exercising on scenarios involving fighting a war across the Taiwan Strait. China has shown a willingness to use military threats to affect public opinion and electoral outcomes in Taiwan, and has made clear it will use military force against Taiwan if it declares independence. The issue of Taiwan has become a focus of nationalism and pride in China. China's leaders also worry about the cohesion of all China as Tibet and Xinjiang province also have separatist movements. If China failed to respond to assertions of independence by Taiwan, its leaders might lose the confidence of the military and risk internal strife. Thus mainland China and Taiwan have serious domestic pressures that could prompt a war both would likely prefer to avoid.

As China has reduced army deployments at its border with the former Soviet Union, much of its capabilities have been reoriented toward Taiwan. China's armed forces of 2.25 million significantly outnumber Taiwan's. China's jet fighters outnumber Taiwan's by ten to one and China has 70 submarines compared to Taiwan's 4. Taiwan has three times the number of fourth-generation jet fighters as China—though Taiwan's pilots are far better trained. In 2006, China lacked significant naval power and, in particular, adequate amphibious landing capacity that would allow it to launch a major invasion across the Taiwan Strait. As China reorients its military capacity for force projection, it has focused on a near-term effort to enhance missile technology to inflict immediate and painful damage in a conflict. China had, by 2003, deployed 450 short-range ballistic missiles in range of Taiwan and was expected to deploy an additional 75 per year. These deployments are likely to include an advanced, medium-range missile which could also strike Japan.[31] China can institute a naval blockade of Taiwan via submarines and fighter aircraft. China also has made significant advances in information warfare, electronic warfare, and special operations.[32]

China has important reasons to avoid military action against Taiwan. For example, an attack before summer 2008 would have put China's hosting of the summer Olympics in jeopardy. China places a high priority on economic growth and thus engagement in the global economy might be viewed as more important than Taiwan. China might thus be more likely to use diplomatic isolation, increasing Taiwan's economic dependence on mainland China, and seek to affect domestic public opinion in Taiwan.[33] American military estimates suggest that the United States does not believe China will have the capacity to engage in a war to unify it and Taiwan before the year 2010. The United States assumes it will be at least that long before China would develop into a major military power and that it will take about five to ten years for it to develop the modern weapons systems necessary for contemporary warfighting. The United States would, however, also be under additional threat from Chinese intercontinental ballistic missiles which would likely grow at least three-fold by 2010. This nuclear potential limits U.S. freedom of action regarding its commitment to Taiwan.

China's major military weaknesses are in naval power and amphibious craft which are both necessary for an invasion of Taiwan. China also lacks sufficient air cover to protect landing craft. While it is looking at innovations in warfighting doctrine and technology, China does not have experience with joint operations coordinated among various services. Chinese logistics would, for example, be vulnerable to confusion and counterattack. The United States does assume that China could win an engagement in Taiwan. However, China would have to be willing to make a massive commitment of capabilities over an extended period, to hope there would be no third-party intervention, and to be prepared to accept significant damage to its economy and global diplomatic standing.[34]

Unconventional War and Strategic Consequences

China may be developing strategies and capabilities consistent with other options besides a conventional invasion. In this scenario, China could rely on strategic surprise designed to cut off the leadership of Taiwan with a direct assault on the capital city of Taipei. Such a decapitation strategy would combine precision attacks by pre-positioned special operations forces, airborne troops, and a barrage of missiles and fast achievement of air superiority—perhaps as fast as 45 minutes. By attacking leadership and command and control capacities in Taiwan as well as selected targeting of civilian infrastructure, China would hope to instill massive confusion. By the time Taiwan's regular army troops could coordinate and respond, it might be too late. China could simultaneously create panic and chaos in the general population by launching missile attacks across the Taiwan Strait—possibly to include a selective use of weapons of mass destruction. Using conventional missiles as well as some with chemical and biological agents would exacerbate the psychological impact and could also temporarily shut down airfields, thus preventing elements of the Taiwanese air force from launching. China might engage in small amphibious attacks to distract the Taiwanese army as a ruse away from the real action, which would remain focused on leadership and command and control facilities.[35] Meanwhile, some form of pro-Beijing uprising could be cultivated as a political showing of public support for China's actions. An early objective would be to capture a major landing strip to deploy Chinese rapid reaction troops who would then conduct operations with air support launched from mainland China.[36] From there China would appeal to a pro-Beijing leader who would then shift policy away from independence and perhaps toward unification on China's terms.

China is not prepared to undertake a front-on invasion of Taiwan and would not likely be for many years, if not decades. Chinese leaders thus frame the question of reunification as a goal for about 2020. In order to actually invade and occupy Taiwan, China would have to combine an effective capacity to land ground troops and use air power to subjugate Taiwanese defenses before reinforcements could be organized. China's existing capability makes this a very difficult proposition. For example, its ballistic missiles are highly inaccurate. To attack Taiwan's runways and prevent its mustering an air defense would require virtually the entire arsenal of Chinese missiles. China's air force would not be able to fly during the night and any massing of Chinese air power would be noticed by American and Chinese intelligence, eliminating the element of surprise. Once an attack began, nightfall would likely be used by Taiwan to make short-term repairs to any damaged airfields. China's planes lack precision and would have to fly at low altitude making them highly vulnerable to antiaircraft fire. Attrition rates as high as 10 percent would not destroy China's ability to attack, but combined with servicing, refueling, and limited duration of missions, its air power would be seriously constrained. Most likely, at least half of Taiwan's aircraft would survive even the best of surprise attacks, allowing them to hinder Chinese efforts to achieve air dominance. China's small amphibious fleet would only be able to move about 10,000 to 15,000 troops plus their equipment. China might be able to airlift more troops into Taiwan but not large pieces of equipment in a rapid manner. If Taiwan had warning time and could coordinate its active-duty ground forces, it would have a significant advantage over Chinese forces with about 100,000 troops facing some 20,000 within the first forty-eight hours. This imbalance would likely be even greater, however, as China would lose as much as 20 percent of its forces just in approaching Taiwan and fighting its way onto land.[37]

Rather than an invasion, China could combine economic and military pressure to force a change in Taiwan's political leadership. A blockade, or punishment with missile attacks, could be used to coerce Taiwan into a pro-Beijing position. Each has drawbacks as it is not clear that China could enforce a blockade and missile attacks carry the risk of escalation and international isolation. If, however, China did launch a form of surprise invasion, there might be little that the United States could do. Washington could scramble airplanes from Japan and the Philippines and move its aircraft carrier in the Pacific toward Taiwan.

Within twenty minutes, the United States could launch air attacks on China's mainland to damage logistical support for ongoing operations. Also, marines based in Japan and on amphibious assault ships in the Pacific might be able to conduct operations inside Taiwan relatively quickly. The problem for the United States is that, by the time it was able to influence events, the facts on the ground might have already been set. The United States would also have to ask whether it wanted to risk an escalation with China, possibly to include nuclear war.

Taiwan has run computer war game simulations which show that, in a surprise attack scenario, China might actually defeat Taiwan in as little as six days. This scenario alarmed Taiwanese officials because it was based on an amphibious landing invasion, which Taiwan has anticipated for some time. The drill showed that in a surprise attack, Taiwan's troops would not be able to stop a Chinese amphibious landing or to halt them from advancing inland. After one day of simulated Chinese attacks, Taiwan's airport bunkers, harbors, and key government buildings were destroyed by extensive bombings including the launch of some 700 missiles from China.[38] Taiwan could hope to preserve the fighting capabilities of the air force and navy and about 80 percent of the army—allowing it to hold on for two weeks while reinforcements were organized.[39] For military success by Taiwan, the United States would have to uphold its promise to defend Taiwan by organizing a response within that two weeks. More likely, the United States would need about one month to organize enough forces to mount a serious counterattack in Taiwan. If, at that same moment North Korea chose to attack South Korea, then the strategic calculation would be dramatically altered. The United States has begun to train for this scenario, conducting a major military exercise in summer 2004. "Summer Pulse 2004" involved seven aircraft-carrier strike groups, 50 warships, 600 aircraft, and 150,000 troops surging simultaneously around the world.[40]

Taiwan's Security Dilemma

Taiwan's dilemmas are complicated by a need to transform its military capabilities. Taiwan's military is organized heavily around its army, which is not integrated into a joint command structure, is not well-trained, and is highly politicized. Budget constraints have made major modernization a difficult proposition. Procurement of missile defense systems has been slow to move forward in Taiwan. Even if missile defenses were put in place, Taiwanese personnel would not be sufficiently trained to operate these systems. Taiwan's budget allocated to purchasing new weapons and equipment has declined in favor of personnel costs. Taiwan does not have a functionally integrated national security and planning system, which makes it hard to coordinate flexible and efficient military planning. Initiative and low-level adaptive strategy are not significantly developed in army training—an essential ingredient to countering a surprise Chinese attack.[41] American officials have suggested improvements that Taiwan needs including better interservice coordination; a joint perspective on military operations; the capability to deter modern air and naval forces; development of missile defense; development of modern anti-submarine warfare capabilities; modernization of command and control systems; appointment or election of effective military and civilian leaders with vision; an effective national security structure; better military responsiveness to civilian control; and a rational procurement system.[42] It is possible that such improvements might actually accelerate an attack on Taiwan should China fear that it would lose strategic initiative if it waited. China might, alternatively, pursue a strategy of purposeful deception regarding its own strengths in order to lull Taiwan into a sense of security and thus forestall any serious Taiwanese build up in defense capability.[43]

Taiwan could also opt for unconventional military action. Taiwanese military experts refer to a "Scorpion Strategy" against China. If, for example, Taiwan attained warning of a Chinese attack, it could launch preemptive attacks against some of China's missile launch capability. China would have to defend its flank, allowing time for the Taiwanese army and American reinforcements to engage. Taiwan also might purchase air defense systems that could help to neutralize a Chinese air assault. Taiwan could also choose not to engage China's troops at all but to attack high-value targets deep inside of China. By presenting a credible threat to the Chinese mainland including its civilian population or major infrastructure like Shanghai's Pudong Tower or the Three Gorges dam project, China might think twice about the relative benefits of conquest. Taiwan's existing capacity to project power at this level is not likely to be taken seriously by China. For example, the Three Gorges dam is 1,500 kilometers from Taiwan while its aircraft have a combat range of only up to about 1,200 kilometers. Such an attack would also likely be labeled by China as a terrorist attack and be used to justify an overwhelming military response against Taiwan.[44]

Given its vulnerabilities Taiwan could develop nuclear weapons. However, this action would certainly provoke a hostile response from China and do serious damage to Taiwan's relationship with the United States. Some analysts and press in Taiwan nevertheless argue that the only way to ensure China knows it will suffer great damage from an attack would be to develop a Taiwanese nuclear arsenal.[45] Taiwan engaged in a nuclear weapons research program in the 1970s but abandoned it under strong American and international pressure. Taiwan does, periodically, make statements that it has the capacity to make nuclear weapons quickly if need be. Taiwan could probably build nuclear weapons, but how fast is uncertain. Taiwan would likely need to import separated plutonium or highly enriched uranium.[46] Taiwan is also not likely to develop sufficient numbers of missiles or long-range aircraft that would allow it to truly inflict pain on China.[47]

Interdependence and the Case against War

An important trend between China and Taiwan could dampen the risks of war. Taiwan has increasingly engaged with economic investment in China. Increasing economic interdependence could eventually make war too costly for both. Despite occasionally intense rhetorical hostility, neither side appears willing to risk all-out war. Nevertheless, the threat of war between the two is real. For Taiwan, the issue is a matter of identity and independence. For China, it is a matter of strategic interest and pride. Most Taiwanese recognize the danger in their situation and public opinion surveys show that nearly 50 percent of Taiwanese oppose fighting to defend the island if a vote favoring independence triggered a conflict with China.[48] Even Taiwan's official position on military power is vague, as their 2002 White Paper on Defense demonstrates: "menaces to our national security include domestic, destabilizing factors. . . . Some of our people, for example, are confusing foes with friends, or are divided on the issue of national identity, undermining the unity of the people against external threats."[49]

THE PERSIAN GULF AND THE MIDDLE EAST

Much of the world's economy depends on the steady flow of Persian Gulf oil, which makes the Middle East an area of vital strategic importance. Tensions in the Middle East have led to serious international crises, particularly over Israel, which found itself in regional conflicts in 1948, 1956, 1967, and 1973 and engaging in interventions in Lebanon in the 1980s. The right of Israel to exist as a state has been widely recognized in the region, though its occupation of territory seized in war and the broader plight of the Palestinian peoples combined with major terrorist attacks against Israel remain an open wound around the Middle East. No single state within the region has the capacity to gain regional dominance—although the United States exercises a heavy external influence. The United States maintains close relationships with a range of countries including Saudi Arabia and the other Persian Gulf kingdoms, and nearby countries Egypt, Israel, Jordan, and Turkey. Meanwhile, the United States has organized international coalitions to isolate Libya, Syria, and Iran for their historical record of support for international terrorism. Most dramatically, the United States invasion and occupation of Iraq in 2003 signaled a dramatic new level of engagement in the region.

American Primacy and the Iraq Conundrum

The United States is promoting democracy in the Middle East. However, the combination of America's support for Israel, strong backing of some authoritarian political leaders as in Saudi Arabia and Egypt, and its 2003 invasion of Iraq have stirred growing anti-Americanism. The United States promotes a "Greater Middle East Initiative" that would advance democratic and economic reform in the region. However, this proposal was met with stiff resistance from governments that are allies of the United States in its international war against terrorism. The United States has staked its credibility on the building of democracy in Iraq—with the hope that this effort would prompt further reform in the Middle East. There is no fundamental reason why the Arab and Muslim countries of the Middle East should not emerge as democracies. By 2005 trends appeared to favor this direction in Lebanon and even to a limited degree in Egypt and Saudi Arabia. However, whether democracy will produce stability, and whether it produces outcomes commensurate to the interests of the United States and the West remains uncertain. Ironically, the very notion that democracy is brought from the West may actually undermine its potential in the Middle East.[50]

The United States is the dominant military power in the Persian Gulf and the broader Middle East. Its distribution of forces includes the U.S. Fifth Fleet which has its headquarters in Bahrain and includes U.S. forces devoted to the Indian Ocean, Persian Gulf, and Red Sea. This grouping includes an aircraft carrier battle group with six surface combatants, three amphibious assault ships, and mine-countermine vessels. The United States also has its Sixth Fleet in the Mediterranean Sea which complements those deployed closer to the Persian Gulf. The Sixth Fleet includes one aircraft carrier battle group, three nuclear fueled submarines, two landing aircraft, and a variety of support and transport craft. Also nearby, the United States keeps long-range bombers at Diego Garcia in the Indian Ocean. In Bahrain, the United States maintains a combined 3,000 navy, marine, and army forces. Some 1,000 army troops are deployed in Djibouti. Kuwait has 23,350 U.S. forces including 19,700 army personnel with a headquarters, logistical units, and pre-positioned equipment for one armed brigade that includes two tank battalions, one mechanized battalion, and one artillery battalion. America's deployment in Kuwait also includes 1,250 navy personnel, 2,700 air force personnel, and 1,600 marines. The United States deploys 6,540 troops in Qatar and 1,300 air force personnel in the United Arab Emirates. Meanwhile, the United States also has long-range force projection capacities deployed in Europe and the continental United States devoted to contingencies including Middle East operations.[51]

One of the major sources of tension in the Persian Gulf during the 1990s was the deployment of American troops in Saudi Arabia which were based

The Middle East

there to contain Iraq. This deployment was a source of frustration for Islamic radicals who saw the holiest areas of Islam being protected by non-Muslims. Removing the regime of Saddam Hussein in Iraq eliminated the need to keep American troops based long-term in Saudi Arabia. The American presence in Saudi Arabia has been reduced significantly from the 20,000 troops and equipment pre-positioned in Saudi Arabia during the 1990s to only 300 by 2006. However, this shift did not resolve the strategic question of America's regional presence given the subsequent occupation of Iraq. By 2005, the United States had ongoing deployment into Iraq including 146,000 troops. This deployment included 133,300 army, 550 air force, 1,550 navy, 8,600 marines, and 2,400 special forces personnel.[52] A small coalition of other countries also sent forces to Iraq to complement U.S. forces.

Once the United States was in Iraq, a premature disengagement of U.S. troops might have been the most destabilizing threat to the Persian Gulf. Without the presence of American forces, Iraq could have erupted into civil war, perhaps leading to intervention by neighboring countries. Conversely, the American presence in Iraq energized Islamic radicals in and outside of Iraq who came to see defeat of America in Iraq as a major part of their ideology. Prior to the American invasion, Iraq had about 389,000 active duty forces and 650,000 reserves. While much of the military's leadership had patronage ties to the Saddam Hussein government, most of the regular forces were either conscripts or professional soldiers. Nevertheless, the United States occupation authority in summer 2003 disbanded the Iraqi military. The result was to make several hundred thousand well-armed people unemployed—many of whom would join a counter-U.S. insurgency. Added to the list of unemployed military was the firing of some 50,000 Baath Party members (Saddam Hussein's political party) from their civil service positions, education, public health, and media jobs. An estimated 90 percent of these people had joined the Baath party purely out of fear of the consequences of not supporting Saddam Hussein. However, they were made unemployed when they could have helped in rebuilding Iraq.[53] Meanwhile, by fall 2004, only $1 billion of $13.6 billion of promised international aid had reached Iraq and only $1.2 billion of $18.4 billion authorized by the U.S. Congress for reconstruction in 2004 had been spent.[54]

The internal situation in Iraq was complicated by the demographic makeup of the country which includes a majority Shiite Muslim (overall about 60 percent) population in the south. Sunni Muslims (overall about 20 percent) dominate Baghdad and surrounding areas in central Iraq. In the northern part of the country, the Kurdish population (the remaining 20 percent) has long sought independence. However, they are now required to remain part of Iraq. In this mix, the United States promised to build a functional representative democracy though it would be hard for any true democratic process to produce anything other than a Shiite majority. Shiite Muslim influence is ascending in Lebanon, Pakistan, and Saudi Arabia. Iran was already dominated by radical Shiite Muslims clerics.[55] The Sunnis, which were the dominant part of the Saddam Hussein government, could be left isolated and the Kurds, unsatisfied with their role in a new Iraqi government, might press for independence. Kurdish independence was especially problematic because the Kurds also have large separatist-oriented populations in southeastern Turkey. Kurds in Turkey might thus be prompted to unite with Kurds in Iraq. Such moves could prompt Turkey to intervene in northern Iraq to prevent the Kurds from gaining independence. Ironically, the United States would have to choose between defending their strongest supporters in Iraq—the Kurds—or aligning with their long-time secular ally, Turkey. An alternative scenario would be that extremist Shi-ite and Sunni Muslims align together in the common cause of evicting the United States from Iraq driven by nationalism and a common desire for inde-pendence.[56] By summer 2004, 80 percent of Iraqis indicated in public opinion polls that they had lost faith in the United States and majorities saw the Amer-icans as occupiers, not liberators. By fall 2005, the United States had lost over 2,000 personnel killed and over 12,000 wounded since the invasion. The esti-mated size of the organized guerrilla fighters was 20,000 and entire towns had to be retaken from insurgents by major military force.[57]

Iran, Israel, and the Geopolitical Balance

The country with the greatest potential to alter the strategic environment around the Persian Gulf is Iran. In 1979, the U.S.-backed government of the Shah of Iran was overthrown in favor of a radical Shiite Muslim political movement. Both the United States and many of its allies in the Middle East saw this kind of radical internal change as the biggest threat to regional secu-rity. In the 1980s, the United States thus aligned with the secular government of Saddam Hussein in Iraq, which fought against Iran and its brand of Islamic fundamentalism. Iran is a significant regional power with 420,000 active duty troops and 350,000 reserves. Its army numbers 350,000 (including 1,613 main battle tanks), its navy 18,000, its air force 52,000 (though with only about 200 operational aircraft of second and third generation), and it has 40,000 paramil-itary forces.[58] Iran invests heavily in missile technology and increasingly in submarines and patrol boats, facilitating power projection and mobility in and around the Persian Gulf. These assets include several Russian Kilo-class sub-marines; 56 patrol and coastal boats, many with anti-ship cruise missiles; about 3,000 shore-based anti-ship missiles with ranges of 20,000 meters; 16 surface-to-air missile sites and 35 ballistic missile sites with over 400 SCUD Bs, Cs and SS-8 missiles. Iran's military is mainly defensive—but if it chooses, Iran is in a position to disrupt shipping lanes in the Persian Gulf at the Strait of Hor-muz as well as around the Gulf Islands of Abu Musa and Tunbs.

In the mid-1990s, Iranian domestic politics underwent a modest political thaw as a new generation of leaders emerged that did not share the revolution-ary passion of the 1979 movement. Iran now had over 20 years of its own autonomous rule, with very little to show for it but international isolation. Iran's support for anti-Israeli terrorists in particular had isolated it from the international community. During the 1990s, Iran also saw declining oil revenue combine with growing population demands on the state to deliver basic serv-ices.[59] Inflation ran at around 15 percent and unemployment reached as high as

25 percent. Gradually, Iran began conditioning its support for international terrorists and condemned the attacks by al Qaeda on the United States in 2001.
Meanwhile, a new generation of younger people exerted pressure for a less
restrictive religious government, and more engagement with international society. According to public opinion surveys, some 70 percent of Iranians have a
favorable view of opening normal relations with the West. The Iranian newspaper *Yas-e Now* in June 2003 asked the question "What are the actual
demands of the Iranian people?" To that, 13 percent chose the answer "continuation of the present political policy"; 16 percent chose "political reforms and
increases in the powers of the reformists"; 26 percent chose "fundamental
changes in management and in the performance of the system for an efficient
growth"; and 45 percent chose "change in the political system, even with foreign intervention."[60] Meanwhile, unlike the majority of the Arab states in the
Middle East, Iran has a legislative democracy, though it is constrained by
heavy influence of religious leaders in the judicial branch of government.

Iran's primary security problem for the last twenty years has been Iraq. Iran
and Iraq fought a devastating war to a stalemate in the 1980s. Iran remained
neutral in the 1991 and 2003 U.S.-led wars against Iraq. Nevertheless, Iran
had a significant interest in the outcome of a post-Saddam Iraq, and a particular interest in the length of the American presence there. Without a strong Iraq,
Iran is left as the most powerful country in the Persian Gulf. However, the
American presence in Iraq is a major problem for any Iranian desire to expand
its influence in the Middle East. If America were to succeed in transforming
Iraq, popular pressure for reform there could also overwhelm the religious
leadership in Iran. Or, Iran's leadership might use the American presence in
Iraq as an excuse to tighten its grip on power and avoid moderate reforms.
Iran would thus have to tread carefully in its relationships with Shiites in Iraq.
If it was perceived as having moved too close, that also could be a precept for
American intervention against Iran. Furthermore, it is not clear that the Shiites
in Iraq would accept heavy Iranian influence in their affairs.[61]

Iran's role in the geopolitical framework of the Middle East has also been
shaped by what appeared by 2004 to be an effort by Iran to build nuclear
weapons. There are a number of incentives for Iran to have nuclear weapons.
First, Iran might seek nuclear weapons as a deterrent against an American preemptive war. Second, Iran's other major enemy in the region is Israel, which is
estimated to have about 200 nuclear weapons. Iran might want nuclear weapons
to deter possible Israeli military action and to achieve strategic parity with
Israel. Third, Iran has a nuclear Russia to the north, nuclear Pakistan and India
to the east, and China is not far away. Should there be a coming conflict over
access to oil flows from the Persian Gulf or Caspian Sea region, nuclear
weapons would be an important asset via which Iran's role would be signifi-

cantly elevated. Fourth, Iran might want to develop nuclear capabilities to further proliferate the assets for money or to hand over weapons to terrorists. It could also be the case that Iran's nuclear program is linked to a general quest for prestige in the international community and a general sense of national pride.

The extent of Iran's nuclear capabilities is in some dispute. Americans say the evidence of nuclear activity is clear. Iran says that it is solely developing civilian energy reactors. American and Israeli intelligence services, however, estimate that Iran would not likely be able to develop a nuclear weapon before 2010. If Iran had access to a variety of external sources of nuclear technology and fuel, then its program could have developed and tested a nuclear weapon as early as 2005. The United States, Europe, and the International Atomic Energy Agency expressed concern that a facility being built at Bushehr was being used as civilian cover for a nuclear weapons program that could produce enough plutonium to make over a dozen nuclear weapons per year. Iran has not hidden its effort to mine uranium deposits in Saghand. Iran has also been constructing a uranium enrichment facility at Natanz. By 2003, Iran had as many as 160 centrifuge machines assembled, parts for another 1,000, and plans for up to 5,000. In Arak, Iran was constructing a heavy water plant that could make up for the lack of this capacity at the Bushehr plant.[62]

During the summer of 2004, the International Atomic Energy Agency found evidence of noncivilian nuclear activity at Iranian facilities. This activity included the use of a laser uranium separation process, an alternative to centrifuges; discovery of plutonium in a facility where it was not declared to be; secret purchases by Iran of advanced centrifuges out of Pakistan; development of a heavy water research reactor; the clearing of a site at Laviszan before an International Atomic Energy Agency (IAEA) inspection; and removing seals on some components which had been fixed by IAEA inspectors.[63] The IAEA reported that Iran was close to testing a facility that could convert raw uranium into weapons-grade material. Additionally, Iran apparently wanted to convert thirty-seven tons of yellow cake uranium into uranium hexaflouride. When spun into centrifuges, this material can create enriched uranium, which generates power for nuclear warheads.[64] Short of nuclear weapons, Iran was estimated to have between several hundred and 2,000 tons of nerve agents and chemicals available for delivery by artillery shells and aerial bombs. Iran has an older generation of missile technology purchased largely from North Korea during the 1980s. This program also includes components from North Korea's *No Dong* program, which could give Iran the foundations for an eventual intercontinental ballistic missile system. Iran has also developed an internal ballistic missile program to reduce its reliance on external technology. This program includes the *Shahab-3* missile, claimed by Iran to have a range of 1,000 miles—which includes all of the Persian Gulf region and Israel.[65]

Iranian acquisition of nuclear weapons would raise significant concern in Israel. In 1981, when Israel learned about Iraq's nascent nuclear program, it launched a preemptive military attack against Iraqi nuclear facilities. Israel could be tempted to eliminate or slow Iran's nuclear advances. Israel does have the capacity to carry out such a policy. Israel's total armed forces number 168,300 and 408,000 reserves. Israel has 125,000 in its army and a relatively small navy numbering 11,000 personnel including 3 submarines and 300 naval commandos. It has a likely nuclear capability of 200 warheads deliverable on *Jericho 1* and *Jericho 2* missiles which can range between 500 and 2,000 kilometers. The Israeli air force is one of the best equipped and trained in the world. It includes 35,000 troops and its pilots have an average of 180 flying hours per year for training. Israel's air force has 402 combat aircraft and 95 armed helicopters. Its air force is divided into 13 squadrons—1 (with 3 forming) with 8 F-16I (102 delivered at a rate of 2/month as of 2004), 8 with 237 F-16, 1 with 25 F-15I, 2 with 64 F-15, and 1 with 39 A-4N for lead-in fighter training.[66] Israel is capable of long-range bombing runs if planes are refueled either in air or on friendly territory. Israel's planes have a high degree of accuracy and thus could likely strike deep inside Iran with confidence of success. Israel's interests in constraining Iran are high given the end of the Saddam Hussein government in Iraq. Before the collapse of the Iraqi army, Israel's combined regular personnel and reserves faced a total of 2,128,000 troops in a variety of countries to its east. After Iraq's defeat, Israel faced a total of 1,054,000.[67]

If the United States grew concerned that Israel might act unilaterally against Iran, it is possible that Washington would step in—perhaps preferring to act rather than face the dangerous consequences of an Israeli war with its neighbors. While a U.S.-led coalition of the willing, or UN-mandated attack on Iran might be somewhat less destabilizing than an Israeli assault, the risks involved remain extremely high. Iran would likely generate a robust defense of its territory and airspace, and possibly counterattack against the locations where attacks were launched against it. Depending on the scale of the attack, Iran would likely place its forces on alert, disperse high-value assets, and implement internal security plans to prevent internal uprising. It might also retaliate by shutting down the Straits of Hormuz. Iran might seek support from other states in the region to attack U.S. assets and threaten oil shipments in the Persian Gulf or impose a general oil embargo against the United States. If attacks on nuclear facilities released radioactivity into civilian population areas, Iran would likely use that to appeal further to world public opinion. In the medium term, Iran would likely pursue a diplomatic strategy which identified it as the victim of external aggression, seeking to sway world opinion toward a position sympathetic to it. Pakistan, in particular, would likely face significant internal pressure on its leadership given its border with Iran and its own nuclear programs. Tehran might also engage in a campaign of asymmetric warfare on high-value Israeli or American targets including promoting the destabilization of Iraq. Those states in the region that aligned with the United States might be pressured by large-scale domestic unrest to distance themselves, perhaps leading to an unraveling of the Arab-Israeli peace process, and even the collapse of U.S.-friendly governments in the region, such as Egypt and Jordan.[68]

The best option for attacking Iranian facilities would be covert action carried out by Iranians perhaps with support from American special operations forces. This option would require highly precise intelligence which is not likely to be available. A direct attack option would be more likely to succeed, but would have to be dramatic in its scale and include a significant air campaign to suppress Iranian air defenses; provide combat search-and-rescue services; eliminate Iran's ability to retaliate immediately with air, missile, or naval units; and conduct follow-on strikes to ensure targets were destroyed.[69] It is possible that such an attack could prompt an uprising to overturn the Iranian government. If so, several hundred thousand external troops might be necessary to halt internal fighting and provide long-term stability. The most problematic outcome of a military option is that the opportunity for a peaceful transition away from nuclear weapons in Iran would be lost. Many Iranian reformers have worked for integration into the world community. Yet, Islamic clerics who currently dominate Iran often use the threat of outside attack as a justification for holding back reform movements and suppressing dissent. Domestic changes in the country could be the best means for prompting an internal rethinking of nuclear efforts in the broader context of a new foreign policy that prioritizes integration with the world economy.[70]

The Saudi Question

The future of Saudi Arabia raises significant questions about the overall stability of the Persian Gulf and has significant regional and global implications. With 25 percent of the world's oil reserves, Saudi Arabia plays a key role in setting global energy prices. It is also home to the holiest of Islamic sites. Challenged by instability to the north in Iraq, growing Iranian influence, and internal threats to the dynasty of the Royal Saud Family, the future of Saudi Arabia is a significant strategic question.[71] The more the Saudi royal family perceives external threats, the more they find themselves reliant on the United States for defensive needs. However, the more the Saudis align with the United States, the more internal threats to the regime arise in the form of radical Islam. Ironically, the greatest threat to the current Saudi government might actually be a successful transition toward a secular democracy in Iraq. If Iraq emerged as a model for a stable representative government, internal pressure for democratic reform could destabilize Saudi Arabia—the outcome of which would be very uncertain. Also, if Iraqi oil were to reemerge on global markets and drive down international prices, then Saudi Arabia's place of primacy in international oil would be challenged. If Iraq were to fail as a state, Saudi Arabia could be drawn into conflict inside Iraq, pitting its relatively small military up against the larger forces of Iran and possibly Syria and Turkey. Given its size and open desert geography, Saudi Arabia might also find that the fastest and cheapest form of deterrent would be to obtain nuclear weapons.

One of the greatest risks to stability in the Middle East would be a gradual failure of Saudi Arabia as a state. Internal strife or a coup by radical Islamists could produce a dramatic shift in Saudi Arabia's strategic priorities and significantly alter the regional, and even global, balance of power. The most dramatic scenario would be an abrupt revolution. However, this also appears the least probable outcome for Saudi Arabia. Despite of the death of the Saudi leader King Fahd in July 2005, there is a working combination of a strong status quo preference in the embedded leadership and ruling elites and strong international support for internal stability in Saudi Arabia.[72] Saudi Arabia could, however, atrophy in an extended and uncertain leadership transition as the older generation of the Saud family passes on, accompanied by internal and external instability, growing population needs, and declining economic conditions for average Saudi citizens.[73]

An Uncertain Future

When the United States invaded Iraq in 2003, it took a dramatic strategic gamble to transform the region. It hoped to eliminate a threat in Saddam Hussein, but there was almost certainly more to the strategy than this. Washington certainly hoped to ensure that oil flows would remain open and at stable prices. However, oil alone could not explain the policy—especially as Washington could have cut a deal with Saddam Hussein and ultimately lifted sanctions. Perhaps by removing a major threat to the east, Israel might feel more comfortable in negotiating with Palestinians for a lasting peace. Washington also appeared to hope to spread democracy through the region so as to produce governments more responsive to their people, and hopefully more amenable to American interests. Two years after the invasion, it appeared that none of these outcomes was any more likely—though very significant first steps toward elections had been accomplished in Iraq. Time—likely measured in decades—will be necessary to know if this American gamble has succeeded or not. The people of this proud and historical region are certainly as prepared for democracy, freedom, and peace as any other region of the world. The tragic irony might be that, as a general peace is in grasp, it could just as easily slip away in a spiral of instability, terrorism, and war.

EURASIA

Eurasia is a geographical term which describes the region spanning from Turkey into western China. The geopolitics of the Eurasian area reflects a nascent and shifting alliance system among states that have competing interests but that tend to reinforce a fragile status-quo.[74] It is also a region that converges on the second largest energy reserves in the world and that could provoke a new area of strategic competition among the great powers. Central Asia is rife with instability driven by weaknesses in state capacity to meet domestic challenges including transnational terrorism, ethnic strife, environmental degradation, and organized crime. The region remains heavily swayed by residual Russian influence left over from the Soviet system that dominated much of the area during the twentieth century. However, smaller former Soviet republics are exerting their independence through efforts to coordinate policy that would hedge or balance against Russian influence. Meanwhile, expanding American influence has prompted nascent great power coordination between Russia and China. All the major countries engaged in the region perceive a shared threat from radical political Islam and international terrorism, which facilitates a shared interest in stability. Thus, while the potential for great power competition exists, it is not assured.[75] The dominance of existing geopolitical trends is illustrated by the three major alignments that have emerged in early twenty-first-century central Asia: the Commonwealth of Independent States (CIS), the GUUAM group, and the Shanghai Cooperation Organization (SCO).

Russian Hegemony and Balancing: The CIS and GUUAM

The CIS is a residual structural legacy of the Soviet Union. Established through the Minsk Treaty of 1991, the CIS emerged as a loose confederation of twelve countries seeking to harmonize various economic and, to a much lesser extent, post-Soviet policies. In 1993, Russia completed a military doctrine defining the frontiers of the former Soviet Union as the strategic frontiers of Russia. In 1995, a presidential statement identified Moscow's goals in the CIS as making the region an exclusive area of Russian influence, minimizing the expansion of external presence and influence on CIS territory, facilitating regional crisis management, and protecting Russians living outside Russia within the CIS.[76] For non-Russian members, support for the CIS has varied

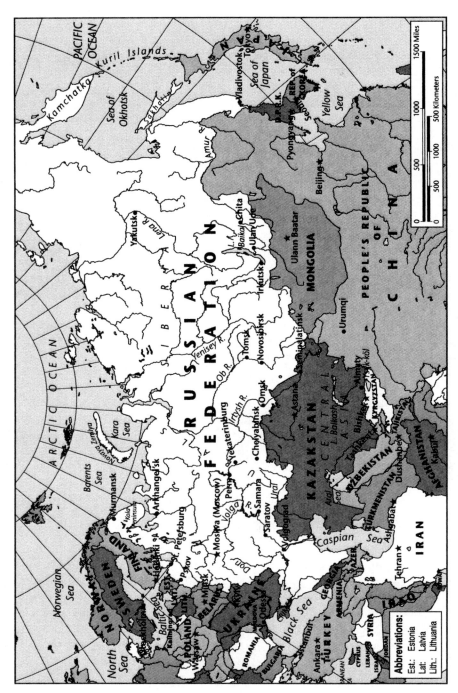

Eurasia

from the enthusiastic embrace of Belarus to the reluctant compliance of Ukraine. In the absence of significant Western assistance, weak states like Ukraine have often been left with little choice but to maintain their deep economic dependence on Russia—which Moscow has used to leverage power within the CIS.

Russia's exercise of power in the CIS is primarily economic and is done through the residual personnel and economic networks of the Soviet era. Power is often exerted through fuel and energy policy which Moscow can turn on and shut off depending on how cooperative CIS members might be. To pressure Georgia into allowing a continued presence of Russian military bases on its territory, Moscow periodically shuts off the flow of natural gas. When Georgia refused to allow Russia to enter the Pankisi Gorge area on the border with Russia's breakaway republic of Chechnya, Moscow retaliated by introducing visa restrictions on Georgian citizens in Russia and halting gas flows until past debts were repaid. Russia has also used the flow of energy supplies as a means of pressuring Ukraine and Moldovà to make payments on debts owed to Moscow.[77]

Russia has sought to develop within the CIS a customs union, economic integration, converging standards of international economic legislation, a payments union, integration of production in science and technology (and the defense industry), common legal conditions, and a common capital market.[78] Russia has sought to destabilize uncooperative CIS states via a range of intelligence activities, blackmail, coercion, subversion of problematic political leadership, and support to violent groups amenable to Russian influence.[79] Russia's overall military power in the region is, however, in significant decline. By 2006, Russia maintained 7,800 troops in Tajikistan (in high combat readiness status), 3,500 troops in Armenia, 3,000 in Georgia, 1,400 in Moldova, and 1,100 in Ukraine.[80] From a base in Tajikistan, Moscow has organized joint exercises with central Asian armies and supplied arms and equipment to Kazakhstan, Kyrgyzstan, and Tajikistan, which Russia sees as important allies. However, Russia has declining capacity to project military power within the CIS area. Russia hopes to develop a 50,000-member rapid deployment corps at the Russia-Kazakhstan border, but whether it can fund and sustain readiness is doubtful. Airlift capabilities are severely limited and what remains from Russia's air capacity are mostly medium-range bombers and operational-tactical missiles.[81] In a worst case, Russia might, given its conventional military weakness, have to rely on tactical nuclear weapons to deter attacks on forward deployed troops.

While Russia's overall military influence in the CIS area is declining, most remaining states continue to lean toward Russia to meet their security concerns. The trade-off for Russian influence is the provision of some degree of stability. This is especially the case for states like Tajikistan, which have post-communist leaders drawing from their Soviet background to gain economic benefits they can then distribute within their own political patronage systems. Even non-CIS states have moved closer toward Russia to enhance their own relative interests. For example, in June 2001, Turkey completed a deal to build the Blue Stream natural gas pipeline with Russia. This pipeline would increase its dependence on Russian natural gas from 66 to 80 percent (Turkey imports 98 percent of its energy needs). This deal was completed over strong objections from Turkey's main ally, the United States.[82] Nonetheless, Russians do not always perceive real gains from dominating the CIS states, which are all weak and dependent on Moscow. For example, to promote integration, Russia has often discounted energy prices to its CIS partners. Seeming to prefer the relative simplicity of bilateral ties, Russian President Vladimir Putin often prioritized Russia's individual relationships with CIS members.

To make Russia's hegemonic goals more receptive within the CIS, Moscow presents its efforts as a cooperative approach to regional security. In 1992, Russia negotiated a "Collective Security Treaty" with most of the CIS members. While little substantive follow-on effort emerged, in 1999 the CIS did develop a Joint Air Defense System based in Moscow and headed by the Russian Air Defense Forces Command. This move largely institutionalized what already existed in the previous Soviet air defense system that covered Russia, Belarus, Azerbaijan, Armenia, Kazakhstan, Kyrgyzstan, Tajikistan, and Uzbekistan. CIS security functions received additional bolstering when an agreement was reached to create a joint rapid reaction force consisting of troops from Russia, Kazakhstan, Kyrgyzstan, and Tajikistan to respond to regional crises and to fortify porous border areas against terrorist incursions. Russia has pushed for the CIS to expand its military role, and also to facilitate the transfer of military equipment and technology and to limit the influence of alternative arms marketers, particularly the United States. In May 2001, the participating CIS members completed planning for a CIS rapid deployment force. Each participant contributes at least one battalion to this force. It includes a 3,000-member contingent for central Asia with contributions from Kazakhstan, Kyrgyzstan, and Tajikistan, and elements of the remaining Russian 201st division deployed for peacekeeping purposes in Tajikistan. A separate arrangement includes Russian and Armenian forces totaling 1,500 for crisis management operations in the Caucuses region.

The mandate of the emerging CIS military capacity stresses broader geostrategic objectives, declaring that: "We, the leaders of the states participating in the Collective Security Treaty, state our strong resolution to promote the formation of a multipolar, fair, and democratic world order based on respect for the United Nations Charter and the norms of international law."[83] For Russia, the CIS was thus also a means of signaling its security interests to the United States and its worries about the expanded influence of the United States in Eastern Europe and areas of the former Soviet Union. The culminating effect of the CIS has been to allow Moscow to extend a defense perimeter away from its borders via air defense, border guards, and the possible development of small-scale rapid deployment forces. The CIS has not emerged to balance the expanded NATO alliance toward its west as some opponents of NATO enlargement predicted. Rather, the CIS has been a vehicle through which Russia maintains its primacy in the area of the former Soviet Union.

The most significant attempt at regional balancing is the GUUAM grouping of Georgia, Ukraine, Uzbekistan (which suspended its membership in 2002), Azerbaijan, and Moldova. The GUUAM members described their alignment as a "strategic alliance designed to strengthen the independence and sovereignty of these former Soviet republics."[84] The GUUAM is significant as the only security institution in the former Soviet space that does not include Russia. Western officials generally view GUUAM as an anti-Russia alliance. This perspective is also shared in Moscow, which watched cooperation in GUUAM accelerate during the 1999 NATO war in Kosovo during side-meetings held at NATO's fiftieth anniversary summit in Washington, D.C. The GUUAM alliance began informal consultations and produced joint declarations beginning at the Conventional Forces in Europe review conference held in 1996. The status of GUUAM was formalized as a cooperative structure at the 1997 summit of the Council of Europe meeting in Strasbourg.[85] The central organizing elements of GUUAM include promotion of political interaction, the avoidance of separatism, peaceful resolution of conflicts, peacekeeping activities, and the development of a Eurasian-Transcaucasian transport corridor. Strategically, GUUAM members signaled their intent to hedge against Russian power through their integration into Euro-Atlantic and European structures of security and cooperation, including "the development of a special relationship and dialogue with NATO."[86] The fluctuating level of member interest in GUUAM prevents it from becoming much more than a loose affiliation of states. Both Moldova and Uzbekistan engaged inconsistently, with Uzbekistan suspending its membership in 2002.

Great Power Alignments: The Shanghai Cooperation Organization

In June 2001, the leaders of China, Russia, Kazakhstan, Kyrgyzstan, and Tajikstan transformed an informal grouping established in 1996 and known as the "Shanghai Five" into a formal international institution, the "Shanghai Cooperation Organization," and was expanded to include Uzbekistan. Its official objectives are to promote trust, stability, and mutual understanding between members, including confidence-building in the military sphere and mutual reductions of armed forces in border areas.[87] The SCO is a potential balancing mechanism that could be used by China and Russia to frustrate American global dominance. The founding document specifies promoting multipolarity as a core institutional objective. Both China and Russia use the advancement of multipolar international relations to balance American power. This objective is reinforced by the specific requirement that each state accept the primacy of the UN, with respect for sovereignty, and noninterference in the domestic affairs of states. While specifying that the organization is not directed against any other states, there are important elements of geopolitical alignment in the SCO. For example, to bolster Russian and Chinese efforts to frustrate U.S. plans for national missile defense, SCO members agreed to preserve the global strategic balance. The members stated that they all saw the 1972 Anti-Ballistic Missile Treaty as crucial to that objective.[88] The orientation of the SCO to this global balancing goal, even with a combined Russian-Chinese position, had little impact as the United States began deployment of a missile shield in 2004. The balancing potential of the SCO can thus be overstated.

Among the participants, Russia had serious misgivings about including Uzbekistan in the group, largely because of its strident commitment to complete independence from Moscow. Russia's interest in the SCO may also be as much guided by a desire to constrain the growth of China's influence in the region as to hedge against American power. Russian-Chinese accommodation must also be viewed in the light of their history of deep tensions and rivalry for influence in northeast Asia. Also complicating the SCO's balancing functions is its members' shared interest with the United States in combating the spread of radical political Islam and international terrorism. The SCO agreed to create an antiterrorist center in Bishkek, Kyrgyzstan, and a 2,000-soldier unit of Russian, Kazakh, Kyrgyz, and Tajik troops was to be organized. Thus the SCO is as likely to move closer to common American interests as it is to balance American power. This trend-line is true for Russia, which has suffered a steady campaign of separatist-oriented terrorism, and China, which has a significant ethnic separatist movement in its northwest Xinjiang province. China asserts that Islamic groups in Xinjiang were supplied by money, arms, and leadership by the al Qaeda terrorist organization and that as many as 1,000 Chinese Muslims may have trained in terrorist camps in Afghanistan.[89] Uzbekistan also has had to combat a significant al Qaeda–affiliated terrorist threat in the Islamic Movement of Uzbekistan (IMU).

Given the proximity of the SCO states to Afghanistan and other areas of terrorist basing, the SCO could even complement American strategic interests as the SCO pursues its own campaign against terrorism. Conversely, the SCO could be used by Russia and China to ensure that the United States does not gain a permanent strategic foothold in Eurasia justified by its counterterrorism efforts. By further institutionalizing the SCO in the area of counterterrorism,

Russia and China would advance their goals of limiting American influence in Eurasia and simultaneously justify efforts to secure their own state authority in Chechnya and Xinjiang. In early 2002, the SCO issued a joint statement declaring that regional and subregional structures were best suited to fighting terrorism, and implied that the threat of international terrorism provided a rationale to deepen SCO cooperation. However, for medium and smaller regional powers, the increased American presence in central Asia—especially support for Uzbekistan, which jealously covets its independence from Russia—might make the SCO less attractive if their security concerns can be more immediately met through cooperation with the United States.

Beyond the Status Quo?

Generally, the status quo in central Asia favors stability, rather than a major confrontation. There is no single power that has the capacity to dominate the region. Current alignments work in concert to hedge against any one country dramatically overturning the existing status quo. Shared common interests in constraining radical political Islam and combating international terrorism favors cooperation rather than competition among the great powers. It is, however, possible that major shifts in energy demand or stoppage of oil flows from the Persian Gulf could create incentives for states to assert their interests in natural resources around the Caspian Sea. A central question for the region will be the extent to which the United States deepens its engagement with Georgia, Uzbekistan, Tajikistan, and Afghanistan. A dramatic heightening of American power in the region could serve to strengthen Russian and Chinese cooperation. Nonetheless, this possibility was put into question both by the overstretch of U.S. forces into Iraq as well as Uzbekistan's decision in July 2005 to not renew American rights to base troops on its territory. Alternatively, a dramatic increase in China's power could move Russia closer to the United States. In an important way, the ability to play this pivot role between the United States and China also gives Russia important leverage through which it can gradually build its own gains in the region over time.

SUMMARY

A close look at these major regional flashpoints illustrates the role that power can play in both conflict and peace. The flashpoints of the twenty-first century are complex regional affairs. Moreover, each of them could have dramatic global consequences. A major dilemma that emerges from these potential crises is that the United States plays a key role in all of these areas. Yet, the

United States cannot be everywhere at once. Thus a central strategic dilemma is the question of whether or not the United States can sustain this level of global engagement. And, if the United States had to choose regional priorities, what would they be? To be certain, none of these flashpoint crises are inevitable and in some cases might even be improbable. They are less likely to become true catastrophes if the risks involved are well understood and creative solutions to them generated.

NOTES

1. International Institute for Strategic Studies, *The Military Balance: 2005–2006* (Oxford: Oxford University Press, 2005), 236–40.

2. International Institute for Strategic Studies, *Military Balance: 2005–2006*, 244–46.

3. Details on nuclear capabilities comes from Michael Quinlan, "How Robust Is India-Pakistan Deterrence?" *Survival* 42, no. 4 (Winter 2000/2001): 145.

4. Quinlan, "How Robust Is India-Pakistan Deterrence?" 147.

5. These war games were reported and summarized by Thomas E. Ricks, "India-Pakistan Nuclear Rivalry," *The Wall Street Journal*, June 24, 1998.

6. International Institute of Strategic Studies, *Strategic Survey: 2003–2004* (Oxford: Oxford University Press, 2004), 233.

7. Alexander Evans, "India, Pakistan, and the Prospect of War," *Current History* 100, no. 645 (April 2002): 160–65.

8. International Institute for Strategic Studies, *Strategic Survey: 2003–2004*, 233–35.

9. The Natural Resources Defense Council, "The Consequences of Nuclear Conflict between India and Pakistan," at www.nrdc.org/nuclear/southasia.asp (accessed Summer 2004).

10. Nuclear Threat Initiative, "The Global Threat," at www.nti.org/e_research//cnwm/threat/global.asp (accessed Summer 2004).

11. "Country Profile: North Korea," *BBC News*. Updated September 30, 2005.

12. Gen. Thomas A. Schwartz, Commander, UNC/CFC/USFK, testimony before the Senate Armed Services Committee, March 5, 2002.

13. United States Department of Defense, *2000 Report to Congress: Military Situation on the Korean Peninsula* (Washington, D.C.: U.S. Department of Defense, 2000), 4.

14. Jonathan Pollack and Chung Min Lee, *Preparing for Korean Unification: Scenarios and Implications* (Santa Monica, Calif.: Rand Corporation, 1999), 67–68.

15. International Institute for Strategic Studies, *Military Balance: 2005–2006*, 282–84.

16. International Institute for Strategic Studies, *Military Balance: 2005–2006*, 284–87.

17. United States Department of Defense, *2000 Report to Congress*, 2.

18. Barton Gellman, "Pentagon War Scenario Spotlights Russia," *Washington Post*, February 20, 1992.

19. Bernard Trainor, "Worst Case Scenario: Suppose North Korea Starts a War," *Boston Globe*, May 24, 1997.

20. United States Department of Defense, *2000 Report to Congress*, 5.

21. United States Department of Defense, *2000 Report to Congress*, 6.

22. Donald MacIntyre, "Kim's War Machine," *Time Asia* 161, no. 7 (February 24, 2003).

23. Andrew Demaria, "North Korea: The Cost of Conflict," *CNN*, January 21, 2003.

24. Hans M. Kristensen, "Preemptive Posturing," *Bulletin of the Atomic Scientists* 58, no. 5 (September/October 2002): 54–59.

25. International Institute of Strategic Studies, *North Korea's Weapons Programmes: A Net Assessment* (Oxford: Oxford University Press, 2004).

26. Bruce B. Auster and Kevin Whitelaw, "Pentagon Comes Up with a Provocative Plan to Face Down North Korea," *U.S. News and World Report*, July 21, 2003, 21.

27. Richard C. Bush, Sharon Yanagi, and Kevin Scott, eds., *Brookings Northeast Asia Survey: 2003–2004* (Washington, D.C.: Brookings, 2003), ix.

28. Phillip C. Saunders and Danial A. Pinkston, "Seeing North Korea Clearly," *Survival* 45, no. 3 (Autumn 2003): 79–102.

29. Chris Rahman, "Defending Taiwan, and Why It Matters," *Naval War College Review* 54, no. 4 (Autumn 2001): 71–74.

30. International Institute for Strategic Studies, *Military Balance: 2005–2006*, 298–300.

31. Thom Shanker, "U.S. Says China Is Stepping Up Short-Range Missile Production," *New York Times*, July 31, 2003.

32. Tim Luard, "Military Balance Goes Against Taiwan," *BBC News*, March 9, 2004.

33. Benjamin Kang Lim, "Taiwan Sees Military Balance Tipping to China by Next Year," *Reuters*, January 11, 2003.

34. Ching Cheong, "China-Taiwan War Unlikely before 2010, Says US Report," *Straits Times*, June 7, 2004; and United States Department of Defense, *2004 Report to Congress*.

35. Richard L. Russell, "What If . . . 'China Attacks Taiwan!'" *Parameters* 31, no. 3 (Autumn 2001): 76–91.

36. Wendell Minnick, "The Year to Fear for Taiwan: 2006," *Asia Times*, April 10, 2004.

37. Michael O'Hanlon, "Can China Conquer Taiwan?" *International Security* 25, no. 2 (Fall 2000): 51–86.

38. "Taiwan Stages War Games as Report Shows China Would Win in Six Days," *Agence France Presse*, August 12, 2004.

39. "Taiwan Could Fend Off China Attack for 2 Weeks," *Reuters*, August 12, 2004.

40. John M. Glionna, "China, U.S. Each Hold Major War Exercises," *Los Angeles Times*, July 20, 2004.

41. Michael D. Swaine, "Deterring Conflict in the Taiwan Strait: The Successes and Failures of Taiwan's Defense Reform and Modernization Program," *Carnegie Papers*, no. 46 (July 2004).

42. Randall Schriver, Deputy Assistant Secretary of State for East Asian and Pacific Affairs, remarks to U.S.-Taiwan Business Council Defense Industry Conference, February 14, 2003.

43. Richard L. Russell, "What if . . . 'China Attacks Taiwan!'" 76–91.

44. Chris Hogg, "Storm across the Taiwan Strait," *BBC News*, June 22, 2004.

45. "Taiwan Needs Nuclear Deterrent," *Taiwan Times*, August 13, 2004.

46. David Albright and Corey Gay, "Taiwan: Nuclear Nightmare Averted," *Bulletin of the Atomic Scientists* 54: no. 1 (January/February 1998): 54–61.

47. Swaine, "Deterring Conflict in the Taiwan Strait," 21.

48. "Poll: Taiwanese Do Not Expect War with China Soon," *Associated Press* (July 22, 2004).

49. ROC Ministry of National Defense, *2002 National Defense Report, Republic of China* (Taipai, Taiwan: Ministry of National Defense, 2002.

50. See Graham E. Fuller, "Islamists in the Arab World: The Dance around Democracy," *Carnegie Papers,* no. 49 (September 2004): 1–15.

51. International Institute of Strategic Studies, *Military Balance: 2003–2004* (Oxford: Oxford University Press, 2003), 26–27; and International Institute of Strategic Studies, *Military Balance: 2005–2006*, 31–35.

52. International Institute of Strategic Studies, *Military Balance: 2003–2004*, 26–27.

53. Judith Yaphe, "Turbulent Transition in Iraq: Can It Succeed?" *INSS Strategic Forum*, no. 208 (June 2004): 5.

54. Nadia Abou El-Magd, "Insurgency Slowing Iraq Reconstruction," *Associated Press*, October 13, 2004.

55. Vali Nasr, "Regional Implications of Shi'a Revival in Iraq," *Washington Quarterly* 27, no. 3 (Summer 2004): 7–24.

56. Yaphe, "Turbulent Transition in Iraq," 2.

57. Michael E. O'Hanlon and Adriana Lins de Albuquerque, "Iraq—By the Numbers," *Los Angeles Times*, September 3, 2004, and U.S. Department of Defense.

58. International Institute for Strategic Studies, *Military Balance: 2005–2006*, 188–91.

59. Institute for National Strategic Studies, *Strategic Assessment 1997* (Washington, D.C.: National Defense University Press, 1997), 83.

60. *Yas-e Now*, June 22, 2003. Referenced by Patrick Clawson, "Reading the Popular Mood in Iran," Washington Institute for Near East Policy, *Policy Watch*, no. 770, July 7, 2003.

61. Anoushiravan Ehteshami, "Iran-Iraq Relations after Saddam," *Washington Quarterly* 25, no. 4 (Autumn 2003): 124–25.

62. International Institute for Strategic Studies, *Military Balance: 2003–2004*, 102–3.

63. Paul Reynolds, "Iran: The Next Crisis?" *BBC News*, July 27, 2004.

64. "Iran Plans to Convert Uranium," *BBC News*, September 1, 2004.

65. Federation of American Scientists, "Iran: Weapons Systems Purchased by Iran," at www.fas.org (accessed Summer 2004).

66. International Institute for Strategic Studies, *Military Balance: 2004–2005*, 126–27; and International Institute for Strategic Studies, *Military Balance: 2005–2006*, 192–94.

67. Gal Luft, "All Quiet on the Eastern Front?: Israel's National Security Doctrine after the Fall of Saddam," *Analysis Paper*, no. 2 (March 2004): 15.

68. Jeffrey White, "Iranian Nuclear Weapons, Part III: How Might Iran Retaliate?" *Policywatch*, no. 762 (May 29, 2003): 1–3.

69. White, "Iranian Nuclear Weapons," 1–3.

70. Shahram Chubin and Robert S. Litwak, "Debating Iran's Nuclear Aspirations," *Washington Quarterly*, 26, no. 4 (Autumn 2003): 99–114.

71. J. E. Peterson, "Saudi Arabia and the Illusion of Security," *Adelphi Paper*, no. 348 (2002).

72. G. Gregoary Gause III and Jill Crystal, "The Arab Gulf: Will Autocracy Define the Social Contract in 2015?" in *The Middle East in 2015: The Impact of Regional Trends on U.S. Strategic Planning*, ed. Judith Yaphe (Washington, D.C.: National Defense University, 2002), 175.

73. Michael Knights, "Saudi Arabia Faces Long-Term Insecurity," *Jane's Intelligence Review* (July 2004): 20–22.

74. Sean Kay, "Geopolitical Constraints and Institutional Innovation: The Dynamics of Multilateralism in Eurasia," in *Limiting Institutions: The Challenge of Eurasian Security Governance*, ed. James Sperling, Sean Kay, and S. Victor Papacosma (Manchester: Manchester University Press, 2003), 125–43.

75. Richard Sokolsky and Tanya Charlick-Paley, *NATO and Caspian Security: A Mission Too Far?* (Santa Monica, Calif.: Rand Corporation, 1999), 13–21.

76. "Strategic Policy toward CIS Published," *Foreign Broadcast Information Service Daily Report: Central Asia SOV-95* (September 28, 1995): 19–20.

77. International Institute of Strategic Studies, *Strategic Survey 2000–2001* (Oxford: Oxford University Press, 2001), 19–20.

78. "Strategic Policy toward CIS Published," 19–20.

79. Stephen J. Blank, *Energy, Economics, and Security in Central Asia: Russia and Its Rivals* (Carlisle Barracks, Pa.: US Army War College, 1995).

80. International Institute of Strategic Studies, *Military Balance: 2005–2006*, 166–68.

81. Dmitri Trenin, "Central Asia's Stability and Russia's Security," *PONARS*, no. 168 (November 2000).

82. Douglas Frantz, "Russia's New Reach: Gas Pipeline to Turkey," *New York Times* (June 6, 2001).

83. Haroutiun Khachatrian, "Creation of Rapid Deployment Force Marks Potential Watershed in Collective Security Development," *Eurasia Insight* (July 2, 2001).

84. "The GUUAM Group: History and Principles: Briefing Paper," November 2000 at www.guuam.org/general/browse.html (accessed Spring 2001).

85. Uzbekistan joined in 1999, at which time the name was formerly expanded from GUAM to GUUAM.

86. Anatol Lieven, "GUUAM: What Is It, and What Is It For?" *Eurasian Insight* (December 18, 2000).

87. "Joint Statement by the Heads of State of the Republic of Kazakhstan, the People's Republic of China, the Kyrgyz Republic, the Russian Federation, the Republic of Tajikistan, and the Republic of Uzbekistan."

88. "Central Asia Bloc United Against Missile Shield," CNN, June 15, 2001.

89. Philip P. Pan, "China Links Bin Laden to Separatists," *Washington Post*, January 22, 2002.

SUGGESTED READING

Victor D. Cha and David C. Kang, *Nuclear North Korea: A Debate on Engagement Strategies* (New York: Columbia University Press, 2003).

Robert E. Ebel and Rajon Menon, eds., *Energy and Conflict in Central Asia and the Caucuses* (Lanham, Md.: Rowman and Littlefield, 2000).

Michael O'Hanlon and Mike M. Mochizuki, *Crisis on the Korean Peninsula: How to Deal with a Nuclear Armed North Korea* (New York: McGraw-Hill, 2003).

Kenneth Pollack, *The Persian Puzzle: The Conflict Between Iran and America* (New York: Random House, 2004).

Victoria Schofield, *Kashmir in Conflict: India, Pakistan, and the Unending War* (London: I. B. Taurus, 2002).

David Shlapak, David T. Orletsky, and Barry A. Wilson, *Dire Strait: Military Aspects of the China-Taiwan Confrontation and Options for U.S. Policy* (Santa Monica, Calif.: Rand Corporation, 2000).

James Sperling, Sean Kay, and S. Victor Papacosma, eds., *Limiting Institutions: Security Governance in Eurasia* (Manchester: Manchester University Press, 2003).

J. J. Suh, Peter J. Katzenstein, and Allen Carlson, eds., *Rethinking Security in East Asia: Identity, Power and Efficiency* (Stanford: Stanford University Press, 2004).

Nancy Bernkoph Tucker, *Dangerous Strait: The U.S.-Taiwan-China Crisis* (New York: Columbia University Press, 2005).

Judith Yaphe, ed., *The Middle East in 2015: The Impact of Regional Trends on U.S. Strategic Planning* (Washington, D.C.: National Defense University Press, 2002).

Chapter Six

Technology and the Business of Security

Astronaut Dale A. Gardner, on an extravehicular mission, holds up a "For Sale" sign referring to the two satellites, *Palap B-2* and *Westar 6*, which they retrieved from orbit after their Payload Assist Modules failed to fire. *Source*: NASA.

Technological advancements can be central to the development of strategy and tactics. For example, in World War II, it took the United States 9,000 bombs, weighing 2,000 pounds each, dropped by 1,500 B-17 aircraft to destroy a 500 × 1,000 foot target. By 1970, it took 176 bombs to do this—flown by 88 F-4 aircraft missions. In the 1991 Persian Gulf War, the same outcome could be achieved with one or two laser-guided bombs launched by just one F-117 aircraft.[1] The networks of globalization allow for the proliferation of entirely new concepts of technology, which can radically shape the dimensions of battle. These networks have, in effect, become part of the modern battlefield—or, more appropriately, battlespace. This chapter examines the relationship between technology, trade, and modern security challenges by surveying the revolution in military affairs, the relationship between information and security, and the military use of space. It then examines how the business of technology and trade relationships affect the supply and demand of weapons proliferation, the role of transnational networks in organized crime and proliferation, the privatization of security, and the security impact of international economic sanctions.

REVOLUTION IN MILITARY AFFAIRS

A revolution in military affairs (RMA) occurs when the combination of technological advances with economic transformation brings about dramatic innovative changes in weapons, tactics, and strategies.[2] There have been at least a dozen revolutionary changes in military capability including the chariot, iron age infantry, Macedonian, stirrup, artillery/gunpowder, Napoleonic, railroad, rifle, telegraph, dreadnought and submarine, air superiority and armored warfare, naval airpower, and nuclear weapons.[3] The twentieth century witnessed dramatic changes in the role of military technology. By the end of World War I, for example, the tank emerged as a new means of combat and was applied heavily in World War II. Yet the tank was of little use to American fighters in the jungles of Vietnam. The nuclear revolution illustrates the enormous strategic implications some technologies can have. The contemporary evolution of technology focuses primarily on the combination of existing tactics integrated into multiple systems utilizing advanced technology to guide precision weapons and to engage in new dimensions of warfare. Information warfare, cyberwar, advanced psychological operations, electronic warfare, biometrics, robotics, and integrated intelligence systems reflect a few of the emerging tools of modern warfare. In some areas, the impact of these changes could be so dramatic as to fundamentally alter core concepts of warfare.

The Limits of Technology in War

The modern revolution in military affairs creates several new dynamics in warfighting for those states that possess the capacity. By integrating information with weaponry, a state with advanced technology can attain dominant situational awareness in a battlefield. Possessing advanced technology, however, does not guarantee success unless it is coupled with advancements in strategic doctrine. In the 1973 Yom Kippur war, Israel emerged victorious—but not because of its significant technological superiority. Israel had surveillance technology which showed that Egypt was massing artillery, tanks, and bridging equipment. However, the Israeli military rejected this information, refusing to believe that Egypt would attack. Even when Egyptian commanders' discussion of invasion plans on open communication channels was intercepted by Israel, it was ignored. Israel had modernized its technological capacity, but not its doctrine. It won the war because of the quality of its military leadership, troops, and national spirit—not technology.[4] Faulty information in 1993 led the United States to bomb, with great precision, a meeting of Somali warlords that it thought was plotting attacks on United Nations peacekeepers in Mogadishu. Actually, it was a gathering of moderate local political leaders planning possible negotiating strategies. This attack stigmatized much of the local population against the United States. In the 1999 Kosovo war, bad information led to an inadvertent targeting of the Chinese Embassy in Belgrade by the United States, killing a number of Chinese and severely damaging the embassy building.

In 2003, the United States and Britain went to war against Iraq on the premise that they had intelligence that Iraq was developing weapons of mass destruction. The U.S. National Security Agency intercepted conversations over e-mail, telephone calls, and military communications, and presented them as proof of illegal weapons. However, they were not actually able to tell who was talking to whom, or about what. Information that had not been confirmed was included in a formal presentation by U.S. Secretary of State Colin Powell at the United Nations. Satellite imagery presented by the U.S. intelligence community showing trucks which were "signature" evidence of nearby chemical weapons use, turned out to be water tankers or fire trucks.[5] After the Iraq war, an inquiry into Britain's use of intelligence showed that (among other problems) (1) there was significant doubt about a "high proportion" of human intelligence sources and the information they gave which was passed on to decision-makers; (2) sources were not adequately double-checked; (3) third-hand information regarding chemical and biological weapons programs was relied on; and (4) information from another country's intelligence agency on Iraqi biological and chemical agents was "seriously flawed." A claim by the British government that Iraq could use weapons of mass destruction within forty-five minutes was based on dubious intelligence.[6]

Despite enormous technological advances, the United States did not have accurate situational awareness before the Iraq invasion in 2003. There was actually abundant public information countering the claims of the United States and Britain regarding Iraq. The information needed to determine that Iraq had no weapons of mass destruction had been largely revealed by UN weapons inspectors and in public media reporting.[7] During the war, poor human intelligence illustrated the limits of technological advantage. The United States launched about fifty air strikes against high-value Iraqi leaders with precision-guided munitions. None of these attacks hit their target, in spite of what was thought at the time to be solid intelligence. Information provided by satellite telephone from an Iraqi source reported that Saddam Hussein was hiding in a bunker at a compound south of Baghdad. This report prompted an acceleration of warfighting with the hope that the leadership could be "decapitated" and thus lead to quick victory. After the war, it was discovered that no such bunker existed.[8] Throughout the war, frontline American troops lacked access to surveillance and intelligence data due to computer failures. In one case, a Lt. Colonel was told to expect one Iraqi brigade advancing south from Baghdad, but instead encountered three separate brigades advancing from three different directions. This was the most significant Iraqi counterattack during the war. While the battle was won by the United States, it did so because of greater firepower, not advanced technology. Often, U.S. troops suffered from a "digital divide," which allowed division commanders to have a good sense of the battlefield but left frontline commanders blind. Basic problems including lengthy computer download times, software failures, and a lack of access to high bandwidth communications were common. In several circumstances, American troops were attacked by Iraqis when they stopped moving to download computer data on enemy locations.[9]

Despite such limitations, advances in information technology are also a significant strategic asset. The contemporary information revolution creates conditions in which the modern military can achieve close to total battlefield situational awareness. The integration of satellite technology with soldiers on the ground can provide information in almost real time to command and control centers. This capacity can help with targeting as well as post-battle damage assessment. Technologically advanced militaries can achieve an integrated analysis of air, land, subterranean, and above- and underwater areas. Thermal imaging and pinpoint satellite technology as well as audio sensors can gain a full spectrum of information about an enemy. Advanced radar imaging and night-vision capability allows an advanced military to do most of its fighting at night. A political decision to employ technology is also often necessary. During the 1994 Rwandan genocide, the United States considered electronic jamming of radio programming that was promulgating the mass murder of civilian populations. Washington decided that it would not take this action because it would have violated international radio broadcasting agreements.

Battlefield awareness can give an attacker significant tactical advantages. For example, the ability to deploy a Tactical Internet system can give a force real-time communications interlinked with command-and-control authorities. A Tactical Internet is an integrated system of computers, radios, satellite terminals, switches, and software, which constantly passes information both horizontally and vertically, automatically and on-demand, throughout a military force.[10] In the United States military, this force integration is able to clarify to units exactly where their friendly allies are in the battlefield while identifying enemy locations through Unmanned Aerial Vehicles and integrated surveillance. These integrated systems can pinpoint, with precision, an accurate and evolving update of a battlefield.[11] The American "Land Warrior" system makes a single troop part of an integrated digital battlefield via a helmet eyepiece that folds down, presents a computer screen with display or sighting from a camera on the soldier's rifle. The Land Warrior then wears a personal computer and two radio systems with a ballistic protection vest that has a folding handgrip that serves as a computer mouse.[12] Applications of technological development for warfighting are both accelerating and radical in their potential implications.

From Science Fiction to Modern War

Scientific and technological advances in fields usually not associated with warfare, such as biology and genomics, increasingly have applications for modern conflict. Biological entities are being found to have military applications as scientists have researched the use of insects, shellfish, bacteria, and weeds to act as "bio-sentinels" which would warn of biological or chemical attacks including heat-sensing beetles and bees that can smell explosives such as TNT and Semtex.[13] In the Persian Gulf, the United States has deployed a team called "Mark 6"—a group of dolphins used to detect, locate, and mark a threat to a swimmer or diver such as underwater mines. Protein-based bacteriorhodopsin is a biological material which undergoes shape changes when exposed to light. Each of these changes has unique spectral properties that might be used in an electronic device. Protein-based electronics could produce three-dimensional memory devices. With this technology, every soldier in a unit could be provided with a wearable computer system. Such a system would store 7 to 10 gigabytes of digital data in a $1 \times 1 \times 3$ centimeter polymer vial and withstand virtually any environmental setting. Another application might include a protein-based photovoltaic converter that could coat a soldier's helmet and generate energy to run a laptop computer in the field. Other future applications of biology currently envisioned by American military planners include engineered bone and accelerated wound-healing. Integrating the biological foundations of organisms such as abalone could, conceivably, lead to materials that are impact resistant for armor. Some bird feathers and fruits have foundations that could be integrated into military clothing and enhance concealment. Biosensors, perhaps based on a wristwatch, might help identify when a soldier has been exposed to a biological or chemical attack, as well as give information about how well a particular soldier might withstand a particular climate or environmental setting, such as altitude.[14]

Technology also has the capacity to mimic or go beyond biology via the emerging science of nanotechnology. Small, minute airborne platforms could, for example, mimic the swarming behavior of insects, having a dramatic impact against an enemy troop concentration or civilian population that lacked countermeasures. Nanotechnology would, if functional, create machines smaller than the microscopic level and produce technology that is fifty billionths of a meter. This would be done by combining individual atoms and molecules into the smallest of mechanical, electrical, and biological machines. Advanced states are investing heavily in nanotechnology research with investments estimated to exceed $1 trillion a year by 2015.[15] Envisioned nanotechnology applications include molecular-sized robots that could repair individual human cells.

Already, in late 2004, Japanese scientists successfully conducted a surgical operation on a single living cell using a "nano-needle" 200–300 nanometers in diameter. This procedure included successful insertion of the needle into the cell's nucleus.[16] Supercomputers could be made so small that they could not be seen even by a powerful microscope. Nanodetectors could be used to identify airborne biological phenomenon such as viruses or noxious chemicals. In theory, billions of nanotechnology-based sensors could be deployed to revolutionize the notion of intelligence. Multidimensional information dominance would be radically enhanced. Via nanotechnology, virtual reality systems might emerge that revolutionize training simulations. Weapons proliferation might be better monitored by nanotechnology sensor nets. Such sensors might also function in missile defense systems.[17] In 2004, *Dust Networks Inc.* concluded a contract with *Science Applications International Corp.* to deliver "smart dust sensors" for perimeter security systems using tiny battery-powered, wireless sensors. These sensors can integrate information to track surrounding conditions and transmit them to a device, which then assembles important data via the Internet. Such sensors can take pictures or serve as a thermometer while some can detect whether an individual is carrying a gun or whether a tank is nearby.[18]

Automation and advanced robotics are already widely available—for example, for diffusing bombs, clearing minefields, or via unmanned airplanes—which allows for combat or activity in dangerous situations without placing troops in harm's way. In Iraq, the United States introduced a robotic airplane called the *ScanEagle*, which carried out more than 1,000 hours of intelligence and reconnaissance work for the Marines in 2003 and 2004. The plane is four feet long with a ten-foot wingspan and flies for up to fifteen hours at a time on just two gallons of fuel. Its surveillance capacity allows it to send to U.S. troops real-time video images with detail such as the facial expressions of enemy soldiers.[19] The potential for further advances in these areas, when combined with nanotechnology, will have dramatic effects on the battlefield.

A range of military research focuses on the development of nonlethal weapons. Research into the bio-effects of beamed energy and sonic wavelengths, which might be able to affect human behavior without killing people, has advanced considerably. Lasers to blind enemy soldiers and sonic weapons to stun individuals, nauseate them, or create severe gastro-intestinal crises have been successfully developed.[20] In 2004, the United States government warned airline pilots that terrorists might seek to crash airplanes by shining lasers (common in a variety of industries including outdoor light shows) into cockpits, thus blinding the pilot during landing or takeoff.[21] Lower-tech concepts include means of delivering electric shocks from a distance, spreading slippery material that makes roads impassable, or dispersing foam to limit access to or disable machinery. Tactics used by domestic police also can have military applications. Such tools include tear gas; pepper spay; rubber bullets and propelled balls or bean bag rounds; flash grenades that make a bright light and bang but with no damage; tasers; and weapons using light, sound, heat, or smell for diversion.[22] These applications would be especially useful in conditions where hostages are being held, where combatants hide amongst civilian populations, and in situations requiring crowd control.

Other nonlethal weapons include audio devices that can disable an enemy. The United States has developed a megaphone that can operate at 145 decibels at 300 yards with an ear-splitting tone. This technology could work to rid a cave or building of terrorists or insurgents hiding inside. While the wider civilian impacts have not been fully vetted, the United States deployed this capability in Iraq in 2004.[23] A simpler version of screeching noise was used to the same effect in Panama in 1989 when invading U.S. forces cornered General Manuel Noriega at the Vatican Embassy in Panama City. U.S. troops set up large speakers in a nearby street and blasted the Embassy with heavy metal rock known to be detested by the beleaguered general. Noriega soon surrendered. In Iraq, American trucks with massive audio equipment were used to blast AC/DC songs that would overpower the sound of mosques calling fighters to jihad against American troops during the battle of Falluja in fall 2004. Lasers used to blind a target on the ground or in the air are already available. New chemical weapons have been used by Russia and are in further development in the United States as tools to put occupants of a building to sleep. The United States is researching a microwave weapon that would work by mounting a millimeter-wave beam on a military vehicle from which the beam penetrates skin to a depth of about one sixty-fourth of an inch, heating water molecules and producing intolerable pain.[24]

The Dilemma of Advanced Technology

Only a few states possess the spectrum of advanced capabilities or research and development methods to deploy advanced military technology. Globalization does, however, allow for the proliferation of technology so that a state might skip entire generations of conventional military evolution and focus on high-tech capabilities. Many of the innovative technologies used to enhance modern military operations have dual-use civilian functions and can be purchased on international markets. Militaries must also struggle to employ technological experts who can make more money in the private sector. Traditional measures of military power might not be adequate for defining the relative power or capability that a particular state possesses. A related problem arises in coalition fighting. If one state makes technological advances, it can become less capable of entering combat interoperable with other nations' military equipment.

During the 1999 Kosovo war, the United States found that communication systems for their pilots were not compatible with older systems used by its NATO allies. The United States could not always utilize its technological advantages in this war. However, this was a cost seen as worth paying to gain the benefit of a larger political coalition. Another operational dilemma posed by advanced technology is the high degree of expertise required to operate modern military systems. A higher education might be at least as important for military recruitment as combat skills. Finally, for all the precision technology, large bombs and conventional ground forces still matter. In 2004, the United States asked defense contractors to develop a precision-guided, 30,000-pound bomb to be called the Massive Ordnance Penetrator—informally known as Big Blue.[25]

As technology makes war more precise, the use of war as a policy option might appear to be a painless exercise perhaps making it more likely as a policy option. Because technology allows military power to be projected from far-off platforms and the appearance of minimal casualties is established among public opinion, war might be more likely. A premature resort to war on such assumptions could lead to quick military solutions to otherwise intractable problems—or just as easily result in an unwinnable quagmire. The latter is a problem in particular if overreliance on technology distracts planning and investment away from important military tools such as land armies. If an impression is created that war can be fought and won via airpower alone and thus ground options are not available, a critical tool for achieving victory can be denied military commanders. Winning a war with air power is possible. However, securing a long-term peace on the ground likely requires ground troops. If the troops on the ground are not there to secure a peace, a war might not have been worth fighting in the first place.

Underdeveloped or collapsing states and rough terrain can reduce target opportunities and make it harder to deploy advanced technology. In the 2001 Afghanistan war there were a very limited number of targets that could be attacked by the United States with precision weapons. Fighting in a desert or mountain environment could make it very difficult, for example, to deploy a Tactical Internet system when high mobility raises the difficulty in establishing a network and rugged terrain is not amenable to effective computer use. The Afghanistan war of 2001 did produce new high-technology innovations such as arming Unmanned Aerial Vehicles (previously conceived as being only for high resolution surveillance) with bombs for pinpoint attacks with conventional munitions. Also, American intelligence agents were able to use satellite communications to guide precision air strikes to create fear among local warlords who needed persuasion to give fuller cooperation with the United States.[26] Enemies, however, might simply choose not to fight against the high-tech aspects of a more powerful adversary and instead draw them into urban areas or jungles where the technology will be less effective. Fighting at night in close quarters, insurgents in Iraq used bright red and blue flares to blind American night-vision equipment. In addition to the problem of location, technology also can be constrained or degraded by atmospheric conditions including weather, dust, and smoke.[27]

As advances occur in the area of communication and observation, surveillance could put privacy at risk among average citizens. The United States had, by 2002, begun using its military surveillance capability to monitor a variety of domestic activities ranging from observing individuals and groups of people at large, symbolic events, to mapping important cities for emergency preparedness. The U.S. National Geospatial-Intelligence Agency has assembled visual information on more than 130 urban areas.[28] Human knowledge and freedom can grow as technology facilitates interconnections and communications across borders. However, knowledge and freedom can also be eroded as states seek modern technological means of military advantage. To modernize both its economy and its military, China is seeking advanced technology. However this technology is also proliferating within Chinese society—allowing citizens to gain access to the outside world. This trend makes it harder for the state to control the flow of information. An example from the Tiananmen Square crisis, where Chinese troops cracked down on public demonstrations for liberty in June 1989, illustrates this challenge. A man named Wang Nan left his home on the morning of June 3 with a camera in hand, innocently thinking he could take some photographs of a historic moment in Chinese history as students and others gathered to protest Communist Party rule. Wang Nan witnessed the military opening fire on civilian protesters and took out his camera. The soldiers firing on the people saw him with the camera and shot him, killing him with a bullet wound to the head.[29]

New surveillance technology known as "Radio Frequency Identification"— or RFID—can allow for instant tracking of goods and people on a global basis in near real-time. RFIDs, for example, have been used on Texas schoolchildren to allow law-enforcement officers to monitor their movements. In the same manner that children's safety would be enhanced, this technology could also be used to invade individual privacy and perhaps violate civil liberties such as the freedom of movement.[30] By 2014, it is possible that one trillion objects will all be linked electronically and remote sensors and radio transponders of microscopic size could be placed virtually anywhere, including inside people's bodies. The degree to which states use technology to enhance control, or to which states will lose control because of technology, remains to be seen. Also, the health and environmental implications of technological advances are uncertain—such as the residual waste of discarded cell phones.

INFORMATION AND SECURITY

Modern developed societies have so dramatically expanded the role of information systems that the meaning of power must incorporate knowledge and communication as key elements. In 2002 there were about 180 billion minutes of international telephone calls made by about 2.8 billion cellular phone and 1.2 billion fixed-line subscribers worldwide—all made possible by several hundred satellites orbiting Earth.[31] It took radio broadcasting thirty-eight years to reach fifty million people and thirteen for television to reach the same amount. It took the Internet four years to reach fifty million users. By March 2000, 300 million people worldwide were using the Internet.[32] In 2002, thirty-one billion e-mails were estimated to have been sent worldwide every day.[33] In 2006, daily e-mail volume exceeded sixty million. E-mail mailboxes were estimated to have grown to 1.2 billion by 2005.[34] The information revolution increases demand for integrating the military and civilian life beyond weaponry. This military-civilian interface includes advanced telecommunications systems and computerized databases. Networks where information storage, transmission, manipulation, and dissemination of electronic digital information, including satellite communications systems of microprocessor production and software development, all transcend this nexus between the civilian and military worlds.[35] From these trends, the dynamics of information power have come to assume a major strategic importance.

Information Power

As information has become a tool to power, it has increasingly become a vital means of modern warfare. Information warfare has five basic elements: intelligence-based warfare designed to attack or confuse an adversary's means of gathering knowledge; electronic warfare using technology to degrade an adversary's information infrastructure; hacker warfare, which includes attacks on or espionage within an enemy's computer system or to turn an enemy's own systems against them with disinformation; command and control warfare using targeted violence to destroy command centers and their links to the battlefield; and psychological operations, which use information to demoralize an enemy's forces or affect an enemy population.[36] While these operational concepts are appealing tools of strategy, they are also complicated and have limitations. For example, knowing how information is used and interlinked by an adversary can be difficult to ascertain. State and private sector activity can be protected by encoding and creating systems redundancy. It is also difficult to know when to strike with information warfare to have the maximum impact and how to assess whether one has been successful or not. Finally, one has to be cautious about crippling an enemy's ability to communicate. For example, if one destroys an enemy's command and control system, it might make it difficult for them to command troops to stop fighting and lay down weapons. Destroying an enemy's telephone and television capacity can make it more difficult to get information out to a public and gain their support for peace-support operations or occupation.[37]

Developing countries like China and India are making significant gains in information support networks which give them increased international leverage that investment in military capabilities might not provide. India is attracting international investment due to relatively low-cost information support systems and it is expanding its own infrastructure investment into the Middle East. China is expanding telecommunications infrastructure projects in emerging economies around Asia and Latin America as well as Africa. In 2004, China announced that it was investing $20 billion in Argentina to build railways, oil and gas exploration, construction, and communications satellites.[38] While Chinese equipment might not be at the same standards as that of the United States and Europe, it is significantly cheaper. This gives China a relative advantage in capturing emerging markets for telecommunications infrastructure development.

In addition to the United States, there are four emerging centers of global communications power—India, China, Europe, and Russia. A periphery of states including Indonesia, Brazil, and Romania also are engaged in communications infrastructure. Power within this system can shift and indicate relative gains for one state or region. For example, in 2002, 85 percent of the undersea communications infrastructure was owned by American companies; by 2004 that had been reversed as China bought control of major assets including *Level 3*, *PSI-Net*, *Asia Global Crossing*, and *Global Crossing*.[39] In December 2004, China's *Lenovo Group* announced that it was purchasing the personal computer business of *IBM Corp*, making *Lenovo* the third-largest seller of personal computers in the world. The shifting geopolitics of the information revolution creates new opportunities for states like India and China to accelerate their economic and political power in the twenty-first century. Meanwhile, this creates vulnerabilities for the United States, which has seen information and technology-driven jobs migrate to these countries that can provide similar services as American systems, but with lower wage workers.

Increasing global reliance on a new generation of solid state electronics and rapid information processing and transmission creates a heavily integrated network of targets for those who might seek to attack an enemy. Banking, stock markets, telephone switching networks, electric power grids, and air traffic control systems can combine so that information can become both a strength and vulnerability of a modern society.[40] Critical security questions arise including: What constitutes an information attack? When is an information attack an act of war? How is an information attack verified? How is the attacker identified and verified?[41] A state or non-state actor can attack information systems from within the territory of a third state, or cross several states in the process of attacking an information system from various directions. There are over 30,000 personal computers each day that are involuntarily recruited into secret networks that spread spam and viruses. Viruses such as *Mydoom* and *Bagle* conduct an online battle over control of information via malicious viruses that can capture and control an individual computer. These particular attacks originated from private sources in Latvia, Macau, and Israel.[42] The American Department of Defense estimates that, in 2001, it faced about 40,000 Internet attacks. While most cyberattacks on the U.S. military fail, in 2000, 715 achieved some degree of access to Department of Defense systems.[43]

The heavy investment in civilian and military systems makes the modern state vulnerable to traditional weapons used in new ways. For example, exploding a nuclear device at a high altitude (about 40 to 400 kilometers above Earth's surface) would do little damage in terms of blast and radioactivity. But the objective could be to generate an electromagnetic pulse (EMP) from the interaction of the nuclear explosion with Earth's atmosphere, ionosphere, and magnetic field. The result would be a general shock within the atmosphere and on the Earth to electronics and destruction or damage to the systems which they drive. The impact would be particularly damaging to electrical power systems and information systems on which modern society depends. The effects on a nation's infrastructure would include a shut-down of a nation's financial system and its means of getting food, water, and medical care to its people. Trade and production of goods and services would also be severely affected.[44]

In a country like the United States, which has its electric power grid interconnected into several regional clusters, an EMP event over the Midwest could expose about 70 percent of America's power grid to disruption. An EMP attack would also significantly damage or disrupt civilian telecommunications systems in areas exposed to the effect. Surviving networks would be stressed beyond their capacity to function properly. Inter-bank fund transfers, securities transfers and payment services would be dramatically affected as would automated banking operators. Even a shut down of a few minutes to a day would have a potentially catastrophic impact on the accounting and flow of wealth in the American economy. Severe effects would also be felt in the transportation sector including massive traffic light malfunctions in major cities, confusion in railway traffic, a breakdown in loading and unloading and security measures at affected seaports, and a breakdown in air traffic control systems leading to a national backup of air travel. The region affected by an EMP event would likely see food distribution problems over a period of weeks or even months. Absent food, the potential for large scale public unrest and disorder would emerge as a major public security crisis.[45] In some major cities where fresh water is generated by electricity drinking water would be in short supply.

Knowledge and Power

The spread of instant communications is exposing regions of the world to a variety of new ideas and information. For example, the Middle East is open to information that has the potential to engage publics in ways that have previously been unknown in the region's politics. Internet technology combines with new uses of older technology such as satellite television and videocassettes to transfer ideas across borders where information has traditionally been controlled by the state. Newspapers are no longer able to serve as mouthpieces of governments as they are challenged by independent voices. Some newspapers are published outside the Middle East such as *Asharq Alawsat* and *al-Hayat* which link Arab communities into a global discussion that bridges ideas from within and outside of the Arab world. Television has also been altered by the *al-Jazeera* network, which uses satellite technology for independent broadcasting.

The Internet is still a relatively rare tool in the Middle East but it is available to varying degrees in every Middle East country.[46] Access to television is likely to play the greatest role in the Middle East where there is an average of 175 televisions per 1,000 people.[47] Clandestine networks, including terrorist organizations, use Internet access and television imagery to get their messages out. The 1979 Iranian revolution was fomented using audiocassette tapes for transferring information.[48] In the modern era, these efforts range from uplifting and diverse public engagement in debates and education, to graphic imagery of beheadings of captives by terrorists. Public debate and grassroots organization could foster democratization and reform, leading to greater regional stability—or it could foster revolution and instability. In Iraq, insurgents used cell phones attached to bombs to kill targets—triggering the device by calling the phone's number. Automatic garage door openers and toy remote control devices were used the same way.

The global proliferation of information technology also allows for an unprecedented awareness of international attitudes via detailed surveys which might help states respond to people's concerns or to anticipate consequences of particular policies. Knowledge of public attitudes also exposes growing international divergences. Opinion surveys, for example, show a growing public perception that the United Nations had become less important at the dawn of the twenty-first century. This was true among majorities in Israel, South Korea, Jordan, the Palestinian Authority, Lebanon, Brazil, France, Pakistan, the United States, Russia, Great Britain, Australia, Morocco, Spain, Germany, Indonesia, and Italy. Majorities of public opinion are very or somewhat worried about a potential U.S. military threat in Indonesia, Nigeria, Pakistan, Russia, Turkey, Lebanon, Jordan, and Kuwait. This perspective was important as these states were key American allies in the war against international terrorism. In Morocco and Jordan, some 66 and 70 percent, respectively, said suicide bombings against Americans and Westerners in Iraq were justified.

Most Muslims express confidence in their ability to operate under Western-style democracy. Yet, most Muslims also believe that this can be done alongside a prominent role for Islam and religious leaders in their political lives. Contradicting televised images of large antiglobalization protests, surveys show general worldwide support for globalization. Majorities in the developed world, but also in places like Uzbekistan, Lebanon, Turkey, Pakistan, Egypt, and Jordan see globalization's impact on their country as either very good or somewhat good. In Africa, people generally have highly favorable attitudes toward multinational corporations as well as international institutions like the International Monetary Foundation and the World Bank. Indeed, people worldwide have a generally negative reaction to antiglobalization protestors. Other key structural trends reflect a deep divergence in the historic transatlantic alliance with favorable attitudes toward the United States registering at 37 percent and 38 percent respectively in France and Germany.[49]

The ability to process information is impacted by a crucial variable—education. Some countries with advanced technological foundations, especially the United States, are historically beacons for international students who come to study these technologies. However, there are increasing economic and cultural incentives to take that knowledge and invest it at home. Countries that invest in their domestic education are themselves likely to gain a strategic edge in the information age of security. The United States has experienced trouble in this area as it has fallen behind Korea, Norway, the Czech Republic, and Japan among countries that have a higher percentage of adults who finish high school levels of education. The Organization for Economic Cooperation and Development shows that those states that have historically fallen below the United States in terms of college educated population are closing that gap.[50] Meanwhile, states that are developing advanced technology are investing that technology into their own education priorities. India, for example, has launched a satellite exclusively for education. The satellite connects classrooms to communications infrastructure in even the most remote areas of the country to train teachers and provide primary and university education around the country. In 2004, some 350 million of India's one billion people were illiterate and only 13 percent finished the equivalent of high school.[51] Application of advanced technology to education in a developing country like India could thus have dramatic implications for the distribution of information and power in the modern international system.

Finally, the purposeful use of disinformation can help a state or other international actors advance a particular strategic objective. For example, in October 2004, the United States military in Iraq let CNN know that it was going to begin military operations in the insurgent stronghold city of Falluja. That particular report was, in fact, not true (though the United States would eventually engage insurgents in a major battle at Falluja). It was, however, an intentional use of the media to confuse the enemy into thinking an attack was imminent and thus exposing its defensive tactics. Blurring the line between confidence and accuracy in military reporting can raise concern about credibility versus propaganda for a state at war. However, as a U.S. official told the *Los Angeles Times*, "Information is part of the battlefield in a way that it's never been before. . . . We'd be foolish not to try to use it to our advantage."[52] If, however, military information were to lose credibility, it risks a loss of prestige and trust among a domestic and international audience. It was largely for this reason that the United States Department of Defense abandoned a plan in 2001 to create an "Office of Strategic Influence" whose work would have included planting pro-American, and possibly even false, news stories in foreign media, including that of allies. Nonetheless, psychological operations utilizing new media sources continued in planning mechanisms. Such planning activities include planting news stories in the foreign press and creating false documents and web sites in Arabic which would discredit mosques and religious groups that promulgate anti-Americanism.[53] The United States confronts a significant dilemma in that its businesses market material goods on a worldwide basis with great success—but its contemporary foreign and national security policy often fails to win the hearts and minds of target audiences. However, overt efforts to influence hearts and minds can just as easily backfire if they are seen as propaganda.

THE MILITARY USE OF SPACE

Space harbors great unknowns, though exploration continues to expand knowledge of the final frontier. The unknown can breed optimism and fear at the same time—but the urge to develop and expand technology to explore space continues to grow. The exploration of Mars and of Earth's moon raise new possibilities for human life. Mars, it appears, might have once held water, the essence of life. The moon could be a major source for energy production through mining of the helium 3 isotope which can be attained there. If accessed, the helium 3 isotope would have a cash value of as much as $4 billion a ton in terms of its equivalent in oil energy production. There is estimated to be as much as one million tons of helium 3 on the moon—enough to power energy on Earth for thousands of years.[54] Hollywood films often show the future of space as requiring defense from external threats as in *The Day the Earth Stood Still, War of the Worlds, Independence Day,* and *Mars Attacks.* But the image of space also portends a more peaceful future in which the exploration of space, as envisioned in *Star Trek,* unites humanity to expand knowledge and embrace diversity. Programs like *Star Trek* have also stimulated thinking about new technology.[55] The growing use of space—including about 500 operating satellites orbiting Earth—creates an additional challenge of space debris and other hazards. There are an estimated 9,000 pieces of space debris that can be tracked from Earth, which pose threats to satellites or spacecraft. There is also considerable "micro-debris," perhaps more than 100,000 particles that can do damage but that are less than ten centimeters in length and are undetectable.[56] Most of this debris comes from intentional and unintentional satellite explosions in orbit. In the most extreme case, space threats can also include meteorites which might have to be diverted from hitting Earth—a ten-kilometer in diameter asteroid hitting Earth likely contributed to the extinction of the dinosaurs.

Spacepower

Outer space—the area beyond Earth's atmosphere—is considered the common heritage of humankind and is—both by tradition and, in part, by treaty— void of military deployment. While space has not been weaponized—with actual weapons used in or from space—it has been militarized for many decades. Indeed, the use of space contributes significantly to increasing security. Satellites provide early warning about nuclear weapons launches, which helps states avoid misinterpretation leading to deadly conflict. The same satellite technology can also be used for monitoring the destruction of weapons according to treaty obligations. Satellite technology can be used to monitor the earth to understand global environmental challenges. International cooperation and communications technology in space facilitates a global perspective on security challenges. Humanity has also been served by the advent of satellites used for enhanced astronomy, atmospheric studies, search and rescue capacity, space exploration, and weather forecasting.

Many countries benefit militarily from space activity: Global Positioning Satellites help with mapping; aerial refueling and rendezvous; geodetic surveys; search and rescue operations; communications; arms control verification; monitoring of non-proliferation activity; early warning satellites; intelligence, surveillance, and reconnaissance; and weather prediction. The United States relies heavily on space activity to support its modern military. American military command and control capacity is enhanced by coordinating troop movements and helping troops on the ground determine their location, facilitate targeting and weapons guidance, and provide communications for unmanned aerial vehicles. New concepts may include antiballistic missile laser technology, precision-guided bunker-buster bombs, kinetic energy antisatellite weapons, space-based lasers, and a new space plane.[57] The future use of space raises questions of how "spacepower" will develop and what new challenges will accompany it. In civilian technology industries, the commercial sector, the defense industries, and intelligence gathering, states are increasingly competing over strategic advances in spacepower—though in every area of space, the United States has near-complete dominance.[58]

Heavy reliance on space also creates new vulnerabilities. For example, a relatively crude satellite could be launched privately or by a country. Already by

2004 relatively heavy private rockets had been tested, which eventually could be launched into space. That satellite or rocket could be packed with pebbles or nails that would disperse and explode on contact with a critical satellite or spacecraft.[59] Such an attack might eliminate an existing space-based advantage or undermine intelligence gathering capabilities as a precursor to other military actions on the ground. While terrorists could not likely gain access to space capacity, they could use conventional weapons or weapons of mass destruction on Earth against critical communications links that control satellite guidance and communication networks. More likely, terrorists might use space-based technology such as the Global Positioning System to target precision attacks or to coordinate locations of cells worldwide. With this concern, the United States has planned for the capacity to disable the entire U.S. network of global positioning satellites during a crisis so as to deny that technology to anyone who might use it to aid terrorist activity.[60] Satellite imagery available for purchase on the Internet can also help in planning attacks on particular targets. Finally, states seeking power in the international system could build advanced space weapons, such as antisatellite or laser technology as a means of achieving strategic parity or advantage.[61]

Space weapons are means of causing harm that are based in space or that have an essential element based in space. Such weapons include directed-energy weapons that can propagate destructive energy at very high speeds, and mass-to-target weapons that deliver a hard device, such as an explosive, to a target in space or on Earth.[62] Space-applicable weapons can also include metal projectiles called "Hypervelocity Rod Bundles" for hitting ground targets from space.[63] These bundles were often referred to in debates over space weapons as "rods from God." Missile defense or antisatellite systems can be based on Earth to be used in space. There are three basic kinds of space-applicable weapons. The first includes ground, sea, and air-based missile defense interceptors which use low-Earth orbital space to destroy ballistic missiles—this kind of system is being simultaneously researched and deployed by the United States. The second area of space-based weapons is under consideration for future development and testing including kinetic kill interceptors designed to destroy missiles by collision and space-based lasers that send high-powered beams at rising missiles to destroy them. The third development is in the area of antisatellite systems, which could include missiles launched into space or space-based systems that would enter the same orbit as deployed satellites to launch or explode some form of conventional explosives.[64]

The capacity to destroy satellites is an area where states have sought to avoid developing capability, but is likely to be increasingly tempting. Even a small-scale disruption of one satellite can have enormous economic and social impact. For example, in May 1998, a single *Galaxy IV* satellite failed. This caused 80 percent of pagers to stop working in the United States and affected twenty-seven million pager users.[65] A worst-case scenario would involve high-altitude nuclear detonations, one of which could disable all of the low-Earth orbit satellites around the Earth by burning out electronics for any satellites in the line of site of the explosion. Eventually, all non-hardened satellites would be exposed to transient-radiation and system generated electromagnetic pulse as satellites orbit near the area of the initial explosion.[66] Attacking American satellites might be an important means for an adversary to gain a degree of parity on the conventional battlefield given the growing reliance of the United States on satellites for coordinating military activity. American reliance on missile guidance technology has increased significantly. In the 1991 Persian Gulf War, the United States launched 228,000 air-to-ground munitions but only 4 percent were laser-guided. In the 1999 Kosovo war, some 23,700 air-to-ground missiles were launched and 30 percent were either laser or GPS guided. In the 2001 Afghan conflict, the United States launched 18,000 air-to-ground missiles of which 56 percent were laser or GPS guided munitions.[67] Since the 1990s, the United States has been engaged in the development and deployment of stealth satellite technology that would make it much harder to detect the location and orbital path of satellites.[68]

Space Dominance

The United States is the dominant space power but there is not an internal consensus as to how it should approach the military use of space. "Space Doves" oppose all military use of space and seek treaties to forestall future development. "Militarization Realists" believe that warfare will eventually entail some form of combat involving space and it is best to prepare for it. "Inevitable Weaponizers" argue that every area of the battlespace has previously been developed for weapons use and thus there is no inherent reason why the same rule should not apply to space. Thus states can be expected reasonably to prepare to conduct military operations involving outer space. "Space Hawks" are enthusiastic about all development of space weapons and oppose most constraints on research and deployment.[69] One key element of the space debate is the financial power of the space industry. Space-technology industries generated $125 billion in profits in 2000 and total American investment in space technology is expected to be $600 billion a year by 2010.[70]

The United States has embarked on a concerted effort to continue, develop, and expand space dominance as a key strategic objective in the twenty-first century. The United States controls 95 percent of all global military spending on space and dominates two-thirds of the commercial space industry. The U.S. budget for military-related space activity was $18 billion in 2003 and expected to rise to $25 billion by 2010. The United States maintains 28 satellites for the Global Positioning System used to coordinate and locate troops and targets. Imagery intelligence is provided by the use of the Kh-11, which has a resolution of four to six inches in daylight and several feet at night, and the *Onyx* system, which provides night and all-weather imaging radar. There are also as many as seven signals intelligence satellites use to intercept radio and television broadcasts, cell phone communications, radar transmissions, and other electronic signals. A satellite network provides real-time communications for the military and includes a nuclear-hardened, anti-jam communication link between the military, the White House, and the Department of State without ground-based assistance. Nine satellites comprise a tactical mobile communications network for naval communications and other fixed and mobile terminals. Early warning systems are provided by a constellation of satellites that detect and track missiles throughout all phases of their flight around the world.[71]

The U.S. Space Command concludes that "just as land dominance, sea control, and air superiority have become critical elements of current military strategy, space superiority is emerging as an essential element of battlefield success and future warfare" and the vision for 2020 is that the United States should succeed at "dominating the space medium and integrating space power throughout military operations."[72] The United States Strategic Command (STRATCOM) identifies space as essential to America's security and well-being and carries the mission of protecting the nation's space capabilities, interests, and investment in space. STRATCOM oversees a global network of satellite command and control, communications, missile warning, launch facilities, and command and control for U.S. space systems. Specific missions are divided into four major categories. Space Force Support includes launching of satellites and high-value payloads into space. Space Force Enhancement provides weather, communications, intelligence, missile warning, and navigation to all aspects of American military service operations worldwide. In the Afghan and Iraqi wars of 2001 and 2003, virtually every military platform used was linked by satellite through STRATCOM. Space Control involves using technological advantage to ensure freedom of movement in, and use of, space and denial of use by adversaries. This function includes surveillance of space, protection of space forces from hostile threats and environmental hazards, and prevention of unauthorized exploitation of space capabilities. This function can include negation of space systems hostile to the United States and its allies. How this is to be done is left unspecified in public literature.

STRATCOM notes that the United States might find it necessary to disrupt, degrade, deny, or destroy enemy space capabilities in future conflicts. The United States does confirm, however, that there is no current means to operate antisatellite weapons. More likely, conventional weapons could be used to strike an adversary's space launch or ground relay facilities while antisatellite research is ongoing. STRATCOM also includes Space Force Application in its planning and operations. It identifies future roles and missions involved in the evolving battlefield, which could encompass combat operations in, through, and from space.[73] Notably, antisatellite weaponry need not necessarily be space-based and, as such, would not necessarily violate existing international understandings on the weaponization of space.[74] Symbolizing, both to supporters and critics, the scope of spacepower, acting Air Force Secretary Pete Teets said in 2004, "We haven't reached the point of strafing and bombing from space—nonetheless, we are thinking about those possibilities."[75] The inherent dilemma is that defensive weapons to protect satellites might be needed for space-faring powers. However, any deployment of offensive weapons in space would risk creating a new arms race in space.

In 2005, the United States began consideration of a new policy that would authorize the Air Force to implement its research, development, and eventual deployment of space weapons. However, it is also possible that while policy might change, implementation might still be a long way off. The extreme difficulty, even danger, of operating in space is a major deterrent to deployment of systems. Additionally, the costs of deployment are likely to be highly constraining on any actual decision to deploy weapons. In fact, it is not guaranteed that the United States will prioritize space as a major investment area beyond its existing dominance. Domestic or other strategic priorities on earth could prompt a redirection of resources away from space programs. Conversely, there is also some evidence that space might not actually be the center of gravity of future military operations that its proponents assert. For example, the American Space Shuttle Fleet has been diminished in value as an expensive safety risk. America's satellite launch capacity is heavily dependent on a declining commercial-sector demand in order to stay economically viable.[76] The U.S. did announce in 2005 that it intended to return to the moon by 2018—though the estimated price tag of $104 billion could prove too high relative to other priorities. How the United States chooses to exercise its spacepower—either as a tool of dominance or as guided by restraint—might be one of the most important strategic questions of the twenty-first century.

The Space Race

France, Japan, and Israel each have self-contained space-launch capabilities. Australia also has the potential to provide launch facilities for Russia and the United States. France, the United Kingdom, Germany, Italy, Japan, and Israel have their own satellite industries and technology. Japan has launched a set of four satellites for information gathering over North Korea. These satellites can also monitor any point on Earth twice a day. Japan is also developing a two-layer missile defense shield which was expected for deployment in 2007.[77] Europe has moved forward with its *Galileo* project which provides a global tracking navigational satellite system allowing any user to know their location with precision accuracy around the world. The European Space Agency (dominated by France) provides Europe with access to launch facilities as well as a variety of remote sensing satellites.[78]

A second tier of space-capable countries includes India, which has its own access to space; Pakistan, which has developed missile technology and deployed a communication satellite (with plans to deploy an observation satellite); and Brazil, which has its own indigenous space launch programs. Among these states, however, only India has a comprehensive space program.[79] India was the first developing nation to achieve space deployment capabilities. The degree of India's military use of space is unclear beyond the development of surveillance capacity. In October 2003, the chief of the Indian Air Force said that India had begun development of a command station for an eventual space platform for nuclear weapons. He later retracted the statement under pressure from his civilian leadership.[80] Brazil maintains a nascent space program and has significant military involvement in a rocket development program. Brazil has also worked with China to develop and launch two remote-sensing satellites for real-time, civilian, environmental monitoring.[81] For these countries, as well as many first tier countries, a major driver of the investment in space technology might also be the ability to sell access or equipment for profit.

The main potential for strategic competition with America's space dominance comes from Russia and China. Russia maintains significant space capabilities left over from the Soviet Union. About two-thirds of Russia's spacecraft in orbit are used for military purposes. Russia has announced plans for modernization of its communications, navigation, and reconnaissance satellites. However, Russia has also cut its overall space programs investment by two-thirds since the end of the Cold War and about 80 percent of its satellites should have expired around 2002. Russia has five types of imagery reconnaissance satellites—but by 2004, none of these were in orbit. Russia also has a series of electronic intelligence satellites, but they have short life-spans which, by 2004, had also begun to expire. Russia does maintain active orbits for its military communications satellites, though not all of those available are operational. Only about 50 percent of Russia's navigation satellite capabilities were running in 2004. Russia's ballistic missile early warning and space monitoring systems have been in significant decline since the collapse of the Soviet Union in 1991. Much of the infrastructure for Russia's early warning satellite network was spread around the former Soviet Union and not all former Soviet republics have cooperated on the upgrading of radar systems. Only in 2003 was Russia able to activate the Volga radar station, based in Belarus. Previously, the entire northwestern sector of missile surveillance had been exposed due to the shutdown of a radar station in Latvia in the mid-1990s.[82]

In 2003, China joined Russia and the United States as having placed a human into orbit around Earth. Chinese leaders say they envision a moon landing by about 2017, and eventually the deployment of a project to measure the capacity for accessing helium-3 on the moon. China also envisions deploying a moon-based telescope and deploying robotic space explorers.[83] China has communications, navigation, and imaging satellites. A number of its communications satellites are integrated into military command, control, communications, computer, and intelligence systems. China has one imaging reconnaissance satellite, one meteorological satellite, and one remote sensing microsatellite, all of which can be used for civilian or military purposes. China has also established an engineering and research center which would allow it to implement large-scale production of small satellites. China envisions being able to produce six to eight small satellites a year with a plan to launch over one hundred by 2020 to provide complete surveillance of the country. According to the Xinhua news agency, the purpose would be to have a "large surveyeing network" to monitor water reserves, forests, farmland, city construction, and "various activities of society."[84]

Strategic Dilemmas in Space: Missile Defense and ASAT

Two technological advancements under development in the early twenty-first century cross the divide between militarization and weaponization of space: missile defense and antisatellite warfare. Missile defenses, the ability to destroy incoming missiles, were banned during the Cold War by the United States and the Soviet Union. The logic behind the ban was that missile defense systems could make a nuclear war more possible if one side felt they could launch a war and survive retaliation. In the 1980s, the United States revisited the idea under President Ronald Reagan, who called for a Strategic Defense Initiative (SDI)—known by detractors as Star Wars. The United States conducted research but agreed not to deploy such systems through the 1990s.

There are serious technological limitations on the idea of building a missile defense system. If accomplished using ground-to-space interceptors, missile defense means effectively "hitting a bullet with a bullet." Space-based options are equally difficult, relying on the creation of lasers to destroy missiles from above. The United States, nevertheless, announced its intent to withdraw from the antiballistic missile treaty in 2001 and accelerated its research and deployment options for missile defense. A system could knock down a missile in its

"boost phase"—just as it is launched and before it enters space and accelerates. At the launch phase, rockets are large and slow, making them easier to
hit. This would, however, require almost instantaneous knowledge of a launch
and a missile defense platform within range. According to the American Physical Society, the feasibility of successfully killing an intercontinental missile
in its boost phase is very limited. A space-based laser intercept sufficient to
kill one ICBM would require one thousand or more interceptors—this element of the U.S. missile shield program was shelved in 2002. There is also
research into an airborne laser program, with the concept being to place lasers
on a Boeing 747–400. However, this capacity would be limited by range,
beam power, the type of ICBM rocket used, and countermeasures.[85]

The United States has thus proceeded with a "layered" missile defense
shield concept that stresses building a ground-based mid-course defense program. This system would track the trajectory of an incoming missile with
radar and launch a countermeasure missile to intercept the inbound missile.
The United States began deploying initial elements for this system in September 2004. The United States intended to have ten interceptor sites spread along
Alaska and California by the end of 2005. Another layer involves a sea-based
system which would focus on intercepting a variety of missiles in their mid-
course phase. The United States planned to deploy twenty sea-based interceptors on three ships beginning in 2005. These layers of missile defense face
serious technological difficulties. Indeed, the deployment has moved forward
in spite of the lack of evidence that any element of the system will work. In its
first test in two years, a December 2004 attempt to shoot down a missile with
a mock warhead failed. The interceptor missile did not take off and was automatically shut down on the launch pad due to what the Pentagon described as
an "unknown anomaly."[86]

Even if fully deployed, the effectiveness of missile defenses would likely
be highly diminished by the use of decoys. Aluminized plastic balloons,
inflated with a propellant, can be used by an enemy to confuse a missile interceptor. The right paint application and fuel would give off an infrared signature confusing the guidance systems on interceptor missiles. An enemy could
launch a barrage of decoys, luring the missile defense system to respond and
use the majority of interceptor missiles—only to then be followed with a real
missile strike against the now defenseless country.[87] Finally, the most likely
way to get a nuclear weapon onto American territory would not be via a missile, which can be traced back to its source, but rather through a ship or a boat
in a harbor. In this sense, the $10 billion a year to be spent on missile defense
between 2004 and 2009, and the possible hundreds of billions that would
eventually be spent on full deployment, raised the question of whether space
weapons would be money well-spent. A state also might detonate a nuclear

weapon just above Earth's atmosphere. If North Korea were to detonate a fifty-kiloton nuclear warhead 120 kilometers over its own territory, within fifty days the number of commercial satellites surviving in low-Earth orbit would decline from about 450 to zero.[88] Consequently, a middle position advocated by some space security experts has been to develop purely defensive capabilities for space deployments, perhaps guaranteed by an international treaty limiting space weapons deployments.

A missile defense capability has a secondary application if these systems are also used to attack satellites orbiting Earth. Attacking satellites, which travel in well-known orbits that can be tracked from ground positions, would be considerably easier than intercepting incoming missiles. If, for example, a ground-based missile defense interceptor was launched straight up, it could lift to an elevation of about 6,000 kilometers and hit satellites in low-Earth orbit with little difficulty.[89] The non-development of antisatellite weapons has been respected as an international norm since the Soviet Union abandoned work on their production in the 1980s. The Soviet systems, of which plans and designs remain in Russian hands, involved launching a missile armed with conventional explosives into an orbit close to a target. When the warhead would explode, the debris would consequently destroy any nearby satellite. The United States developed some nascent antisatellite programs in the 1980s and 1990s but has not deployed such capability. These programs included Air-Launched Miniature Vehicles, ground-based kinetic energy, and Mid-Infrared Advanced Chemical Laser programs.[90] In February 2004, the U.S. Air Force released its *Transformation Flight Plan* which identified antisatellite weapons and weapons which could strike the Earth from space as areas for research and eventual deployment after 2015. Specific weapons systems mentioned are: Air Launched Anti-Satellite Missile, Ground Based Laser, Orbital Transfer Vehicle, Space-Based Radio Frequence Energy Weapon, Space Maneuver Vehicle, Space Operations Vehicle, and Hypervelocity Rod Bundles.[91] Once developed, antisatellite weaponry potentially opens a new era of arms races in space because it is hard to imagine countries standing idly by while others advance the capacity to destroy their satellites and other space assets.

THE BUSINESS OF SECURITY

Global military spending by 2005 totaled $1.035 trillion a year, which is about 2.6 percent of the world's gross domestic product. The United States accounted for about 50 percent of global defense spending.[92] The United States outspends the next fifteen nations combined on military capabilities. The increase in U.S. defense spending for 2002—about $40 billion—was equal to the entire annual

defense budget of the United Kingdom. The total value of global arms trade for
2000–2003 was about $148.2 billion. Developing nations accounted for $13.6
billion of all international arms deliveries. The United States ranks first in
global weapons sales—accounting for about 47.5 percent of all deliveries. The
United Kingdom is second in worldwide arms deliveries totaling $4.7 billion
and Russia is third with $3.4 billion. These top three suppliers accounted for
75.7 percent of all arms delivered in 2003.[93] Such expenditures can be opportunity costs that weaken a society in other vital areas such as investments in
education. Even for the United States, the investment in military spending has
economic costs as growing defense expenditure contributes to rising budget
deficits. The International Monetary Fund issued a warning in January 2004
that the American preference for borrowing could push up global interest rates
and slow international economic growth.[94]

Supply, Demand, and the Networks of Trade

Conventional weapons and support systems transfers are the dominant source
of security commerce between states including weapons, logistics, and communication tools. Some recipients of weapons systems purchase older
weapons to modernize for their use or further arms sales.[95] Illustrating the
complicated dynamics of the arms enhancement trade, Israel agreed to buy
Illushin-76 cargo aircraft from Uzbekistan in March 2004. These planes were
then to be sent to Russia to get new high-powered engines. After this outfitting, they would be sent to Israel where they would be equipped with the Airborne Warning and Control System of radar tracking—which then would, in
turn, be sold to India for profit. The system, known as the *Phalcon*, would be
able to pick out low-altitude enemy aircraft hundreds of miles away and 24-
hours-a-day in all weather. The aircraft would also have communication inter-
ception capability and decoding of radio transmission equipment.[96]

While much attention rightly focuses on the fear of weapons of mass
destruction proliferating, conventional weapons have had much more damaging effects. During the latter half of the 20th century, there were some 160
wars in the world and 24.5 million killed in those conflicts—primarily
through the use of conventional weapons.[97] The dangers posed by conventional weapons proliferation were illustrated for the United States in post-
invasion Iraq. Though the United States invaded Iraq to rid it of weapons of
mass destruction, the major threat to American forces were from conventional
weapons. Most of the over 2,000 American troops killed by late 2005 resulted
from revolvers, rifles, pistols, rocket propelled grenades, and improvised
roadside bombs. By one estimate, Iraq had three million tons of bombs and
bullets, millions of AK-47s and other rifles, rocket launchers and mortar

tubes, and thousands of more sophisticated arms including ground to air missiles. As many as eight million small arms might have fallen into citizens' hands, which were either used by or sold to insurgents.[98]

Another danger of small arms proliferation includes MANPADS (Man Portable Air Defense Systems) which are a threat to military and civilian aircraft. These portable systems are light, hard to counter, and can fire infrared guided missiles targeting a heat source such as an airplane engine. There are estimated to be 500,000 shoulder-fired surface-to-air missiles of about thirty different types worldwide. An estimated 6,000 are considered to be outside governmental control, including some 4,000 that were unaccounted for following the U.S. invasion of Iraq in 2003. In illegal weapons markets, MANPADS have been known to sell for between $1,000 and $100,000 each.[99] By one estimate, MANPADS were responsible for four hundred casualties in twenty-seven incidents involving civil aircraft during the 1980s and 1990s. During the Soviet invasion and occupation of Afghanistan, some 2,698 Soviet aircraft were shot down and MANPADS accounted for 56 percent of these hits and 79 percent of aircraft damage. In November 2002, an Israeli passenger plane was fired at by two rockets launched via MANPADS in Mombasa, Kenya.[100] A related proliferation concern is cruise-missile technology. There are some 70,000 cruise missiles in arsenals around the world that can be launched without detection from private vessels or ships in waters nearby a target.[101]

West Africa illustrates the challenge of conventional proliferation. In 2003, the government of Guinea imported mortar rounds and ammunition from Iran in boxes whose shipping manifestos were labeled as "detergent" and "technical equipment." From Guinea, these weapons were forwarded to rebels inside Liberia who used them to fire indiscriminately on civilians in Monrovia. Mortar shells were even fired at civilian refugee camps for displaced individuals. The Liberian government also imported weapons via illicit arms traders and, in turn, sent weapons to rebels in Sierra Leone. In 2002, the Nigerian Customs Service reported that it had intercepted small arms and ammunition valued at $30 million over a six-month period. In one catch in November 2003, they confiscated 170,000 rounds of ammunition.[102]

The supply and demand example of conventional weapons trade is but one example of the globalization of international transactions that drive the world economy. This system relies heavily on a complex web of transnational networks which are the lifeblood of the global trading system. These networks include the flows of goods and services, people, and the transportation nodes on which they all interconnect. Such networks can be identified by their physical characteristics such as roads, pipelines, shipping lanes, and ports. They can also be thought of as less tangible identities such as the flow of money, the Internet, and ideas.[103] Such networks can become a target for attack in a global security dynamic. These networks are highly vulnerable to disruption by states or non-state actors seeking a strategic advantage in a conflict. Disruption of trading networks can be done through direct attacks on transportation nodes. For example, the use of a nuclear weapon in the port of Los Angeles would disrupt 50 percent of America's imports and exports. More than 95 percent of America's non-North American foreign trade (and 100 percent of some commodities such as oil) arrives by ship. Some 8,000 ships make more than 51,000 U.S. port calls every year.[104] Alternatively, destruction of major geographical chokepoints where shipping transits, through the South China Sea, the Panama Canal, or the Straits of Hormuz, can do major damage to the flow of international goods and services.

The Internet also provides new means of stealing, moving, or hiding financial resources by criminals or terrorists engaging within the networks of global trade. In February 2000, two major websites were subjected to denial of services attacks, illustrating the power available to cripple major Internet industry. By securing access to a number of unprotected computers, hackers then instructed them to send a massive number of e-mail messages to websites, which overloaded capacity and caused collapse. This happened to *Yahoo!* which was shut down for five hours—leading to a major disruption for its 8.7 million daily users and to its service as a portal to other web pages and search engines. *Buy.com* was also attacked the same day and shut down for six hours. The next day, *Amazon.com*, which was then visited by 892,000 users a day, was shut down for nearly four hours; the *CNN* website, with 642,000 users daily, was shut down for 3.5 hours; and *eBay* with 1.68 million users each day was shut down for five hours. A day later, the *E*Trade* brokerage site, with 183,000 users each day, was closed for nearly 3 hours and *ZDNet* with 734,000 daily users closed for over 3 hours. The financial costs of these attacks were estimated at a minimum to be hundreds of millions of dollars.[105] In October 2000 a group of 20 people—working with an inside contact—created a digital clone of a Sicilian bank's online function. The group planned to use this to divert $400 million and then launder it through other financial institutions including the Vatican bank and banks in Switzerland and Portugal. This scheme failed, but only because one of the plotters informed the police.[106]

Transnational Networks and Organized Crime

The use of transnational networks for illicit activity, particularly organized crime, represents a new security challenge fomented by globalization. Such networks are communication channels and interconnected nodes, which can be individuals, organizations, firms, and computers that are connected in significant ways.[107] Networks can range in size from a few individuals to hundreds, and in their activity from drug trafficking to money laundering to prostitution to trade in weapons. A United Nations study concluded in 1999 that "from the perspective of organized crime in the 1990s, Al Capone was a small-time hoodlum with restricted horizons, limited ambitions and merely a local fiefdom."[108] The United Nations notes three classifications of transnational organized crime: (1) groups that can be specifically identified; (2) clusters of criminal groups that originate from specific geographic localities; and (3) the market factors toward which transnational organized crime groups gravitate and within which they operate.[109]

Transnational criminal networks can operate clandestinely or hide behind legitimate front groups. They are inherently dispersed and lack an identifiable physical infrastructure. Such groups are able to exploit differences in national laws and regulations and are highly resilient and redundant. If one part of the network is taken down, the remainder will stay in place. Transnational criminal networks tend to have a core, based around some form of kinship or close operational ties among a leadership group. This core is often located in weak states which serve as safe-havens. The core group then tends to have peripheral affiliates that range from organizational leaders to couriers and transportation personnel. Such networks organize to gather information as an early warning against infiltration by law enforcement and might engage in collaboration with other networks while also exploiting corrupt officials within governments for both means of operating and information gathering. These networks thus can become virtual entities including organizers, insulators, communicators, guardians, extenders, monitors, and crossovers who are recruited from legal activity and maintain their official positions.[110]

Transnational organized crime is especially problematic as a conduit for illegal weapons trade. For example, North Korean officials have openly boasted that they will sell fissile nuclear material and even weapons for the right price. North Korean intelligence agents have already been identified in the international illegal drug trade and counterfeiting. Some North Korean ambassadors fund their embassies through black-market trading in methamphetamine, heroin, and cocaine. North Korea also brings in about $500 million a year by selling missiles and related missile technology.[111] North Korea could exploit its ties to the global criminal underworld to open black-market trade in nuclear weapons and related materials. In 2004, inspectors from the International Atomic Energy Agency discovered evidence that North Korea had secretly supplied Libya with nearly two tons of uranium, which could have been enriched to weapons grade via centrifuges Libya was also seeking. While no evidence had emerged of North Korean assistance with Iran's nuclear ambitions, North Korean nuclear experts had been monitored by Western intelligence at Iranian nuclear facilities.[112]

Russia presents the most serious danger for the convergence of organized crime and proliferation. The rise of organized crime within Russia during the 1990s was extensive. Some estimates showed that as much as two-thirds of the Russian economy was under some sort of influence from organized crime. Many private enterprises and banks found themselves having to pay large margins from their profits to protection rackets—criminal gangs seemed to replace the rule of law in some areas of the economy. By the late 1990s, there were an estimated 8,000 criminal gangs in the former Soviet Union of which 200 had global ties.[113] Much of this emergence of organized crime resulted from the end of the Cold War when the Soviet security apparatus, the KGB, was reduced in size. Downsizing the KGB left a cadre of about 100,000 people with expertise in international clandestine activity, such as money laundering, looking for employment. The rise of transnational organized crime could further erode state stability, and if combined with dilapidated conditions in the Russian military, lead to the theft or sale of nuclear materials and conventional weapons. There were at least eighteen known attempts of nuclear weapons trafficking from Russia in the decade following the Soviet collapse. Military trucks have been used by narcotics and weapons smugglers, including the smuggling of short and medium-ranged missiles, as they are not typically searched by Russian internal security forces.

The technology of nuclear weapons presents a particular challenge created by the nexus of supply, demand, and transnational networks. There are some 30,000 strategic and tactical nuclear weapons in the world. Stockpiles of separated plutonium and highly enriched uranium are estimated to include about 470 tons of separated plutonium—enough for roughly 100,000 bombs. There is nearly 1,600 tons of highly enriched uranium, which is enough for over 130,000 additional bombs. Aside from the nuclear states or suspected nuclear states, there is enough plutonium for civilian use for more weapons in Belgium, Germany, Japan, and Switzerland and about 20 tons of civilian highly enriched uranium at over 130 operational, and an unknown number of closed, civilian research facilities in more than thirty countries.[114] There are, overall, some 20,000 nuclear weapons in assembled form in Russia alone, though only a small number of those—about 5,000—are operationally deployed along with several thousand tactical warheads. The remaining weapons are waiting for either deployment or destruction at sixty-five to seventy-five storage facilities in Russia. There is an estimated 600 tons of weapons grade separated plutonium and highly enriched uranium located in 252 buildings at fifty-three sites spread across eleven time zones.[115] Russia had made significant improvements at protecting its nuclear facilities. Basic security upgrades include placing bricks over windows and blocking access to sites on about 40 percent of its nuclear storage sites and about 17 percent of the sites had received comprehensive security and accounting upgrades.[116] While that was an improvement, the large percentage left to be secured remains a serious concern.

Most attempts at smuggling nuclear material from Russia have been relatively small-scale criminal efforts. The network of organized criminal activity has, however, moved closer to nuclear facilities. For example, at Russia's main storage facility for plutonium and highly enriched uranium, counterintelligence officers closed down an organized crime ring supplying illegal drugs to security forces there. Russia and its surrounding former Soviet republics all have significant weaknesses at their customs and border patrols. Few border crossings have nuclear weapons detection equipment and even less have personnel trained to use it.[117] The biggest problem from Russia has, nevertheless, been the illegal transfer of conventional weapons and equipment. By 2004, an estimated 27,000 firearms had been stolen from military units in Russia and 53,900 crimes involving illegal trading in weapons were reported in 2001 alone.[118] According to the United States' General Accounting Office, 1,500 Russian customs officers were fired in 1998 for corruption and at one border crossing personnel agreed to turn off radiation detection equipment in exchange for alcohol.[119]

The A. Q. Khan Nuclear Shopping Center

Transnational networks facilitate a growing danger of a black market in nuclear weapons technology. In 2004, this risk was exposed in the form of the nuclear trading network of Pakistani scientist A. Q. Khan. Khan was the scientific pioneer of the Pakistani nuclear weapons program. Khan, who the Pakistani government says worked without their approval, developed, over several decades, a covert transnational network to profit from the sale of nuclear weapons technology and designs. The market focused on obtaining non-weapons-grade uranium, which can be legally purchased, combined with illicitly traded centrifuges. These centrifuges can process uranium into weapons-grade material by spinning away impurities and retaining U-235, which can then be used to create atomic reactions used to detonate nuclear warheads. Uranium can be found widely around the world and efforts to keep it under control have not been successful. For example, in Congo the mining operation that provided uranium for the atomic bombs dropped on Japan in 1945 is closed for operations. Yet thousands of diggers continue every day to hack at open earth, filling thousands of burlap sacks with soil rich in cobalt, copper, and radioactive uranium. This activity provided $1 billion in business in 2002 for poverty-stricken Congo. Near to the mines, businessmen from Africa, India, and China have set up smelting mills through which the products are shipped to Zambia and then overseas.[120]

The role of A.Q. Khan illustrates the danger that, once the scientific knowledge of how to build nuclear weapons is attained, it can be hard to keep it contained. Mr. Khan gained expertise in nuclear design technology in the 1970s when he worked on centrifuge designs in the Netherlands. He returned to Pakistan, where it is believed he soon applied his knowledge, via stolen designs, to the Pakistani nuclear program. Khan became well known in Pakistan as a strong supporter of the global Islamic movement and a critic of restrictive positions of the existing nuclear powers. Khan widely publicized information in scholarly papers about how to make centrifuges effective. In the 1990s, he began to advertise sales of used equipment from his laboratory in Pakistan. Contacts between Pakistani nuclear experts and potential recipients began as early as 1987, when Pakistan transferred centrifuge design information to Iran, North Korea, and Libya. Mr. Khan apparently made at least thirteen personal trips to North Korea, which offered to send its missile technology to Pakistan in exchange for centrifuge designs and equipment.[121]

The Khan network was small, efficient, and profited enormously from the transfer of nuclear weapons technology. It began to unravel when, in April 2003, a ship with a cargo of super-strong aluminum tubing was stopped in the Suez Canal by German authorities who determined it was headed toward North Korea. The tubes were consistent with Mr. Khan's centrifuge designs. In October 2003, a German-registered ship bound for Libya was stopped by the United States, which discovered thousands of parts for uranium centrifuges linked to businesses in Turkey and Malaysia. This exposure combined with diplomatic pressure on Libya so that it soon thereafter announced it was abandoning its nuclear weapons program. The International Atomic Energy Agency was granted access to Libya's programs and it thus was possible to explore how this network of nuclear weapons proliferation operated.

The shipment to Libya had come from Dubai, via a middleman working for Khan. This same agent had previously offered Iraq assistance on its nuclear program in 1990.[122] This representative offered to provide Iraq with nuclear bomb designs and uranium enrichment equipment in exchange for $5 million. Iraq rejected the offer, believing it likely to be a scam.[123] The Khan network, working out of about a dozen different locations, was organized to trade components for uranium-enriching gas centrifuges. Libya acknowledged that it purchased parts for at least 4,000 advanced centrifuges. This would have allowed it to enrich enough uranium to make several nuclear bombs a year—though only a small amount of the necessary parts actually reached Libya. Libya also lacked rotors, rapidly spinning tubes needed for the core of a centrifuge.[124]

The Khan network consisted mostly of legitimate businesses spread around a variety of countries. Khan largely served as a salesman negotiating the parameters of a nuclear technology deal and then promising delivery of parts in exchange for money. A variety of middlemen would then find suppliers for the necessary components and finished parts were shipped to Dubai where they were assembled. The suppliers included businesses in Malaysia, South Africa, Japan, the United Arab Emirates, and Germany. Components were produced independently and included a range of electronics, vacuum systems, and high-strength metals.[125] In Malaysia, *Scomi Precision Engineering* (a subsidiary of *Scomi Group Berhad*, a prominent and public trading conglomerate) manufactured components for export to Libya. They produced fourteen semifinished components, shipped in four deliveries to Libya between December 2002 and August 2003 in exchange for $3.4 million.[126] This business produced a total of 330 tons of quality aluminum purchased from a German firm in Singapore legally.[127]

Chartered flights were used to deliver the cargo organized by a network of middlemen that included three German businessmen and a Sri Lankan. The Sri Lankan associate, Buhary Syed Abu Tahir, told Malaysian police that he had been asked by Khan to send two shipping containers of used centrifuges to Iran from Dubai aboard a merchant vessel owned by an Iranian company. The Iranian individual receiving the shipment provided two briefcases with $3 million cash which was then stashed at a residence owned by Khan in Dubai. A British national living in France also helped obtain material for Libya via Spain and Italy. Tahir described the Khan organization as a "loose network without a rigid hierarchy or a head and a deputy head" with some associates of Khan dating to the early 1970s.[128]

Khan, who pled guilty and was then pardoned by Pakistan's military leader Gen. Pervez Musharraf, insists that the only material transferred was old, second rate technology of little actual use. In the case of Libya, however, nuclear weapon blueprints were included—for $50 million. This information would have allowed Libya to bypass considerable steps in developing a self-run uranium reprocessing program and given it explicit detail on how to assemble an implosion-type nuclear bomb to place atop a large ballistic missile. The blueprints were detailed down to the level of what torque to use on the bolts and what glue to use on the parts.[129] Some of these blueprints were well-engineered, but second generation, documents originating from China.[130] Through the transfers, Khan earned millions of dollars and lived a lavish lifestyle beyond the means of a Pakistani governmental scientist.[131] Hundreds of millions of dollars were exchanged in this nuclear technology network over a period of about fifteen years.[132]

The dangers of the network were illustrated by the high degree of legal activity that was integrated into an illicit and dangerous illegal trade. As a Malaysian police report on the network's activity concluded, "to untrained eyes, such components would not raise any concern as the components are similar to components that could be used by the 'petro-chemical industry' and 'water treatment' and various other industries."[133] When the International Atomic Energy Agency received documents at the center of its investigations in Libya, they were handed over in two white plastic shopping bags from a Pakistani clothing shop called "Good Looks Tailor."[134]

Countries like Russia or networks like the Khan smuggling ring are not the only challenge regarding the proliferation of nuclear weapons technology. In 2004, government auditors in the United States disclosed that the U.S. had made insufficient effort to recover large quantities of weapons-grade uranium—in total enough to make about 1,000 nuclear bombs. This material had been distributed to forty-three countries over several decades—including to Iran and Pakistan. This uranium was loaned, leased, or sold to countries beginning in the 1950s to help promote the peaceful use of nuclear energy. The intention was to recover the materials but the effort to do so was lax. The audit estimated that the government had recovered only about 2,600 kilograms of 17,500 dispersed—leaving about 15,000 remaining overseas. The material is currently under the control of governments, universities, and private companies in twelve countries that are not expected to participate in programs to facilitate the material's return including Iran, Pakistan, Israel, Mexico, Jamaica, and South Africa.[135]

SECURITY PRIVATIZATION

The expansion of transnational networks in security reflects an increasing trend toward the privatization of security. This particular trend poses significant challenges to the ability of nation-states to control the security agenda. Private companies have filled a void left by the historic role played by mercenaries. Some states are ceding direct control over important security operations to the private sector.[136] These private contractors have played an especially important, and sometimes illegitimate, role in recent wars in Afghanistan and Iraq. Finally, private interest groups have also played a growing role in agenda-setting by focusing international attention onto particular security problems that states might otherwise have ignored.

Private Security Companies

Private security firms are increasingly present in international conflict situations where states find it easier to outsource some security operations. Private security companies can be less costly than training large numbers of troops. Moreover, as contractors exist outside the control of nation-states, they lack accountability that military or intelligence personnel might have. Private contractors might thus do things that states otherwise might not get away with. Private contractors can, alternatively, venture into war zones where states might not be willing to go, provide security protection for humanitarian aid groups and for political leaders seeking to consolidate peace but who are at risk.[137] Contracting to private logistics firms might also save governments money or allow them to assign more pressing tasks to formal soldiers.[138]

American companies have taken the lead among private military functions. Military Professional Resources, Incorporated (MPRI) employs seventeen retired U.S. generals and sent 182 former Special Forces personnel to train and equip Bosnian military forces in the 1990s. This operation was supplied with $100 million worth of surplus American military equipment. Vinnel Corporation, which is a branch of the large military manufacturer Northrop Grumman, has trained the Saudi National Guard and received a $48 million contract to train the Iraqi military. Executive Outcomes, which eventually went out of business, sent 600 soldiers to Angola and 300 to Sierra Leone to combat insurgency movements that local governments were unable to manage. Executive Outcomes included its own air force with MI-8, MI-17, and MI24 helicopters and MiG-23 fighters. This group was central to outcomes in a number of African conflicts during the 1990s. Comprised primarily of former South African military officials, Executive Outcomes had a permanent staff of only thirty people, but could deploy a fully supported battalion of 650 fighters within fifteen days. Between 1993 and 1998, the number of private security companies operating in Angola alone grew from six to eighty.[139]

The total profit taken in by private security companies is estimated to be $100 billion a year. Some $87 billion of money spent by the United States in Afghanistan and Iraq in 2004 was allocated to private companies. Halliburton, which does a range of logistical support for military operations including security operations for the oil industry, had $5 billion worth of contracts in Iraq by 2004. The Halliburton subsidiary Kellogg, Brown & Root was a major logistics component in U.S. operations in Somalia in the early 1990s. This company became the number one employer in Somalia by 1993 with 2,500 locals on its payroll. By September 2003, Kellogg, Brown & Root had billed over two years about $950 million for work done under contracts in Iraq which are capped at $8.2 billion. Kellogg, Brown & Root was also set to earn additional income from contracts to maintain U.S. bases ranging from the Balkans to the Horn of Africa stretching east to Afghanistan and Kyrgyzstan. It also built the U.S. detention facility for captured terrorists in Guantanamo, Cuba. A number of specific operating systems are heavily dependent upon contracting for their operations including the American F-117 stealth fighter, M1A1 tank, Patriot missile, and Global Hawk unmanned drone aircraft.[140]

Other companies in Iraq included DynCorp which was given a $50 million contract for law-enforcement support, police training, and prison guard duty.

DynCorp also won a lucrative contract to provide security for the leading government figures in Afghanistan. Custer Battles received a $16 million contract to provide security at the Baghdad airport, and the British firm Erinys received $39 million to protect Iraqi oil fields.[141] Not accounting for the Iraq spending, as much as 8 percent of the regular U.S. defense budget (about $30 billion) is spent each year on contracts for private security operators. Budgetary outlays to American private companies have replaced or complemented major support activity including, by 2003: $35 billion allocated to the private sector for information technology (growing at a rate of 10–15 percent annually), $191 million for military supply operations run at seven locations, $171 million for soldier recruitment in seven states, and $4 billion for soldier training and running war games.[142] In Colombia, six different companies have received a share of $1.2 billion annually from the United States to fly planes that spray coca fields and monitor smuggling with radar. British firms also account for a large number of private security companies, such as Global Risk International, which provided Nepalese Gurkhas, Fijian paramilitaries, and former British SAS veterans to guard the American headquarters in Iraq.

The increasing role played by private security companies in military operations raises questions about the ability of states to control and protect personnel who act on the states' interest but are not subject to oversight or even direct legal liability. For example, if a soldier wearing a uniform commits a crime in a foreign land, they would be legally the responsibility of their command authority—the military under which they serve. If, however, a private security employee commits a crime, even while employed by another country, they would be subject to local laws of the state they are in. Because many of the places where such private security forces operate are, in effect, failed states with no local legal apparatus, they often operate outside the rule of law.[143] In one case, a number of American contract employees in Bosnia-Herzegovina were implicated in criminal activity including rape and operating a sexual slavery racket involving trade in girls as young as twelve years old. Several of these contractors were fired from their jobs, but none were prosecuted. The only court case involved the whistleblowers who were fired for publicizing the illegal activity.[144] Military command and control questions arise: Should contractors carry weapons? If they abandon their work, are they deserters? Do they get rights as prisoners of war if they are captured? Do they have to obey the laws of war if they are doing guard duty at a prison?

Outsourcing War

In the post-invasion peace-support operations in Iraq, private security companies were assigned significant roles in the U.S.-led military occupation.

Numerically, private contractors were the second largest coalition member—with about 20,000 working in Iraq. By spring 2004, assignments for private security companies in Iraq included guarding reconstruction projects; providing security for senior American officials; escorting supply convoys through hostile territory; and defending key locations, including fifteen regional authority headquarters and the primary American base in central Baghdad. The costs of these private security companies were about 25 percent of $18 billion that had been authorized for reconstruction in Iraq by the United States government in 2004. This was significantly more expensive than an initial estimate that contractors would only account for 10 percent of spending.[145] As much as 30 percent of primary military support services were being supplied by private contractors in the Iraq mission by 2003. Included in this mix were eleven work orders valued at $66.2 million awarded to CACI International Inc. which provided interrogation support and analysis work for the U.S. Army. These contractors were assigned tasks including debriefing of personnel, intelligence report writing, and screening and interrogation of detainees at established holding areas. Interrogators were assigned to coordinate and work in conjunction with military police and military intelligence interrogation units. Because of a lack of trained interrogators, the U.S. Army contracted this task—only to find that few of the CACI personnel had any formal training in military interrogation policies and techniques.[146] Some of these contractors were hired by CACI after five-minute phone interviews and with no resume, fingerprint, or criminal background checks.[147]

Using private contractors for intelligence activities carried a high risk as private contractors could be co-opted by, and working for, other governments. These individuals' loyalty, accountability, or professional training could not be as guaranteed as in formal military command structure. In a December 2000 internal memo, the U.S. Assistant Secretary of the Army gave instructions to the Deputy Chief of Staff for Intelligence that contractors' involvement in intelligence should be restricted. The memo noted that "private contractors may be acquired by foreign interests, acquire and maintain interests in foreign countries, and provide support to foreign customers" and that "reliance on private contractors poses risks to maintaining adequate civilian oversight over intelligence operations."[148] Yet, no formal effort was made to place such restrictions into field manuals for the U.S. military that govern the activity of private contractors. In fact, a private contractor, Military Professional Resources, Inc., was hired by the Pentagon to write the rules for contractors in the field.

The role of private contractors in Iraq was publicized when the burnt bodies of several private contractors doing security duty in the city of Falluja were hung from a bridge and shown in newspapers and on television around the world. In September 2004, two Americans and one British contractor were kidnapped and then beheaded in Iraq. The suffering that private contractors underwent exposed the fact that many had gone there desperate for the income. But most private contractors also believed very much in helping the Iraqi people. These individuals were often highly capable and had some degree of serious military background including retired Navy SEALS working for Blackwater Security Consulting, retired Army Rangers working for Special Operations Consulting-Security Management Group, and retired Green Berets and Delta Force personnel working for Triple Canopy. The typical recruits for a private security company work on average 80 hours a week and earn about $15,000 a month. Their ability to serve for short-term deployments and then leave after a high salary payout would increasingly pose a challenge for U.S. National Guard and Reserve retention, as they could lose recruits to these private outfits.[149]

Private contractors in Iraq participated in human rights abuses at the Abu Ghraib prison. In summer 2004, it became known that American personnel had used torture and psychological tactics to humiliate Iraqi prisoners of war. While a number of U.S. military personnel were tried for their involvement in these activities, none of the contractors present were violating the Geneva Conventions on prisoners of war. CACI International provided more than half of all the analysts and interrogators at Abu Ghraib and all the translators there were employees of Titan Corp. Contractors were put into positions where they were actually supervising military officers.[150] The only investigation of abuse by contractors was carried out by CACI itself. Even before that investigation was complete, the U.S. government extended an additional $23 million contract to CACI. Another company, Erinys, discovered that four of its guards killed while working in Iraq were former members of governmental security forces from the Apartheid era in South Africa. One of these employees had admitted to crimes in an amnesty application to the Truth and Reconciliation Commission there.[151] In Afghanistan, three Americans were sentenced to extended prison sentences for running a private prison and torturing Afghan detainees. The leader of the group, Jonathan Idema, a former member of the U.S. Army Special Forces, presented a defense that showed video of him being greeted by high-level Afghan officials and meeting with a U.S. Army officer. Idema asserted that all of their operations had been approved by either corps commanders or regional governors. However, the Afghan court concluded that there had been no authorization for these men's activity.[152]

The New Agenda Setters

An additional expanding private component of twenty-first century security is the role played by international nongovernmental organizations. Activist movements and independent research institutes generate transparency about the activity of states and their military-security activities. This work complicates the ability of states to act, but also provides citizens with information on which to judge their governments. Issues such as human rights and the environment owe their place on the world's strategic agenda to the efforts of nongovernmental activist movements such as Amnesty International, Human Rights Watch, Freedom House, the Rainforest Action Network, and the World Watch Institute. In the early 1990s, a hunger strike by American activist Randall Robinson brought the attention of the United States government onto Haiti—the kind of place that a great power would have previously ignored. The Nobel Peace Prize was awarded in 1997 to Jody Williams who worked to coordinate the International Campaign to Ban Landmines. This effort resulted in a global treaty banning the production and use of these weapons which kill indiscriminately. Meanwhile, websites offer for private use satellite imagery and information on a wide array of technology, tactics, and strategy that once were the classified domain of nation-states. Indeed, there is little information about international security that cannot be found via a good Internet search engine. As such, a wide range of possibilities exist for multiple actors to engage in agenda-setting in international security.

SANCTIONING SECURITY

The relationship between security and trade is heightened by the use of sanctions to enforce international standards or to project state power. International economic sanctions entail the stoppage of any trade or financial relationship between two or more international actors, typically by one state or international organization targeted against another state or group of states. Sanctions are a popular tool of exercising power because they help to send a serious political message without resorting to force. International sanctions have been seen as a legitimate tool of modern diplomacy since they were enshrined in the League of Nations Covenant and used by the United Nations as instruments of collective action among states. States have applied multinational sanctions or bilateral sanctions to promote or compel change in international behavior. With the end of the Cold War, sanctions became a popular tool of the United States, which imposed over sixty different sanctions on countries during the 1990s.[153] The United Nations also imposed economic sanctions on Iraq, Libya, the Balkans, and North Korea. A number of states placed sanctions on India and Pakistan after they tested nuclear weapons in 1998.

The Sanctions Dilemma

Despite the increasing use of sanctions as a policy tool, there is considerable disagreement on their utility. The question as to whether sanctions work depends largely on what states seek to accomplish. Evidence suggests that sanctions have been the least successful at promoting the fall of governments or the overthrow of dictators. There has also been minimal success at getting governments to change policies that are perceived as being fundamental to their interests. However, sanctions might have played a more positive role as an inducement to achieve policy change over positions that states are not fundamentally committed to. Sanctions have been shown to play a role in weakening a government's ability to carry out aggressive plans by denying key resources.[154] Sanctions are also thought to have had a number of unintended consequences and thus are increasingly controversial.[155] For example, sanctions are often thought to hurt those people that they are intended to help—such as in the case where a dictatorship is being punished. The denial of goods and services to a dictatorship is more likely to pass on the pain of sanctions to the population rather than to those who hold power. Sanctions can also hurt the interests of the state imposing sanctions if they are not universal. Those who are most negatively damaged in that circumstance are producers inside the sanctioning country who lose access to markets. By 1998, the United States was estimated to be losing about $20 billion a year in export profits due to sanctions. This cost American workers about 200,000 well-paying jobs.[156] Sanctions can also deny states the tool of diplomatic engagement and economic leverage to work with countries to get them to change particular policies.

According to a survey of international sanctions conducted by the Institute for International Economics, sanctions have been most effective when the goals are relatively modest; the target is much weaker than those imposing the sanctions; there is a significant amount of trade to cut off; they are sustained for a long time; force is used to implement them; and they are multilateral. The institute surveyed 116 cases of international sanctions and found them to be effective about 33 percent of the time.[157] The direct correlation between sanctions and increases in security is limited. The most well-known case is South Africa, which had a comprehensive sanctions regime imposed on it by the United Nations in the 1980s for its official policy of segregation between whites and blacks. Sanctions worked, largely because they were universal and because those who were suffering under them—the black majority in South Africa—were willing to bear the costs as a path to long-term change.

There are numerous cases where well-intended sanctions have led to significant decreases in security. In 1991, the United Nations imposed sanctions on the Balkans via an embargo on the sale of weapons into the region. The problem, however, was that one side in the conflict, the Serbs in Yugoslavia and their Serb brethren in Bosnia-Herzegovina, inherited the majority of weapons and associated equipment from the collapse of the Yugoslav national army. This left the Croatians and Muslims, who had seceded from Yugoslavia in search of independence, largely undefended. By 1993, the United Nations had sent 25,000 peacekeepers, mainly British and French, into the region to uphold ceasefire agreements. Once these troops were on the ground, these countries became deeply opposed to lifting the arms embargo because they feared that their troops would be caught in a spiraling crossfire of ethnic payback. Once the arms embargo had been put in place, it was not possible for it to be lifted without the approval of Britain and France in the United Nations Security Council. These same countries had also recognized the legal independence of Slovenia, Croatia, and Bosnia-Herzegovina. They were granted statehood but denied the most important component of legal sovereignty—the right to self-defense. The end result was an ethnic slaughter in which over 200,000 went dead or missing.

The case of Iraq in 1990 illustrates both the opportunity and the danger of using trade sanctions as a security tool. The United Nations Security Council levied severe economic sanctions on Iraq following its invasion of Kuwait. Only food and humanitarian goods were permitted to flow into Iraq. The sanctions, it was agreed at the UN, could not be lifted until the Security Council had determined through intrusive weapons inspections that Iraq had met a number of postwar requirements including complete elimination of weapons of mass destruction programs. However, the primary victims of these sanctions were the citizens of Iraq, and not the leadership. While Saddam Hussein lived comfortably in his palaces, the UN estimated that the sanctions had contributed to the death of over 576,000 children and that Iraq had its infant mortality rate double in the 1990s.[158] By 1998, it appeared that the sanctions were simply not working. The Iraqi government told UN weapons inspectors it had complied with their mandates and then kicked them out. The period between 1998 and 2003 would lead to a growing sense of insecurity, particularly in the United States, that Iraq had reconstituted its weapons of mass destruction program. Only after the United States invaded and overthrew the government of Saddam Hussein did it become clear that, regarding weapons of mass destruction, the sanctions had actually worked—there were no weapons of mass destruction in Iraq. As one senior Iraqi scientist put it after the war, the material condition for developing weapons of mass destruction was considerably worse than when the programs had been in full development in the 1980s. Abdul Noor, a major developer of Iraq's earlier nuclear program, said: "We would have had to start from less than zero. . . . The country was cornered. We were boycotted. We were embargoed. The truth is, we disintegrated."[159]

Are Sanctions Better Than Nothing?

The use of sanctions as a tool of leveraging trade for security illustrates a moral dilemma. The United States, for example, imposed harsh sanctions on

Burma to punish the military for denying basic human rights to its people. Yet the denial of trade contributed to some 100,000 Burmese people losing their jobs while the military dictators remained in power. This economic dislocation occurred in a country where one child in ten dies before age 5, 44 percent of children are malnourished, and 58 percent of pregnant women do not receive adequate medical care. Many of the women made unemployed as a result of U.S. sanctions had little choice but to earn their living in the sex industry, thereby risking exposure to and proliferation of HIV/AIDS.[160] Yet, even in such a circumstance, alternative policies such as doing nothing or using military power are unpalatable.[161] The case of Iraq also suggests that, while morally abhorrent for the Iraqi people, the sanctions had accomplished their purpose of forcing the disarmament of Iraq. In the case of India and Pakistan, the world community could not agree on effective sanctions as regarding either potential nuclear development or nuclear testing. After India and Pakistan tested nuclear weapons in 1998, the immediate international response was to apply sanctions. Yet this reaction raised a major strategic question—what gain was there in sanctioning India and Pakistan when they already had the weapons? They were not going to roll back their weapons programs. Sanctions only served to make already poor and potentially unstable countries even poorer and more unstable. Under harsh international sanctions they would be poor, unstable countries armed with nuclear weapons and isolated from engagement with the international community. Indeed, Pakistan emerged as a vital ally in the U.S.-led war on terrorism beginning in 2001 and became a major recipient of foreign economic assistance. Notably, the threat of sanctions had done nothing to deter either country from pursuing nuclear weapons technology nor were they persuaded to give up their weapons by the threat of sanctions.

SUMMARY

This chapter illustrates ongoing transformations in the nature of technology and the business of global security. The intersection between the evolving network of ties between the civilian and security world of trade is illustrated by the challenges of commerce mixing with transnational organized crime and nuclear proliferation. The particular power dynamics of the supply and demand equation are illustrated both by the demands for proliferation and also by the growing privatization of security operations. Finally, the relationship between trade, and the stoppage of trade via sanctions, and security outcomes shows that actions that states take to exert their power in this integrated network of transnational information and commerce can have unintended consequences. These examples of new dimensions of security show that there is an encroaching nexus between the civilian and military world, which blurs the two and creates a host of new targets for anyone engaged in conflict, but also new opportunities for peace.

NOTES

1. Abe Singer and Scott Rowell, "Information Warfare: An Old Operational Concept with New Implications," *INSS Strategic Forum*, no. 99 (December 1996): 1–3.

2. Theodor W. Galdi, "Revolution in Military Affairs?" *CRS Report for Congress*, Congressional Research Service, 95–1170-F, December 11, 1995.

3. "Historical Examples of RMAs," Center for Strategic and Budgetary Assessments, at www.csbaonline.org/2Stretegic_Studies/1Revolution-in-Military_Affairs/REvolution-Military_Affairs.htm (accessed Summer 2004).

4. Robert S. Bolia, "Over-reliance on Technology in Warfare: The Yom Kippur War as a Case Study," *Parameters*, 34, no. 2 (Summer 2004): 46–56.

5. Bob Drogin, "Spy Work in Iraq Riddled by Failures," *Los Angeles Times*, June 17, 2004.

6. "At-a-Glance: Butler Report," *BBC News*, July 14, 2004.

7. Joseph Cirincione, Jessica T. Mathews, and George Perkovich, *WMD in Iraq: Evidence and Implications* (Washington, D.C.: Carnegie Endowment for International Peace, 2004).

8. Douglas Jehl and Eric Schmitt, "Errors Are Seen in Early Attacks on Iraqi Leaders," *New York Times*, June 13, 2004.

9. David Talbot, "How Technology Failed in Iraq," *Technology Review*, October 31, 2004.

10. Mark Hanna, "Task Force XXI: The Army's Digital Experiment," *Strategic Forum*, no. 119 (July 1997): 2.

11. Hanna, "Task Force XXI," 2.

12. Thomas K. Adams, "The Real Military Revolution," *Parameters* 30, no. 3 (Autumn 2000): 54–55.

13. Caroline Drees, "US Military Taps Bugs and Weeds in War on Terror," *Reuters*, November 24, 2004.

14. Robert E. Armstrong and Jerry B. Warner, "Biology and the Battlefield," *Defense Horizons*, no. 25 (April 2003): 1–8.

15. John L. Peterson and Dennis M. Egan, "Small Security: Nanotechnology and Future Defense," *Defense Horizons*, no. 8 (March 2002): 1–2.

16. "Nano-needle Operates on Cell," *BBC News*, December 15, 2004.

17. Petersen and Egan, "Small Security," 2–3.

18. Robert O'Harrow Jr., "Tiny Sensors That Can Track Anything," *Washington Post*, September 24, 2004.

19. "Marines Aided by Robotic Airplane in Iraq," *Associated Press*, November 29, 2004.

20. Douglas Pasternak, "Wonder Weapons," *U.S. News and World Report*, July 7, 1997.

21. Curt Anderson, "Government Says Terrorists May Use Lasers," *Associated Press*, December 9, 2004.

22. Graham T. Allison and Paul X. Kelley, *Nonlethal Weapons and Capabilities* (New York: Council on Foreign Relations, 2004).

23. William B. Arkin, "The Pentagon's Secret Scream: Sonic Devices Are Being Deployed," *Los Angeles Times*, March 10, 2004.

24. William M. Arkin, "Pulling Punches," *Los Angeles Times*, January 4, 2004.

25. Barbara Starr, "Bunker Busters May Grow to 30,000 Pounds," CNN, July 21, 2004.

26. Bob Woodward, *Bush at War* (New York: Simon and Schuster, 2002).

27. Michael E. O'Hanlon, "Beware the 'RMA'nia!'" paper presented at the National Defense University, September 9, 1998.

28. Katherine Pfleger Shrader, "Spy Imagery Agency Watching Inside U.S.," *Associated Press*, September 27, 2004.

29. "Tiananmen: A Picture Which Cost a Life," *BBC News*, June 4, 2004.

30. Daniel B. Wood, "Radio ID Tags Proliferate, Stirring Privacy Debate," *Christian Science Monitor*, December 15, 2004.

31. Michael A. Wertheimer, "Crippling Innovation—And Intelligence," *Washington Post*, July 21, 2004.

32. Ben Charny, "World Net Population Nears 300 Million," ZDNet News, September 8, 2000.

33. Nua Internet Surveys, www.nua.ie/surveys (accessed December 2005).

34. Available at www.nua.com/surveys/?f=VS&art_idz905358417&rel=true (accessed December 2, 2005).

35. Dan Kuehl, "Defining Information Power," *Strategic Forum*, no. 115 (June 1997): 5.

36. Martin Libicki, "Information Dominance," *Strategic Forum*, no. 132 (November 1997): 4.

37. Libicki, "Information Dominance," 4.

38. Larry Rohter, "China Widens Economic Role in Latin America," *New York Times*, November 20, 2004.

39. Bob Nonow, "Global Networks: Emerging Constraints on Strategy," *Defense Horizons*, no. 43 (July 2004): 1–4.

40. Singer and Rowell, "Information Warfare," 4.

41. Richard E. Hayes and Gary Wheatley, "Information Warfare and Deterrence," *Strategic Forum*, no. 87 (October 1996): 5.

42. "Net Security Threats Growing Fast," *BBC News*, September 21, 2004.

43. Jacques S. Gansler, "Protecting Cyberspace," in *Transforming America's Military*, ed. Hans Binnendijk (Washington, D.C.: National Defense University, 2002), 336.

44. John S. Foster Jr. et al., "Report of the Commission to Assess the Threat to the United States from Electromagnetic Pulse (EMP) Attack," at house.armedservices .gov/ (accessed Fall 2004).

45. Foster et al., "Report of the Commission."

46. Jon B. Alterman, "The Information Revolution and the Middle East," in *The Future Security Environment in the Middle East*, ed. Nora Bensahel and Daniel L. Byman (Santa Monica, Calif.: Rand Corporation, 2004), 227–51.

47. Alterman, "Information Revolution," 238–39.

48. Alterman, "Information Revolution," 245.

49. Pew Research Center for the People and the Press, "Views of a Changing World 2003," Washington D.C., June 3, 2003; and "A Year after Iraq War," Washington D.C., March 16, 2004.

50. Organization for Economic Cooperation and Development, "Education at a Glance," Paris, 2004.

51. "India Launches Satellite to Boost Education, Stem Illiteracy," *AFP*, September 20, 2004.

52. Mark Mazzetti, "PR Meets Psy-Ops in War on Terror," *Los Angeles Times*, December 1, 2004.

53. Thom Shanker and Eric Schmitt, "Pentagon Weighs Use of Deception in a Broad Arena," *New York Times*, December 13, 2004.

54. Jim Wolf, "U.S. Eyes Space as Possible Battleground," *Reuters*, January 19, 2004.

55. See Lawrence M. Krause, *The Physics of Star Trek* (St. Helens, Ore.: Perennial, 1996); and Lawrence M. Krause, *Beyond Star Trek* (St. Helens, Ore.: Perennial, 1998).

56. James Clay Moltz, "Reigning in the Space Cowboys," *Bulletin of the Atomic Scientists* 59, no. 1 (January/February 2003): 6–8.

57. The Eisenhower Institute, "The Historical Context: Some Scientific, Commercial and Military Uses of Space," at www.eisenhowerinstitute.org/programs/global-partnerships (accessed Fall 2004).

58. Peter L. Hayes, "Current and Future Military Use of Space," in United Nations Institute for Disarmament Research, *Outer Space and Global Security* (New York: United Nations, 2003), 21–27.

59. Clay Moltz, "Future Space Security," Nuclear Threat Reduction Initiative, June 2002.

60. "Bush Plans for Shutdown of GPS Network During Crisis," *Associated Press*, December 16, 2004.

61. MAB, "On the Role of Outer Space in Confronting Aggressive Threats," The Eisenhower Institute, Washington, D.C., October 2002.

62. Bob Preston et al., *Space Weapons: Earth Wars* (Santa Monica, Calif.: Rand Corporation, 2002), 23–36.

63. Marc Lallanilla, "U.S. Military Takes First Step towards Weapons in Space," ABC News, March 30, 2004.

64. Moltz, "Future Space Security."

65. Michael Krepon, "Lost in Space: The Misguided Drive toward Antisatellite Weapons," *Foreign Affairs* 80, no. 3 (May/June 2001): 2–8.

66. Peter Hays, "United States Military Space: Into the 21st Century," *INSS Occasional Papers,* no. 42 (2002): 101.

67. Lt. Col. Peter Hays, "Space Arms Control and Regulation: Opportunities and Challenges," presentation at the George Washington University, Space Policy Institute, June 10, 2002.

68. Jeffrey Richelson, *The Wizards of Langley: Inside the CIA's Directorate of Science and Technology* (Boulder, Colo.: Westview Press, 2002).

69. Lt. Col. Peter Hays, "United States Military Space: Into the 21st Century," *INSS Occasional Papers*, no. 42 (2002): 98–99.

70. Krepon, "Lost in Space," 2–8.

71. "United States: Military Programs," Monterey Institute of International Affairs, at cns.miis.edu/research/space/us/mil.htm (accessed Fall 2004).

72. United States Space Command, "Vision for 2020," United States Space Command, Peterson Air Force Base, Colorado.

73. U.S. Strategic Command Public Affairs, *Fact File*, Offutt Air Force Base, Nebraska, March 2004.

74. Theresa Hitchens, "Weapons in Space: Silver Bullet or Russian Roulette?" a paper for the George Washington University Security Space Forum, April 18, 2002, 1.

75. Sean Kay and Theresa Hitchens, "Bush Policy Would Start Arms Race in Space," *Cleveland Plain Dealer*, May 25, 2005.

76. John M. Logsdon, "A Vital National Interest?" *Space News*, August 12, 2002, 12.

77. Norimitsu Onishi, "Japan Support for Missile Shield Could Tilt Asia Power Balance," *New York Times*, April 3, 2004.

78. Onishi, "Japan Support for Missile Shield."

79. Preston, *Space Weapons: Earth Wars*, 91–98.

80. David Rohde, "India's Lofty Ambitions in Space Meet Earthly Realities," *New York Times*, January 24, 2004.

81. "Brazil's Military Programs," Monterey Institute, at cns.miis.edu/research/space/brazil/mil.htm (accessed Fall 2004).

82. "Russia's Military Programs," Monterey Institute, at cns.miis.edu/research/space/russia/mil.htm (accessed Fall 2004).

83. "China Eyes 2017 Moon Landing," *Reuters*, November 4, 2005.

84. "China Plans Big Production of Small Satellites," *Reuters*, December 14, 2004.

85. Report of the American Physical Society Study Group on Boost-Phase Intercept Systems for National Missile Defense: Scientific and Technical Issues, July 15, 2003, at www.aps.org/public_affairs/?popa/reports/nmd03.cfm (accessed Summer 2004).

86. "Missile Defense Shield Fails Test," *BBC News*, December 15, 2004.

87. M. Elaine Bunn, "Deploying Missile Defense: Major Operational Challenges," *INSS Strategic Forum*, no. 209 (August 2004): 1–6.

88. Peter D. Zimmerman and Charles D. Ferguson, "Sweeping the Skies," *Bulletin of the Atomic Scientists* 59, no. 6 (November/December 2003).

89. David Wright and Laura Grego, "Anti-Satellite Capabilities of Planned US Missile Defense Systems," *Disarmament Diplomacy*, no. 68 (December 2002/January 2003).

90. Laura Grego, "A History of US and Soviet ASAT Programs," at www.ucsusa.org/global_security/space_weapons/a-history-of-asat-programs.html (accessed Fall 2004).

91. Theresea Hitchens, "USAF Transformation Flight Plan Highlights Space Weapons," Center for Defense Information, February 19, 2004, at www.cdi.org/program/document.cfm?DocumentID=2080&StartRow=1$ (accessed Summer 2004).

92. "Military Spending on Rise," *Associated Press*, June 8, 2005.

93. Richard F. Grimmett, "Conventional Arms Transfers to Developing Nations, 1996–2003," *CRS Report for Congress*, Congressional Research Service, August 26, 2004.

94. Elizabeth Becker and Edmund L. Andrews, "I.M.F. Says Rise in U.S. Debts Is Threat to World's Economy," *New York Times*, January 8, 2004.

95. Michael T. Klare and Lora Lumpe, "Fanning the Flames of War: Conventional Arms Transfers in the 1990s," in *World Security: Challenges for a New Century*, ed. Michael T. Klare and Yogesh Chandrani, 3rd ed. (New York: St. Martin's Press, 1998), 160–79.

96. "India and Israel Sign One-Billion-Dollar Defense Deal," *AFP*, March 6, 2004.

97. Ruth Leger Sivard, *World Military and Social Expenditures: 1996* (Washington, D.C.: World Priorities, Inc., 1996), 18–19.

98. Rachel Stohl, "Forget WMD—It's Conventional Arms That Are Killing GIs and Iraqis," *Los Angeles Times*, July 19, 2004.

99. Dana Priest and Bradley Graham, "Missing Antiaircraft Missiles Alarm Aides," *Washington Post*, November 7, 2004.

100. "Infrared Countermeasures Systems," at www.globalsecurity.org/military/systems/aircraft/systems/ircm.htm (accessed Fall 2004).

101. Bradley Graham, "Cruise Missile Threat Grows, Says Rumsfeld," *Washington Post*, August 18, 2002.

102. "Small Arms and Conflict in West Africa," *Testimony of Lisa Misol, Human Rights Watch Researcher, Before the Congressional Human Rights Caucus*, May 20, 2004.

103. Martin C. Libicki, "Global Networks and Security: How Dark Is the Dark Side?" in *The Global Century: Globalization and National Security*, ed. Richard Kugler and Ellen Frost (Washington, D.C.: National Defense University Press, 2001), 809–24.

104. Department of Transportation, "An Assessment of the Marine Transportation System: A Report to Congress," September 1999, 2.

105. Stephen J. Lukasik, Seymour E. Goodman, and David W. Longhurst, "Protecting Critical Infrastructures against Cyber-Attack," *Adelphi Paper*, no. 359 (London International Institute of Strategic Studies, 2003).

106. Phil Williams, "Organized Crime and Cybercrime: Synergies, Trends, and Responses," at usinfo.state.gov/journals/itgic/0801/ijge/gj07.htm (accessed Fall 2004).

107. Phil Williams, "Transnational Criminal Networks," in *Networks and Netwars: The Future of Terror, Crime, and Militancy*, ed. John Arquilla and David Ronfeldt (Santa Monica, Calif.: Rand Corporation, 2001), 61–97.

108. "Fighting Transnational Organized Crime," Tenth United Nations Congress on the Prevention of Crime and the Treatment of Offenders, Backgrounder, No. 1.

109. "Fighting Transnational Organized Crime," Tenth United Nations Congress.

110. Williams, "Transnational Criminal Networks," 61–97.

111. Graham Allison, *Nuclear Terrorism: The Ultimate Preventable Catastrophe* (New York: Times Books, 2004), 80–81.

112. David E. Sanger and William J. Broad, "Evidence Is Cited Linking Koreans to Libya Uranium," *New York Times*, May 23, 2004.

113. William Webster, *Organized Crime in Russia* (Washington, D.C.: Center for International and Strategic Studies, 1997 and 2000).

114. Matthew Bunn, "The Global Threat," November 14, 2002, at www.nunnturner.org/e_research/cnwm/threat/global.asp (accessed Fall 2004).

115. "Matthew Bunn, "The Threat in Russia and the Newly Independent States," October 28, 2002, at www.nunnturner.org/e_research/cnwm/threat/russia.asp (accessed Fall 2004).

116. "The Threat in Russia and the Newly Independent States."

117. "The Threat in Russia and the Newly Independent States."

118. Radio Free Europe/Radio Liberty, "Crime, Corruption and Terrorism Watch," November 12, 2001.

119. U.S. General Accounting Office, Nuclear Nonproliferation: U.S. Assistance Efforts to Help Other Countries Combat Nuclear Smuggling Need Strengthened Coordination and Planning, GAO-02–426 (Washington, D.C.: General Accounting Office, May 2002), 24.

120. Todd Pitman, "Miners Drawn to Illegal Congo Uranium," *Associated Press*, March 31, 2004.

121. David E. Sanger and William J. Broad, "From Rogue Nuclear Programs, Web of Trails Leads to Pakistan," *New York Times*, January 4, 2004.

122. Sanger and Broad, "From Rogue Nuclear Programs."

123. Peter Slevin, "Pakistani Scientist Tied to Illicit Nuclear Supply Network," *Washington Post*, February 5, 2004.

124. Joby Warrick, "Libyan Nuclear Devices Missing," *Washington Post*, May 29, 2004.

125. Peter Slevin, John Lancaster, and Kamran Khan, "At Least 7 Nations Tied to Pakistani Nuclear Ring," *Washington Post*, February 8, 2004.

126. Peter Slevin, "Pakistani Scientist Tied to Illicit Nuclear Supply Network."

127. Ellen Nakashima and Alan Sipress, "Insider Tells of Nuclear Deals, Cash," *Washington Post*, February 21, 2004.

128. Nakashima and Sipress, "Insider Tells of Nuclear Deals, Cash."

129. William J. Broad and David E. Sanger, "Warhead Blueprints Link Libya Project to Pakistan Figure," *New York Times*, February 4, 2004.

130. Joby Warrick and Peter Slevin, "Libyan Arms Designs Traced Back to China," *Washington Post*, February 15, 2004.

131. John Lancaster and Kamran Khan, "Musharraf Named in Nuclear Probe," *Washington Post*, February 3, 2004.

132. George Jahn, "Nuclear Black Market Is Small, Covert," *Associated Press*, February 2, 2004.

133. Nakashima and Sipress, "Insider Tells of Nuclear Deals, Cash."

134. Warrick and Slevin, "Libyan Arms Designs Traced Back to China."

135. Joel Brinkley and William J. Broad, "U.S. Lags in Recovering Fuel Suitable for Nuclear Arms," *New York Times*, March 7, 2004.

136. Peter W. Singer, *Corporate Warriors* (Ithaca, N.Y.: Cornell University Press, 2004); and Lawrence W. Serewicz, "Globalization, Sovereignty and the Military Revolution: From Mercenaries to Private International Security Companies," *International Politics*, no. 39 (March 2002): 75–89.

137. Al J. Venter, "Market Forces: How Hired Guns Succeeded Where the United Nations Failed," *Jane's International Defense Review*, March 1, 1998.

138. David Shearer, "Outsourcing War," *Foreign Policy*, no. 112 (Fall 1988): 68–81.

139. Herbert Howe, "Global Order and Security Privatization," *Strategic Forum*, no. 140 (May 1998): 1–7.

140. "Outsourcing War," *BusinessWeek*, September 15, 2003.

141. David Lazarus, "Taking the War Private," *San Francisco Chronicle*, January 21, 2004.

142. Nelson D. Schwartz, "The War Business: The Pentagon's Private Army," *Fortune*, March 17, 2003.

143. Ian Traynor, "The Privatization of War," *The Guardian*, December 30, 2003.

144. Traynor, "Privatization of War."

145. David Barstow et al., "Security Companies: Shadow Soldiers in Iraq," *New York Times*, April 19, 2004.

146. Andre Verloy and Daniel Poloti, "Contracting Intelligence," *Center for Public Integrity*, July 28, 2004, at www.publicintegrity.org/wow/report.aspx?aid=361 (accessed Fall 2004).

147. Peter W. Singer, "The Contract the Military Needs to Break," *Washington Post*, September 12, 2004.

148. "Private Contractors," *Center for Public Integrity*, June 13, 2004, at www.publicintegrity.org/wow/report.aspx?aid=328 (accessed Fall 2004).

149. T. Trent Gegax, "Military Moonlighting," *Newsweek*, June 8, 2004.

150. Singer, "The Contract the Military Needs to Break."

151. Barstow et al., *Security Companies*.

152. Pamela Constable, "U.S. Men Guilty in Afghan Case," *Washington Post*, September 16, 2004.

153. Richard Haass, "Sanctioning Madness," *Foreign Affairs* 76, no. 6 (November/December 1997): 74–85.

154. Institute for National Strategic Studies, *Strategic Assessment: 1996* (Washington, D.C.: National Defense University Press, 1996), 56–60.

155. Robert A. Pape, "Why Economic Sanctions Do Not Work," *International Security* 22, no. 2 (Fall 1997): 90–136.

156. Gary Clyde Hufbauer, "Sanctions-Happy USA," *Institute for International Economics*, Policy Brief no. 98, 4.

157. Gary Clyde Hufbauer, Jeffrey J. Schott, and Kimberly Ann Elliott, *Economic Sanctions Reconsidered*, 2nd ed. (Washington, D.C.: Institute for International Economics, 1991).

158. Barbara Crossette, "Iraq Sanctions Kill Children, U.N. Reports," *New York Times*, December 1, 1995.

159. Barton Gellman, "Iraq's Arsenal Was Only on Paper," *Washington Post*, January 7, 2004.

160. Nicholas Kristof, "Our Man in Havanna," *New York Times*, November 8, 2003.

161. David Baldwin, "Sanctions Have Gotten a Bum Rap," *Los Angeles Times*, August 18, 2004.

SUGGESTED READING

Graham Allison, *Nuclear Terror: The Ultimate Preventable Catastrophe* (New York: Times Books, 2004).

John Arquilla and David F. Ronfelt, *Networks and Netwars: The Future of Terror, Crime, and Militancy* (Santa Monica, Calif.: Rand Corporation, 2002).

Jacques S. Gansler and Hans Binnendijk, eds., *Information Assurance: Trends in Vulnerabilities, Threats, and Technologies* (Washington, D.C.: National Defense University Press, 2005).

Theresa Hitchens, *Future Security in Space* (Washington, D.C.: Center for Defense Information, 2004).

Gary Clyde Hufbauer, *Economic Sanctions Reconsidered* (Washington, D.C.: International Institute of Economics, 2005).

Richard O. Hundley, *Past Revolutions, Future Transformations: What Can the History of Revolutions in Military Affairs Tell Us about Transforming the U.S. Military?* (Santa Monica, Calif.: Rand Corporation, 1999).

Leigh Armistead, ed., *Information Operations: Warfare and the Hard Reality of Soft Power* (Washington, D.C.: Potomac Books, 2004).

Janne Nolan, Bernard I. Finel, and Brian D. Finlay, eds., *Ultimate Security: Combating Weapons of Mass Destruction* (New York: Century Foundation, 2004).

P. W. Singer, *Corporate Warriors: The Rise of the Privatized Military Industry* (Ithaca, N.Y.: Cornell University Press, 2004).

William Webster, ed., *Russian Organized Crime* (Washington, D.C.: Center for Strategic and International Studies, 2000).

Chapter Seven

Asymmetrical Conflict

U.S. and Saudi military personnel survey the damage to Khobar Towers caused by the explosion of a fuel truck outside the northern fence of the facility on King Abdul Aziz Air Base near Dhahran, Saudi Arabia, June 25, 1996. *Source*: U.S. Department of Defense.

The diffusion of global power in the twenty-first century provides new avenues with which to apply strategy in conflict. States, substate groups, terrorists, and individuals have new and profound opportunities to shape the political outcomes of conflicts. Conventional military conflict may no longer be the most useful tool for winning wars—and could even be a liability if not used with precision. This chapter examines the dynamics of asymmetrical power as applied in the cases of genocide, ethnic cleansing, terrorism, and insurgency movements. It shows that responding to asymmetrical threats creates new security demands involving military intervention and preemptive war, homeland defense, and peace-keeping and peace-support operations. In a world where asymmetries in conflict are increasing, the effort to increase security can inadvertently create more insecurity. When the likelihood of asymmetrical threats is high, the quest for power and the search for peace can become increasingly complicated for as security in one area might be accomplished, entirely new sets of threats can emerge. Moreover, traditional responses to security threats derived from conventional military power can have declining value and inadvertently create new threats.

STRATEGY AND TACTICS OF ASYMMETRICAL CONFLICT

Asymmetrical threats are best understood as stemming from a relationship between strategy and tactics conducted outside accepted international norms, often by non-state actors. Asymmetrical tactics are employed to make a weak actor strong in the pursuit of a strategic gain. Not playing by the rules is not new and it can be an effective means of leveling a major imbalance of power. The story of the Trojan horse shows what can happen when an enemy fights with tactics that enhance surprise. American revolutionary minutemen hid in forests and attacked in a way that the British could not adapt well to. Mohandas K. Gandhi fought an asymmetric battle against the British by refusing to fight them with weapons, but rather with nonviolent action. Some asymmetric acts use barbaric behavior to shock a society—as with the Rwandan genocide or the al Qaeda attacks on the United States in 2001. The key to understanding asymmetric conflict is that it is a tactic in the exercise of power and that the proliferating networks of globalization make asymmetric conflict more likely and considerably more dangerous.

Asymmetrical warfare is the application of tactics in conflict that are outside the norms of accepted rules of combat designed to weaken an enemy's resolve or ability to fight. When asymmetrical warfare is engaged, traditional defensive barriers such as military power and deterrence may decline in value. Asymmetrical attacks might take advantage of an opponent's unwillingness or inability to adapt to asymmetrical challenges due to self-imposed restraint. The use of asymmetric warfare is driven by the perception of relative power available to a combatant. It also might be driven by expectations as to what an attacked country or group of people will tolerate when confronted with a choice of fighting or capitulating. An attacking group or country might, for example, employ barbaric tactics which violate the laws of war to achieve a particular objective. Examples of offensive asymmetrical tactics can include the murder of noncombatants, the use of concentration camps, and strategic bombing of nonmilitary targets. Defensive strategies can also apply asymmetric tactics such as guerrilla insurgency, which seek to impose costs on an occupying adversary without marshaling a massive military force. Such offensive or defensive strategies are not designed to bring about conventional military defeat of an enemy, but rather to target the enemies' hearts and minds and to destroy their will to fight.[1]

Those who use asymmetrical warfare are often engaged in what they see as a heroic struggle for life and death not only for themselves but for a larger worldview. Nationalism and religion can, for example, help those who use barbaric tactics convince themselves that their efforts are just. Extreme forms can include terrorism; hostage taking; biological, chemical, and radiological warfare; deliberate wide-scale attacks on civilians; indiscriminate targeting; hiding military or paramilitary forces near schools or churches; false representation; cyberwarfare or infrastructure attacks; and deliberate environmental destruction.[2] Every conflict situation has some degree of asymmetry—symmetry of power balance is rare, and in fact more likely to produce stability than conflict because of mutual deterrence. Thus asymmetrical conflict is best understood in both strategic and tactical terms.[3]

Asymmetrical tactics are often conducted against states that have self-imposed constraints on their own concepts of strategy and warfighting. Terrorists or insurgents might have no reservations about killing large numbers of innocent civilians whereas modern states operate under legal, public, and moral constraints that prevent them from responding in kind. Nevertheless, states also can use asymmetrical tactics to attain strategic objectives such as using technological advantages that an enemy does not possess. Asymmetrical tactics can thus be force multipliers in the exercise of state power. The major asymmetric challenges of the twenty-first century often combine strategic objectives with attacks on civilian society in a combustible and deadly mix of tactics and proliferating targets.[4] There can be direct targets such as attacks on large civilian populations via nonmilitary techniques ranging from ethnic cleansing to the use of rape and torture to psychologically terrorize a population into some form of concession or capitulation. In the extreme, genocide can be used to destroy an entire population. Rather than fighting against large armies, a country or group can draw an enemy into urban conflict where the advantages of heavy armor, artillery, air power, and technology are substantially affected. In such settings, those fighting with asymmetrical tactics of insurgency have an advantage as they know the terrain and have mobility within it. Asymmetrical warfare also includes a target audience to be impacted by the visual consequences of asymmetrical attacks. News media, the Internet, and other forms of mass communication can help movements draw attention to their causes. In this sense, asymmetrical attacks might be limited in their physical effects, but various media dramatically multiply the intended political impact of asymmetrical attacks.

Understanding the dynamic between strategy and tactics is essential for engaging in asymmetric conflict because wars are not won by defeating an enemy's tactics. Wars are won via winning strategies. For example, in the 1993 Battle of Mogadishu in Somalia, the American troops won the battle, killing scores of Somali fighters. However, battlefield victory turned into strategic retreat for the United States when scenes of dead American soldiers being dragged through the street were shown on worldwide television. Creating chaos and fear in the streets for a television audience was the tactic—forcing an American withdrawal was the strategic goal. Destroying the World Trade Center in September 2001 was an asymmetrical tactic by al Qaeda—mobilizing Muslims against the West and prompting internal regime change in Saudi Arabia and Pakistan was a likely strategic objective.[5]

Asymmetrical warfare is a tactical tool that might be employed at the periphery of a conflict but with the intent of striking at the center of gravity of an enemy.[6] Generally, the goal is to effect the will of an enemy to continue a fight or to effect some other form of change in policy behavior. Will to fight can also have an operational component that drives asymmetrical tactics. Those who are desperate in a conflict or face overwhelming weaknesses might be more willing to take huge losses in conflict and to pursue dramatic and escalating forms of violence. Certain virtues can enhance asymmetrical strategies and tactics. For example, the will to persist and fight on against overwhelming odds can often serve stronger than the will of a state to bear the human and financial costs of certain policies. Patience is a particular advantage and one where religious groups employing asymmetrical strategy and tactics have an advantage. If one side in a conflict expects quick and easy outcomes, they might be defeated by an adversary that sees conflicts as being fought over years, if not decades.[7] Organizational functions can also provide asymmetrical opportunities. NATO's virtue in fighting Serbia was that it was an alliance of democracies functioning on the basis of consensus. However, these dynamics simultaneously provided opportunities for the Serbs to exploit by seeking to affect public opinion in NATO member states and exploiting differences over strategy and tactics in the democratic consensus process of NATO decision-making. NATO set out against Yugoslavia believing it could win a war in a matter of days. However, the enemy, Serb leader Slobodan Milosevic could, in effect, "win" by outlasting the fragile consensus of democracies in NATO. Some states also might engage in support of asymmetric tactics to achieve objectives without directly engaging in conflict themselves.[8] Iran and Syria have, for example, each engaged in third-party support for anti-Israeli terrorist networks.

Combating asymmetric challenges requires using unconventional frameworks for conceptualizing security challenges. Linear strategic thinking can risk perpetuating dangerous outcomes and even make an asymmetrical threat worse. For example, Russia responded to Chechen demands for independence with a massive conventional military campaign of punishment. However, this did nothing to sway the ambitions for independence among Chechen rebel fighters. For example, after Russia intervened with military force in Chechnya in 1994, one of its tanks got lost from its main unit. When the driver stopped to ask a group of civilians where he might buy some cigarettes, they shot and killed him.[9] Ten years later, some 200,000 Chechens were killed and Russian citizens were dying in a barrage of Chechen-backed terrorist attacks around Russia. Heavy reliance on conventional military power in a world where asymmetrical opportunities are proliferating can be self-defeating. In effect, combating unconventional warfare requires both conventional and unconventional methods if it is to be defeated. Ultimately, fighting a war against a tactic, rather than developing a clear plan to defeat a strategy, can play into the hands of those whom one is trying to defeat.[10] A campaign against a strategy, which takes battle to the center of gravity of an enemy, has a real prospect for success.

GENOCIDE AND ETHNIC CLEANSING

Barbaric tactics, such as genocide and ethnic cleansing, exist far outside norms of acceptable international behavior and can have major strategic consequences. Genocide is the purposeful targeting for murder of a particular group of people based on shared political, ethnic, national, or religious identity. Ethnic cleansing is the purposeful movement by force or threat of force of a population from a particular piece of territory. The Holocaust of World War II, in which six million Jews as well as gypsies and other minorities were killed in Nazi death camps, led the international community to define such actions as crimes against humanity. Nevertheless, genocide and ethnic cleansing remain a major tactic in warfare as an asymmetric method to achieve a strategic objective. These kinds of attacks are asymmetrical because they include the purposeful use of military force or other forms of violence specifically targeted against unarmed civilian populations.

Nationalism oriented around ethnic or religious traditions has been a common factor behind the resort to genocide or ethnic cleansing. Nationalism is a doctrine in which the most important source of conflict is identification with a particular group—either ethnic or religious, or both. Nationalism arises as a historical phenomenon in which acquisition of a particular piece of territory with the symbolic value of being a "homeland" for a group of people is achieved. Such a group wants then to defend that land against external threats. Religion can play an important, though not always essential, part in heightening a sense of difference between one group and another's desire to control territory. Over time, a mythology of victimization and superiority can emerge within a group, leading to overt tension or even conflict with outsiders. Modern communication can facilitate and accelerate the expression of such ideas surrounding identity, culture, and religion. Nationalism is not necessarily a negative phenomenon. Nationalism can be a crucial means of establishing a cultural identity. The modern nation-state owes much of its existence to the organizing role that nationalism plays in identification with a particular state. Nationalism, however, also can be a substate or transnational phenomenon that can erode the authority of states and even contribute to state collapse. Close proximity among ethnic and religious groups can heighten an emotional sense of threat or victimization which can lead to independence movements, transborder disputes, and the more dramatic policies of genocide and ethnic cleaning.[11]

The use of genocide or ethnic cleansing as a tactic in warfare is particularly likely when there is no clear distinction between offensive or defensive military capability among parties to a conflict. In this condition, fear of the future for one's group can be heightened when there are multiple identities and weak states where activists or political leaders use fear to mobilize people to defend against a perceived threat. Such actions can then create similar fears in other groups.[12] One group that feels threatened by another thus would have an incentive to strike first and decisively. The other group is therefore also given an incentive to strike first.[13] A side choosing to use offensive action will have an incentive to use any power advantages they have to eliminate the threat posed by their opponent—either through shocking tactics leading to capitulation, ethnic or religious relocation, or genocide. The result is a model of conflict reflecting a spiraling path toward severe tactics that can be both massive and intractable in their consequences.[14] A weaker side will have equal incentive to inflict pain and psychological trauma on the more powerful side to reduce their will to fight. As each side engages in barbaric tactics, they will likely both feel victimized and their positions can harden into immutable worldviews that can only be satisfied with total annihilation of the enemy.

The Balkans

A decade of ethnic-nationalist conflict in the Balkans illustrates the severe dangers inherent in some forms of nationalism that apply asymmetric tactics to achieve political outcomes. In 1991, Slovenia and Croatia withdrew from the constitutional architecture of Yugoslavia. These former-Yugoslav republics used democratic processes to create their own self-determination, though in the case of Croatia there was a sizeable Serb minority population. Meanwhile, Serb politicians had, since the mid-1980s increasingly used nationalism as a rationale for their ongoing control over the remaining Yugoslav government. The Serbs responded with a short war in Slovenia and a more extended conflict in Croatia. Croatia reacted by displacing several hundred thousand ethnic-Serbs in Croatia. Another former Yugolav republic, Bosnia-Herzegovina, was roughly divided between three major ethnic groups—43 percent Muslim; 32 percent Serb; and 17 percent Croatian. By summer 1993, Serb forces in Bosnia, aided by Serbs in Yugoslavia began a major campaign against the largely defenseless Bosnian Muslims. Serb forces ethnically cleansed entire regions of the country, organized death camps, used rape as a tool of warfare, and regularly shelled civilians in major cities. Serb authorities have admitted to having committed Europe's worst atrocity since World War II—the killing of 7,000 Muslims in the city of Srebrenica in 1995.

Eventually, a Croat-Muslim alliance beat back Serb forces in Bosnia which created a new balance of power on the ground and facilitated peace negotiations in 1995. Once war ended, the depth of the damage in Bosnia became clear. Entire cities had been cleansed of male populations of fighting age. There were an estimated six million landmines needing to be cleared. The impact on the country's infrastructure was dramatic with some 80 percent of power generators damaged or out of operation; 40 percent of bridges destroyed; no national telecommunications system; 30 percent of health care facilities, 50 percent of schools, and 60 percent of housing had been destroyed or seriously damaged. Average citizens were surviving on a per capita income of $500 a year and 80 percent of the population was dependent upon external humanitarian assistance. An estimated two million people were displaced from their homes within Bosnia-Herzegovina and another one million had fled as refugees. In addition to the over 200,000 estimated dead, there were also 200,000 wounded—of which 25 percent were children.[15] The entire population—Muslim, Croat, and Serb—suffered severe psychological impacts of warfare and destruction that can only be measured in terms of generations.

The Balkans story did not end, however, after the negotiated cease-fire in Bosnia. In 1987, Serb nationalist leader Slobodan Milosevic visited a site in the region of Kosovo. Kosovo is an area inside Serbia, a province of what remained of Yugoslavia, with a 90 percent ethnic Albanian population living under Serb rule. Milosevic delivered an impassioned speech which stirred the historical memories of Serb nationalism as a tool to establish his political power in Yugoslavia. During the 1990s, the Kosovo situation simmered as local Albanian rights were usurped by Serb authorities. In response, a violent Albanian independence movement grew—the Kosovo Liberation Army (KLA). Targeting Serb military and civilians, the KLA hoped to raise the costs of Serb control and provoke international intervention on their behalf. By spring 1998, the KLA had prompted a growing Serb backlash. The Serbs relied primarily on paramilitary forces to frighten Kosovar Albanians into giving up their claims to independence—culminating in a gruesome attack on Albanian civilians in January 1999 killing about two dozen in a grotesque fashion. The Serb forces hoped to deter a NATO intervention to stop human rights abuses by suggesting that, if NATO attacked, Serbs would ethnically cleanse the entire province. When NATO did go to war, the Serbs forcefully expelled some 800,000 Albanians from Kosovo into neighboring Albania and Macedonia.

Rwanda

The Balkans story was somewhat less tragic than it might have been because it took place in the backyard of modern Europe. The conflict simply could not escape the attention of the United States and its European allies. This condition stood in contrast to the completely unchecked genocide in Rwanda that occurred at the same time. In this case, the world stood by while an estimated 800,000 people were killed in barbaric ethnic and tribal warfare. The conflict in Rwanda culminated from years of power struggles between Hutus and Tutsis—the dominant tribal makeup in the country. By 1990, these struggles took the form of a movement by Rwandan Tutsi refugees (who had been trained by and fighting for Uganda) which invaded Rwanda in October 1990. As these rebels were combated, prominent Tutsis were arrested and the Hutu government looked askance while private militias carried out escalating harassment, in some cases massacring Tutsis. A near-term settlement was negotiated by the Rwandan Hutu leaders and Tutsi rebels; and France, Belgium, and Zaire sent peacekeeping forces. By 1993, however, the Tutsi rebels regrouped, and the Hutu leadership of Juvenal Habyrarimana was challenged internally by militant nationalists. In April 1994, his plane was shot down. Hutus blamed Tutsis, though it has not been determined who shot down the plane and it could have been Hutus looking for a reason to begin an organized plan of genocide.[16]

Genocide resulted from a decision by dominant Hutu forces to use paramilitary militias to kill and terrorize Tutsis. These forces were specially trained in tactics including the burning of houses, tossing of grenades, and the hacking up of dummies with machetes.[17] According to a United Nations informant, whose warnings were passed on to but ignored by senior UN officials, military and paramilitary training was focused on discipline, weapons, explosives, close combat, and tactics. This training, the informant indicated, was designed to take advantage of the registration of all Tutsis in the Rwandan capital of Kigali—most likely for the purposes of extermination. The informant estimated that the personnel he was working with could kill 1,000 Tutsis in twenty minutes.[18] Additional evidence that the actions were premeditated to achieve a strategic objective against Tutsis included: ethnic entries on identity cards; numerical codes painted on homes in the capital city; radio broadcast of violent, anti-Tutsi messages; a Hutu extremist party operating with presidential backing; civilians being armed through party militias; militia members keeping surveillance over Tutsi families; and the preparation of death lists. The Hutu militias were armed and supplied by the Hutu-led Rwandan ministry of defense.[19]

Hutu militias promulgated an ideology of "Hutuness" for all of Rwanda. They presented a "final solution" of mass murder—not as a way to create suffering, but what they claimed was a strategy for alleviating it.[20] The strategic intent behind the killing was made evident in that it was not limited to Tutsis, but also targeted moderate Hutus.[21] An American intelligence assessment done as the genocide raged concluded that the strategy appeared designed to eliminate all potential opposition, including those who favored negotiation, and to "raise the costs" of any Tutsi takeover of Rwanda.[22] The conditions for genocide were set as a spiral that quickly grew out of control. Hutu propaganda, broadcast over national radio, identified Tutsis repeatedly as "animals," "cockroaches," and "snakes"—and asserted that Tutsis were not true Rwandans. Tutsis were depicted as invading Ugandans who had a superiority complex. All Tutsis were thus seen as a direct threat to all Hutus and, in this view, had to be stopped by killing them before they could kill average Hutus.[23] A perspective had grown within each tribal community that the other was a threat to its survival and thus the solution was to eliminate the other. The balance of forces favored the Hutus who were on the offensive. Genocide was carried out by about 30,000 active-duty Rwandan army forces and an additional 15,000 to 30,000 Hutu militia organized against about 20,000 Tutsi rebel forces. The Tutsi force was not able to do much to counter Hutu movements, however, as the Tutsis were located in one small area of northern Rwanda.[24]

About 800,000 were killed in one hundred days during the Rwandan genocide—an average of 333.3 murders per hour, or 5.5 lives taken each minute. Added to this were uncounted numbers of maimed who lived with their wounds. Many survivors were raped as a tool used to systematically terrorize Tutsi women.[25] The situation had accelerated rapidly, as initially Tutsis gathered together in groups, so that within several days, more than 500,000 Tutsi were gathered in large concentrations throughout the country. This gave the Tutsi an advantage in the short-term as the initial Hutu attackers were poorly armed. However, gathering in large numbers soon turned against the Tutsis when Hutu regular army, reservists, and the Presidential Guard arrived at these Tutsi locations. The result of this congregation and tilt in the balance of power toward the better armed Hutus resulted in 250,000 Tutsis killed in just two weeks.

Hutus systematically avoided attacking Tutsis in areas where the world community was likely to witness the events. In areas where Tutsis survived, it was most likely due to the presence of international observers. Hutus also cut landline telephone service in the country to prevent outside communication and set up roadblocks to check civilian identification and prevent people fleeing the country.[26] After the major fighting ended, an international response was organized by the United Nations to set up refugee camps. However, during this time thousands of Hutus were killed in retaliatory attacks by Tutsis. The pure brutality of the tactics used by each side was described in one account as including the use of machetes which "often resulted in a long and painful agony and many people, when they had some money, paid their killers to be finished off quickly with a bullet rather than being slowly hacked to death. . . . Mutilations were common."[27]

Like in the Yugoslav case, the Rwandan application of genocide as a tactic failed as strategy. The initial Hutu goal appeared to be to create enough of an unstable situation so that any international presence would withdraw and Tutsi leaders and Hutu moderates could then be systematically eliminated. In the near term this approach appeared to succeed. Several weeks into the campaign, with the number of people killed around 100,000, the UN Security Council agreed to withdraw 90 percent of its peacekeepers. UN military officials on the ground, however, said the rapid deployment of about 5,000 UN troops might have prevented the entire genocide. Absent even a signal of intent to engage from the international community, the violence spiraled out of control while the UN had only 450 poorly trained and lightly equipped troops left. Six weeks after atrocities began, and with 328,000 dead, the UN authorized 5,000 African peacekeeping forces to deploy into Rwanda— though few countries offered troops. This deployment was, however, also delayed as the United States bickered with the UN over who would pay for the use of American armored personnel carriers. Eleven weeks into the genocide, the UN Security Council authorized France to create a safe area within Hutu controlled regions. By July 17, Tutsi rebels regained the initiative and fought their way to the Rwandan capital of Kigali. The Hutu government eventually fled to Zaire along with a massive exodus of Hutu refugees. In one hundred days of fighting, the Hutus succeeded in their barbaric tactic of killing innocent civilians. The tactic also worked in that the horrific nature of the activity prevented the international community from reinforcing what minimal presence it had in Rwanda. Indeed, as the crisis escalated, UN forces withdrew. Yet, in the end, the Hutus lost the war and fled.

Never Again?

Genocide and ethnic cleansing are far more common than the world would have expected following the promise that it would never happen again after the World War II Holocaust. Often the meaning of "genocide" is disputed in part to avoid having to take responsibility for stopping it when there are no high national interests involved. Nevertheless, the organized mass murder of innocent civilians is reasonably well-identified when it happens. In Bangladesh, Cambodia, Equatorial Guinea, Ethiopia, the Balkans, and Rwanda, the organized mass killing of innocents has happened since World War II. Millions of innocent men, women, and children have been killed, abused, or dislocated as a result of genocide or ethnic cleansing. When the international community noted the tenth anniversary of the Rwandan genocide in 2004, strong lessons were debated as to why it happened and how it could have been prevented. Yet at the very same time, genocide was happening again in Sudan.

TERRORISM AND INSURGENCY

Terrorism and insurgency are asymmetrical tactics applied toward strategic objectives. Historically, the impact of terrorism and insurgency movements are more confined than the larger tactics of genocide and ethnic cleaning. However, if combined with the proliferation of weapons of mass destruction, terrorism and insurgency movements could create catastrophic consequences. Both terrorism and insurgency are asymmetrical strategies available to weak actors seeking to level the strategic playing field through dramatic and shocking political events. Terrorism targets innocent civilians without discrimination. Insurgency is a tool used by clandestine fighters to attack military targets during an occupation. Complicating the dynamics of terrorism versus insurgency is the dilemma that one person's insurgent, which might gain local political sympathy against an occupying power, is often another person's terrorist. Context matters when identifying the role that terrorism and insurgency play as tactics. Nonetheless as tactics, both are asymmetrical, and both are barbaric in nature.

The Meaning and Use of Terror

Terrorism is a tactic designed to achieve a political objective by using violence against innocent civilians to generate fear. The objectives of terrorism have evolved over time, as have the tactics and targets. What has remained constant are the dynamics of asymmetrical power that drive it—as a struggle along a continuum of central power versus local power, big power versus small power, modern power versus traditional power.[28] The principal purpose of a terrorist attack is to destroy the tactical objective or target, but also to reach an audience through the use of dramatic and shocking acts which create fear.[29] In that sense, selection of a target and how and when it is hit are critical components of both tactics and strategy. Such was the case with the use of airplanes as missiles on September 11, 2001 and in the choice of the World Trade Center and the Pentagon as highly symbolic targets. The medium for fear would be the proliferation of the imagery of the attacks on worldwide television. Targets are thus generally selected consistent with the strategic objective in conjunction with available resources and relative potential for success in an attack.[30]

The use of terror has been commonplace as a means of securing power and stability for governments. After the French Revolution, terror was used to restore order following the overthrow of despotism. Modern terrorism, however, specifically uses the murder of private citizens and the destruction of public and private property to achieve a broader political objective. The purpose can range from the use of violence for nationalist ends or state ends, to advancing specific transnational interests such as drug cartels or other organized crime.[31] Religious zealots, many of which project philosophy ranging from dominance to Armageddon—and take it on themselves to bring it about—add a new dimension to the use of terrorism. While terrorism can be defined differently based on context, it is best understood as an asymmetrical tactic designed to advance a strategic goal. Terrorism is most often associated with a political objective; uses violence or the threat of violence; is intended to have a psychological repercussion beyond the actual tactical target; is conducted by organizations with a chain of command and organization, though acting without uniform or insignia; and most often has been perpetrated by a subnational group or non-state entity that seeks to overcome power disparities in order to shape a public agenda.[32]

Insurgency and guerrilla war also have increasingly adopted asymmetrical tactics of terrorism as a tool of attrition. Insurgency and guerrilla movements are campaigns of small armed groups fighting for a particular piece of land or political objective. They are often differentiated from terrorists in that insurgent and guerrilla fighters generally confine their attacks to military targets, rather than killing innocent civilians. Nevertheless, civilians have been directly affected by these movements. In its struggle for Algerian independence, the Front Liberation Nationale (FLN) killed about 16,000 and kidnapped about 50,000 civilians. The FLN also killed an estimated 12,000 of its own members in internal purges. Similar activity took place among the Vietcong movement during the Vietnam War.[33] The Irish Republican Army (IRA) in Northern Ireland saw itself as a legitimate guerrilla campaign, but many of its targets over several decades were civilians. The IRA bombed bars and timed attacks to do serious economic damage to the United Kingdom—including conducting bombing campaigns in advance of Christmas holidays. Insurgents and guerilla fighters have in some circumstances gained legitimacy—depending on the conditions under which they operate. During the Cold War, the United States and the Soviet Union supported insurgent and guerrilla movements in the underdeveloped world to advance their competing strategic and ideological agendas. Insurgents and guerrilla movements in Nicaragua fighting a socialist government in the 1980s were deemed by the United States to be "freedom fighters." The right wing government of El Salvador was also backed by the United States in its campaign to suppress insurgents and guerrilla fighters. Yet the government of El Salvador supported right-wing paramilitary groups that used barbaric tactics including rape, disappearances, and other forms of violent intimidation.

Insurgent and guerrilla movements can, thus, take on a variety of rationales. These movements are, however, increasingly turning to terrorism as a tool for accomplishing their objective. While insurgency and guerrilla movements are not regular armies, they organize and operate and select targets as if they were in a military campaign. The goal of insurgency is often to prevent an external power or a local government from exerting effective control over a piece of territory, or even a whole country. Thus a central objective of insurgents is to create confusion, chaos, and fear to show that those in power cannot govern effectively. Whether such movements are global (such as the al Qaeda terrorist movement) or local (such as the groups advocating the Palestinian cause, Basques in Spain, or Chechens in Russia), all are aided dramatically by the dynamics of the global security environment. Transportation technology accelerates the pace and capacity for such movements to organize and act. Communication technology has had a similar role as a force multiplier for communications among members of an organization, and also as a means of publicizing via the media. The deregulation of the international economy and the means through which global trade is exercised helps to weaken the traditional role of the state and facilitate the flow both of money and weapons. Migration also plays an important role as expatriot organizations can provide members of such movements with support or safe-harbor. The spread of modern culture, especially the western versions which dominate contemporary popular television, movies, art, and food, serve to fuel backlash. This reaction can tip someone toward insurgency or at least provide a rallying cry from those who claim to defend local cultures against intrusion from outside forces.[34]

Terrorist tactics applied by insurgent and guerrilla forces are potent when employed in weak states or states experiencing major internal transitions. Weak or failing states are fertile ground for armed gangs or militias to coalesce into organized insurgent or guerrilla movements seeking to consolidate power. As an asymmetric tool, these tactics can be crucial means to redress substantial power imbalances. The Liberation Tigers of Tamil Eelam in Sri Lanka, for example, developed a well-organized campaign which recruited and trained individuals to carry out terrorist attacks including bombing an airplane in 1987 killing sixteen people, in 1997, targeting a ship killing thrity-two, and a truck bombing in 1997 killing eighteen. The Tamil Tigers had, by 2003, conduced over 200 bombings of places of religious worship, office buildings, and transportation centers. The Tamil Tigers asserted that these kinds of attacks were the only means available to fight given the military dominance of the Sri Lankan army.[35]

States in transition toward democracy are vulnerable to insurgent movements and guerrilla forces which can use terrorist tactics to intimidate civilians and harass or kill political opposition. Moreover, targets in transition states might also include international aid workers, and the staff of organizations seeking to build civil-society such as UN employees. The objective in this case would be to create the circumstances in which outside forces withdraw, leaving a political and security vacuum for insurgents to fill. This was the case in post-Saddam Iraq, where an insurgency opposed to American occupation emerged in 2003 and grew steadily through 2005. Their targets for terrorist attacks included bombing average Iraqi citizens lining up to join Iraqi police forces, the headquarters for United Nations operations, and civilian aid workers and contractors. Many of these innocent victims were kidnapped and then killed by beheading, which was on occasion videotaped and sent out for viewing on the Internet. Such attacks are consistent with an asymmetric strategy driven by a combination of will, capability, and goals. In the case of Iraq, the strategic objective appeared to be to facilitate the conditions in which Iraqis would abandon support for outside intervention, or possibly to prompt a civil war, from which insurgents might emerge to govern.

The Evolution of Modern Terrorism

Terrorism took modern form during the decolonization movement after World War II. During the 1960s, terrorism grew among some substate groups expressing opposition to particular policies or advancing particular ideologies. While many movements professed their commitment to revolutionary ideological zeal, there was no single case where it actually succeeded as part of a strategy to advance an ideological doctrine.[36] In the 1970s, a number of organizations emerged using terrorist methods to bring attention to causes advancing independence for particular territories or to protest the actions of particular governments and their policies. Movements such as the Irish Republican Army, the Palestinian Liberation Organization, and ETA Basque separatists in Spain became well-known for their use of brutal terrorist methods in sustained campaigns designed to weaken the resolve of public will to support existing policies. These movements did have some degree of sympathy within their own community and saw themselves as advancing a legitimate case against oppression. Terrorism thus fostered a vicious cycle of attack, retribution, attack, retribution. Some elements in this cycle would become deeply entrenched to the point where they would favor war over peace. When the Israeli leader Yitzak Rabin negotiated a peace settlement with the Palestinians, he was assassinated—by a Jewish zealot.

By the 1980s, these anticolonial trends in terrorism were accompanied by the growth of state sponsorship of some terrorist organizations. Some states, such as Iran and Syria, had direct ties to anti-Israeli groups. However, other states were labeled as sponsoring terrorism in the international community though their ties to terrorist groups were minor or nonexistent. Some states that did have ties to terrorist groups were often not identified as such because they were allied with great powers—especially the United States. The United States conducts an annual review of what states sponsor international terrorism. If a state appears on this list, it is to be denied trade and approval of international loans among other penalties. During the 1990s, the primary states on this list were Cuba, North Korea, Iran, Iraq, Syria, Sudan, and Libya. The list was complicated because, among these states, only Iran, Libya, and Syria were actively engaged in terrorism during this time. Yet to varying degrees, all three softened their support for terrorism as they attempted to find paths to join the international community of nations. Cuba and North Korea were largely on the list as a consequence of their domestic leadership. Iraq was connected to one incident in 1993 when it was shown to have engaged in a plot to assassinate former U.S. President George H. W. Bush—but there was no evidence of direct Iraqi involvement with international terrorist organizations. Two states that did provide some support for international terrorist groups were not on the list as they were American friends. Saudi Arabia was known to have provided financial resources to anti-Israeli groups while profiting from the sale of oil to American consumers. Prior to September 2001, Pakistan provided recognition and support for the Taliban government in Afghanistan, which harbored al Qaeda. Pakistan also had been engaging in informal support of cross-border terrorist organizations operating against India in Kashmir.

Overall, the relative incidents of international terrorism declined during the 1990s, with an average of 382 attacks per year down from 543 in the 1980s. At the same time, however, casualties from terrorism have risen, from 344 worldwide in 1991, to 6,693 in 1998.[37] Two key dynamics illustrate a major change in the role of international terrorists in modern international security. First, some major international terrorist networks have gone global, and moved beyond limited objectives. At the same time, these movements work closely with more local political movements to extend their web of influence. In this sense, globalization provides multiple means through which terrorists can organize and operate. Terrorist groups are increasingly able to use the international financial system to move and hide money, and to use the Internet to transmit messages via encoded communications. Dispersed ethnic groups can provide local cover and recruitment for terrorist operatives. Moreover, the perceived negative effects of globalization have expanded the number of discontents looking for some means, if even symbolic, to defend local cultures and traditions. The rise of global finance, the 24–7 global economy, the ability to hide financial resources in safe havens, the ability to traffic in illicit items, the ability to encode communications with advanced technology, and the growth of transnational ethno-religious communities are key manifestations of the global networks where terrorists can now work.[38]

Second, religion plays an increasingly important role as an inspiration for terrorists. The appeal of religious convictions helps leaders of terrorist networks motivate people into the tactic of suicide terrorism. Earnest religiosity can quickly spiral to fanaticism when combined with other key factors such as economic deprivation and a sense of social humiliation and isolation. Whether it is a Muslim fanatic or the American right-wing Christian who blew up the Oklahoma City federal office building in 1993, violence is seen by religious terrorists as a moral act that brings them closer to salvation. Religious terrorists are absolutist in their worldviews and thus do not necessarily seek stature beyond the notoriety of their sacrifice.[39] Nevertheless, even those people that are advancing a religion have a strategic goal, and have convinced themselves that their actions are rational.

The trend toward more religious-driven terrorism is rising. In 1968, there were no religiously motivated international terrorist organizations identified in a study by the Rand Corporation. By 1994, one-third of forty-nine international terrorist groups were classified as primarily religious.[40] Religion is particularly used as a recruitment and motivational tool by terrorist organizers to bring people into their cause as operatives or political and financial supporters. While terrorism might appear to reflect acts of desperation, they can be rational acts as understood by those who carry them out. In some cases extended terrorist campaigns have led to some political gains—once the movement chose to abandon violence.[41] Irish Republican Army terrorist leaders Gerry Adams and Martin McGuinness became acceptable international actors following the end of their struggle against British occupation of Northern Ireland. Likewise, the leader of the Palestinian Liberation Organization, Yassar Arafat, became a widely accepted international figure after his group called a cease-fire, condemned terrorism, recognized Israel's right to exist, and engaged in negotiation.

Religion is an element in, but not the sole driver of suicide terrorism. The main group in the world that practices suicide terrorism is not a religious movement, bur rather the Tamil Tigers (LTTE) in Sri Lanka. The LTTE is mostly motivated by Marxist/Leninist ideology. Of 186 suicide terrorist attacks worldwide between 1980 and 2001, the LTTE accounted for 75.[42] Nevertheless, the mix of religion and terrorism can be extremely dangerous. Religious terrorists see themselves locked in a permanent struggle of good versus evil. They use violent behavior to please a perceived commitment required by a higher being. As such, religious terrorists consider themselves unconstrained by secular rules or laws. Generally alienated from the dominant social system, religious terrorists are dispersed and have dispersed supporters within society making them harder to locate and making it harder to prevent them from taking violent actions.[43]

An important and dangerous combination regarding the relationship between religion and terrorism is the role of religious cults. Some cults have charismatic leaders that draw support from the concept of coming Armageddon and salvation. These leaders demand total faith in a god-like figure which instills the belief that it is the follower's duty to facilitate the end of times. The Aum Shinrikyo movement in Japan held such a commitment to its leadership and Armageddon during the 1990s. This group also had considerable financial resources and scientists seeking to develop weapons of mass destruction. The cult included scientists trained in microbiology and who experimented with Anthrax, botulinum toxin, Q-fever, and Ebola virus. In the early 1990s, they sought to disseminate biological weapons by outfitting a car to distribute botulinum toxin via the exhaust pipe. They also tried to spread Anthrax via a spray system on a roof in Tokyo. Aum Shinrikyo failed in the use of biological weapons distribution, so they resorted to the use of sarin nerve agent in the Tokyo subway killing eleven people and wounding hundreds while instilling fear within the entire country. On a smaller scale, in the United States in 1984, the Rajneeshee religious movement sought to affect the outcome of local elections in Wasco County, Oregon, by spraying salmonella poison on salad bars in restaurants leading to about 750 cases of digestive poisoning, though no deaths. The cult's plan was discovered and their effort failed.[44]

How an individual turns into a terrorist can result from a variety of factors. Some terrorists see themselves as legitimate actors advancing political or religious values in a war so important that they cannot afford to differentiate between military and civilian targets. Others justify their actions on the basis of historical actions taken by their enemy. Still others are alienated from society as a result of some direct experience that brought them to a belief that violence against innocents is legitimate. In many cases, a vicious cycle develops—for example, a Palestinian might kill an Israeli, Israel responds with violence, killing Palestinians, and thus more terrorists emerge. One woman who carried out a suicide bomb in early 2004 against Israeli citizens did so after her brother had been killed by Israeli forces.

Such stories are common in a world where a passion for revenge can overtake a willingness to resolve differences peacefully. Timothy McViegh, for example, was a loner who developed deep resentment for the United States government following a stay in the U.S. military and a tour of duty in the first Persian Gulf War—where he learned to work with explosives. He was seen as too radical in his worldviews, even for some of America's most virulent antigovernment militia movements that McViegh had come to idealize. He and a friend conspired and blew up the Oklahoma City federal building killing 168 people. Among the dead included school children attending class on the second floor. One high-level leader of al Qaeda, Dr. Iman al Zawahiri, was in his youth a political activist in Egypt. He was arrested by the Egyptian government for his activity where he was reportedly tortured over several years in prison. It was there that his hatred appeared to have grown deep enough that he took to arms. Indeed, prison has become an important place for terrorist recruitment—particularly for Islamic terrorist networks.

Some anti-Western and pro-Islamic terrorist movements have evolved into a broader ideological context that also serves as a significant inspirational tool for local radical activists to carry out terrorist attacks. This rise toward an ideologically dispersed international terrorist movement is based on an overarching belief that Muslims should take up arms in a holy war against the Judeo-Christian West, a profound sense of indignation at the deaths and perceived oppression of Muslims in Palestinian areas and in Iraq, and a growing conviction that moderate secular governments should be replaced by Islamic political movements. This trend complicates terrorist coordination and makes attacks more likely to be regionally based, smaller in scale, and hitting "soft" (i.e., easy to kill) civilian targets. While the scale of the threat might be small and more diffuse, it also makes the strategic threat more difficult to combat.[45] There were, by 2004, at least over a dozen, and perhaps as many as forty, regional Islamic groups whose capabilities and ambitions were growing. These groups had established training camps in Kashmir, the Philippines, and

West Africa—and their ambitions were growing beyond the local concerns that initially spawned them.[46]

A measure of one element of the success of terrorism as an asymmetrical tactic is the degree of attention that it gets from modern media. Following the horrific attacks against the United States on September 11, 2001, terrorism was understandably elevated to the number one international issue in world politics. Empirical data on terrorism, however, suggests a disconnect between the attention terrorist acts receive and the individual fear they create relative to the actual threat to any particular individual. During the entire twentieth century, less than twenty terrorist attacks killed as many as one hundred people and, aside from the September 11 attacks, none had killed more than four hundred in a single attack. Excepting for the one-day horror of September 11, more Americans are killed by lightning strikes in any given grouping of years than by all forms of international terrorism combined.[47] As a relative comparison of risk, 1 of every 400 Americans is injured each year by simply lying in bed and having the bed break.[48] Yet between fall 2001 and fall 2005, no Americans were killed by terrorist attacks on American soil.

Defining terrorism is highly contextual. Most Americans would not view themselves as having resorted to policies designed to produce mass civilian casualties and widespread fear. And yet around the world, this is how America is viewed in many societies. Indeed, the United States did use its own asymmetrical advantages in warfare when it dropped nuclear bombs on Japan at the end of World War II. That act was purposefully intended to target civilians and produce enough fear to achieve a political outcome to end the war. Of course, context provides a better understanding, however, of the choice between dropping nuclear bombs to end the war versus a land-invasion and its likely toll. The United States could have merely tested a weapon or dropped one in the sea near Japan. However, it was judged that the best way to maximize fear was to target large civilian populations. The gamble was that this would end the war faster—but it was, nevertheless, a tactic derived around terror and civilian destruction.[49]

In terms of global security threats, terrorism pales in comparison to the impact of other global challenges. The potential costs of war between India and Pakistan, the 8,000 Africans that die every day from the spread of HIV/AIDS, and the 800,000 that died in the Rwandan genocide provide a stark contrast to the reality of the fear terrorism generates relative to its consequences. In the United States, 40,000 Americans die every year in automobile accidents whereas between fall 2001 and fall 2005, none died in the United States from terrorist attacks. This data does not in any way undermine the barbarism of what murderers of innocent civilians did on September 11. Rather, it illustrates the devious impact of the tactic. Americans developed a high degree of fear—which is what the terrorists hoped to generate with the use of a tactic disproportionate to their actual power. This fear has spread as waves of follow-on attacks occurred around the world from Indonesia to Morocco to Spain. The fear is understandable as terrorism brings home to average people the sense that there are motivated and dangerous individuals walking among society. As the leader of the anti-Israeli Hezbollah terrorist group said in 1992: "We are not fighting so that the enemy recognizes us and offers us something. . . . We are fighting to wipe out the enemy."[50]

Al Qaeda

Despite the relatively low incidence of terrorism, its catastrophic potential has been made clear by al Qaeda, which killed nearly 3,000 Americans in September 2001. Before September 11, large-scale terrorism rarely involved more than a few hundred casualties in only a handful of massive-scale events: 325 killed in a 1985 crash of an Air India flight; over 300 killed in 1993 by car bombs in India; 270 killed in the 1988 explosion of Pan Am flight 103; 241 killed in a 1983 truck bombing of an American marine barracks in Lebanon; 171 killed in the crash of a UTA flight in 1989; 168 killed by the Oklahoma City truck bombing in 1995; and 115 in the 1987 destruction of a Korean jet-liner. Of more than 10,000 terrorist events between 1968 and September 11, 2001, only 14 resulted in 100 or more fatalities.[51] Terrorists were, nonetheless, able to kill nearly 3,000 people within several hours on September 11. In bringing down the World Trade Center, al Qaeda achieved the equivalent damage of a small nuclear bomb. On that single day, nearly half as many people were killed as had been among all nationalities in terrorist attacks around the world during the 1980s and 1990s. During that same two-decade period, 856 Americans had died abroad or at home from terrorist attacks.[52] Al Qaeda's methods and determination to obtain weapons of mass destruction nevertheless illustrate the growing danger of this kind of operation. Moreover, while its tactical capabilities have been reduced in the years since September 11, al Qaeda has evolved into a larger, more ideological movement—exacerbated by the American invasion of Iraq in 2003.

Al Qaeda, which means *the base*, is a transnational terrorist movement inspired by the Saudi national Osama bin Laden. Bin Laden brought the organization considerable financial resources and organizational skills that he had developed as an engineer. Bin Laden was well-educated, experienced in the ways of the West, and lived a wealthy lifestyle via his upbringing in a prominent Saudi family. The al Qaeda organization grew out of the anti-Soviet Mujahadeen movement in Afghanistan and in the 1990s engaged in a close relationship with the fundamentalist Islamic Taliban movement. By the late 1990s, the Taliban had come to control most of Afghanistan. The al Qaeda network also expanded during this time by forging an alliance with a similar Islamic terrorist movement based in Egypt. Al Qaeda set up training bases in Afghanistan, perhaps more than a dozen, where as many as 100,000 fighters committed to a holy war went through training. Not all who went through these camps, however, were committed al Qaeda terrorists, and most went on to fight in the Afghan civil war, not to take up a global crusade. Al Qaeda's core group of followers likely numbered at the time of the 2001 attack about 2,000 and had an even smaller group of leadership structure numbering several hundred.

Al Qaeda took on the form and rhetoric of a military organization including a high-level political committee which authorized actions; a military committee that proposed targets, gathered ideas for and organized support for operations, and managed training camps; a finance committee that provided budgetary resources for training, housing, costs of living, travel, and the movement of money worldwide; a foreign purchases committee that acquired weapons, explosives, and technical commitment; a security committee that provided physical protection, intelligence collection, and counterintelligence; and a public relations committee that organized propaganda strategies and made public statements for the organization.[53] Al Qaeda was known to even possess a number of seagoing vessels which would help with the movement of people and supplies around the world. The organization was not, however, a hierarchical chain of command. Rather, it would identify operations and assign responsibility to very carefully selected clandestine operatives. Of the hijackers on September 11, bin Laden boasted after the attack that only a handful actually knew they were on a suicide mission. Following the collapse of the Taliban in Afghanistan, al Qaeda's known numbers were reduced by an estimated two-thirds who were either killed or captured by American and allied forces. It had also lost its home base of operations in Afghanistan.

By 2004, al Qaeda appeared to have transformed from a tightly controlled tactical operation to a larger anti-Western ideological movement. Al Qaeda appeared to rely on an expanding group of regional and local terrorist movements with which it could associate. Rather than having command decisions made centrally by bin Laden and his closest associates, his legacy appears to have been as an inspiration for a hybrid of smaller-organized, regionally-based, terrorist operations. By 2005, a diverse proliferation of local al Qaeda leadership were making command decisions and coordinating its efforts with radical local Islamic movements. Attacks in Morocco and Spain in 2003 and 2004 were carried out not by highly trained terrorists organized by Osama bin Laden, but rather by uneducated slum dwellers or small shopkeepers with little previous involvement in extremism. These people justified their attacks as part of a global religious war. They had been recruited and trained by an experienced Moroccan veteran of al Qaeda's Afghanistan operations.[54] The Morocco attacks were complex in their number of targets, but on a small scope in ambition. These attacks included the destruction of a Jewish community center, a Spanish restaurant and social club, a hotel, a Jewish cemetery, and a Jewish-owned Italian restaurant. In the Morocco attack, forty-five were killed, including twelve of the fourteen terrorist bombers. When suicide bombers hit London in July 2005, killing fifty-two people on the Tube and a bus, it quickly was discovered that the bombers were not international terrorists but rather home-grown British citizens inspired by the al Qaeda message if not organization.

For many citizens around the world, September 11, 2001 was the first time they had heard about al Qaeda, but it was by no means its first attack. Al Qaeda members were involved in the first effort to collapse the World Trade Center in 1993. Al Qaeda members also were involved in a failed plot to blow up a number of airliners flying over the Pacific Ocean several years later. In 1998, al Qaeda operatives destroyed American embassies in Kenya and Tanzania, killing hundreds of workers—mostly local Africans. As the 2000 New Year approached, an al Qaeda member was arrested at the U.S.-Canadian border. He was caught with operational devices and plans to explode a bomb at the Los Angeles airport. Later in 2000, al Qaeda members used a small boat to bring explosives alongside the *USS Cole* which was at harbor in Yemen, killing over a dozen soldiers and severely disabling the ship. In fact, al Qaeda formally declared war on the United States in 1996. Yet, aside from the expert community which focused on international terrorism, the warnings did not register with a sense of urgency. Even when, in August 2001, American President George Bush received a classified briefing from the Central Intelligence Agency titled "Al Qaeda Determined to Attack Inside the United States," little was done and the president continued a vacation to Texas. The American media focused heavily that summer on the dangers of shark attacks.

The Globalization of Terror

Globalization provides modern terrorist networks new means to finance, carry out, and publicize attacks. Al Qaeda illustrates the way in which its relatively small inner circle was able to multiply its power by forging alliances with Islamic groups in other countries including Egypt, Libya, Algeria, Saudi Arabia, Oman, Tunisia, Jordan, Iraq, Lebanon, Morocco, Somalia, and Eritrea.[55] While bin Laden brought considerable financial resources to al Qaeda, most of the money raised by their operations was generated via legal global fundraising networks. Al Qaeda relied on well-placed financial facilitators and diversions of funds from Islamic charities including large amounts of money diverted to al Qaeda without the knowledge of those giving money. While no government, besides the Taliban, overtly supported al Qaeda, it did benefit from some governments turning a blind eye toward its fundraising efforts.[56] Al Qaeda's money was moved through what is known as the *hawala* architecture, a traditional and informal system of transferring money in the Islamic world. Couriers operating in Pakistan, the United Arab Emirates, and around the Middle East also served as a means of transferring funds. Al Qaeda had an operating budget before 2001 of about $30 million, most of which went to supporting the Taliban in Afghanistan—as specific terrorist operations were relatively inexpensive. The 2001 attack against the United States was estimated to have cost $500,000. The much lower scale, but still very deadly, al Qaeda bombings in Morocco that killed forty-five people in May 2003 only cost about $4,000.

A unique attribute of modern transnational terrorist movements is the growing use of the Internet as a tool of tactical communication and strategic propaganda. One observer in Afghanistan during November 2001 said that he watched "every second al Qaeda member carrying a laptop computer along with a Kalashnikov" as they dispersed around the globe.[57] In December 2003, al Qaeda supporters published on the Internet a manifesto articulating both the strategy and the timing of what became attacks on commuter trains in Madrid, Spain, the following March. The Internet posting clearly stated the desired strategy: "Withdrawal of Spanish or Italian forces would put immense pressure on the British presence in a way that Tony Blair might not be able to bear. . . . In this way the dominoes will begin to fall quickly." The March 2004 attacks killed 191 people—a week later, the pro-American Spanish government was ousted in a popular vote. The Internet has served as a virtual base to unite al Qaeda members using encoded programs to facilitate the exchange of information, discussion of strategy, and provide instructions and training methods for terrorist recruits. Also in 2004, the Saudi Arabia branch of al Qaeda began publishing an online magazine. Overall there are an estimated 4,500 terrorist-related websites in the world. Not only do such Internet sites facilitate coordination and communication, they also have become virtual training camps—including postings of how to build explosives and carry out attacks.

The role of the Internet in al Qaeda's network was detailed in summer 2004, when Pakistan detained Mohammed Naeem Noor Khan, a key computer engineer for the terrorist network. The seizure of his computer led to the arrest of thirteen terrorist suspects in Britain and exposed electronic links between al Qaeda operatives or sympathizers in Pakistan, Europe, and the United States. His computer files included extensive detail on surveillance and information about target preferences that al Qaeda hoped to attack. The tactics al Qaeda employed in using the Internet were not especially sophisticated. The group avoided detection by not using the same Internet café too often and writing a message first on a word processor, then pasting that into an e-mail so that the computer would not be connected for an extended period to the Internet.[58] The advantage provided by the Internet is that it has no center of gravity and yet unites terrorist operatives from around the world. This interconnectedness gives terrorists global reach in recruitment, communication, and coordination. The Internet can also be a tool for spreading false information that might heighten defenses in a country like the United States, costing it billions of dollars in preparedness even if there is no actual attack planned. Terrorists can thus use the Internet to produce strategic "chatter" that creates economic and psychological damage on a target society without firing a shot. When the United States elevates its terrorist warning alert level from "yellow" to "orange," it costs on average $1 billion a week from the American economy. Such provocations can also show what kinds of threats a target is preparing to defend and how, and that information can be used for further tactical planning by terrorists.

A particularly gruesome application of the Internet to spread terror is the broadcast of recorded images of the killing of hostages. The images of the murder of American journalist Daniel Pearl by al Qaeda members in Pakistan was spread worldwide around the Internet. During the occupation of Iraq, images of Western hostages seized by insurgents were quickly spread over the Internet. Barbaric images of beheadings were used to incite others to support a cause and to create humiliation and a sense of helplessness among the target audiences. These images also appear to have been used to deter nongovernmental organizations and international organizations from sending workers into the areas where their assistance was most needed to provide long-term stability. Meanwhile, radical Islamic websites could be further used for incitement by projecting propaganda. For example, photos of American soldiers mistreating Iraqi prisoners were widely distributed on the Internet to advance political arguments that the United States sought to humiliate Muslims. Individuals or activists who support the goals of terrorist movements, but who do not want to engage in terrorism directly, have quietly engaged in an "electronic holy war" by distributing anti-Western propaganda.[59]

The virtual battlespace of global terrorist networks also has included the advanced technology of cellular telephones—which create both opportunities and vulnerabilities for terrorist networks. For some time, for example, the United States had intercepted the cellular phone communications of Osama bin Laden. This ability became known after a press leak from the American intelligence community seeking to show off the capability to intercept. Subsequently, bin Laden went deep underground and resorted to more basic forms of communication such as couriers. American intelligence also apparently intercepted communications made by bin Laden during the 2001 war in Afghanistan at the battle of Tora Bora. It is possible, however, that such conversations were previously taped and broadcast to deceive the United States over bin Laden's actual location. In April 2002, several al Qaeda operatives used a cell phone call as a means of alerting a senior al Qaeda leader of an attack on a synagogue in Tunisia which killed twenty-one people—mostly German tourists. The phone call was traced to a particular kind of cellular phone used by the senior al Qaeda operative. German officials were able to locate the origin of the phone conversation to a Polish-born Muslim living in Germany whom officials had been monitoring because of an association with known militants at a local mosque. This intercept revealed a preference among al Qaeda operatives for a particular kind of cell phone that included a Swiss chip, known as Subscriber Identity Modular cards, which al Qaeda apparently thought would keep their conversations untraceable. By narrowing their monitoring of traffic to cell phones in Pakistan, they were able to track the senior al Qaeda figure's general location.[60] Eventually, the terrorist, Khalid Sheikh Mohammed—the operational leader of al Qaeda and the mastermind of the September 11 attacks—was captured.

The capture of Mohammed led American intelligence agents to his computers, cell phones, and a personal phonebook. From this source, authorities traced up to 6,000 phone numbers, which provided a virtual map of al Qaeda's existing international operations.[61] Central to the application of understanding the al Qaeda network was a tiny Swiss communications chip. Al Qaeda members thought this particular chip would hide them, but it actually facilitated the monitoring of Mohammed and a number of his associates. Use of cell-phone information also helped Switzerland break up a Yemeni and Somali ring of document forgers engaged in human smuggling who had ties to a high-level al Qaeda operative. A cell phone obtained from a bomber involved in an attack in Saudi Arabia in May 2003 helped to break up this ring of terrorists. The extent of the network was exposed to have included contact with operatives in France, Italy, Germany, Great Britain, Belgium, the Netherlands, Turkey, Georgia, Saudi Arabia, Yemen, Bahrain, Qatar, Syria, Iraq, Iran, Malaysia, Ethiopia, Somalia, and the Maldives.[62]

The decline of some states' capacity to meet basic human needs and to enforce the rule of law can serve as fertile recruiting ground or training areas for terrorist sympathizers or operatives. Al Qaeda, having lost Afghanistan, increasingly looked to other failing states as new areas for basing activity. Consequently, problems of local governance can quickly become global issues. Historically, the collapse or weakening of states in the underdeveloped world did not merit much attention from great powers. However, the absence of the rule of law in some states allows terrorist networks freedom to organize, train, and carry out terrorist attacks. Somalia, for example, has suffered a prolonged crisis of state capacity, a significant rise in criminality, and faces large-scale disease and drug problems. Somalia has large numbers of internal and externally displaced refugees—many of whom have found their way to the United States. Somalia also has a long, unpatrolled coastline with a high incidence of piracy. Added to this mix, Somalia has a growing radical Islamic movement from which have stemmed small, but significant terrorist actions, primarily carried out by the Al-Ittihad al Islami. This is one of at least seven significant Islamist movements in Mogadishu, which has been identified as having facilitated financial transfers to training camps where al Qaeda members have been based.[63] West Africa has seen considerable movement of financial resources, especially from diamond investments made by al Qaeda. West Africa was a particularly popular location as al Qaeda appeared to conclude that such areas provide opportunities to organize outside the purview of traditional Western intelligence operations.[64] Meanwhile, by 2004, Afghanistan and some areas of Pakistan remained areas where al Qaeda could roam unencumbered. Leaders of Iraq's anti-American insurgency declared an allegiance to al Qaeda in 2004. By summer 2005, the American CIA concluded that Iraq had become a new training ground for Islamic terrorists who were gaining skills there that they could then bring back to their home countries or use for training further terrorist networks.

Terrorism and Weapons of Mass Destruction

The United States invaded Iraq on the premise that Iraq had a relationship with al Qaeda and so it might transfer weapons of mass destruction to the terrorist network. On both accounts, the United States was wrong, but the risk of terrorists with weapons of mass destruction is a legitimate concern. Attaining and using weapons of mass destruction are not the same thing as wanting them or being able to use them effectively. However, the demand for them by terrorists does exist. There are five primary reasons for concern over the nexus between terrorists and weapons of mass destruction. First, these weapons are the most dramatic means a movement can use to attain a sense of massive or divine retribution. Second, the motivations of some terrorists have changed, with the increased role of religious groups fanatically committed to the perceived "just" nature of their cause. Third, the supply-side of weapons persists and manifests serious security problems, particularly in Russia, Pakistan, and North Korea. Fourth, chemical and biological weapons capabilities are proliferating and many dangerous communicable diseases grow naturally and could be utilized by terrorists. Fifth, the technology with which to develop weapons of mass destruction is proliferating through the networks of globalization.[65]

The prospect of a transnational terrorist group developing an outright functional nuclear weapon is most likely very low. It is, however, somewhat more possible that one could be stolen or purchased. More likely, the combination of a variety of components from existing weapons would be of value—if only to build something that looks like a functional weapon to use for blackmail. Built-in safeguards in American and Russian nuclear weapons programs are a significant complication in using a full nuclear weapon if one was stolen. Nevertheless, there are at least 200 locations worldwide where terrorists could acquire a nuclear weapon or the fissile material to make one.[66] The development of nuclear weapons generally requires the apparatus of a nation-state to build and deliver them effectively. A terrorist's standard of success for a nuclear blast, damage, and generation of fear is, however, likely to have a much lower threshold than that of a state acting according to traditional military doctrine. Chemical weapons are a battlefield tool that most militaries see as a dangerous hindrance to be avoided if possible. However, a chemical weapon dispersed in a subway would produce dramatic panic and fear—highly consistent with terrorist objectives. The use of biological agents for targeted attacks was proved in fall 2001 when five people were killed by Anthrax sent through the U.S. mail. While these small-scale attacks created significant fear, the limits of Anthrax as a weapon of mass destruction were also highlighted. Large states, including the United States and the Soviet Union, worked to weaponize such biological agents but abandoned these programs in the 1970s largely because of the difficulty of delivering them.

The dangers of biological weapons are, nevertheless, real and serious. Biological agents such as viruses are especially problematic because many grow in nature and are hard to detect until someone has been infected. Among the most virulent of biological threats, smallpox and forms of the plague could be spread by terrorists. A terrorist group could infect an operative who would try to use the global travel system to infect unknowing victims who might contract the disease and spread it further. Of course, this assumes that people who saw someone obviously infected with smallpox would come into direct contact with them rather than run away. In addition, smallpox has a vaccine, effective after exposure if administered within several days. The vaccine is possibly even more dangerous than the risk of the disease if an outbreak is successfully contained. In the last American outbreak of smallpox in the United States in the 1940s, more people died from the vaccine than did from the infection. While its effects were limited, the 2001 Anthrax attacks in the United States still caused considerable damage by shutting down parts of the U.S. Congress and Supreme Court, infecting eighteen and killing five people, requiring 33,000 people to take preventive antibiotics, and doing $3 billion in damage to the U.S. postal service. While Anthrax is extremely dangerous if inhaled, it is also treatable with antibiotics if one knows the symptoms. Anthrax must be finely processed using sophisticated laboratory technology to be effective in its most virulent form. Even then, it is vulnerable to wind currents and low levels of radiation (such as from the rays of the sun). Another biological agent that terrorist groups have experimented with is ricin, which grows naturally. However, its likely use is limited to an attack on one individual, not as a weapon of mass destruction. A ricin attack would be horrifying. If inhaled, ricin causes death within forty-eight hours from a failure of the respiratory and circulatory systems and if injected, it causes immediate destruction of the muscles and lymph nodes near the injection site with major organ failure and death quickly following. However, to equal one kilogram of Anthrax, one would need to have four metric tons of ricin.[67] Ricin is relatively simple to weaponize—but Anthrax and smallpox are not. To apply such tools as weapons of mass destruction, the apparatus of a modern state would be necessary. A longer-term concern is that in the future, states or individuals might be able to alter the genetic code of such diseases, making them resistant to vaccines or antibiotics.

In a nightmare scenario, a functional nuclear weapon would be smuggled, most likely through a shipping container, into a country and exploded—either in a port or an urban area. Alternatively, parts of a nuclear device could be delivered in a variety of different component forms and then assembled domestically. The threat is serious for a country like the United States which has on the road daily about 300,000 trucks, 6,500 rail cars, and 140 ships that deliver some 50,000 containers holding more than 500,000 items from around the world.[68] In 2004, *ABC News* reported that for two consecutive years, their reporters successfully shipped depleted uranium into the United States. Though harmless, depleted uranium would give off a signature similar to that of enriched uranium used in nuclear bomb devices. In the second test, the reporters shipped the depleted uranium in a teak trunk from Jakarta, Indonesia. It was then placed in a shipping container bound for the United States. Despite newly placed radiation detection devices, the uranium went unnoticed during a three-week passage across the Pacific and through the port of Los Angeles.[69] The numbers of weapons-grade materials in the former Soviet Union, the risk of leakage or a coup in Pakistan, and the growth of clandestine markets combined with vulnerable ports and other transportation modes is a serious global security challenge. Just one nuclear bomb exploded by a terrorist group could do extraordinary physical, economic, and psychological damage. A relatively small nuclear bomb, exploded in a major American West Coast shipping port, could shut down as much as 50 percent of America's international trade, having devastating effects on the global economy.

The difficulties of nuclear bomb building and delivery, however, make alternative forms of radiological terrorism more likely. For example, a terrorist attack on a nuclear power plant, such as the Indian Point nuclear power station thirty-five miles north of New York City, could have dramatic consequences. Though nuclear power stations are hardened against airplanes, it is not clear what a sustained air attack combined with explosives would do. Alternatively large ground assault teams could, in theory, seize a power station and destroy it from the inside. Any circumstance in which a terrorist group instigated a nuclear meltdown at a power station would have devastating consequences. A study of the consequences of an attack on Indian Point estimates that, depending on weather conditions, a core meltdown and radiological release could result in 44,000 near-term deaths from acute radiation syndrome and 518,000 long-term deaths from cancer for people within fifty miles of the plant. Economic damage, within one hundred miles would exceed $1.1 trillion in a worst-case.[70] The probability of creating a successful meltdown scenario is low—but there is a variation on the threat. Rather, for example, than crashing a large jet-liner into a nuclear reactor, the target could instead be the building that houses spent fuel rods. The fuel rods are by-products of the production of nuclear energy and are stored in cooling pools of water not far from reactors. A fire created in such a pool by jet fuel could spread radioactivity into the atmosphere equal or beyond that released in the Soviet Chernobyl disaster.[71] A successful attack on a nuclear power plant would be very difficult for terrorists to achieve—assuming it would want to. On September 11, 2001, al Qaeda could have flown into any number of nuclear power stations that their hijacked air-planes flew near. Al Qaeda instead remained focused on the targets they had selected and the political impact of that selection.

Also more likely than a nuclear explosion would be the release of radioactivity via a conventional explosive device—a so-called "dirty bomb." The purpose of a dirty bomb is not the actual destruction, but rather to cause panic and economic damage. In a simulation of a successful dirty bomb attack on London, via an explosion of a handful of cesium chloride wrapped around a ten-pound conventional explosive, the potential effects were shown to be significant. Exploding such a device in Trafalgar Square might immediately kill only about ten people. Heated air from the blast would likely carry millions of minute flakes of cesium chloride into the breeze over London. Depending on the wind direction, this would cover Whitehall's government offices, Charring Cross, and then the City of London. Within a half an hour, radioactive dust would reach about six miles toward London's suburbs. As the air cooled, the invisible radioactive particles would fall on people, parks, gardens, pavement, and cars. People within about three miles from the blast would be exposed to a small risk of cancer—about 1/1000 people would get some increased risk. At the point of the blast, however, the risk would be about 1/50. The main damage would be economic as panic among millions of people that did not realize the relatively small radiation risks could severely damage the economy. In fact, some people might die in panic from heart attacks, or even being trampled on if a bomb were exploded during a large gathering. The costs of a cleanup operation, however, would be unknowable as radiation would linger for some 200 years if left undisturbed. It might actually be more effective to demolish entire sections of the city and remove the rubble completely.[72]

Even the risk of a dirty bomb—while more likely than a nuclear bomb blast—has to be taken in context. Constructing such a bomb is not an easy task. Absent conditions only a state can provide, terrorists constructing or transporting a device would be exposed to radiation. They would likely quickly become sick and die from radiation exposure. Among known terrorist organizations, al Qaeda has attempted to purchase uranium, but with no success. Documents were also discovered by the United States in Afghanistan which contained accurate information on how to most effectively build a dirty bomb. However, uranium would be of little value for a dirty bomb since the key ingredients would be cesium 137, cobalt 60, and radioisotopes that are hard to come by. Also, in terms of the effects of a dirty bomb's radioactive dispersion, humans live every day with tolerable levels of radiation simply by traveling on jets or walking in the sun. Just four medical CAT scans create an increased cancer risk of 4/,1000—a greater risk that the London dirty bomb scenario. Thus, while a radiological device would be an effective tool of terror, it is not a weapon of mass destruction.[73] In reality, a terrorist would likely do far more human and economic damage by using some sort of air or ground assault on a petro-chemical facility or stealing and exploding a truck full of chlorine gas. As an example of the dangers of what a leak, let alone an explosion, can do at a chemical plant, in 1984 a toxic leak at a pesticide factory in Bhopal, India, led to the death of 7,000 people. An additional 15,000 people died in Bhopal from related diseases between 1984 and 2004.[74]

It is not entirely clear that terrorist groups would benefit from the kind of indiscriminant destruction that a weapon of mass destruction would create. While there are doomsday terrorists, most groups have strategic objectives that are dependent on recruitment and winning hearts and minds. It is not clear that the mass killing of innocent civilians is an effective recruiting tool as it would as likely produce a worldwide negative reaction. The decision to engage a nuclear or radiological device by any terrorist group would face the severe difficulty of acquiring and delivering it. Having decided to organize and engage in nuclear terrorism, a group would then have to either get a weapon or get the components necessary to build one, while bypassing the safeguards designed to make getting a weapon or materials highly difficult. A terrorist organization would have to move these materials through a wide array of transportation nodes, bypassing existing (and improving) detection capabilities. Finally, terrorists would have to successfully detonate the weapon. At any one point, a disruption of this effort would make the entire project fall apart, making it a high risk and high cost venture.[75]

Consequently, while the risk of terrorists with weapons of mass destruction is not zero, terrorists appear to prefer the most achievable and least expensive means—such as car bombs, assassinations, and suicide bombers. The reality behind this risk remains a significant threat to modern states. Indeed, the bombs exploded in London in July 2005 were built from materials that anyone could get at local stores. Looking at a country like the United States, there are 600,000 bridges to protect and 14,000 small airports that could be used by terrorists. There are 4 million miles of paved roadways, 95,000 miles of coastline, and 361 ports to be policed in addition to an open 4,000-mile border with Canada. There are some 260,000 natural gas wells and 1.3 million miles of pipeline that could be attacked. In terms of transportation, 1.2 billion people ride the subway system in just New York City every year and more than 77 million people use its three airports each year. While the United States has hardened its government and military targets, the private sector remains highly vulnerable to attacks designed to generate fear—movie theaters, shopping malls, hotels, sporting events, concerts, and schools are just a small list of possible places for feeding fear with violent terrorist acts.[76]

DEFENSIVE DILEMMAS

Asymmetrical threats create significant defensive dilemmas. By their very nature, asymmetrical challenges are difficult if not impossible to deter. From genocide to terrorism, these strategies and tactics are driven by deep passions that cannot be easily overcome. Deterrence in the classic sense does not work when the attacker is willing, even wanting, to die. In fact, the very strength that many nation-states might have in terms of conventional deterrence is why they are more likely to be attacked asymmetrically. Any strategy that seeks to stop asymmetrical threats is challenged to identify the proper center of gravity as to where to engage most effectively. A response to terrorism that relies on conventional military power actually risks playing into the hands of terrorists. Yet doing nothing, or capitulating to demands, would signal weakness and invite more attacks. Striking a balance between offensive and defensive measures for managing asymmetrical challenges is a central dilemma for states in the twenty-first century.

One of the most important lessons of genocide, ethnic cleansing, and the rise of terrorism and insurgency is that early, proactive engagement by the international community can be a means of preventing escalation. However, prevention creates a variety of challenges that heighten the dilemma posited by asymmetrical threats. For example, the conditions that can lead to genocide and ethnic cleansing might be best managed by preventive diplomacy, and if necessary the use of force to uphold diplomatic settlements. However, as was the case with Kosovo, many of these crises occur within sovereign states. In this sense, sovereignty is a barrier toward preventing genocide and ethnic cleansing. Had NATO done in 1992 what it did in 1995 and 1999, tens of thousands of lives might have been saved in the Balkans. Had the United Nations moved forces into Rwanda as the violence was breaking out there, genocide might have been prevented. Early international engagement is essential for preventing local or regional violence from escalating. However, such conflicts often occur in parts of the world where there is low strategic interest for great powers beyond a moral appeal. Additionally, regional organizations and countries often do not have the capacity to handle such crises without the help of larger international states. This dilemma is further heightened as it is in some of these no-man's-lands where terrorist organizations are able to move with impunity.

This intervention dilemma is also true regarding the relationship between terrorism and weapons of mass destruction. In 2003, the United States invaded Iraq based on a new doctrine of preemptive war. This doctrine justified offensive attack against a sovereign country based on possible future threats. While the fear that the United States had of such a linkage was understandable, it was proven to have been unfounded. By focusing on a symptom of the problem in Iraq, the larger nuclear threat was left unattended—the risk of proliferation of weapons of mass destruction from Russia and Pakistan. Meanwhile, Iran, which did have direct links to international terrorist organizations, would proceed toward a nuclear weapons program. A 2001 study by a bipartisan commission, the Baker-Cutler Report, showed that the problem of weapons security in the former Soviet Union could be managed with a total expenditure of $30 billion spread out over ten years. However, the United States was surpassing $300 billion spent in Iraq as it moved into the year 2006.

In Iraq, the United States exercised a universal right of preemption in the event of an imminent clear and present danger. However, the United States did this without making a compelling public case that the threat was imminent. Such a case would likely have gained the approval of the international community. The United States, like any state, would have reserved for itself the right to act how it deemed necessary according to its national security interests. However, the absence of an international stamp of approval also meant that acting alone in warfighting also meant acting alone after the war period was over. Following the invasion of Iraq, the United States thus supplied 90 percent of the international troops for Iraq, paid 90 percent of the costs, and sustained 90 percent of the casualties. Additionally, as the intelligence upon which the United States based the rationale for invasion was proven wrong, it could be more difficult to persuade allies in the future to support American claims about states with weapons of mass destruction.

The United States embarked in Iraq on the biggest nation-building effort since World War II. American occupation troops confronted a growing insurgency seeking to destabilize an emerging national government and to push Americans out of the country. By summer 2004, American intelligence agencies estimated that the best case for Iraq's future would be a tenuous status quo, and civil war more likely. Insurgents and terrorists had an advantage in that their fight, to them, is a struggle for basic life-and-death, identity, or religion. Also, they benefit by fighting on terrain they know—their homeland. To them, time was on their side, particularly when combating an occupying power. In defeating such a threat, the center of gravity where victory is won will be the hearts and minds of a nation's population.[77] This can mean that while conventional military power has a role in defending against asymmetrical threats, nonmilitary tools are equally important including diplomacy, intelligence, and economic aspects of power.

Good intelligence, which exposes genocidal planning, ethnic cleansing operations, terrorist plots, or early trends toward an insurgency, is essential to identify opportunities for early intervention to preempt attacks. If local communities can be convinced to turn against those who perpetrate barbaric acts of violence, then culprits can be captured or killed. As the insurgency in Iraq grew in late 2003, the United States increased the numbers of prisoners at the Abu Ghraib prison from 5,800 in September 2003 to 8,000 five months later.[78] By arresting large numbers of Iraqis, and then using interrogations combined with humiliation techniques and torture, the United States might have hoped to compel prisoners to give up information. Some prisoners who were released to go back into society might even provide intelligence information if they feared that their treatment in prison would become public in a society where shame, particularly regarding sexual issues, is a major part of life. The humiliation tactic was a deep psychological intrusion into basic morays of Iraqi culture and religion. Photos were taken of men simulating sex with each other, naked men touching each other, and being placed in a variety of compromising sexual positions while being handled on dog leashes by women prison guards.[79] Other elements of interrogation included the use of dogs, dog collars on inmates, wires and electrodes attached to genitals, and physical abuse. U.S. Marines in Iraq used mock executions of juvenile prisoners to frighten other prisoners, burned and tortured other detainees with electric shocks, and warned a Navy doctor that if he treated the prisoners, he would be killed.[80] If defeating insurgents who use the barbaric tactic of terror meant winning hearts and minds, the United States had landed a major defeat on itself.

It is possible to fight asymmetric tactics with asymmetric tactics, without giving up the moral or legal constraints that define the civilized world. Israel, for example, has come to realize that, in its battle with Palestinian insurgents using terrorist tactics, every death is a defeat. The deaths of Israelis make it much harder to negotiate with moderate Palestinian leaders, and the deaths of Palestinians only serve to further radicalize the Palestinian movement. Israel has pursued a strategy that focuses on precision capabilities including Apache helicopters, unmanned aerial vehicles, and long-range optics while issuing its infantry with plastic bullets and riot control gear to deal with disorder in the streets without lethal force. When a conflict could not be avoided, Israel issued restrictive rules of engagement, for example, using snipers to respond to armed opponents.[81] When Israel perceived that the Palestinian leadership had not sufficiently acted to end violence against Israelis, Israel took military pressure straight to the heart of the Palestinian center of gravity, using heavy military equipment to isolate Palestinian leader Yassar Arafat. Israel's dilemma, however, has been that it was not battling a unified threat. Israel confronted a Palestinian political movement that had splintered into a moderate faction which wanted stability and radical Islamic terrorist movements such as Hamas and Hezbollah which wanted no part of negotiations.

Pakistan has applied another unique approach to rounding up terrorist suspects that is sensitive to local cultures and traditions. When confronting an area around the town of Wana near the Pakistan border with Afghanistan, the Pakistani army told local leaders that if they did not hand over suspected al Qaeda terrorists, the entire tribe would be punished. Houses would be demolished, government funds withdrawn, and tribal members detained for questioning. The Pakistani forces left it up to the local leaders themselves, rather than outsiders, to do the dangerous and difficult work of apprehending suspected terrorists while maintaining their tribal dignity. When these tribes cooperated, they reaped economic benefits paid from a $67 million budget made available for development in tribal areas.[82] It is thus possible to apply an array of tactics to fight asymmetrical warfare with asymmetrical means. Public relations, economic investment, intelligence, diplomacy, special operations forces, and military intervention are all available tools of power that can be applied to erode the center of gravity of those who would incorporate asymmetrical tactics to make strategic gains.

One of the most successful, and positive, asymmetrical tactics in modern history was the Marshall Plan after World War II. Through the Marshall Plan, the United States transferred large amounts of its wealth to help rebuild Europe. This approach to winning hearts and minds in Western Europe was central to the effort to combat nationalism and communism. As a more contemporary tactical example, should a network of terrorist communication be infiltrated, such as an e-mail list, false information could be sent out as a means of exposing or further infiltrating transnational terrorist networks. The ability to get inside transnational financial networks used by terrorists to move money is also key to undermining terrorist plots. The United Nations has attempted, for example, to require its members to freeze assets of any person or group linked to the al Qaeda terrorist network. Yet the costs of actual terrorist acts are small. Al Qaeda attacks in Spain, Bali, Kenya, Tanzania, and Turkey cost just $150,000 combined.[83]

Interrogation of prisoners can lead to direct and actionable intelligence. One tactic used by the United States has been to render terrorists to friendly countries whose intelligence agents do not have the same restrictions on the use of violent tactics to gain information as does the United States. Other methods, which are also controversial yet short of direct physical harm, have included American agents in Guantanamo Bay, Cuba, having certain detainees strip to their underwear, sit in a chair while shackled hand and foot to a bolt in the floor, have them face strobe lights and loud rock and rap music while the temperature was adjusted to maximum levels—all for up to fourteen hours at a time. Other techniques included allowing a captive to fall into deep sleep, then moving them to another cell, waiting for deep sleep, waking them and moving them again—up to six times a night.[84] Yet, even in these cases, there is considerable dispute over whether such pressure works to gain good information. Ultimately, the person being physically or mentally coerced is as likely to tell what they think the captor wants to hear. Or, a person being interrogated might give up some actionable information combined with information that is terrifying but untrue. This would give credence to bad information that could further the cause of spreading fear without actual acts of terrorism.

Defensive postures against asymmetrical warfare also create unique dilemmas. Using power to balance suicide terrorists is not possible because suicide terrorists do not fear death. Power in this case is useful, but only if exercised with the ability to kill the suicide terrorist before he or she can reach their target. It is possible to create layers of perimeter security which can dissuade a terrorist organization from wasting scarce resources and recruits on certain targets within a state's home territory. For example, the United States has created an integrated data system for using finger scans and photos to match identities of any suspicious visitors who come into the country at its airports, seaports, and border crossings. This program was expected to affect about thirteen million travelers from twenty-seven countries and to eventually cost $15 billion to implement fully by 2014.[85] At the same time, as states perform their most traditional functions of national defense, human rights and civil liberties of citizens are at risk of being encroached upon. Once, for example, the International Civil Aviation Organization implements an international standard for facial recognition on all passports, it will have established a database of information on over one billion people.[86] In the United States, hundreds of citizens were detained without reasonable evidence following the September 11, 2001 attacks. In 2004, a federal judge ordered Drake University in Iowa to provide records of students who attended an antiwar meeting. Reconciling the tension between security and freedom thus is a significant challenge of the twenty-first-century security dynamic.

SUMMARY

Asymmetrical conflict challenges the foundations of traditional approaches to power and peace. Wars between nation-states can be significantly altered by the variety of means that small, less powerful, but very dangerous actors have to set the agenda of international security. The dangers posed by such new threats are severe to nation-states and to average citizens. Threats of genocide and ethnic cleansing are containable, and, if international society chooses to engage them, preventable. The horrors of genocide and ethnic cleansing are real and continue despite international norms that promise intervention to halt these barbaric acts of brutality against civilian populations. In this sense, the solution lies in the willingness of the international community to act in cases of genocide and ethnic conflict. Terrorism too can be both reduced and defeated—but it requires an application of an equally aggressive asymmetrical strategy that undermines the objectives that terrorists seek to achieve. Meeting asymmetrical threats requires creative thinking that applies a range of tactics. Asymmetrical threats will thus have to be engaged in the new battlespace of global security with unconventional tactics at the service of clearly conceived strategic objectives.

NOTES

1. Ivan Arreguin-Toft, "How the Weak Win Wars: A Theory of Asymmetric Conflict," *International Security* 26, no. 1 (Summer 2001): 100–105.

2. Roger W. Barnett, *Asymmetrical Warfare* (Dulles, Va.: Brassey's Inc., 2003), 18.

3. Stephen J. Blank, *Rethinking Asymmetric Threats* (Carlisle Barracks, Pa.: United States Army War College, Strategic Studies Institute, 2003), 18.

4. Montgomery C. Meigs, "Unorthodox Thoughts about Asymmetric Warfare," *Parameters* 33, no. 2 (Summer 2003): 4–18.

5. Blank, *Rethinking Asymmetric Threats*, 41.

6. Steven Metz, *Asymmetry and U.S. Military Strategy: Definition, Background, and Strategic Concepts* (Carlisle, Pa.: US Army War College, 2001).

7. Metz, *Asymmetry and U.S. Military Strategy*, 5–12.

8. Kenneth F. McKenzie Jr., *Revenge of the Melians: Asymmetric Threats and the Next QDR*, McNair Paper, no. 62 (November 2000).

9. Stasys Knezys and Romanas Sedlickas, *War in Chechnya* (College Station: Texas A&M Press, 1999), 105.

10. Shahram Chubin and Jerrold D. Green, *Terrorism and Asymmetric Conflict in Southwest Asia* (Santa Monica, Calif.: Rand, 2002).

11. See Michael E. Brown, ed., *Ethnic Conflict and International Security* (Princeton, N.J.: Princeton University Press, 1997).

12. David A. Lake and Donald Rothchild, "Containing Fear: The Origins and Management of Ethnic Conflict," *International Security* 21, no. 2 (Fall 1996): 41–75.

13. Barry Posen, "The Security Dilemma and Ethnic Conflict," in *Ethnic Conflict and International Security*, ed. Michael E. Brown (Princeton, N.J.: Princeton University Press, 1993), 103–24.

14. Stuart J. Kaufman, "Spiraling to Ethnic War: Elites, Masses, and Moscow in Moldova's Civil War," *International Security* 21, no. 2 (Fall 1996): 108–38.

15. Christine Wallach, "Policy Forum: Bosnia—After the Troops Leave," *Washington Quarterly* 19, no. 3 (Summer 1996): 3–6.

16. Alan J. Kuperman, *The Limits of Humanitarian Intervention: Genocide in Rwanda* (Washington, D.C.: Brookings, 2001), 9–12.

17. Philip Gourevitch, *We Wish to Inform You That Tomorrow We Will Be Killed with Our Families: Stories from Rwanda* (New York: Farrar Straus and Giroux, 1998), 93.

18. FAX NO: MOST Immidate-Code, Cable-212, Subject "Request for Protection of Informant," BARIL/DPKO/UNATIONS, January 11, 1994.

19. Arthur J. Klinghoffer, *The International Dimension of Genocide in Rwanda* (New York: New York University Press, 1998), 112–13.

20. Gourevitch, *We Wish to Inform You*, 95.

21. "Interview: General Romeo Dallaire," *Ghosts of Rwanda*, PBS Frontline, at www.pbs.org/wgbh/pages/frontline/shows/ghosts/interviews/dallaire.html (accessed Fall 2004).

22. United States Department of State, Bureau of Intelligence and Research Assessment, "Roots of Violence in Rwanda," April 29, 1994.

23. Klinghoffer, *International Dimension of Genocide in Rwanda*, 113.

24. Kuperman, *Limits of Humanitarian Intervention*, 38–42.

25. Gourevitch, *We Wish to Inform You*, 134–35.

26. Kuperman, *Limits of Humanitarian Intervention*, 14–16.

27. Shaharyar M. Khan, *The Shallow Graves of Rwanda* (New York: London, 2000), 17.

28. Audrey Kurth Cronin, "Behind the Curve: Globalization and International Terrorism," *International Security* 27, no. 3 (Winter 2002/2003): 34.

29. Bruce Hoffman, *Inside Terrorism* (New York: Columbia University Press, 1998), 15.

30. C. J. M. Drake, "The Role of Ideology in Terrorists' Target Selection," *Terrorism and Political Violence* 10, no. 2 (Summer 1998): 53–85.

31. James Der Derian, "The Terrorist Discourse: Signs, States, and Systems of Global Political Violence," in *World Security: Trends and Challenges at Century's End*, ed. Michael T. Klare and Daniel C. Thomas (New York: St. Martin's Press, 1991), 237–65.

32. Hoffman, *Inside Terrorism*, 43.

33. Ariel Merari, "Terrorism as a Strategy of Insurgency," *Terrorism and Political Violence* 5, no. 4 (Winter 1993): 215.

34. John Mackinlay, *Globalization and Insurgency*, Adelphi Paper, no. 352, International Institute for Strategic Studies, (November 2002): 17–27.

35. Joey Hanzich, "Dying for Independence: World Separatist Movements and Terrorism," *Harvard Business Review* (Summer 2003): 33.

36. Ted Robert Gurr, "Some Characteristics of Political Terrorism in the 1960s," in *The Politics of Terrorism*, 3rd ed., ed. Michael Stohl (New York: Marcel Dekker, 1988).

37. U.S. Department of State, *Patterns of Global Terrorism*, U.S. Department of State, Washington, D.C., 2002.

38. Phil Williams, "Eurasia and the Transnational Terrorist Threats to Atlantic Security," in *Limiting Institutions: The Challenge of Eurasian Security Governance*, ed. James Sperling, Sean Kay, and S. Victor Papacosma (Manchester, U.K.: Manchester University Press, 2003), 69–85.

39. Hoffman, *Inside Terrorism*, 94.

40. Bruce Hoffman, "Viewpoint: Terrorism and WMD: Some Preliminary Hypotheses," *Non-Proliferation Review* (Spring/Summer 1997): 48.

41. Robert Pape, "The Strategic Logic of Suicide Terrorism," *American Political Science Review* 97, no. 3 (August 2003): 343–61.

42. Pape, "The Strategic Logic," 343.

43. Cronin, "Behind the Curve," 41–42.

44. W. Seth Carus, "The Threat of Bioterrorism," *Strategic Forum*, no. 127 (September 1997): 1–4.

45. Douglas Frantz et al., "The New Face of Al Qaeda: Al Qaeda Seen as Wider Threat," *Los Angeles Times*, September 26, 2004.

46. Raymond Bonner and Don van Natta Jr., "Regional Groups Pose Growing Threat," *New York Times*, February 8, 2004.

47. John Meuller, "Harbinger or Aberration? A 9/11 Provocation," *The National Interest*, no. 68 (Summer 2002): 45–50.

48. Jessica Stern, *The Ultimate Terrorists* (Cambridge: Harvard University Press, 1999), 32.

49. Barton Bernstein, "Eclipsed by Hiroshima and Nagasaki: Early Thinking about Tactical Nuclear Weapons," *International Security* 15, no. 4 (Spring 1991): 149–73.

50. Walter Laqueur, "The New Face of Terrorism," *Washington Quarterly* 21, no. 4 (Autumn 1998): 171.

51. Brian M. Jenkins, "The Organization Men: Anatomy of a Terrorist Attack," in *How Did This Happen? Terrorism and the New War*, ed. James F. Hoge Jr. and Gideon Rose (New York: Public Affairs, 2001), 4–5.

52. Paul R. Pillar, *Terrorism and U.S. Foreign Policy* (Washington, D.C.: Brookings Institution Press, 2001), 19.

53. 9/11 Commission, Staff Statement, no. 15, "Overview of the Enemy," June 2004.

54. Frantz, "The New Face of Al Qaeda."

55. 9/11 Commission, Staff Statement, no. 15.

56. 9/11 Commission, Staff Statement, no. 15.

57. Steve Coll and Susan B. Glasser, "Jihadists Turn the Web into Base of Operations," *Washington Post*, August 7, 2005.

58. Douglas Frantz, Josh Meyer, and Richard B. Schmitt, "Cyberspace Gives Al Qaeda Refuge," *Los Angeles Times*, August 15, 2004.

59. Sarah el Deeb, "Extremists Using Web to Spread Terror," *Associated Press*, June 13, 2004.

60. Don van Natta Jr. and Desmond Butler, "How Tiny Swiss Cellphone Chips Helped Track Global Terror Web," *New York Times*, March 4, 2004.

61. van Natta and Butler, "How Tiny Swiss Cellphone Chips Helped."

62. Michael Isikoff and Mark Hosenball, "Like Clockwork," *Newsweek*, August 25, 2004, at www.newsweek.com (accessed Fall 2004).

63. Ken Menkhaus, "Somalia: State Collapse and the Threat of Terrorism," *Adelphi Paper* no. 364, International Institute for Strategic Studies, London (2004): 54–56.

64. Douglas Farah and Richard Shultz, "Al Qaeda's Growing Sanctuary," *Washington Post*, July 14, 2004, A19.

65. Stern, *Ultimate Terrorists*, 8–10.

66. Graham Alison, *Nuclear Terrorism* (New York: Times Books, 2004), 67, 83–86.

67. "What Is Ricin?" CNN, October 23, 2003.

68. Stephen E. Flynn, "The Fragile State of Container Security," testimony before the Senate Governmental Affairs Committee, March 20, 2003.

69. Brian Ross, "New Report Reveals Gaps in Port Security," *ABC News*, October 13, 2004.

70. Edwin S. Lyman, "Chernobyl on the Hudson? The Health and Economic Impacts of a Terrorist Attack at the Indian Point Nuclear Plant," Union of Concerned Scientists, September 2004.

71. Alison, *Nuclear Terrorism*, 7–8.

72. "What If a Dirty Bomb Hit London?" *BBC News*, February 14, 2003.

73. Peter D. Zimmerman with Cheryl Loeb, "Dirty Bombs: The Threat Revisited," *Defense Horizons*, no. 38 (January 2004): 1–11.

74. "World 'Failed' Bhopal Gas Victims," *BBC News*, November 29, 2004.

75. Charles D. Ferguson and William C. Potter, *The Four Faces of Nuclear Terrorism* (Monterey, Calif.: The Monterey Institute, 2004), 6.

76. Matthew Brzezinski, *Fortress America* (New York: Bantam Books, 2004), 8.

77. Andrew Krepinevich, "The War in Iraq: The Nature of Insurgency Warfare," Center for Strategic and Budgetary Analysis, June 2, 2004, 1–2.

78. Scott Wilson and Sewell Chan, "As Insurgency Grew, So Did Prison Abuse," *Washington Post*, May 10, 2004.

79. Seymour M. Hersh, "The Gray Zone," *The New Yorker*, May 15, 2004, 38.

80. Richard A. Serrano, "Details of Marines Mistreating Prisoners in Iraq are Revealed," *Los Angeles Times*, December 15, 2004.

81. Wesley K. Clark, "How to Fight an Asymmetric War," *Time Canada*, October 23, 2000, 30.

82. David Rohde and Ismail Khan, "Pakistan Adopting a Tough Old Tactic to Flush Out Qaeda," *New York Times*, January 31, 2004.

83. "Al Qaeda Sanctions 'Ineffective,'" *BBC*, August 27, 2004.

84. Neil A. Lewis, "Broad Use Cited of Harsh Tactics at Base in Cuba," *New York Times*, October 17, 2004.

85. Christopher Lee and Sara Kehaulani Goo, "U.S. VISIT Program to Add 27 Countries," *Washington Post*, April 3, 2004; and Eric Lichtblau and John Markoff, "U.S. Nearing Deal on Way to Track Foreign Visitors," May 24, 2004.

86. "Concern over Biometric Passports," *BBC News*, March 30, 2002.

SUGGESTED READING

Roger W. Barnett, *Asymmetrical Warfare: Today's Challenge to US Military Power* (Washington, D.C.: Potomac Books, 2003).

Peter I. Bergen, *Holy War Inc.: Inside the Secret World of Osama Bin Laden* (New York: Free Press, 2002).

Ivo Daalder and Michael O'Hanlon, *Winning Ugly: NATO's War to Save Kosovo* (Washington, D.C.: Brookings, 2000).

Bruce Hoffman, *Inside Terrorism* (New York: Columbia University Press, 1999).

Stuart Kaufman, *Modern Hatreds: The Symbolic Politics of Ethnic War* (Ithaca, N.Y.: Cornell University Press, 2001).

Alan Kuperman, *The Limits of Humanitarian Intervention: Genocide in Rwanda* (Washington, D.C.: Brookings, 2001).

National Commission on Terrorist Attacks, *The 9/11 Report* (New York: St. Martin's Press, 2004).

Robert A. Pape, *Dying to Win: The Strategic Logic of Suicide Terrorism* (New York: Random House, 2005).

Samantha Power, *"A Problem from Hell": America and the Age of Genocide* (New York: Perennial, 2003).

Jessica Stern, *Terror in the Name of God: Why Religious Militants Kill* (New York: Ecco, 2004).

Chapter Eight

Human Security

A boy who lost his hand after picking up a mine. *Source*: UN Photo by Armineh Johannes.

Human security focuses analytical and policy attention onto the problems that affect the basic safety and well-being of individuals. In this case, the quest for power and the search for peace focuses on the conditions of those people who themselves do not have power or are victims of international conditions outside their control. Approaches to human security stress the protection of human rights and democracy as well as physical challenges such as population size, food availability, disease, and the human costs of war. This approach also, however, has significant strategic applications. Even those people who live comfortably are challenged by pressures from external human insecurity crises which can spill over into modern and developed societies. Individuals are often threatened in the context of asymmetrical attacks on civilian populations. This chapter examines the meaning of human security in the context of human rights and democracy, population and migration, food and health, and the human costs of war.

WHAT IS HUMAN SECURITY?

The question of the security, safety, or rights of the individual is not fundamentally new. What are new, however, are the increasing number of challenges to human security, and the increasing number of states and non-state actors who work to put it at the top of the international agenda. Canadian Foreign Minister Lloyd Axworthy notes that Canada explicitly adopted a foreign policy focused on human security after the Cold War to advance a "new foreign policy paradigm."[1] The result was, Axworthy noted (in 2001), that "Several years ago, few were talking about human security. . . . Today, at every forum I attend or meeting I participate in, states of all station and tradition are using the term, and more important, are accepting the usefulness of the idea."[2] A range of countries including Canada, Ireland, and the Scandinavian countries pursues a foreign policy that emphasizes human security. International organizations and advocacy groups have also played a major role working outside the traditions of the nation-state system as a major part of a growing human security network.

Human security research seeks to identify conditions under which the actions of states' internal and external policies threaten the safety and security of individuals. The concept can also be applied to non-state actors and transboundary phenomena that can affect the human condition. Such an approach becomes even more applicable in the era of global security as individual rights often go unprotected in the absence of international guarantees. For example, as many as 800,000 people are trafficked each year in an illegal trade of humans. Most of these people are women and children placed into forced labor or prostitution.[3] The human security concept is also an advocacy agenda—promoting freedom from pervasive threats to people's rights, their safety, or even their lives.[4] How to measure human security, however, is a significant methodological challenge. Generally, human security can be thought to be achieved when and where individuals and communities: (1) have the options necessary to end, mitigate, or adapt to threats to their human, environmental, and social rights; (2) have the capacity and freedom to exercise these options; and (3) actively participate in attaining these options.[5] The United Nations uses a Human Development Index focusing on levels of economic development, life expectancy, and level of education as indicators of human insecurity. The application of various data shows that it is possible to achieve relatively significant increases in human security via even small increases in economic development.[6]

Human security analysis suffers from a divergence among relative expectations of how much security is necessary for any individual to be said to have attained a measure of security.[7] A family living in Mozambique or Ethiopia might have significantly different human security expectations than one living in Egypt or South Africa. Any African citizen might have a completely different set of expectations as regarding human security than a citizen from Europe or North America. Within Europe or North America, there are dramatic differences in expectations, for example, between western Europe and southeastern Europe and between the United States and Mexico. Citizens in the developed world might worry about a general threat such as terrorism or global climate change. Citizens in the underdeveloped world might worry more about where their next meal might come from. The era of global security also poses new challenges to human security. For example, Africa is highly vulnerable to the spread of disease such as HIV/AIDS. However, Africa is less vulnerable to a transnational disease like SARS, which spread in large part in 2002–2003 as a consequence of global air travel and therefore mostly affected developed countries.

The United Nations Development Program (UNDP) 1994 report on human development, defines a variety of areas of human security. The UNDP report identified the core elements of human security as being economic security, food security, health security, environmental security, personal security, community security, and political security.[8] Building on these core aspects of human security, the Commission on Human Security defined human security in 2003 as "protecting the vital core of all human lives in ways that enhance human freedoms and human fulfillment."[9] According to Sadako Ogata and Johan Cels, this means "protecting vital freedoms—fundamental to human existence and development. . . . Human security means protecting people from severe and pervasive threats, both natural and societal, and empowering individuals and communities to develop the capabilities for making informed choices and acting on their own behalf."[10] Caroline Thomas notes that human security is about the "achievement of human dignity, which incorporates personal autonomy, control over one's life, and unhindered participation in the life of the community."[11]

Fen Osler Hampson and his colleagues identify three general approaches to human security. The first approach focuses on liberty, human rights, and the rule of law as a source of security. The second focuses on achieving mechanisms to provide for the safety of peoples and to create freedom from fear. Such an approach seeks proactive ways to end war and to eliminate the underlying causes of international conflict and violence. The third approach stresses the need for "sustainable human development" by alleviating the economic sources of human insecurity and treating the new sources of insecurity such as AIDS, drug trafficking, poverty, and environmental problems. The sustainable human development approach has three distinct dynamics: (1) the definition extends to a large number of problems that have not been traditionally associated with the concept of security; (2) the new understanding of these threats marginalizes those of an exclusively military nature; and (3) those threats considered to be the most relevant—such as environmental degradation and population growth—are considered to be so relevant within a global context that the national interest itself is a diminishing point of reference.[12]

A catalogue of potential threats to human security could result in an endless list of harmful aspects of the human condition. As Andrew Mack writes: "Conflating a very broad range of disparate harms under the rubric of 'insecurity' is an exercise in re-labeling that serves no apparent analytical purpose. . . . If the term 'insecurity' embraces almost all forms of harm—from affronts to dignity to genocide—its descriptive power is extremely low."[13] In his pioneering work, Mack limits the definition of human security to the study of the direct consequences of war and conflict on the human condition. Alternatively, some approaches take such a broad definition so as to include the general distribution of power in the structure of the international system. Caroline Thomas, for example, asserts that when power is distributed unevenly, human insecurity results when one person (or group of persons) exercises power in a purposeful manner that harms other people. "Human security," writes Thomas, "is understood not as some inevitable occurrence but as a direct result of existing structures of power that determine who enjoys the entitlement to security and who does not."[14] While there is a range of specific issue areas that can be assessed to measure degrees of human security, dominant issues include human rights and democracy, population and demographic change, food and health, and the human cost of war.

HUMAN RIGHTS AND DEMOCRACY

Human rights have been a major element of the international security agenda since World War II and were enshrined in the establishment of the United Nations in 1945. There is, however, considerable debate over what human rights are, what degree of rights are sufficient for all people, and the extent to which the exercise of one individual or group's human rights might impinge on the rights of others. Human rights advocacy also raises strategic questions about the moral imperative to protect human rights versus the tradition of sovereignty. Moreover, a particularistic concept of human rights—such as the Euro-American concept of individual liberty—might be seen as an infringement on cultural or religious rights of other societies. Military intervention to stop human rights abuses can also create entirely new sets of humanitarian problems simply by nature of the use of force. Closely related to the question of human rights is the degree of political freedoms that are assured and protected by governments—and as such the degree to which governments are responsive to the needs of their peoples. Thus the degree of democracy has also become an important measure of human security.

Contemporary Challenges to Human Rights

The global human rights situation improved dramatically with the end of the Cold War. Hundreds of millions of people were liberated from dictatorships in central and eastern Europe. The end of direct superpower competition led to a resolution of proxy conflicts for example in Latin America, where human rights were persistently violated. The end of the Cold War, however, also resulted in a resurgence of the quest for self-determination in ethnically complex regions. Culture and religion also have emerged as significant human rights questions—particularly in the Islamic world. Is it a human right to exercise religious freedom if that denies individual liberty? Are Islamic women denied human rights because they often cannot show their faces in public, attain higher education, drive cars, or vote? Or, is such a perspective derived from a Western concept of human rights and thus an expression of cultural imperialism and Western domination? Even in the Western world, religious differences highlight a human rights dilemma. In Ireland a woman cannot legally attain information about how to get a safe abortion—a law consistent with the religious beliefs of Ireland's 90 percent Catholic population. Some girls who have been raped and seek to travel abroad to attain abortions have been stopped by Irish tribunals which required the girls to finish the pregnancy. In this case, however, Ireland would be in violation of human rights doctrine as codified in the European Union—which guarantees the freedom to travel. Conversely, in China the government provides strong incentives for women to have only one child—and the end result is a very high rate of abortions. In this case, China has been criticized for advocating a draconian population control policy that denies the right to procreate. In these cases, which human priority should take precedence: the interests of society or the right of an individual?

States which advocate international human rights have not responded well when the light is shined in their direction. In the United States, California banned birth-rights to people who are rightful citizens under the fourteenth amendment of the U.S. Constitution if their parents were illegal immigrants. The United States allowed Cuban exile refugees to remain in the United States, but forced Haitian refugees to return. The Haitian return policy was especially problematic because it allowed for children born in the United States from Haitian refugee parents to remain. However, this meant that parents had to choose between taking their children back to Haiti—the poorest country in the Western Hemisphere—or abandoning them in America in hope of a better future. The United States has also been accused by international human rights groups of violating rights of immigrants seeking to cross the border at Mexico. Suspected illegal immigrants have suffered arbitrary detention, withholding of water, and even murder by state officials. European states will not extradite criminals to the United States out of opposition to America's death penalty policy, which is seen as a cruel and unusual punishment. Human Rights Watch identifies a range of areas where the United States faces human rights deficiencies including children, criminal sentencing and drug laws, death penalty, discrimination against gays and lesbians, immigration and treatment of noncitizens, labor rights, police brutality, prison conditions, racism and discrimination, and women's rights.[15]

The United States has also served as a beacon of human rights during the twentieth century. It has had its soldiers die to protect the rights and dignity of other peoples. It also continues to place pressure on states like China and Burma to respect human rights. As a state with interests, however, the United States had to choose priorities and thus supported authoritarian governments in Pakistan, Saudi Arabia, and Uzbekistan in order to defeat international terrorism. In 2002, U.S. Secretary of Defense Donald Rumsfeld visited Afghanistan and declared the Herat-based warlord Ismail Khan an "appealing person." Khan had eliminated dissent, controlled the press, and forced women to wear burqas—something Washington had heralded would end with the liberation of Afghanistan.[16] Europeans also share this dilemma as they confront a significant increase in European anti-Semitism and anti-immigrant attitudes reflected in increased incidents of violence against North African and Middle Eastern immigrants and against gypsies.

The standards for assessing human rights are the guarantees articulated in the Universal Declaration on Human Rights. As Jack Donnelly notes, these rights provide a basis on which to organize action for remedies—such as the values of nondiscrimination and an adequate standard of living for individuals. The rights (with the exception of the right to self-determination) are specifically rights which are indivisible and not merely a menu from which one can pick and choose. Nevertheless, there is a core tension between such universal rights and the historical right of sovereignty.[17] As Donnelly writes: "Internationally recognized human rights impose obligations on and are exercised against sovereign territorial states. . . . 'Everybody has a right to x' in contemporary international practice means 'Each state has the authority and responsibility to implement and protect the right to x within its territory.'"[18]

The scope of human rights challenges spans all regions of the globe, though some areas are clearly more violation-free than others. Human Rights Watch summarizes regional human rights trends in its annual *World Report*.[19] According to their survey, Africa has some of the most severe human rights challenges among the regions of the world. Africa hosts 3.3 million refugees, has almost 30 percent of the world's refugee population and about 13.5 million, or more than half of the world's twenty-five million internally displaced persons. Africa also is challenged by the relationship between transnational disease (especially HIV/AIDS) and basic human needs (such as access to medical treatment more readily available in the developed world). Between 2000 and 2020, some 25 million Africans will die prematurely. Meanwhile extremely violent conflict ravages areas of Africa. In ongoing wars in the Democratic Republic of Congo, Sierra Leone, and Sudan, warring parties have employed gang rape, violent abduction followed by repeated rapes, and amputation of breasts and sexual organs. Africa's efforts to advance a continent-wide human rights agenda were complicated by Libya's role as the region's representative on the United Nations Commission on Human Rights. Libya has a long record of detaining government opponents without charge or trial, prohibiting the formation of political parties or independent nongovernmental groups, constraining press freedoms, and torture of governmental opponents.

Latin America has seen a general improvement in regional human rights trends with the end of the Cold War. Limitations on political dissent remain a particular problem in Cuba and public protests have produced violent government reactions in Venezuela, Paraguay, and Bolivia. Haiti has severe problems resulting from a lack of governance and general instability with competing militias combating each other for power. Antigovernment rebels in Columbia (the FARC) have carried out a persistent terrorist campaign that includes targeting of civilians. In one circumstance, these rebels launched a gas cylinder bomb that hit a church in Bojaya where displaced persons were gathered. This attack killed 119 people including nearly 50 children. Conversely, the government has also used severe tactics against captured rebel members and their sympathizers.

While states in Asia have moved away from the argument that "Asian values" justify strong state power over liberties, the global war on terrorism has given many leaders a new rationale to deny individual freedoms. In Afghanistan, however, the human rights condition improved considerably with the ouster of the oppressive Taliban government in 2001. In Bangladesh and Sri Lanka, massive numbers of displaced persons must worry daily about their personal security—let alone access to education, clean water, and health care. In Malaysia, a political opponent of the prime minister was arrested and given a flawed trial, imprisoned, and suffered physical mistreatment. In Burma, the military government placed the country's elected leader and longtime dissident, Aung San Suu Kyi, under arrest. The government in Burma also conscripted large numbers of child soldiers and forcibly relocated entire ethnic communities. Hindus have been especially targeted with their homes often looted, vandalized, and burned; temples and sacred sites destroyed; and scores of Hindu women and girls gang-raped in front of male relatives while the government did little or nothing to investigate or prosecute these crimes. In China, political and religious freedoms were repressed by the Communist Party government. Meanwhile, North Korea was effectively a massive prison camp under the rule of the world's last remaining totalitarian government.

Europe has demonstrated a deepening commitment to human rights and a desire to expand them more broadly through Eurasia. When NATO and the European Union expanded to include new members from Central and Eastern Europe, these countries had to meet specific criteria for respecting human rights. In a historical reversal, Russian minority populations in former Soviet republics have sought, and received, due regard and protections for their status. Ethnic cleansing in the Balkans has been halted—though the seeds of conflict remain unresolved. Throughout the Caucuses and central Asia, the human rights situation, however, is grim. The combination of rule by former Soviet crony-dictators; competition over oil-driven economic growth in the Caspian Sea region; ethnic conflict and civil war in a number of states; and the general preference toward stability over human rights dominate the war on terrorism in this area. Uzbekistan, in particular, is ruled by an authoritarian government that has imprisoned poets and other citizens in a crackdown on political Islam, which has terrorist support in the Islamic Movement of Uzbekistan. Meanwhile, Belarus remains stuck in a Soviet era political circumstance, and Ukraine sits on the margins of instability. In Ukraine and Russia, press freedoms have been severely curtailed. Journalists investigating sensitive governmental activity have been harassed and several murdered. The Russian government continues to press a military solution to the problem of Chechnya where as many as 200,000 may have been killed. Meanwhile, Chechen separatists continue to wage a well-coordinated campaign of terrorism, killing innocent civilians throughout Russia. Throughout the European region, there is growing tension regarding the need to protect the rights of immigrants—especially the cultural and religious rights of those coming from North Africa and the Middle East.

The Middle East is one of the world's most problematic areas for human rights abuses. A failure to resolve the long-standing Palestinian question, both in the Palestinian areas and for refugees who fled Israeli occupation, plagues the region. Between 2000 and 2002, some 2,500 Palestinians and over 650 Israelis were killed and at least 21,000 Palestinians and 2,000 Israelis were injured in ongoing conflict. Some of the most dramatic violations of human rights in the region come from the hands of Arab governments against their own peoples. The lack of legitimately elected and supported governments in Jordan, Morocco, Saudi Arabia, and the smaller Gulf states—combined with the unilateral rule of long-standing political parties in Egypt, Libya, Syria, Tunisia, and Yemen—make progress toward advancing regional human rights difficult. Throughout the region, justice is poorly administered and often takes place outside the rule of law. Peaceful critics of governments have been imprisoned, and press and publishing freedoms severely restricted. If Iraq stabilizes and eventually functions as a representative democracy, then other governments in the area might feel pressure to reform. However, if the Iraq project fails, the region could see chaos and war of the kind not witnessed in generations. Meanwhile, since the 1980s, secular and Western-leaning Turkey killed 25,000 of its own people in its campaign against Kurdish separatist fighters. Islamists in Turkey wishing to display their faith publicly were barred from public service and the Turkish military intervened and overthrew a popularly elected pro-Islamist national government.

The human rights dimension of human security reflects a mixed record. Improvements might occur in one part of the world, while significant declines occur in others. Much progress depends also on the priority that the world community puts on advancing human rights. When concern about national security is high, then respect for human rights tends to decline. There is a serious dilemma in this approach as near-term support for authoritarian government tends to stir violent opposition in the long-term. In supporting authoritarian governments who are helping in the campaign against terrorism, the world simultaneously risks the emergence of a new generation of terrorists grown from the resentment that oppression can breed.

Degrees of Democracy

The expansion of democracy, and the functions of representative government, have become an important measure of human rights. Democracy is seen as increasing human security because well-functioning democracies facilitate the peaceful resolution of internal disputes. In democracies, political and military leadership are held accountable for their actions and it is therefore harder to pursue policies that violate human security needs. Democratic institutions alone do not guarantee stability or peace. Indeed, the process of democratization can be highly destabilizing if political, ethnic, or religious groups position themselves—often violently—to attain power via elections. Also, the democratic principle of self-determination can stir separatist movements that often result in violent conflict or civil war. Generally, however, democracies protect basic political freedoms, particularly minority rights, which accord a higher sensitivity to the cause of human security.

Since 1973, Freedom House has done annual surveys measuring the level of freedom worldwide—which provides a standard for measuring effective democracy. *Freedom House* generates rankings of degrees of freedom by evaluating the electoral process; political pluralism and participation; the functioning of government; freedom of expression and belief; associational and organizational rights; the rule of law; and personal autonomy and individual rights. A country with a score of 1–2.5 is understood to be "free"; 3 to 5.5 is "partly free"; and 5.5 to 7.0 is "not free." The areas that are ranked 6 and 7 are those with the lowest degrees of democratic freedom. A ranking of 6 means that people in a country have severely restricted rights of expression and association, and there are almost always political prisoners and other manifestations of political terror. These countries are characterized by a few partial rights, however, such as some religious and social freedoms, business activity, and relatively free private discussion. Countries with a score of 7 are those having virtually no freedom and in which there is an overwhelming and justified fear of repression. States ranked in 2004 as "not free" on political rights and civil liberties were: Afghanistan, Algeria, Angola, Belarus, Bhutan, Brunei, Burma, Burundi, Cambodia, Cameroon, Chad, China, Congo, Côte d'Ivoire, Cuba, Egypt, Equatorial Guinea, Eritrea, Guinea, Haiti, Iran, Iraq, Kazakhstan, North Korea, Kyrgyzstan, Laos, Lebanon, Liberia, Libya, Maldives, Oman, Pakistan, Qatar, Rwanda, Saudi Arabia, Somalia, Sudan, Swaziland, Syria, Tajikistan, Togo, Tunisia, Turkmenistan, United Arab Emirates, Uzbekistan, Vietnam, Yemen, and Zimbabwe.

Over thirty years of *Freedom House* surveys, the Western Hemisphere and Western Europe rank as having the highest degrees of freedom. Worldwide, the number of "free" countries grew from 43 in 1973 to 89 in 2003 while the number of "not free" states declined from 69 to 48. The area with the highest number of "not free" states is sub-Saharan Africa, though that too has dropped from 28 in 1973 to 16 in 2003. In non-Muslim countries, the number of "not free" has declined from 46 in 1973 to 14 in 2003 while the number of "free" countries has risen from 41 to 87. Muslim majority countries have not, however, witnessed considerable change with 23 countries not free in 1973 and a decline toward 27 not free countries in 2003. In 2003 there were only 9 countries in the Muslim world with electoral democracies whereas 112 non-Muslim countries have such systems. Thus the global trend has been toward more democracy—with the exception of the Muslim world. Importantly, *Freedom House* notes that, as a percentage of the global gross domestic product, "free" countries account for 89 percent or $26,759,070,650,480 annual economic output. Meanwhile, "not free" and "partly free" countries account for a combined 56 percent of the world's population—a decline from 65 percent in 1973.

The relative degree of democracy is an important measure of human security at several levels. First, as a general rule, democracies have been better suited at holding governmental authorities accountable for human rights abuses. Second, there is a correlation between lack of democracy and inhibited economic development. Third, in democracies the ability to set the agenda and win arguments via persuasion diffuses power away from central authority and into the hands of citizens who choose to engage in the democratic process. Fourth, there has been negative growth in the degree of freedom and civil liberty in the Muslim world. Often contemporary terrorism is associated with Islamic movements, but it is also the case that many movements evolve out of a sense of oppression from their governments and religion plays a minimal role.

Reform of authoritarian governments in the Islamic world provides new outlets for legitimate political expression and can be an important means of undermining terrorism. This approach presents dilemmas because strong governments can be necessary for combating some terrorist groups. At the same time, strong governments that repress citizens' rights can spawn new terrorist movements. Democracies might risk sacrificing some political freedoms in the name of safety from fear of international terrorism. In that case, while seeking protection from external attacks, governments gain in power at the expense of individual freedoms. This too can spark a backlash and even lead to violence against governments. When he blew up the Federal Building in Oklahoma City in 1993, Timothy McViegh was, in his view, protesting the encroachment of the federal government on the private lives of citizens. Democracies are uniquely vulnerable to terrorists because the freedoms that they protect can be used by terrorists and other criminals to move about freely. Reconciling the demand for safety and the maintenance of freedom has become one of the most significant challenges for human security in the twenty-first century.

POPULATION AND DEMOGRAPHIC CHANGE

The Earth has finite resources and finite space, yet the population grew by exponentially massive rates during the twentieth century. The world population of 6.2 billion in 2004 was over 3.5 times that of the population at the beginning of the twentieth century. The time required for global population to grow from 5 to 6 billion—twelve years—was shorter than the interval between any of the previous one-billion increases. In 2002, the global population grew at the rate of 371 million per five-year periods—the equivalent of a new Western Europe.[20] India and China each have over 1 billion people. China is expected to add over 10 million people per year through 2015. Overall, the world will add 80 million people a year or 960 million in total by 2015.

There are four main approaches to understanding the relationship between population and security. First, states face resource scarcity problems and might seek to capture new territory to meet the needs of their population. Second, lateral pressure can result when a state extends its interests outside territorial boundaries leading to a combination of high population growth, high technological capacity, and inadequate resources.[21] Third, military capability is closely related to population in that, for population growth to cause expansionist behavior by a state, some military capacity is necessary. Traditionally, population is also seen as a vital source of power and an important means of raising large armies. A fourth approach sees positive security consequences from population growth. The growth of population might force innovation and reduce conflict as free-trade, technology, and human ingenuity foster cooperation, increased productivity, and efficiency.[22] It is indeed the case that, while there is enormous poverty and depravation globally, more people in the twenty-first century are living in comfort and relative wealth than in any time in human history.

While population can exacerbate a conflict situation, significant military capabilities may be a necessary ingredient. Thus population pressure alone may not explain expansionist or aggressive behavior.[23] Also, countries with low technology are more subject to population pressures and resulting conflict than more technologically advanced states. Finally, states do not actually appear to engage in conflict for purposes of acquiring new land for a population. Rather, this is more often used as an excuse for expansion rather than an actual cause.[24] Overpopulation is most likely to be a security problem when rapid demographic change within or among populations occurs. Rapid changes among or within populations can be indicators of coming violence that might result in international or civil wars. An expanding agrarian population might rise up to protest how land is used by owners of the land or their treatment of the population on that land. An expanding urban population combined with declining economic growth might turn publics toward protest, crime, and violence. An expanding population of higher educated youth facing limited opportunities can enter into conflict with each other as they compete for elite status within society. A large "youth bulge" in which the numbers of people aged 15–25 come to have a disproportionate role within a population can also lead to large-scale mobility or public dissatisfaction with a status quo. Migration of a population into an area already settled by another distinct ethnic or political identity can breed conflict.[25] Finally, declining population rates can be a sign of an inability of a state to meet basic human needs.

Population movements can become a security issue for several reasons. First, international migration is increasing, either as a result of a desire to flee conflict areas, or as an effort by people to pursue a better economic future. These movements are aided by advances in global networks of communication and transportation. Other factors such as environmental degradation or natural disasters also generate cross-border or internal movements of people. Second, more people want to leave their countries than there are countries willing or capable of accepting them. Third, most of the world's population movement is from one underdeveloped country to another and the world's largest refugee flows have been within Africa, south Asia, southeast Asia, and the Persian Gulf.[26] Governments might force emigration as a means of achieving cultural homogeneity or asserting the dominance of one ethnic community over another. Governments have also forced outward migration as a means of dealing with political dissidents and class enemies. Under Fidel Castro, Cuba managed some of its internal dissent by opening up prisons and allowing political opponents to depart Cuba for the United States. This policy removed a threat to the Castro government and put significant strain on America's immigration capacity. States might also force a population movement as a strategic objective—perhaps to use emigration as a tool for putting pressure on a neighboring state or states. States have also relocated their national populations to secure territory they have seized. For example, the Soviet Union moved significant Russian populations into the Baltic states after World War II. By the time of the Soviet collapse in 1991, there were 22 million Russians living in the non-Russian areas of the former Soviet Union.

Economic migration can also become a security problem if migrant workers' presence fuels nationalist reactions. Legal immigrants have been harassed and treated violently even in advanced democratic societies such as the United States and Western Europe. This condition occurs for several reasons. When migrants are actively opposed to the regime of their home country, they can skew political discourse within their country of residence. Migrants or refugees can also be perceived as political, economic, or security risks to their host country if they strain state capacity or are there to conduct violence such as terrorism or other criminal activity. Immigrants can also be seen as a cultural threat to a host society exacerbating social, racial, or religious tensions. A host country might turn on those visiting within it and use them as hostages or human shields to threaten or blackmail their country of origin.[27] The movement of populations across borders also provides new networks of globalization as money flows back and forth between émigrés and their home families. While the vast majority of such financial transfers are legitimate, some have been used as cover for financing international terrorist movements.

Population Trends and Demographic Developments

Data available from the United Nations Fund for Population Assistance demonstrates the difficulties of and regional disparities in population trends.[28] Sub-Saharan Africa has the most severe population challenges. The region is rife with health problems, human displacements, violent conflicts, and political, strife all of which are compounded by ongoing increases in population. Over the past thirty years, sub-Saharan Africa's population has grown faster than any other region. The population there doubled between 1975 and 2000—rising from 325 to 650 million. Annual growth rates are 2.5 percent. Even accounting for the impact of HIV/AIDS, the United Nations Population Division projects that sub-Saharan Africa's population will be about 1.1 billion by 2025. Over 47 percent of Africa's population is between ages five and twenty-four, thus future growth in population is likely to remain very high. Only recently has a general acceptance of the need for reproductive health awareness, family planning, and the use of contraception emerged. The region faces a severe shortage of health professionals, managers, researchers, planners, and technicians to implement population assistance programs. The absence of significant infrastructure makes it difficult to bring the best means of coping with these challenges into the region—even for the purposes of gaining good data on the nature of the population problem.

The Middle East, spreading from North Africa to the Persian Gulf, has an overall population of about 300 million with annual population growth rates of 2.7 percent. Average economic growth rates in the region are lower than the population growth rate. The Middle East's population is young—with almost 39 percent below the age of fifteen and 50 percent under twenty-five. The number of women of reproductive age grew from 50 million to 69 million during the 1990s. These population trends exacerbate the human security problem in the Middle East by compounding the challenge of economic underdevelopment. Sixty-two million people in the Arab world live on under $1.00 a day and 145 million live on under $2.00 a day. There have also been positive demographic trend-lines in the Middle East at the dawn of the twenty-first century. The death rate and infant and child mortality rates have declined in most Arab countries. Fertility rates have also fallen significantly. Nevertheless, poverty has worsened throughout the region with a significant effect on reproductive health services, education, and employment. Rapid urbanization, changing migration patterns, dwindling financial resources for population programs, and increasing rate of HIV infection make the rapid population growth all the more challenging.

Sixty percent of the world's population resides in the Asia-Pacific region, which has also made considerable progress on establishing and implementing goals of reducing population growth. The current growth rate is 1.3 percent—the lowest in the developing regions of the world. Life expectancy is a relatively high sixty-five years. Nevertheless, five countries in the area are expected to account for nearly 45 percent of the world's population growth between 2002 and 2050: Bangladesh, China, India, Indonesia, and Pakistan. Other specific problems include maternal mortality ratios exceeding 400 per 100,000 births and high infant and toddler mortality rates in Afghanistan, Bhutan, Cambodia, India, Laos, Nepal, and Timor-Leste. There are also some 600 million illiterate adults in the region. Rapid urbanization, high levels of water and air pollution, and the rapid rise in the level of HIV/AIDS infections are all serious manifestations of population problems in this region. While there were a high number of people under the age of twenty-five, Asia also had the largest percentage of elderly. In Asia, 8.8 percent of the population was over the age of sixty in 2000 and this number was projected to rise to 14.7 percent by 2025.

Eastern Europe and central Asia represent a diverse group of countries with many states benefiting from membership in the European Union while others are threatened by declining population spurred by poor health care and a growing spread of HIV/AIDS. Countries like Azerbaijan and Kazakhstan are especially challenged by the combination of population and development. Some states such as Bosnia-Herzegovina and the Kosovo region of Yugoslavia are almost entirely dependent upon the external provision of security. There is also a large discrepancy between life expectancy of males and females and an aging population and declining capacity to care for them. Low paying jobs and unemployment have also led to a rise in illegal trafficking of women and girls for prostitution. In Russia, average life expectancy for men is in the mid-fifties and overall the population is in decline.

By 2003, Latin America and the Caribbean had a total population of 534 million. The rate of population growth was 1.46 percent, which was a decline from 1.72 percent during the 1990s. Women's risk of dying during childbirth is high—with a ratio of 1:160. Moreover, high risk of HIV/AIDS infection and a high teenage fertility rate (between 2000 and 2005, 71 births per 1,000 girls aged 15–19) adds to a significant pressure on states to do more to meet basic needs of their populations. Latin America is particularly challenged by large population movements toward massive urban centers. Some of these megacities exist on the margins of a complete breakdown in health services and have high incidents of child prostitution and other illegal activity. Trends in Latin America reflect a global increase in urban populations since 1950 when only .75 billion lived in cities (about 29 percent of world population). By 2000, the United Nations was projecting that the number had quadrupled to about 2.93 billion (48.5 percent of the world's population). Among this new urban citizenry, by 2003, 89 percent lived in underdeveloped countries where the number of urban citizens has multiplied more than six times—to about 40 percent of the world's urban population. The United Nations projects that by 2025 to 2030, people living in underdeveloped countries will account for 98 percent of all new urban dwellers. The UN also estimates that, by 2015, there will be as many as 523 cities with a million inhabitants containing 40 percent of the world's population. By 2000, there were 14 cities with 10 million inhabitants with a projected 26 (22 in underdeveloped countries) by the year 2015.[29]

Nearly 50 percent of all people in the world are under age twenty-five, and about 20 percent are between ages ten and nineteen.[30] Among adolescents, 87 percent live in developing countries. Overall, some 238 million children (one of every four) live in conditions of extreme poverty while many live without their parents or are marginalized by humanitarian disaster, migration, disability, or poor health conditions. About 13 million children under age fifteen have lost one or both parents to HIV/AIDS. Between 100 million and 250 million children live on the streets. One in every 230 people worldwide is a child or adolescent forced from their home as a result of war. Meanwhile, 57 million young men and 96 million young women aged fifteen to twenty-four in developing countries cannot read or write. Children have also been used widely as soldiers in warfare—particularly in Africa. Women of all ages confront unequal power relations relative to men and human rights abuses affecting women have proliferated to include forced marriage, child marriage, sexual violence and coercion, sexual trafficking, and female genital mutilation. There are an estimated 14 million young women between age fifteen and nineteen who give birth each year. For this age group, complications of pregnancy and childbirth are a leading cause of death—with unsafe abortion being a major risk factor.

By 2002, the world's population was 6.2 billion and over two people are added to the world's population every second.[31] Relative population growth has actually been declining with some 74 million people added to the world's population in 2002 compared to 87 million in 1989–1990. The annual average growth rate was approximately 1.2 percent in 2002, a decline from 2.2. percent in 1963–1964. This decline in growth is driven mainly by declining fertility among the world's women who now give birth to 2.6 children over their lifetime. Nevertheless, this number is less than one-half of a child more than the level that is needed to assure the replacement of the population. This level will likely drop below replacement level by 2050 as fertility rates continue to decline. At the same time that fertility is declining, the numbers of women in their childbearing years are increasing relative to the rest of the population of the world. These women represented about three-fourths of the global population growth in 2002. Moreover, age demographics show trends toward growth of younger populations resulting from a relatively high but declining fertility rate combined with a moderate but declining mortality rate. Children (0–14 years of age) represent 29 percent of the world's population, and young adults (15–29 years of age) and women of childbearing age (15–49 years of age) each comprise 26 percent of the world's population.

A critical nexus between demographic challenges and security exists in the Middle East where young males are becoming dominant among the overall population. The United Nations estimates that, by 2010, in Egypt and Saudi Arabia the population aged thirty or younger will approach 60 percent. Young males represent 70 to 90 percent of first-time job seekers and they often lack marketable skills. There are twice as many new workers emerging as there are jobs available which can lead to strong pressures for economic migration.[32] The impact on already unstable and underdeveloped societies is one of economic dislocation, low wages, social free time, anger, and possibly violence. Historically, such demographic pressure troughs have been associated with unrest and even war in Russia (1910s), Japan (1920s), Germany (1930s), and Cambodia (1970s), and similar patterns are repeating in Iran and Saudi Arabia.[33] The population in the Middle East is also aging. Over 20 percent of the population in Egypt and Iran is expected to be over age sixty by 2050 and nearly 15 percent in Saudi Arabia.[34] Even in modern developed countries, the aging of the current young population will present serious population pressures. Japan, for example, is estimated to have about 25 percent of its population over age seventy-five by the year 2050. The pressure to sustain expensive welfare benefits for this aging generation in Europe and Japan will likely significantly strain budgets and can impact long-term economic growth and stability.

Migration and Refugees

As the amount of young people expands in places like the Middle East, and as population declines in Europe and the former Soviet Union, migration pressure will increase significantly in the twenty-first century. As it is more difficult for people of Middle East origin to come to the United States, Europe will most likely feel a high impact of migration. The result is projected to be the growth of an ethnic socioeconomic underclass in Europe. Instability can thus be imported as immigrants maintain their homeland links. Such links could be sustained by protecting insurgencies, supporting sides in conflicts in their place of origin, and solidifying transnational movements.[35] The migration problem is especially problematic for underdeveloped countries as the pull to leave is highest among the most well-trained and capable people— leading the best and brightest to leave and not invest their skills in the advancement of their home country's development. According to the Arab Inter-parliamentary Union, some 54 percent of doctors and 26 percent of engineers migrate, and more than 50 percent of Arab and African students who study abroad do not return.[36]

The United States is increasingly affected by Latino immigration which has prompted some controversial strategic assessments. Samuel Huntington, in particular, argues that "the persistent inflow of Hispanic immigrants threatens to divide the United States into two peoples, two cultures, and two languages."[37] Huntington asserts that the basic values enshrined in American civil culture are those that reflected white, British and Protestant traditions in the seventeenth and eighteenth centuries. These values gave America a clear definition in terms of race, ethnicity, culture, and religion. Huntington sees that tradition being threatened by a new intellectual preference for multiculturalism, combined with the pressures of globalization. The end result is what Huntington calls "the single most immediate and most serious challenge to America's traditional identity" coming from the "immense and continuing immigration from Latin America, especially from Mexico, and the fertility rates of these immigrants compared to black and white American natives." Huntington juxtaposes the scenario of what would happen if Mexican immigration abruptly stopped to the United States. The annual flow of legal immigrants would drop by about 175,000; illegal entries would diminish dramatically; and the wages of low-income U.S. citizens would improve and those who did immigrate to the United States would represent a much higher educated spectrum of Latin America's population.

Huntington differentiates Hispanic immigration into the United States from other movements of ethnic groups by focusing on six factors. First, contiguity of the U.S.-Mexican border makes the issue of immigration an immediate and ongoing problem. Second, the scale of the movement south to north is immense to the point where Latin Americans have outpaced blacks as the largest ethnic group in the United States. Third, much of the immigration from Latin America is illegal with estimates of the number of Mexicans who enter the United States illegally each year being as high as 350,000 during the 1990s. Fourth, the settling of Hispanic immigrants has a strong regional concentration in the American southwest, creating a particularly strong influence on the local economy and politics there. Fifth, the movement of Hispanics northward is persistent. Sixth, there is a historical claim to the territory that Hispanics are settling—having lost the land initially in the Texas War of Independence and the Mexican American War. Huntington notes that the immigrants from the Hispanic world do not assimilate into the traditions of American political and cultural norms, but rather persist in maintaining their own traditions. This trend has sparked a growing debate over whether English should be an official language or whether Spanish should be adopted as well. Huntington concludes that "continuation of this large immigration (without improved assimilation) could divide the United States into a country of two languages and two cultures" which would "not necessarily be the end of the world; it would, however, be the end of the America we have known for more than three centuries" and that "Americans should not let that change happen unless they are convinced that this new nation would be a better one."

America was, of course, built by immigrants including Europeans, Hispanics, and Asians. Raul Yzaguirre, President of the National Council of La Raza, used a quote of Benjamin Franklin's to assert limitations in Huntington's focus. Franklin said: "I have great misgivings about these immigrants because of their clannishness, their little knowledge of English, their press, and the increasing need of interpreters. . . . I suppose in a few years [interpreters] will also be needed in the [Congress] to tell one-half of our legislators what the other half say." Franklin was referring not to the Hispanic immigrants Huntington fears, but rather to Germans. Yzaguirre concludes that "Today's immigrants, their children, and grandchildren believe in America. Why can't Samuel Huntington?" However, some observers such as Fouad Ajami agreed with Huntington's analysis. Ajami wrote that, when he immigrated to the United States, "the door was open (I walked through it four decades ago), but the assumption was that older loyalties would be set aside. . . . It was, after all, the 'newness' of the New World that had created its magnetic appeal" and "in saying there is no 'Americano dream,' Huntington restates the case for that simpler and older American dream." Another admirer, Patrick Buchanan, wrote, "even as one welcomes the eminent Harvard professor to the oft-derided ranks of those resisting the mass invasion of the United States, let us concede the hour is late. Huntington may have just climbed over an adobe wall only to find himself inside the Alamo."

While much of the world's migration is driven by socioeconomic pressures, much of it is also the result of forced population movements due to human action or natural disaster. Refugees are, as defined by the United Nations, "persons who are outside their country and cannot return owing to a well-founded fear of persecution because of their race, religion, nationality, political opinion, or membership of a particular social group."[38] Other "persons of concern" can include asylum seekers, refugees who have returned home but still need help in rebuilding their lives, local civilian communities which are directly affected by the movements of refugees, stateless persons, and growing numbers of internally displaced persons.[39] At the beginning of 2003, the United Nations agency responsible for monitoring data and assisting such individuals estimated that there were a total of 17,093,400 refugees or otherwise displaced people worldwide. Regionally, this includes 6,187,800 in Asia; 4,285,100 in Africa; 4,268,000 in Europe; 1,316,400 in Latin America and the Caribbean; 962,000 in North America; and 74,100 in Oceania.[40]

In its 2003 report, *Refugees by Numbers*, the United Nations High Commissioner for Refugees (UNHCR) noted positively that about 3.6 million refugees and other groups assisted by the United Nations had recently returned home. This included nearly 2 million Afghan refugees from Pakistan and Iran as well as about 750,000 internally displaced people within Afghanistan. Other major homeward population movements occurred in Angola, Sierra Leone, Burundi, Bosnia and Herzegovina, Sri Lanka, and the Russian Federation. The number of new refugees dropped by 69 percent in 2002 compared with 293,000 in 2001. The major focus of refugee outflow has been in Africa, with Liberia and Côte d'Ivoire being especially problematic. In Latin America, Colombia has been a source of growing numbers of internally displaced peoples. Meanwhile, nearly half of the total people of concern are in Asia. There were, in 2002, a total of 1,014,300 people who sought protection from another state for fear of persecution at home. The United Kingdom processed 110,700 asylum applications with main countries of origin being Iraq, Zimbabwe, Afghanistan, Somalia, and China. The United States received 81,100—mainly from China, Mexico, Colombia, Haiti, and India. Even a small country like Ireland, which has had fairly liberal asylum laws, has grappled with a proportionately high number of asylum seekers with about 11,600 coming from Nigeria, Romania, Moldova, Zimbabwe, and Ukraine. Meanwhile, there are also an estimated 951,000 "stateless" individuals globally—such as war-affected populations permanently displaced or ethnic groups such as the Roma gypsy population in Europe.

Insecurity can result for refugees and displaced peoples at several levels. First, those who have fled their homes often do so as a result of severe violence and are forcibly expelled from long-standing homelands. Second, refugee camps have notoriously poor security and overall conditions. Refugees often must flee a situation with only what they have on their backs and in their pockets. Basic human needs must be met upon their arrival—often into dangerous and poorly maintained refugee camps. Third, refugees often find themselves turning to petty crime or getting caught up in organized criminal rackets—with women often having to turn to forms of slavery or forced prostitution. Fifth, refugees and asylum seekers often become targets of hatred and persecution based on race or religion in the country that is hosting them. Sixth, some international actors might use the threat of violence against refugees as a deterrent or other tool of warfare.[41] Refugees returning to their homes after conflicts end can have deep psychological scars—especially among children. Refugees often need assistance in rebuilding, restarting their lives, and restoring their lost traditions. Even more problematic, refugees returning home can mean displacing those who did the displacing in the first place—potentially sparking new conflict. Military conflict is a primary cause of refugees but other factors can include land reform policy, agricultural development, or natural disasters such as droughts, floods, earthquakes, or large tropical storms. The World Commission on Dams estimates that between forty and eighty million people have been displaced by dam construction alone.[42] Solving such broader problems is thus also essential to resolving challenges posed to long-term displacement of peoples.

The problem of internally displaced peoples is also a major threat to human security both inside states and because of spillover effects beyond state borders. The United Nations estimates that, by 2003, there were approximately twenty-five million people forcibly displaced within fifty countries.[43] An illustration of internal displacement is summarized in this comment from a displaced person inside Turkey:

> Soldiers came to our village, they started [with] the village guards. Then the [guerrillas] attacked and killed three village guards. After that, those who had joined the village guards decided that they did not want to be village guards. They wanted to turn their guns back to the army. At that point, the soldiers came and burned the village. . . . There was no possibility to resist. They didn't allow us to take our things. We couldn't gather our animals. They forced us all out. . . . After a few days no one was left. We left everything in our house. It was completely destroyed. They burned everything, the school, the mosque. They burned our fields, our grapes. . . . No one is living in that area now. It is completely empty. . . . We don't have permission to go back.[44]

Internally displaced people are the legal responsibility of their government. But often it is the government, or individuals supported by a government, that causes the problem. Internally displaced peoples often suffer from some of the bleakest manifestations of the human condition. As the United Nations reports, internally displaced peoples are "to be found in urban slums, squatter settlements, camps for the internally displaced, host families, railroad boxcars, converted public buildings—and a majority of internally displaced are women and children, ethnic or religious minorities, indigenous people and the rural poor."[45]

Responsibility for managing the plight of displaced peoples lies with governments and the United Nations. However, the United Nations is limited by sovereignty as to what it can do other than facilitating relief. Even in cases where international relief is agreed to, aid agencies are often attacked by combatants, held hostage, or find it very difficult to operate due to difficult terrain or a lack of infrastructure. Between January 1992 and March 2001, 1,998 United Nations civilian staff members—including staff from UNICEF, the World Food Program, and UNHCR—were killed and 240 were kidnapped or taken hostage. The International Committee of the Red Cross has also been attacked with six medical staff killed in Chechnya in 1997, four killed in Burundi in 1997, and six delegates killed in 2001 while delivering supplies in the Democratic Republic of Congo.[46] A symbolically tragic and personal loss for such aid workers came in the murder of Silvio de Mello and many of his staff in a terrorist attack carried out by insurgents in Iraq. Mr. de Mello, the former United Nations director for humanitarian issues, had deferred his appointment to head the UNHCR in order to develop humanitarian assistance programs in post-invasion Iraq in 2003. Even when humanitarian relief can be established, there remains high danger, for example, in camps set up for internally displaced people. Insurgents or government forces often attack refugee camps to seek out their enemies. Alternatively, some governmental or non-state groups raid displaced persons camps seeking to steal relief supplies.[47]

FOOD AND HEALTH

Food security is affected by the relationship between supply of food and the growing demands of the world's rising population. Some regions of the world face immediate and severe food shortages. In Africa, thirty-five countries have significant food security problems. Worldwide, over 800 million people are undernourished—including 170 million children. Each year, 15 million people die around the world from malnutrition. On average, a child dies of hunger somewhere in the world every five seconds. Malnutrition makes societies vulnerable to famine and disease as people's immune systems are weakened when they are poorly nourished. In the underdeveloped world, this dilemma is made worse by the lack of adequate medical services. Even for those who are well-fed and have excellent medical care, transnational disease has become a significant human security challenge as the networks of globalization accelerate the spread of deadly diseases such as HIV/AIDS and SARS. Transnational disease also contributes to declining state capacity to meet basic human needs, possibly leading to large-scale instability in a country or region. Also, diseases could be used as an asymmetrical tool of warfare by states or terrorists.

Food supplies have, overall, become more plentiful worldwide due to technological advances in food production. However, major disparities exist around the world. For example, in 2004 the average person in developed countries consumed 10 percent more calories daily (2,947) than the average person in the developing world consumed each day (2,675). As a relative comparison, in Tanzania, per capita household expenses were $375 in 1998, of which 67 percent went to food. In Japan, per capita household expenditures were $13,568 in 1998, but only 12 percent was spent on food. This disparity of income and food between the developed and underdeveloped world is illustrated by the $17 billion that is spent in the United States and Europe each year on pet food, versus the $19 billion needed in annual investment to reach United Nations development goals for elimination of hunger and malnutrition.[48] Given annual medical costs of an estimated $30 billion for treating medical ailments associated with malnutrition, the United Nations estimates that an annual funding increase of $24 billion in international support for food programs would result in a five-fold increase in global productivity and income.[49]

As per capita incomes increase worldwide, households are purchasing more meat and animal products—the consumption of which doubled in the developing world between 1995 and 2000. As incomes grow and basic consumption improves, other demands will increase—for example, grain production will need to increase 40 percent by 2020 to keep pace with population growth. Even if food production and trade evolve progressively with growing demand, an estimated 135 million children under the age of five are likely to remain hungry in 2020 with Africa and south Asia being hit especially hard.[50] Food security also has immediate relevance to the quality of food that is eaten. A variety of diseases affecting farm animals can have an impact on humans. Just the fear of such disease can have dramatic consequences for food availability. The fear of mad cow disease in the United Kingdom has done significant damage to the beef industry there. Many countries have since established strict criteria to keep out beef from countries where mad cow disease has been found. New food technology raises questions regarding the quality of food, particularly the creation of genetically engineered food products. While some states explore new means of designing foods, others are opposed to the idea both in principle and on possible health grounds. Pesticides, while necessary to keep crops free of insect infestation, also can contribute to a range of diseases. Food supplies could also be targets of attack by terrorists.

The spread of disease within and across borders poses an immediate threat to those people who are exposed. The Spanish flu of 1918–1919, for example,

killed 50 million people worldwide. By 2004, tuberculosis infected about 8.7
million people every year and killed 2 million. One-third of the world's population is estimated to have the bacteria which can be triggered into the infection. Left unchecked, an estimated 1 billion people could be infected with
tuberculosis by 2024 with 35 million people dying from these contagious airborne bacteria.[51] Malaria, a parasitic disease carried by mosquitoes, killed on
average 1 million people every year of which 700,000 were children.[52]
Influenza, a highly contagious viral infection, causes outbreaks every year,
resulting in between 3 and 5 million cases of severe illness and between
250,000 and 500,000 deaths annually.[53] In 2004, the World Health Organization warned that avian flu could prompt an international pandemic killing an
estimated 7 million people.[54]

Each year, millions of people die from these preventable, curable, and treatable diseases. Most of these deaths occur in regions of the world where there
are other weaknesses including lack of vaccines and basic sanitation. Two
million people die each year from water-related diseases. This represents 80
percent of all illness in the underdeveloped world. Every day, 10,000 people
die from a water-borne illness.[55] The United Nations estimates that nearly 10
million children under the age of five die every year from preventable diseases
such as diarrhea, measles, and acute respiratory infections.[56] Among the
greatest preventable threats to human security is self-inflicted—5 million people around the world died from smoking cigarettes in the year 2000 alone.[57]

Some disease outbreaks are localized but so severe that they strike widespread fear. Ebola hemorrhagic fever, for example, is an illness spread by
direct contact with the blood, secretions, organs, or other body fluids of
infected people. Infection is thought to have spread from infected gorillas or
chimpanzees in Africa. Mourners burying dead Ebola victims as well as
health workers are frequently infected while handling the dead. The disease
incubates within two to twenty-one days and outbreaks spread rapidly. Someone stricken with Ebola virus will have sudden onset of fever, intense weakness, muscle pain, headache, and sore throat. These symptoms are followed
by vomiting, diarrhea, rash, impaired kidney and liver function, and possibly
internal and external bleeding. While considerable attention is given to this
disease, its numbers killed are minor compared to common viruses and bacterial infections. Striking primarily in central African rainforests, there were
1,850 cases of Ebola with over 1,200 deaths between 1976 and 2004.[58]

Among infectious diseases, HIV/AIDS is the world's most serious human
security threat given its impact on those who suffer from the illness and the
strategic consequences. Originally noticed in homosexual communities in the
developed world in the 1980s, HIV/AIDS has spread worldwide as a consequence of sexual contact and infections of blood supply. HIV is the virus

which is spread and AIDS is the resulting breakdown in immune systems. Medical breakthroughs can halt or slow the spread of the disease in individuals. However, once AIDS develops it is incurable. Between 1981 and 2004, some 20 million people worldwide died of AIDS and almost 38 million were living with HIV. By 2004, 50 percent of all people in the world with HIV infection were women and fifteen- to twenty-four-year-olds represented almost 50 percent of all new HIV infections. In developing countries, only 12 percent of the people who would benefit from drug treatments receive them. In low and middle income counties in 2003, only one in ten pregnant women were offered services for preventing mother-to-child HIV transmission. AIDS has wiped out entire families in some countries—with 12 million children orphaned by AIDS in sub-Saharan Africa—where on average 8,000 people die from AIDS every day.[59] In 2004, there were an estimated 15 million children worldwide orphaned by the AIDS epidemic. This number was expected to rise to 18.4 million by 2010.[60] With the best of medical care, the AIDS death is gruesome, painful, and prolonged. In countries lacking adequate medical facilities, the situation is worse. For example, in Cambodia, only one of five of the 25,000 AIDS patients near death receives basic care with most victims left rotting to death.[61]

By 2000, AIDS was increasingly viewed as a threat to international security. In April 2000, the United States formally identified the disease as a security problem. The United States noted that the spread of AIDS can weaken foreign governments, contribute to ethnic conflict, and undermine efforts to expand international trade. According to the U.S. National Intelligence Council, "At least some of the hardest-hit countries, initially in sub-Saharan Africa and later in other regions, will face a demographic catastrophe" by 2020. The United States further projected that dramatic declines in life expectancy were a strong risk factor for "revolutionary wars, ethnic wars, genocides, and disruptive regime transitions" in the developing world and that the social consequences of AIDS has "a particularly strong correlation with the likelihood of state failure in partial democracies."[62] This concern has been especially high in Africa, where there are an estimated 25 million people living with HIV in the sub-Saharan region.

Sub-Saharan Africa has about 10 percent of the world's population and about two-thirds of all people living with HIV. In 2003, 3 million people were estimated to have been infected and 2.2 million died—which was 75 percent of the 3 million global AIDS death that year. In some African countries, such as Swaziland, 35 percent of the population is infected with HIV.[63] African countries are further hindered by a stark decline in life expectancy across the continent as a direct result of AIDS. In seven countries—Zimbabwe, Swaziland, Lesotho, Zambia, Malawi, Central African Republic, and Mozambique average life expectancy is less than forty years.[64] Between 2001 and 2003, there was a global rise of AIDS-orphaned children from 11.5 million to 15 million with eight of ten of these children living in sub-Saharan Africa. In Botswana, which has a population of only 1.5 million, 10 to 15 percent of all children were orphans and 37.4 percent of all pregnant women were HIV-positive by the end of 2003.[65]

While Africa entered the twenty-first century in a full-blown AIDS crisis, other regions of the world also confront a pending catastrophe if the disease is left unchecked. In Asia, there have been dramatic increases in HIV infections in China, Indonesia, and Vietnam. By 2004, some 7.4 million people in Asia and southwest Asia were living with HIV including an estimated 5.1 million in India alone. In Eastern Europe and central Asia there were 1.3 million people living with HIV, with more than 80 percent under age thirty. Latin America had about 1.6 million living with HIV and there were about 430,000 in the Caribbean. Haiti had the highest percentage (5.6 percent) of people outside Africa that were infected. In the United States there were about 950,000 people living with HIV and about 580,000 in Western Europe. Among these countries, China, Russia, and India were on the verge of having catastrophic HIV/AIDS conditions by the year 2025. According to one projection, a mild epidemic in China would produce 32 million new HIV cases and a severe epidemic would produce 100 million. In India the same conditions would produce 30 million new cases of HIV in a mild epidemic and 140 million in a severe epidemic. In Russia, a mild epidemic would result in 4 million infected and a severe epidemic 19 million. Among these three countries, a mild epidemic would project a cumulative total of 43 million AIDS deaths and a severe epidemic would produce a total of 155 million dead by 2025. Even a mild epidemic in Russia would lead to a level of economic output in 2025 that was lower than in 2000. For India, a mild epidemic would depress predicted economic growth by about two-fifths. For China, a mild epidemic would cut anticipated economic growth by about 50 percent.[66]

HIV/AIDS also impacts the military dimension of security. Average infection rates of soldiers around the world are significantly higher than the same age groups in the civilian population. By 2002, the average HIV infection rate of African militaries was about 30 percent. In some states, it was more than two-thirds of the military. In Malawi 75 percent and in Zimbabwe 80 percent of the military have the disease. In Africa, AIDS was the primary cause of death in many armies. This was true even for a state like Congo, which had frequent and severe military conflicts during the 1990s.[67] In the Rwandan genocide, between 200,000 and 500,000 women were raped in a matter of weeks. This raised the risk of the spread of the disease, and in some cases was seen as a legitimate tool of war. The weakening of militaries can place severe strains on state abilities to defend against external attack or to maintain domestic order. The disease also reaches deep into some of the most central functions provided by the most productive members of society. In Africa, 10 percent of all teachers were expected to have died from AIDS by 2005. In some countries, as many as 25 to 50 percent of health-care workers will die from the disease.[68] While HIV/AIDS is not likely to be the sole cause of failed states, it is a major factor compounding already existing weaknesses.

The networks of global security also provide new mechanisms through which disease spreads. A person who becomes sickened with a viral or bacterial infection in one part of the world can travel by plane to another part of the world within twenty-four hours and infect people while in transit and on arrival. This scenario occurred during the global spread of a new virus—SARS—in 2002 and 2003. SARS is an upper-respiratory viral infection related to the common cold and similar to pneumonia. SARS has no known treatment and while many victims survive, it is often fatal. SARS spread because of poor public health services and a lack of public transparency and accountability in China. In February 2003, a doctor who had become infected in China traveled to Hong Kong where he unknowingly infected a dozen people. Some of these infected people then traveled and spread the disease to Vietnam, Singapore, and Toronto where it spread farther. Healthcare workers treating the unknown illness also became ill and took the disease home, spreading it to their families.[69] By May 2003, the total number of SARS cases had reached 8,000 worldwide and over 800 had died.

The SARS pandemic was relatively limited, when contrasted against the risk to human security that other diseases posit. However, the spread of the disease caught public health officials off guard and illustrated the potential dangers lurking in the networks of globalization. For example, terrorist groups could use a small amount of a natural occurring disease such as the plague, Anthrax, or smallpox to create panic and instill fear in multiple locations at the same time. Developing a disease as an effective tool for projecting fear is far more likely to occur than the ability to disseminate diseases as a weapon of mass destruction. Many diseases are not resistant to the atmosphere and thus do not easily survive. Any use of disease as a weapon of mass destruction would require complex and highly expensive weaponization procedures that terrorist groups are not likely to posses. Viruses, bacteria, fungi, parasitic organisms, and toxins that are by-products of living organisms can all have very dangerous effects on a human population.[70] While each of these have been developed or considered as warfare agents, by 2004, no case of large-scale biological warfare had been confirmed in history.[71] A terrorist might, however, be more interested in spreading fear than the actual damage of the disease. Thus biological agents could be used in limited conditions to create psychological results—as with the use of Anthrax mailed in letters in the United States in fall 2001. Perhaps more dangerous is the risk of major outbreaks of new versions of disease such as influenza. The Center for Disease Control in the United States estimates that a "medium level epidemic" of avian flu would kill 207,000, hospitalize 734,000, and sicken one-third of the American population. Such an outbreak would cost $166 billion in direct medical expenses in the U.S. economy.

THE HUMAN COSTS OF WAR

The use of military force can have a major impact on human security. War often includes the purposeful or accidental targeting of civilians and related critical civilian infrastructure such as hospitals or electric power grids. War includes the use of weapons, which do not discriminate between soldiers and civilians. Weapons of war can also have lasting environmental consequences. The World Health Organization showed that in 1998 alone, there were some 588,000 war deaths and 736,000 homicides worldwide.[72] War and violence cause various threats to human security: the immediate effect of combat on individuals, the social effects of war, and the effects of war on the environment.

The Impact of War on Individuals

Historically, most wars were fought primarily among soldiers. Over time, the world has agreed to legal restrictions on who and what is targeted in war. Nevertheless, in modern war, these constraints are regularly violated and with a range of consequences. During the twentieth century, the extent of damage to civilian life grew extensively so that by the end of the century, over 80 percent of casualties in conflicts were civilian. During World War I, parts of the battlefield of Verdun were so wasted with artillery shells that even weeds will still not grow in some spots. A generation of French peasants was emptied from the French countryside at Verdun.[73] Plunder associated with war has included the destruction of priceless property, art, and other irreplaceable aspects of culture. But the most severe example of destructive violence, the use of the nuclear bomb against Japan in Hiroshima and Nagasaki, showed the immediate and horrific consequences war can have on civilian population. Other human costs include the opportunity costs of planning for war. Money spent on weapons and training people for war is money not spent on education, roads, hospitals, and other improvements in the human condition.

Small arms such as handguns, mortars, submachine guns, grenades, and landmines have a unique impact on civilian populations. Small arms account for 90 percent of all civilian casualties and they kill in the tens of thousands, if not hundreds of thousands, every year. Small arms in private hands are often leftovers from military conflicts or sold from military stockpiles. These weapons kill an additional 200,000 people every year. In Brazil, the United States, and South Africa, guns are a leading cause of death among young men. Worldwide, an estimated 2 million children were killed with small arms between 1990 and 2003 and an estimated 1.5 million are wounded by small arms every year.[74] There are over 600 million small arms and light weapons in global circulation. Of forty-nine major conflicts during the 1990s, forty-seven were waged with small arms as the weapon of choice.[75] The United Nations reports that "small arms and light weapons destabilize regions; spark, fuel and prolong conflicts; obstruct relief programs; undermine peace initiatives; exacerbate human rights abuses; hamper development; and foster a 'culture of violence.'"[76] West Africa is especially affected by the relationship between small arms and persistent violence. Nigerian customs services reported that in 2002 they confiscated $30 million worth of small arms and ammunition over a six-month period. In November 2003 some 170,000 rounds of ammunition were seized. By May 2004, Nigeria had seized 112,000 illegal firearms.[77] According to Human Rights Watch, these weapons were used in the massacre of several hundred people in May 2004.[78] In the Delta State area of Nigeria, militia groups have used automatic and semiautomatic rifles along with fishing spears and cutlasses to kill hundreds of people, displace thousands, and destroy property.

Cluster bombs and landmines, which do not discriminate between soldiers and civilians, have a uniquely negative impact on civilian society. Cluster bombs are small explosives combined in a large dispersal area against troop concentrations. These weapons can miss their target and land on civilians or they might not explode at all but sit on the ground unexploded. Unexploded cluster munitions have been a serious problem in Kosovo, Afghanistan, and Iraq. Often, these munitions are discovered by children who see them as toys and touch them, and then are maimed or killed when they explode. In Afghanistan, their use was especially problematic because their appearance resembled ready-to-eat meals that the U.S. military was dropping from the air as part of its humanitarian mission. Landmines have a similarly negative impact on civilians during or after conflicts. They are left, often unmapped, in fields where people congregate or children play. On average, one person is killed or maimed by a landmine every day worldwide.

Even wars which are ostensibly fought for just causes can have negative human costs. In September 2003, U.S. President George Bush called the war in Iraq "one of the swiftest and most humane military campaigns in history."[79] Yet during the three weeks of major hostilities, thousands of Iraqi civilians were unintentionally killed by U.S. forces. A significant cause of these civilian casualties during the war was persistent violations of the rules of war under the guidance of Saddam Hussein's military leadership. These violations included the use of human shields, abuse of the red cross and red crescent emblems, use of antipersonnel landmines, location of military objects in protected areas (mosques, hospitals, and cultural property), and failure to take adequate precautions to protect civilians from military activity. Some Iraqi military also wore civilian clothes, creating confusion between combatants and noncombatants.

The United States also contributed to civilian casualties in Iraq with the widespread use of cluster bombs. The United States reported that it used 10,782 cluster munitions which would contain at least 1.8 million submunitions. Both the United States and the United Kingdom regularly used these weapons to attack Iraqi positions in civilian residential neighborhoods. With an average failure rate of 5 percent, there would have been about 90,000 dud bombs still sitting on the ground in Iraq following the invasion. Among the civilian casualties of the Iraq invasion, more than 400 civilians are known to have died in al-Nasiriyya, including at least 72 women and 169 children; more than 700 additional women and children were injured. Baghdad had high casualties from ground-fire—with perhaps as many as 1,700 civilians killed and 8,000 wounded there. In al-Hilla, U.S. ground-launched cluster munitions caused 90 percent of all civilian casualties.[80]

The postwar American occupation of Iraq confronted significant human security challenges. During the occupation, an insurgency movement attacked American soldiers, international aid workers, and Iraqis. By 2005, insurgents were estimated to have killed 12,000 Iraqi civilians and security forces.[81] An independent British study described the Iraq war as a public "health disaster." After the war, previously well-controlled diseases returned to Iraq including diarrhea, acute respiratory infections, and typhoid while more children were underweight or malnourished in 2005 than in 2000. After the war, the quality of health services had declined due to chronic under-funding, poor physical infrastructure, mismanagement of supplies, and staff shortages.[82] Another study by UNICEF showed that malnutrition among children ages six months to five years had grown from 4 percent before the U.S. invasion to 7.7 percent in the first two years after.[83]

The Social Effects of War

War also can have long-term social effects. For example, many modern warriors are neither modern nor warriors—they are children. There are as many as 300,000 children around the world serving either voluntarily or involuntarily in militaries or private militias. Children under the age of eighteen fought in Sierra Leone, Liberia, Congo, Sudan, Sri Lanka, Afghanistan, and Burma in the 1980s and 1990s. In Sierra Leone's civil war, children fight for both sides. Often rebels will attack a village and abduct the surviving children. Many of these children have already witnessed the horrors of seeing their parents murdered. They are then taken to special camps where they are trained and prepared to fight on behalf of their captors. Those few who escape often sign up to fight with a progovernment militia force. Children and small arms mix together in these conflicts as a child with a light weapon can move quickly and close to an enemy. Children are also seen as less costly, and easier to influence than adults. Indeed, many children are sent into battle high on drugs provided to them by adult officers or paramilitary elders. In Burma, children are not only used in combat, but also in slave labor camps, carrying army supplies to soldiers, and working involuntarily on government construction projects used by the military.[84] Nearly 50 percent of 3.6 million total people killed in war between 1990 and 2004 worldwide were children.[85]

Testimonials of child warriors and refugees taken by the British Broadcasting Corporation (BBC) illustrate the severe impact of war on children. Zaw Tun, a Burmese veteran at age 15, says, "An army recruitment unit arrived at my village and demanded two new recruits. Those who could not pay 3,000 kyats had to join the army." Charles, a 12-year-old Rwandan refugee, says, "I was so afraid of dying. But my friends warned me if the rebel commanders detected any fear in me they would kill me. So I had to pretend to be brave." Asif, a 12-year-old Afghan refugee, says, "When I get older, I will organize a gang and seek my father's revenge." An ex-Burmese army soldier, Htay says, "I joined the army when I was young [at 15] without thinking much. I admired soldiers, their guns and crisp, neat uniforms. I just wanted to fight the way they did in the movies and so I joined the army." Charlie, a 10-year-old Sudanese refugee, says, "Two hundred gone, we pray that war in our country will stop quickly. We also pray for their souls to rest in peace." Christopher, 12, from Uganda says, "I just want to go home and be with my family."[86]

In some conflicts, children are seen as legitimate military targets. A Rwandan radio station broadcasted in 1994 that "to kill the big rats, you have to kill the little rats." During that conflict, 300,000 children were killed. For a child the age of five in 1991 in the former Yugoslavia, the odds are very high that up to the age of ten life was defined by the physical and visual horrors of war and the psychological fear it generated—if not the actual violence. A child growing up in Iraq during the 1980s and 1990s would have known nearly constant war including the Iran-Iraq conflict, the Iraq invasion of Kuwait, American and British air strikes and sanctions, followed by the 2003 American invasion and subsequent occupation and insurgency. The United Nations Children's Fund estimates that between 1993 and 2000, worldwide two million children were killed in war, four to five million disabled, twelve million left homeless, more than one million orphaned or separated from their parents, and ten million psychologically traumatized.[87] Meanwhile, children were used as fighters in at least twenty-two conflicts between 2001 and 2004. Even the United States sent sixty-two children aged seventeen into combat in Iraq and Afghanistan.[88]

While most child soldiers are young boys, girls are also inducted into military life. Girl soldiers are vulnerable to rape, sexual slavery, and abuse both from captors and by the militias or militaries they are recruited into—though the same is done to boys as well. A 14-year-old girl soldier abducted from Kitgum in Uganda by the Lord's Resistance Army (LRA) said, "we were distributed to men and I was given to a man who had just killed his woman. . . . I was not given a gun, but I helped in the abductions and grabbing of food from villagers. . . . Girls who refused to become LRA wives were killed in front of us to serve as a warning to the rest of us." Another girl gave birth on open ground to a daughter from one of her LRA abductors: "I picked up a gun and strapped the baby on my back and continued to fight the government forces."[89] Even in the advanced militaries in the United States and Britain, female soldiers are periodically sexually harassed or discriminated against. Crimes including rape often occur, but are not reported for fear of losing promotion opportunities.

Women have also increasingly become targets of fighting and are highly vulnerable to sexual violence in war. As one study shows: "In certain villages bordering conflict young girls have admitted that armed men come in at night—these girls are used as sex workers—they are not allowed to protest—they are not allowed to lock their doors and the whole community tolerates this because these armed men protect the community—so it is a trade-off."[90] In Sudan, police officers who were sent to restore order in the Darfur region were found by the United Nations to have systematically sexually exploited refugee women. For example, women refugees were promised safety when hunting for firewood in exchange for sexual favors.[91] Vulnerability for women can vary from direct violence to socioeconomic disruptions as they are traditionally left behind during major conflict to manage day-to-day routines, but can often emerge widowed and without support after a war.

The psychological impact of war can have a durable impact on society long after conflict ends. Post-traumatic stress disorder, associated with depression and anxiety, is common for those who have been in or around combat. As a doctor (one of five psychiatrists in the city of Quetta during the Afghan war in 2003) said of such victims: "They are depressed and anxious, they are irritable, have lost their appetite. There is a real feeling of loss—loss of body, loss of money, loss of friends and family." The doctor added, "Their psychological trauma is deep. Their basic needs have been ignored. They feel insecure, have no stability, and are suffering the effects of war, deficiency in food."[92] While the actual number of individuals who are permanently psychologically disabled by war might be small, exposure to war among young people creates a particular risk of long-term psychological disability. In Chechnya, Human Rights Watch reports, "There was no water, electricity or food: only constant explosions. In the refugee camps in Ingushetia, many children suffered extreme cold throughout the winter and start to cry when the warplanes fly over on their bombing missions in Chechnya." As the report's author summarizes:

> In one hospital, I met a five-year-old girl, the only survivor in her family, thrashing around in her bed from the shrapnel wounds which had become infected with gangrene. In the next room was a wounded father, who recounted to me how his younger daughter had died in his arms from an exploding bomb. . . . [As the reporter was leaving he received a letter from a child saying,] All these wars fell hard on my studies. The school year started very well. I was attending school, and was fond of music and fond of English. But one day the war crossed it all out. We became refugees in Ingushetia. I am missing my school year. . . . Peter, when you are in America, please ask all children to write letters to [Vladimir] Putin to stop the war in Chechnya and not to kill civilians, especially children. During the first war, I spent 20 days in the cellar with my parents. In fact, it is not as romantic as it appears to be in the action movies. Our house was hit by a bomb.[93]

Addressing such long-term psychological needs in postconflict situations can thus be a crucial component of attaining long-term peace and reconciliation. For many societies, it is hard to invest in peace if the perpetrators of wartime abuses against civilians remain at large. War crimes tribunals have served to alleviate such long-term issues as a means of vetting justice on those who commit atrocities in warfare. However, even then the psychological scars of war can linger for generations.

The Impact of War on the Environment

War can significantly damage the environment and lead to near- and long-term complications for nature and its inhabitants. Even in peacetime, military presence, planning, and exercising can impact the environment. In the United States, for example, the war on terrorism and the invasion of Iraq prompted the military to seek new exemptions from previous environmental restrictions around some of its bases. Such exemptions were viewed by military planners as necessary. Yet they also place endangered species at risk, allow for avoiding cleaning up toxic rocket fuel, allow for ocean testing which can jeopardize marine mammals, and provide exemptions from clean air laws and hazardous waste regulations. These requests came in spite of a report from the

U.S. General Accounting Office that there was no evidence that environmental rules impair military readiness. The head of the U.S. Environmental Protection Agency told Congress that there is no evidence of "a training mission anywhere in the country that is being held up or not taking place because of environmental protection regulation."[94]

There are four central challenges presented by the relationship between warfighting and the environment.[95] First, the production and testing of nuclear weapons is a significant environmental problem. The release of radioactivity during production and testing threatens general public health when people are exposed. During the twentieth century nuclear weapons were tested 423 times above ground and 1,400 times under ground. These tests led to a release of radionuclides estimated to be at 16–18 million curies of strontium-90; 25–29 curies of cesium-137; 400,000 curies of plutonium-329; and in atmospheric tests, 10 million curies of carbon-14. There is some scientific dispute about the impact of tests. However, the U.S. government has awarded compensation awards to 3,000 current and former employees adversely affected.

A second major environmental challenge from war is bombardment from air or sea. The advent of air power in World War II allowed for the large-scale bombing of civilian populations. During conventional bombing of Tokyo in 1945 between 100,000 and 200,000 people were killed. Between 1943 and 1945 the allied bombing of seventy German cities led to the death of between 500,000 and 800,000 people. The destruction of forests, farms, and irrigation networks resulted in some fifty million refugees at the end of World War II. In Japan, severe food shortages followed the end of the war due to the failure of the 1945 rice harvest causing significant malnutrition and hunger. Landmines represent a third major environmental consequence of war with 70–100 million active mines worldwide by 2000. In the years since World War II, 400 million total landmines have been deployed worldwide. The fear of landmines accelerates environmental damage: Denied access to abundant natural resources and arable land, populations are forced to move into marginal and fragile environments to avoid minefields, this migration speeds depletion of biological diversity. Also, landmine explosions disrupt soil and water processes.[96]

The purposeful destruction of the environment has also been a tool of modern warfare. During World War II, sabotage was used to destroy dikes and dams. In the Vietnam War, defoliants were used to clear forests. From 1965 to 1971, the United States sprayed 3,640 kilometers of cropland with herbicides to deny the enemy sources of food and cover.[97] Contemporary conflicts including wars in Central Africa and conflicts in Mozambique, Sudan, and Afghanistan have contributed to deforestation, encroached on vulnerable ecosystems and national parks, and caused water pollution and sanitation degradation, air pollution, and loss of endangered species.[98] Klaus Toepfer,

Executive Director of the United Nations Environment Program (UNEP), wrote: "Warring factions and displaced civilian populations can take a heavy toll on natural resources. . . . Decades of civil war in Angola have left its national parks and reserves with only 10 percent of the original wildlife. . . . Sri Lanka's civil war has led to the felling of an estimated five million trees, robbing farmers of income." Toepfer notes that greed over the environment has fueled conflict as "some individuals and groups can make a fortune under the cloak of an ideologically motivated war. . . . It is estimated that UNITA rebels in Angola made over $4 billion from diamonds between 1992 and 2001. . . . The Khmer Rouge was, by the mid-1990s, making up to $240 million a year from exploiting Cambodia's forests for profit."[99]

The 1991 Persian Gulf War provides an illustration of the danger to the environment of a purposeful act of war. Saddam Hussein ordered that 789 oil wells be set on fire in Kuwait as Iraqi forces retreated. By burning Kuwaiti oil fields, Iraq hoped to cripple the Kuwaiti economy and punish coalition forces that had ousted Iraq from Kuwait. Possibly these fires were set to make it more difficult for coalition troops to march farther onto Baghdad. By March 1991, six million barrels of oil were burning per day. A massive cloud of fire, smoke, and soot rose up high into the air covering a 1,000-mile radius around the Persian Gulf. While the fires were put out and postconflict studies showed the immediate damage was not as great as initially feared, there was lasting damage. Approximately 500 million tons of carbon was released into the atmosphere. The damage included an estimated 250 million gallons of oil pumped into the Persian Gulf—roughly twenty times that which was spilled in the Exxon Valdez accident in Alaska in 1989. The end result was severe damage to the biological diversity and the coastline of Saudi Arabia.[100] Large pools of oil were left behind in Kuwait, including a half-mile long and twenty-five-foot deep oil reservoir—nine times bigger than the Exxon Valdez spill. As one report showed, "some 6 million to 8 million barrels of oil dumped into the Indian Ocean created oil slicks that coated the shoreline. . . . Bird Life International, a global partnership of non-governmental conservation organizations, estimates the layers of thick, black goop killed 35,000 wintering birds and tens of thousands of wading birds."[101] Also during the first Iraq war, the movement of Iraqi and American troops altered up to 90 percent of the Kuwaiti desert surface. Unexploded bombs left in the sand killed herds of wild camels and other animals.

During the 2003 Iraq war, the United Nations Environment Program noted that burning oil wells in southern Iraq and oil-filled trenches and fires in Baghdad further exacerbated the environmental consequences of war for Iraq. According UNEP: "The black smoke that we see on television and in satellite pictures contains dangerous chemicals that can cause immediate harm to human beings—particularly children and people with respiratory problems—and pollute the region's natural ecosystems."[102] Nevertheless, the environmental impact of war in 2003 was less significant than in 1992—especially given a concern that Iraq might release water from dams and flood valleys, and then blame it on the United States. There was also concern that Iraq might again set oil fields ablaze as well as sabotaging oil producing platforms and pipelines. In the 2003 war, the U.S. military placed a high value on rapid movement toward protecting oil fields. Meanwhile, however, large ammunition dumps went unprotected—providing a source of weapons for the emerging insurgent conflict. UNEP indicated by spring 2005 that it would be almost impossible to achieve improvement in Iraq's environmental situation because of the declining security situation there. UNEP officials noted that key weapons storage facilities had been looted after the U.S. invasion, including a facility south of Baghdad where 5,000 barrels of chemicals were "spilled, burned, or stolen."[103]

The use of particular materials that help to advance military technology can also have a lingering environmental or health impact. Depleted uranium has been a significant source of concern in this context. Depleted uranium is used to harden conventional shells, such as those used for artillery. After the conflict in Bosnia-Herzegovina, UNEP did a postconflict environmental assessment and discovered that NATO's use of depleted uranium shells left traces of uranium in soil samples. Contamination was widespread, but not at levels significant enough to cause safety concerns. However, during the war, the use of depleted uranium had also contaminated local drinking water. The UNEP study found four key lessons about how depleted uranium impacts the environment. First, ground contamination occurs at depleted uranium penetration impact points at low levels and is highly localized. Second, shells buried near the ground surface corrode rapidly and will disappear completely in twenty-five to thirty-five years. Third, where groundwater was contaminated, it is necessary that alternative water sources be found and regular sampling and measurements continued for an extended period. Fourth, contamination of the air occurrs due to wind or human actions.[104] While the UNEP study showed relatively minimal impact of depleted uranium, there remains dispute over its use. A number of NATO peacekeeping troops in areas where depleted uranium was found suffered from diseases including cancers that otherwise would not likely have occurred.

Afghanistan illustrates the extensive long-term environmental costs of war—in this case, resulting from over two decades of conflict. UNEP's postconflict assessment unit found that the pressures of warfare, civil disorder, lack of governance, and drought dramatically impacted natural and human resources. War in Afghanistan had a major impact on usable water—essential to agricultural productivity in this arid land. UNEP found that many of the country's wetlands were completely dry and no longer supported wildlife populations. Similar declines have occurred in forestry areas, leading to losses of fuel wood and construction materials needed for cooking, shelter, and overall survival. Loss of forests and vegetation, combined with excessive grazing and dry land cultivation, has led to soil erosion from wind and rain. In the Badghis and Takhar regions there are almost no trees. In 1977, the area had been covered by 55 percent forest and 37 percent forest for each area respectively. The value of the land is declining and driving people from rural to urban areas. This population migration placed pressure on the weak post-Taliban Afghan government, which struggled to meet the most basic of human needs for its citizens while also building a democracy. Within the cities, there are no proper landfills and no proper means of ensuring against groundwater contamination or toxic air pollution. Safe drinking water in urban areas reaches only 12 percent of the people. Kabul's water system is losing up to 60 percent of its supply because of leaks and illegal use. In the city of Herat, dumpsites were found located in dry riverbeds upstream from the city. At the first sustained rain, the dump would likely wash down through the city. UNEP also shows that the natural wildlife heritage of the country is under threat. Flamingos have not bred in Afghanistan for four years and the last Siberian crane was seen in 1986.[105] Also, after the United States overthrew the Taliban government, Afghanistan returned to its role as the world's primary exporter of opium—providing 87 percent of the world's supply. Opium trade accounted for $2.8 billion in trade and was 60 percent of Afghanistan's gross domestic product—an increase of 64 percent between 2003 and 2004. An average farmer could earn ten times more by growing opium than wheat.[106]

SUMMARY

Human security is a somewhat contentious paradigm as it risks being applied in an overly broad manner so that virtually everything can become a security issue. Nevertheless, the human security agenda has made a major contribution to the study of global security by refocusing the traditional emphasis on the security of the nation-state onto the question of security of the individual or groups of individuals. The substantive focus on the human security agenda provides an important basis for addressing both research and policy aspects of some of the most important challenges to international peace and stability in the global security dynamic of the twenty-first century. The study of human security also paves the way for a new assessment of the issues of environmental and energy security.

NOTES

1. Lloyd Axworthy, "Introduction," in *Human Security and the New Diplomacy*, ed. Rob McRae and Don Hubert (Montreal: McGill-Queen's University Press, 2001), 3.

2. Axworthy, "Introduction," 3.

3. Anne Gearan, "U.S.: 14 Nations Not Stopping Trafficking," *Associated Press*, June 4, 2005.

4. "A Perspective on Human Security: Chairman's Summary," 1st Ministerial Meeting of the Human Security Network, Lysoen, Norway, May 20, 1999.

5. "The Index of Human Insecurity," *AVISO*, no. 6 (January 2000): 1–2.

6. "Index of Human Security," 1–2.

7. Roland Paris, "Human Security: Paradigm Shift or Hot Air?" *International Security* 26, no. 2 (2001): 67–102.

8. United Nations Development Program, *Human Development Report* (New York: Oxford University Press, 1994).

9. Commission on Human Security, *Human Security Now*, New York, May 2003.

10. Sadako Ogata and Johan Cels, "Human Security—Protecting and Empowering the People," *Global Governance* 9, no. 3 (2003): 274.

11. Caroline Thomas, "Introduction," in *Globalization, Human Security and the African Experience*, ed. Caroline Thomas and Peter Wilkin (Boulder, Colo.: Lynne Rienner, 1999), 3–4.

12. Fen Osler Hampson et al., *Madness in the Multitude: Human Security and World Disorder* (Oxford: Oxford University Press, 2002), 16–34.

13. Andrew Mack, "The Human Security Report Project," draft, November 2002.

14. Thomas, "Introduction," 4.

15. Human Rights Watch, at www.hrw.org/about/ (accessed Fall 2004).

16. Human Rights Watch, *2003 World Report* (New York: Human Rights Watch, 2003), xxi.

17. Jack Donnelly, *Universal Human Rights: In Theory and Practice*, 2nd ed. (Ithaca, N.Y.: Cornell University Press, 2003), 23.

18. Donnelly, *Universal Human Rights*, 23.

19. Annual Human Rights Watch reports, from which this data is compiled, are at www.hrw.org.

20. U.S. Census Bureau, "Global Population at a Glance: 2002 and Beyond," *International Population Reports* (March 2002), 1–4.

21. See Nazli Choucria and Robert C. North, "Population and (In)security: National Perspectives and Global Imperatives," in *Building a New Global Order: Emerging Trends in International Security*, ed. David Dewitt (Oxford: Oxford University Press, 1993), 229–56.

22. Chucria and North, "Population and (In)security," 229–56.

23. Jaroslav Tir and Paul F. Diehl, "Demographic Pressure and Interstate Conflict," in *Environmental Conflict*, ed. Paul F. Diehl and Nils Potter Gleditech (Boulder, Colo.: Westview Press, 2001), 58–83.

24. Tir and Diehl, "Demographic Pressure," 58–83.

25. Jack A. Goldstone, "Demography, Environment, and Security," in *Environmental Conflict*, ed. Paul F. Diehl and Nils Potter Gleditech (Boulder, Colo.: Westview Press, 2001), 84–108; and Charles B. Keeley, "Demographic Developments and Security," in *Grave New World: Security Challenges in the 21st Century*, ed. Michael E. Brown (Washington, D.C.: Georgetown University Press, 2003), 197–212.

26. Myron Wiener, "Security, Stability, and International Migration," *International Security* 17, no. 3 (Winter 1992/1993): 91–126.

27. Wiener, "Security, Stability, and International Migration," 91–126.

28. United Nations Fund for Population Assistance, Country Profiles, at www.unfpa.org (accessed Summer 2004).

29. John I. Clarke, "The Growing Concentration of World Population from 1950 to 2050," in *Human Population Dynamics: Cross-Disciplinary Perspectives*, ed. Helen Macbeth and Paul Collinson (Cambridge: Cambridge University Press, 2002), 56–59.

30. This data and that in the following paragraph are from the United Nations Fund for Population Assistance, *State of World Population 2003*, at www.unfpa.org/swp/2003/english/ch1/ (accessed Fall 2004).

31. The data in this and following paragraphs come from United States Census Bureau, *Global Population Profile 2002* (Washington, D.C.: United States Census Bureau, 2002).

32. Jon B. Alterman, "On the Brink? Middle East Demographic Challenges and Opportunities," at www.csis.org/media/csis/events/030403_wilton.pdf (accessed Summer 2004).

33. Alterman, "On the Brink?"

34. *United Nations Report on World Population and Aging*, United Nations, 2002, at www.unfpa.org (accessed Summer 2004).

35. Alterman, "On the Brink?"

36. Alterman, "On the Brink?"

37. Samuel P. Huntington, "The Hispanic Challenge," *Foreign Policy* (March/April 2004), the text and the debate are at www.foreignpolicy.com/story/cms.php?story_id=2495 (accessed Summer 2004).

38. Detail is available at www.unhcr.ch/cgi-bin/texis/vtx/home (accessed Summer 2004).

39. United Nations High Commissioner for Refugees, *Refugees by Numbers* (New York: United Nations, 2003).

40. United Nations High Commissioner for Refugees, *Refugees by Numbers*.

41. Wiener, "Security, Stability, and International Migration," 91–126.

42. World Commission of Dams, at www.worldwatch.org/features/vsow/2003/06/12 (accessed Summer 2004).

43. United Nations High Commissioner for Refugees, *Refugees by Numbers*.

44. Office for the Coordination of Humanitarian Assistance, *No Refuge: The Challenge of Internal Displacement* (New York: United Nations Press, 2003), 1.

45. Office for the Coordination of Humanitarian Assistance, *No Refuge*, 4.

46. Office for the Coordination of Humanitarian Assistance, *No Refuge*, 4.

47. Office for the Coordination of Humanitarian Assistance, *No Refuge*, 64.

48. Erik Assadourian et al., *State of the World: 2004* (New York: Norton, 2004), 8–10.

49. Food and Agriculture Organization, "The State of Food Insecurity in the World: 2004," at www.fao.org (accessed Summer 2004).

50. C. Ford Runge and Benjamin Senauer, "A Removable Feast," *Foreign Affairs* 79, no. 3 (May/June 2000): 39–51.

51. Anthony Mitchell, "U.N.: HIV/AIDS Fuels Tuberculosis Crisis," *Associated Press*, September 21, 2004.

52. Donald G. McNeil Jr., "Malaria Vaccine Proves Effective," *New York Times*, October 14, 2004.

53. World Health Organization, "Influenza," *Fact Sheet*, no. 211 (March 2003), 1.

54. "WHO Warns of Dire Flu Pandemic," CNN, November 25, 2004.

55. Margaret Wertheim, "Drying the Tears of Thirsty Nations," *Los Angeles Times*, September 12, 2004.

56. Sadaqat Jan, "UNICEF Says 170M Malnourished Children," *Associated Press*, December 5, 2004.

57. "Smoking Killing Millions Globally," *BBC News*, November 24, 2004.

58. World Health Organization, "Ebola Hemorrhagic Fever," Fact Sheet, no. 103 (May 2004), 1–5.

59. UNAIDS, *2004 Report on the Global AIDS Epidemic* (New York: United Nations, 2004), 3–4.

60. Patricia Reaney, "AIDS Robs 15 Million Children of Parents—UN Report," *Reuters*, July 13, 2004.

61. Jason Burke, "AIDS, the New Killer in the Fields," *The Observer*, October 17, 2004.

62. Barton Gellman, "AIDS Declared Threat to U.S. Security," *Washington Post*, April 30, 2000.

63. UNAIDS, *2004 Report*, 7.

64. Celia W. Dugger, "Devastated by AIDS, Africa Sees Life Expectancy Plunge," *New York Times*, July 16, 2004.

65. UNICEF, "The State of the World's Children: 2005," at www.unicef.org/publications/index_24432.html (accessed Fall 2004).

66. Nicholas Eberstadt, "The Future of AIDS," *Foreign Affairs* 81, no. 6 (November/December 2002): 34–38.

67. Peter W. Singer, "AIDS and International Security," *Survival* 44, no. 1 (Spring 2002): 147–48.

68. Singer, "AIDS and International Security," 149.

69. Elizabeth M. Prescott, "SARS: A Warning," *Survival* 45, no. 3 (Autumn 2003): 211–12.

70. Laurie Garrett, "The Next Pandemic?" *Foreign Affairs* 8, no. 4 (July/August 2005): 4.

71. Jessica Stern, *The Ultimate Terrorists* (Cambridge: Harvard University Press, 2001), 22–23.

72. World Health Organization, "Facts about Injuries," 2000, at www.who.int/violence_injury_prevention/publications/other_injury/en/ (accessed Summer 2004).

73. Gail Russell Chaddock, "War's Legacy and the Human Condition," *The Christian Science Monitor*, April 27, 2000.

74. Intergovernmental Action Network on Small Arms, "Background Sheet," at www.iansa.org (accessed Summer 2004).

75. Intergovernmental Action Network on Small Arms, "Background Sheet."

76. United Nations, "Small Arms and Light Weapons" at disarmament.un .org:8080/cab/salw.html (accessed Summer 2004).

77. This data comes from "Testimony of Lisa Misol, Human Rights Watch Researcher, Before the Congressional Human Rights Caucus," *Small Arms and Conflict in West Africa*, Human Rights Watch, May 20, 2004.

78. "Testimony of Lisa Misol."

79. George W. Bush, Address to the Nation, September 7, 2003.

80. Human Rights Watch, "Off Target: The Conduct of the War and Civilian Casualties in Iraq," at www.hrw.org/reports/2003/usa1203/ (accessed Summer 2004).

81. Ellen Knickmeyer, "Iraq Puts Civilian Toll at 12,000," *Washington Post*, June 3, 2005.

82. Patricia Reaney, "Iraq War Is a Public Health Disaster," *Reuters*, November 30, 2004.

83. Matt Moore, "Malnutrition Rising among Iraq's Children," *Associated Press*, November 22, 2004.

84. BBC World Service, "Children of Conflict," at www.bbc.co.uk/worldservice/ people/features/childrensrights/childrenofconflict/ (accessed Summer 2004).

85. UNICEF, "State of the World's Children: 2005."

86. BBC World Service, "Children of Conflict."

87. Anup Shah, "Children, Conflicts, and the Military," at www.globalissues.org/ geopolitics/children.asp (accessed Summer 2004).

88. "New Drive against Child Soldiers," *BBC News*, November 17, 2004.

89. "Child Soldiers: An Overview," at www.child-soldiers.org/childsoldiers/ (accessed Summer 2004).

90. Charlotte Lindsey, "Women Facing War: ICRC Study on the Impact of Armed Conflict on Women," no. 839, International Committee of the Red Cross, 561–79.

91. "U.N.: Sudan Police Sexually Exploiting Darfur Women," *Reuters*, August 14, 2004.

92. Martin Parry, "Mounting Concern over Human Cost of War in Afghanistan," *Agence France-Press*, November 16, 2001.

93. Human Rights Watch, "The War through My Eyes: Children's Drawings of Chechnya," at www.hrw.org/campaigns/russia/chechnya/children (accessed Summer 2004).

94. "At War with the Environment," editorial, *San Francisco Chronicle*, April 3, 2003.

95. This summary is from Jennifer Leaning, "Environment and Health: Impact of War," *Canadian Medical Association* 163, no. 9 (October 2000): 1157–61.

96. Jennifer Leaning, "Environment and Health," 1157–61.

97. Jennifer Leaning, "Environment and Health," 1157–61.

98. Jennifer Leaning, "Environment and Health," 1157–61.

99. Klaus Toepfer, "In Defense of the Environment, Putting Poverty to the Sword," at www.unep.org/documents.multilingual/Default.asp?ArticleID=38108doc-umentID=288 (accessed Summer 2004).

100. Trade and Environment Database (TED) at www.american.edu/ted/KUWAIT.HTM (accessed Summer 2004).

101. Amanda Onion, "Battle Scars: Considering Possible Environmental Fallout from a New Gulf War," *ABC News*, March 5, 2003.

102. "Air Pollution from Baghdad Fires Poses Risks for Human Health and Environment Says UNEP," UNEP News Release: 2003/18, March 3, 2003.

103. Khaled Yacoub Oweis, "Postwar Iraq Paying Heavy Environmental Price," *Reuters*, June 2, 2005.

104. United Nations Environment Program, *Bosnia and Herzegovina: A United Nations Environment Program Post-Conflict Environmental Assessment on Depleted Uranium* (New York: United Nations, 2003).

105. United Nations Environment Program, *Afghanistan: A United Nations Environmental Program Post-Conflict Environmental Assessment* (New York: United Nations, 2003).

106. "UN Warns of Afghan Drug State," *BBC News*, November 18, 2004.

SUGGESTED READING

Jared Diamond, *Guns, Germs, and Steel: The Fate of Human Societies* (New York: W. W. Norton, 1999).

Jack Donnelly, Universal Human Rights, 2nd ed. (Ithaca, N.Y.: Cornell University Press, 2003).

Laurie Garrett, *Betrayal of Trust: The Collapse of Global Public Health* (New York: Hyperion, 2001).

Fen Olser Hampson, Jean Daudelin, John B. Hay, Holly Reid, and Todd Martin, *Madness in the Multitude: Human Security and World Disorder* (Oxford: Oxford University Press, 2001).

Human Security Centre, *Human Security Report: 2004* (Oxford: Oxford University Press, 2005).

Samuel Huntington, *The Third Wave: Democratization in the Late Twentieth Century* (Norman: University of Oklahoma Press, 1993).

Philip Longman, *Empty Cradle: How Falling Birthrates Threaten World Prosperity and What to Do About It* (New York: Basic Books, 2004).

Helen MacBeth and Paul Collinson, eds., *Human Population Dynamics: Cross-Cultural Perspectives* (Cambridge: Cambridge University Press, 2002).

Brian McDonald, Richard Anthony Matthew, and Kenneth R. Rutherford, eds., *Landmines and Human Security* (New York: SUNY Press, 2004).

Rob McRae and Don Hubert, eds., *Human Security and the New Diplomacy* (Montreal: McGill-Queen's University Press, 2001).

Chapter Nine

The Environment and Energy Security

Cracked earth from lack of water and baked from the heat of the sun forms a pattern in the Nature Reserve of Popenguine, Senegal. *Source*: UN Photo by Evan Schneider.

The global environment and the demand for natural resources, particularly energy, are two of the most significant security challenges of the twenty-first century. The relationship between the environment and energy as security issues challenges many preexisting concepts about both power and peace. The very definition of security and what is to be secured is open to question when the environment and energy are placed into the security context. Environmental conditions can have a major impact on economic development, shaping security needs and requirements. Similarly, energy consumption and access to resources can have major security implications. Environmental and energy security also goes beyond the impact of the environment on humans. Security also applies to the safety and well-being of the environment. Increasingly, national security, technology, new forms of conflict, and human security are all linked together around global environmental and energy trends. It is in the area of the environment and energy that some of the most significant threats and opportunities for positive outcomes lie in the twenty-first century. This chapter surveys major conceptual approaches to environmental and energy security. It then examines specific environmental threats that have global and regional security implications.

WHAT IS ENVIRONMENTAL SECURITY?

If the environment is not adequately maintained for human life, humanity will have to adapt or face severe hardship. Even those countries that currently have considerable wealth and resources are not immune from environmental challenges. Environmental threats are not amenable to traditional security responses such as deterrence, and the meaning and role of power and peace are made, at best, ambiguous by environmental security questions. Military power has little utility in resolving environmental security problems. Conversely, some threats, such as global warming, have the potential to damage the world's environment on par with a global nuclear war. Local environmental problems can spill over state borders and exacerbate existing security challenges such as refugee crises, urban development, and disease. Acting alone to achieve national security is generally not a functional means of managing environmental challenges—and can make them worse. Managing environmental security problems thus places a high demand on international governmental and private cooperation. Yet such cooperation on long-range environmental challenges is often subsumed by other more immediate perceptions of traditional security threats. The result is a gathering storm of environmental catastrophe that risks being left unchecked by major world powers at the very moment when preventive solutions are available.

The Environment as a Source of Conflict

There are a variety of ways to conceptualize environmental security. Richard A. Matthew defines environmental security as a clear and distinct concept applicable to the entire world at the highest levels of generalization. Matthew defines environmental security as: (1) a condition in which environmental goods—such as water, air, energy, and fisheries—are exploited at a sustainable rate; (2) a condition in which fair and reliable access to environmental goods is universal; and (3) a condition in which institutions are competent to address inevitable crises and manage the likely conflicts associated with different forms of scarcity and degradation.[1] Thomas Homer-Dixon asserts that it is necessary to separate the line of inquiry between the social effects of environmental change and examining what kinds of conflicts are most likely to result from such effects.[2] Homer-Dixon provides a set of variables to consider in assessing environmental security. The impact of human activity on the environment within an ecological area is treated as a function of two main variables—the product of total population and its physical activity per capita, and the vulnerability of an ecosystem to those human activities. Activity is also a function of available physical resources and ideational factors. This social and psychological context is immensely broad and complex: It includes patterns of land and wealth distribution; family and community structures; the economic and legal incentives to consume and produce goods (including the system of property rights and markets); perceptions of the probability of long-run political and economic stability; beliefs of people in government, industry, and academe about the patterns of trade and interaction with other societies; the distribution of coercive power within and among nations; the form and effectiveness of institutions of governance; and metaphysical beliefs about the relationship between humans and nature.[3]

Environmental change can cause scarcity conflicts in which states or groups of people compete over resources such as river water, fish, and agriculturally productive land. Group identity conflicts can occur when various ethnic groups are intermixed as a result of some sort of dislocation caused by environmental problems. Also, relative-deprivation conflict can occur within, and spill over from, societies when domestic conflicts emerge between social groups. Groups that do not have political or economic power might reach a threshold of human insecurity to the point where they will engage with violence against those who have power and wealth. Alternatively, those who do have power and wealth might fight to keep their relative status as a response to a decline in environmental conditions.[4] People who are deprived of natural resources and military capabilities might find it structurally impossible to challenge an existing status quo. Consequently, the developed world might ultimately find an interest in not addressing environmental challenges on a global basis.[5] However, Homer-Dixon cautions that "the North would surely be unwise to rely on impoverishment and disorder in the South for its security."[6]

Homer-Dixon and Jessica Blitt demonstrate that, under some conditions, scarcity can lead to conflict. They frame the question of environmental security by focusing on scarcity. Homer-Dixon and Blitt note that there are several kinds of scarcity. Supply-induced scarcity is a direct result of a degradation or depletion of environmental resources. Demand-induced scarcity is the result of population growth or increase in consumption of a resource. Structural scarcity results from an unequal social distribution of a resource.[7] Each of these scarcities can be exacerbated by the inability of markets to adjust to new challenges, by social friction, or by the availability of capital for meeting new challenges generated by environmental complexities. By surveying Chiapas (Mexico), Gaza, South Africa, Pakistan, and Rwanda, Homer-Dixon and Blitt show that there is a correlation between poor countries and environmental scarcity contributing to conflict. Their study found that environmental scarcity is caused by the degradation and depletion of renewable resources, the increased demand for these resources, and/or their unequal distribution. These three sources of scarcity often interact and reinforce one another. Environmental scarcity also can encourage powerful groups to capture valuable environmental resources and prompt marginal groups to migrate to ecologically sensitive areas. These two processes—called "resource capture" and "ecological marginalization"—in turn reinforce environmental scarcity and raise the potential for social instability.[8]

Water is an area of potential conflict that has received increasing attention for its security implications. For example, Peter H. Gleick measures the conditions under which states might be vulnerable to water-related conflict.[9] Gleick identifies threats to security as "resource and environmental problems that reduce the quality of life and result in increased competition and tensions among sub-national or national groups."[10] In the case of water, such threats include several sources. First, water resources can be a direct military and political objective in conflict. In cases where access to water is an important measure of economic or political strength, ensuring access to it can be a justification for war. Conditions where water is likely to become a strategic objective include: the degree of scarcity, the extent to which the water supply is shared by more than one region or state, the relative power of the basin states, and the ease of access to alternative fresh water sources. Second, water resource systems can be an instrument of war—both as targets and as tools of war. Gleick notes the targeting of water supplies in A.D. 689 when Assyria destroyed a city by attacking water supply canals. In the twentieth century, hydroelectric dams were bombed during World War II. Iran bombed hyrdropower stations during its war with Iraq in the 1980s. In the 1990s, Iraq destroyed much of Kuwait's hydropower when it invaded there. Iraq suffered its own water supply and sanitation problems in the aftermath of America's bombing campaign to expel it from Kuwait. Meanwhile, Saddam Hussein was reported to have poisoned and drained water supplies in southern Iraq to punish a revolt against his leadership.

Some countries could reach an absolute limit on the type and extent of development due to the lack of access to fresh water. Such limits depend on the absolute availability of water, the population needing to be supplied, and the level of development desired, as measured by the need for water and the efficiency with which water is used.[11] Gleick points to a variety of other water-related conflicts that have secondary security consequences such as water development, irrigation, hydroelectric projects, and flood control. Water management issues can lead to large population displacements and do significant damage to ecosystems with related secondary effects for populations. Gleick shows that water-resources vulnerability is a function of economic and political conditions, water availability, and the extent to which a source of water supply is shared and vulnerable to hydrologic conditions, which impacts total electrical supply.[12]

The Middle East provides an important example of the relationship between environmental scarcity and water conflict. Israel has a significant dependence on water located below the West Bank of the River Jordan. The Palestinian Arabs tend not to want to work on even small water projects in the region until larger issues driving the Arab-Israeli conflict are settled. Of the three main aquifer groups in the area, only one is located in Israel. Miriam Lowi notes that "from the outset of the Zionist movement's endeavors, unrestricted access to water resource was perceived as a non-negotiable prerequisite for the survival of a Jewish national home."[13] Lowi shows that the occupation of the West Bank by Israel "guarantees the state control over vital water supplies that originate in the West Bank but are consumed, for the most part, in Israel."[14] Between 1967 and 1993, no new Palestinian Arab individual or village received drilling permission. Israel's policy ensures that "only existing uses" of water are recognized using the 1967–1968 years as the baseline for existing uses. Water allocations to Arab agriculture had, by 1993, remained at their 1968 levels with only a slight margin for growth. Technology for deep-drilling and rock-drilling remained in Israeli control and West Bank Arabs were not allowed to use water for farming after 4:00 pm. While Israeli water projects were heavily financed by the Israeli government, the Arab population received no subsidy and paid as much as six times higher for water than Israeli settlers in the West Bank.[15] Perception of power and control over resources can thus shape the context of negotiating peace. This constraint is important because, as Robert North demonstrated, resource conflicts are not only about actual scarcity but also involve the political and psychological expectations of whether the supply will be there in the future and what reasons it might not.[16]

An Evolving Environmental Security Paradigm

The protection of the environment has been a major international issue since the 1970s when states met in Stockholm to build a process of shaping international environmental policy. The general international emphasis has been on sustainable development and the protection of sovereignty rights in terms of economic development and against transboundary environmental damage. With the end of the Cold War, the search for a new security agenda quickly encompassed environmental issues. A common interest was seen among environmentalists, who would welcome a new direction of governmental resources into environmental security and government bureaucracies, which would continue to justify their budgets. By the end of the 1990s, most states had factored at least some aspects of the environment into their foreign and security policies. A series of major international conferences, treaties, and national security policy statements signaled that environmental concerns were becoming priorities for nation-states. The new state-driven focus placed the environment within the traditional terms of national security. In this sense, the question was mainly how to sustain development in the context of diminishing resources. Such an approach was eventually viewed by critics as treating the security of the state as a means to defend a status quo, rather than to adjust policies which lead to environmental damage.

The environment—measured in terms of the quantity and quality of resources—can be seen as important to state interests. The idea that international environmental problems are threats to be managed enhances the role of the state as a barrier against international anarchy. In this context, Michel Frederick defines environmental security as representing "an absence of nonconventional threats against the environmental substratum essential to the well-being of its population and to the maintenance of its functional integrity."[17] Frederick identifies four key analytical components for measuring and assessing the core elements of environmental security. First, environmental security is placed within a state perspective. Such an approach recognizes the reality that the state remains the predominant actor in the international system and within international institutions. This context does not imply that the state will hide behind sovereignty to blindly destroy the environment. Rather, it offers a basis from which to organize coalitions of states that share common interests in managing environmental threats. Second, the natural environment can pose dangers that threaten the quality of life of a state's population or limit policy options for advancing the national interest. Third, damage—either natural or human-generated—to the environment and ecosystems can pose a threat to a state and its interests. Fourth, a state's social and economic well-being requires regular assessment of the degree of risk when faced with particular environmental problems.[18]

Contrasting the question of national interests in environmental security is the view that the environment must be secured against abuse by states or private actors. Overconsumption of resources on the path toward economic development is common. Sustaining economic development and the advancement of the human socioeconomic condition in light of scarce resources can be an important balance to strike. However, beyond the general social good of economic growth, greed and power have often motivated people and states to undertake activities that damage the environment.

Some activists have sought to expose this situation as being one of exploitation by the few that damages the interests of the many. Mahatma Gandhi stressed living a simple life that required only what was necessary to live as part of nature. Gandhi possessed minimal clothing and material objects, and he recycled paper and other goods to make maximum use of them. Gandhi also focused his attention on how industrial agriculture served as a basis for exploitation. In an American context, dangers of people who would exploit the environment were described by John Muir who wrote:

> In the settlement and civilization of our country, bread more than timber or beauty was wanted; and in the blindness of hunger, the early settlers, claiming Heaven as their guide, regarded God's trees as only a larger kind of pernicious weed, extremely hard to get rid of. Accordingly, with no eye to the future, these pious destroyers waged interminable forest wars; chips flew thick and fast; trees in their beauty fell crashing by millions, smashed to confusion, and the smoke of their burning has been rising to heaven [for] more than two hundred years. After the Atlantic coast from Maine to Georgia had been mostly cleared and scorched into melancholy ruins, the overflowing multitudes of bread and money seekers poured over the Alleganies into the fertile middle West, spreading ruthless devastation ever wider and further over the rich valley of the Mississippi and the vast shadowy pine region about the Great Lakes. Thence still westward the invading horde of destroyers called settlers made its fiery way over the broad Rocky Mountains, felling and burning more fiercely than ever, until at last it has reached the wild side of the continent, and entered the last of the great aboriginal forests on the shores of the Pacific.[19]

At the core of Muir's vision was a moral belief that it is wrong to do unnecessary harm to the environment. Such universal perspectives place the security of humankind and nature as one. As Muir wrote: "The universe would be incomplete without man; but it would also be incomplete without the smallest transmicroscopic creature that dwells beyond our conceitful eyes and knowledge." Placing the concept in terms of battle, Muir wrote in 1896 that "the battle we have fought, and are still fighting, for the forests [of the Sierra] is a part of the eternal conflict between right and wrong, and we cannot expect to see the end of it."[20]

In 1962, Rachel Carson warned in her book *Silent Spring* of the impact of man-made chemicals on the environment and public health. Carson showed that scientific and technological specialization promoted a narrow look at progress without factoring for a more holistic scientific assessment. When this trend was combined with the dominance of industry and associated greed, humankind faced a danger.[21] By 1970, the environmental cause had become ingrained in American political activism with the advent of the first "Earth Day" held on April 22, 1970. Protection of the environment has also been at the core of research into the role of international institutions and global governance. Oran Young, for example, explains the demand that drives states toward multinational cooperation over environmental policy. Young assesses the environment in the context of global commons in that the environment is of benefit to all humankind. In that context a number of issues force a reconsideration of interests beyond those strictly defined by national borders. Shared natural resources are those natural ecological systems that either cross the boundaries or are shared boundaries between two or more states. Transboundary externalities are those activities undertaken within a state which spread outside that state with a potentially negative impact on other states. Finally, linked issues are those areas in which the effort to manage environmental problems creates new challenges. For example, economic development can be hindered in the near term by efforts to set standards for environmental protection.[22] Within this framework, Marc Levy has shown that it is possible to gain both a global and a local assessment of threats to the environment and solutions. Such a new awareness of the nature of environmental harm can establish the framework for cooperation on solving challenges.[23]

States that identify their common interest in overcoming environmental challenges might seek forms of cooperation, which can also help them overcome more traditional security dilemmas. To a large degree this trend has been affirmed with the creation of the United Nations Environment Program (UNEP). Other major institutions, such as the World Bank, have come to factor in environmental impact assessments into their loan programs for the developing world. However, it is equally probable that states will not think more holistically about their interests. In that case, nongovernmental organizations, international scientific communities, and transnational popular movements have played a role beyond nation-states in advancing information about threats to the environment. Movements like the Rainforest Action Network seek to advance transparency about state and business activity by informing the public through grassroots information campaigns. Activist groups such as Greenpeace have staged large public protests and used civil disobedience—for example, by placing a flotilla of boats inside French nuclear test areas in the South Pacific. This publicity significantly raised the political costs of a decision to test nuclear weapons by France. The Greenpeace ship *Rainbow Warrior* was targeted for violent attack in 1985 by French security forces seeking to punish Greenpeace and dissuade it from future protest activity. Fringe elements of environmental radicals have applied eco-sabotage and even violent eco-terrorism to advance their worldviews. Violent groups, however, remain at the margins of the environmental movement, which generally views itself as part of a larger agenda of civic awareness and civic responsibility.

Some conceptual approaches see environmental challenges as providing new incentives for human adaptation which will better both humanity and the environment. Julian Simon places the environment within the context of human ingenuity and the competitive forces of the market that create innovation. More people create more pressure for technological advancements which allows for more progressive adaptation.[24] This approach acknowledges massive population growth but notes that, nevertheless, people are living (overall) in much more wealth and better conditions than ever before. While there are inequities in the distribution of that wealth, environmental pressures will, over time, produce adaptation for the better. For example, humankind has developed cleaner ways of generating power with nuclear energy. Modern societies are exploring solar and wind sources for clean energy. Innovative and positive adaptations are essential for addressing environmental challenges and preventing them from becoming severe security challenges in the future. Some crises, however, might emerge too quickly for humans to adjust to, while others might take so long to develop that humans might not recognize the relationship between current activity and long-term impact. It is also possible that humankind has reached the limits of its capacity to further advance technological and economic adaptation for environmental protection.

Beyond Environmental Security

Comprehensive environmental security, some experts assert, can never be attained because of a fundamental disconnect between human needs or desires and the general welfare of the environment. If so, then the only way for environmental security to be achieved would be for humankind to undergo a paradigm shift in terms of its relationship to the environment. The environment is increasingly seen among the world's population and their governments as something worth protecting. However, this interest is often related to maintaining and securing the existing level of economic and social well-being. So long as humanity sees the environment as something to manage, tame, or control as part of its own global hegemony among species, human kind would not attain a true harmony or peace with nature. On the other hand, perhaps human dominance is the natural order and justified in its economic and social development guided by survival of the fittest. In this context, some analytical frameworks seek to expose more fundamental power dilemmas regarding the relationship between the environment and security.

Some critics of the concept of environmental security believe that equating the environment with security creates new conceptual and policy problems. The challenge, in this view, is to transcend the concept of security entirely. A critical analysis suggests that resolving environmental problems in a security context prohibits a comprehensive and inclusive approach necessary for resolving environmental problems. Simon Dalby, for example, critiques the application of security discourse to the environment.[25] Dalby questions what is being secured in relation to the environment. Dalby focuses analytical attention on the context in which society values something— and thus prioritizes that which must be secured. To Dalby, violence and other forms of disruption affect trans-state politics by way of an emergent sphere of political activity linking human rights, environment, gender, and development issues. "Discussions of global security," writes Dalby, "are premised on the modern assumptions that the state is the provider of security, that legal systems uphold individual human rights, that the latter have been universalized to provide a benchmark for political conduct globally, and that—implicit to much of the conventional security discourse—modernity has to be extended to the poor and backward parts of the world for the greater benefit of all."[26] As an example, sports utility vehicles are marketed in terms of their ability to enhance individual security. The Chevy Blazer was shown in advertising as conquering natural environmental challenges only to emerge unscathed at a beach or a large suburban home. The slogan marketing the Blazer was "a little security in an insecure world."[27] However, Dalby notes a

> very powerful irony here in that the vehicle uses fossil fuels to propel itself and its passengers through storms, the frequency of which may be increased by the global climate changes brought on precisely by the use of fossil fuels. Big vehicles, specifically the popular sport utility vehicles like the Chevy Blazer, are fuel inefficient and, if buying trends at the turn of the century are maintained, will ensure that many states have little hope of meeting carbon dioxide emissions levels agreed to in international climate change agreements in the 1990s.[28]

Dalby observes, "our quest for 'security' in modern economic production is currently undermining the conditions for terrestrial habitability. . . . This is the [environmental] security dilemma in its largest form."[29]

Jon Barnett similarly challenges the application of security discourse to the environment. Barnett instead advocates a "Green Theory" approach. Barnett bases his approach around three core assumptions. First, there is a suspicion that modern anthropogenic and utilitarian cosmology is responsible for environmental degradation as a consequence of human social development in the twentieth century. Second, there is a particular philosophy of space and scale built around the core notion of interconnectedness. Third, there is sensitivity toward the complexity and interdependence within and between social and ecological systems.[30] Barnett views the general cause of environmental insecurity as being the exploitative exercise of power of the developed world. This position of power was attained by patterns of trade, colonization, and resource extraction from the underdeveloped world. He notes that the wealthiest 20 percent of the world's population consume 84 percent of all paper and 45 percent of all meat and fish; they own 87 percent of the world's vehicles and emit 53 percent of carbon dioxide. The underdeveloped world will feel the main negative security consequences of these activities that the developed world seeks to secure for itself.[31] Protection of this status quo is now seen as part of the "environmental security" needs of the developed world. Thus, Barnett writes, "the processes that create environmental insecurity may be defended so that the relatively secure remain so."[32] Barnett promotes "ecological security," focusing on the "ecosystems and ecological processes that should be secured; the *prima facie* referent is therefore non-human."[33] Barnett concludes that a failure to move beyond "environmental security" perpetuates insecurity derived from a concept that "propagates the environmentally degrading security establishment; it talks in terms of, and prepares for, war; it defends the environmentally destructive modern way of life; and it ignores the needs and desires of most of the world's population."[34]

In a postmodern perspective, "securing" the environment requires policy actions placed within a larger social transformation. The "defense" against environmental insecurity would not, therefore be defense of the nation-state. Rather, the solution would lie in the evolution toward a "global civil society." Ronnie Lipschutz develops an approach to global civil society in which agents act collectively through networks of knowledge and practice and work in opposition to some states and in concert with others.[35] Constitutive of a general change in social thinking about the environment are four major elements of global civil society: organizations or alliances that practice at the international or global level or across national borders; organizations that provide technical assistance to local groups engaged in resource restoration; individual groups that belong to national or transnational alliances; and groups and organizations "in touch" with their counterparts elsewhere around the world or simply sharing an ecological epistemology.[36] Such movements can serve as new transmitters of knowledge, information, and power, which can shed light on environmental problems and further raise consciousness of the need to make environmentally necessary adjustments. Importantly, such approaches emphasize information, education, and wisdom as the path to environmental security. Such movements can increasingly use the channels of globalization to proliferate their networks and shift the focus of power further beyond that traditionally held by governments.

CONCEPTUALIZING ENERGY SECURITY

Energy is a highly strategic element of environmental security. Access to energy is central to modern life. Thus resource wars might be fought among great and small powers as nonrenewable energy sources become increasingly scarce. Also, the use of particular kinds of energy can have serious effects on human security. Energy security additionally raises the question of security for whom? For example, as China pursues economic development, its one billion people will consume increasing amounts of energy. This development will increase the standard of living for millions of Chinese. However, growth will place pressure on already developed economies like the United States, Europe, and Japan. The significantly increased energy demands from China and India will likely significantly impact the supply availability among those states which have benefited from relatively inexpensive energy supplies. Such ebb and flow of energy power could be the major cause of the rise and decline of great powers in the twenty-first century. Who controls energy resources, where energy resources are allocated, and how energy use impacts both human and ecological systems are major determinants of global security.

Securing Energy Resources and Flows

The expansion of energy interdependence has been on the international security agenda since oil and gas shocks created a significant energy crisis in the United States during the 1970s. As the developed world took note of the vulnerability that energy interdependence creates, the future of energy moved to the forefront of national security policy. American President Jimmy Carter declared in April 1977 that energy supply shortages presented a problem unprecedented in history. Carter asserted, "With the exception of preventing war, this is the greatest challenge that our country will face during our lifetime. . . . The oil and gas that we rely on for 75 percent of our energy are simply running out."[37] Carter noted that it was necessary to promote "permanent renewable energy sources like solar power." Nevertheless, the world's reliance on oil, gas, coal, and nuclear energy has grown since the 1970s. New strategic priorities focusing on protecting the flow of energy resources from the Persian Gulf and opening new areas of resource extraction have had a major impact on national security planning.

In the 1980s, energy policy was elevated to a primary national security issue in the United States. Donald J. Goldstein, from the U.S. Defense Department, illustrated this trend when he noted that energy security had direct bearing on questions of territorial integrity, political independence, and the physical well-being of populations. Goldstein argued that treating energy as a unique security issue would help to frame strategy and organize governmental efforts for dealing with energy-induced political, economic, or geostrategic difficulties. By moving the question of energy into the security arena, "greater resources can also be brought to bear than exist in the economic area alone," and public opinion would be more readily mobilized for energy-related security engagement.[38] According to Goldstein, "Diverse questions such as the future of nuclear energy, energy-environmental tradeoffs involving coal, natural gas import patterns, domestic stability in [lesser developed countries], and the development of oil resources in the [then] Soviet Union all become linked in a vast security affairs matrix."[39] Goldstein noted the dual-use potential in the development of nuclear energy for the development of nuclear weapons capabilities. He also noted the need to focus policy on the stability of governments that produced energy supplies. The flow and safety of pipelines and potential regional conflicts in areas with energy production capabilities would likely shape the future security agenda. Goldstein concluded that "the energy crisis is not merely the moral equivalent of war, it is the extension of war by other means."[40]

Similarly, Howard Bucknell III stressed the uncertainty and lack of predictability that the demand and supply equation of oil placed on the needs of modern society. Energy insecurity thus results from strategic vulnerabilities of competition such as competition for control of oil in the Middle East among great powers. Bucknell used the oil embargoes imposed on the United States by energy producing countries in 1973–1974 to show how serious the domestic dislocation was on American society. He concluded that the embargoes' effects, and America's reaction to them, caused a 10 to 12 percent reduction in the immediate availability of liquid fuels, a rise in the price index of 5 percent, and the immediate unemployment of about 500,000 people in the United States.[41] Ultimately, the United States and its allies would face three significant choices: find new sources of oil and natural gas, produce more of its own resources, or find alternative energy sources. Getting beyond the existing framework has been difficult as entrenched interests make investment in new energy sources difficult to prioritize, particularly as demand increases create short-term profits for energy companies.

Energy dependence on strategic regions of the world forces states to place access to energy reserves, particularly oil and gas, at the high-end of national security. In the late 1970s, the United States promised to support friendly oil-producing governments in the Persian Gulf and to secure the unfettered transit of oil. To make such an approach feasible, the United States created a rapid military deployment capability to project military power into the Persian Gulf. During the 1980s, the United States deployed power into the Persian Gulf to escort oil-bearing ships during the Iran-Iraq war. In 1990–1991, the planning was put to large-scale effect following Iraq's invasion of Kuwait. Defending Kuwait was important, but the larger concern was Saudi Arabia. Since the 1970s, Saudi Arabia has been the key swing state in oil production—setting the price of oil by controlling its flow. A strategic interdependence emerged as the United States would defend the Saudi government while the Saudis would provide relatively low-cost oil.

There are a variety of threats to the regular supply of energy—either from direct or asymmetrical attack. First, transportation is a major vulnerability. Pipelines often flow across unstable areas and ships pass through narrow lanes where they might be exposed to military or terrorist attack. Sabotage of shipping can lead to a halt in the flow of energy supplies and significantly raise the costs of energy transport. Writing in 1981, Bucknell forewarned of significant security risks to oil transit:

> To mention but a few opportunities available to those interested in the rapid demise of the existing Western order of things: the tankers could be attacked by submarine; the straits could be mined surreptitiously or openly; with properly organized support, a sabotage effort could be mounted in the Persian Gulf itself that could convert it into a sea of flames inextinguishable for perhaps a year. As an alternative the oil extracted from the Persian Gulf region could be rendered radioactive by covert chemical treatment and thus made useless at the ports of debarkation in Europe, Japan, and the United States. The forces of terrorism are abroad in our international society. To ignore them is dangerous. To employ them as surrogates may be a tempting possibility to some nation.[42]

Second, in extreme circumstances of strangulation or blackmail of the developed world's economies by oil-producing states, it might be necessary to intervene with force to gain access to oil. Third, during the twentieth century, defining national interest became equated with oil. For the United States this relationship forced it to abandon principles over interest as it has supported a number of oppressive governments in the Middle East that provided cheap oil.

Michael Klare has shown how access to energy supplies has come to dominate major power interests and affect military planning. Klare notes that "whereas weapons technology and alliance politics once dominated military affairs, American strategy now focuses on oil-field protection, the defense of maritime trade routes, and other aspects of resource security."[43] Klare sees the focus on energy security as reflecting a fundamental rethinking of how power and influence matter in international security after the Cold War. "Whereas, in the past, national power was thought to reside in the possession of a mighty arsenal and the maintenance of extended alliance systems, it is now associated with economic dynamism and the cultivation of technological innovation."[44] Klare identifies several kinds of insecurity that can emerge because of resource conflict. First, conflict can develop over the allocation of a particular source of supply that extends across international boundaries—such as a large river system or underground oil reserves. Second, contested claims to offshore areas that have significant resources can lead to conflict. Third, disputes can arise over access to bodies of water that are essential for the transportation of vital natural resources.[45]

The expansion of global energy requirements, supply and refinery shortages, and ownership conflicts are all likely to place new stresses on the stability of the international system. Klare uses the Persian Gulf to show that the presence of large reserves of oil increases the likelihood and intensity of interstate conflict. Writing before the U.S. invasion of Iraq in spring 2003, Klare noted three scenarios for oil-driven war in the Persian Gulf. First, a recurrence of the 1990 Iraqi drive on the oil fields of Kuwait and Saudi Arabia would have threatened the largest supply of oil in the region. Second, an effort by Iran to close off the Strait of Hormuz or otherwise constrain the flow of shipping from the Persian Gulf would likely prompt an American military intervention. A third scenario might be an internal revolt against the Saudi royal family leading to major domestic instability.[46]

Some critics of the 2003 U.S. invasion of Iraq asserted that the war was guided mainly by an attempt to gain strategic dominance over Persian Gulf oil supplies. Such a strategic move would, in theory, give the United States a continued advantage in relative energy capabilities into the twenty-first century. This would be especially important to counter the influence of the rising demand for energy from China and India. Compelling as this theory might be, there was also reason for skepticism. First, the United States had a significant interest in ending the need to place its troops in Saudi Arabia to contain Iraq. By removing Saddam Hussein as a threat to regional stability, the United States could extricate itself from Saudi Arabia. The American presence in Saudi Arabia had, during the 1990s, become a particularly virulent propaganda tool for extremist fundamentalist Islamic movements. Second, the United States could have had access to Iraqi oil at far lower cost than via an invasion. Washington simply could have cut a deal with Saddam Hussein that allowed the UN to lift sanctions. This would have let Iraqi oil reenter world markets without a war. Also, there are other major areas of the world with strategic energy reserves besides the Middle East which, if more fully developed, would have provided alternatives to accessing Iraqi oil.

With massive proven and unproven reserves, the Caspian Sea region has looked to many observers as a future source of resource wars. There has been a significant amount of posturing over whether pipelines would flow west (a benefit to the United States and Europe): north (a benefit to Russia); east (a benefit to China and Japan); or south (a benefit to Iran). Any major power that could exert primacy in this region might be able to wield significant global power in the twenty-first century. Moreover, the Siberian area of Russia might look attractive for future oil and natural gas development if technology will permit access into the frozen ground that covers much of the resource supply there. The South China Sea, which also has significant energy reserves, also holds potential for conflict should China expand its naval capacity. Some extreme scenarios posit a future war between China and Russia over Siberia's natural gas and oil reserves. Meanwhile, parts of Africa and Latin America also offer potential for future energy development, depending on the degree of stability in states such as Nigeria and Venezuela. Finally, the deep sea bed could prove to be an area of competition for energy resources should technology permit regular access to deep sea drilling.

The more energy demands grow, the more vulnerable societies are to security challenges involving energy. The one-day loss of electric power around the northeastern United States in summer 2003 showed the seriousness of the energy demand problem in modern society. Much of the eastern United States was merely inconvenienced without power for several days. However, the situation was potentially severe in Cleveland, Ohio, which could not start its water purification capacities as they were generated by electricity. A city area of over a million people faced the prospect of losing fresh drinking water supply. The electricity was restored in time to avoid such a crisis. However, the Ohio National Guard was on call to ration drinking water in affected areas. Energy security is a problem with multiple sources and vulnerabilities ranging from overuse to sabotage as populations expand and become more urban-centered. Each kind of energy has its own unique vulnerabilities. Oil is especially vulnerable to transportation disruptions and attack; threats to imports and shipping capacity; infrastructure weakness; collaborative policies of the countries that produce oil (OPEC); the use of oil as a policy leverage against states that need it; and rapid fluctuations in prices due to location-specific or broader structural crises.[47] Electricity is vulnerable to a variety of purposeful or demand-driven disruptions and reliability problems; weak infrastructure; risks associated with nuclear energy; and specific policies and pricing set by states that produce electricity. Natural gas also is vulnerable to disruptions;

infrastructure problems; and state policies and pricing strategies affecting those who rely on the import of natural gas.[48]

Economic Development and Energy Security

The use of energy can help to maximize state power and raise the standard of living among populations by contributing to economic development. However, as Jose Goldemberg notes, despite technological advances modern energy supplies are not accessible to some two billion people around the world. Unreliable energy supplies are a hardship and an economic burden for a larger portion of the world's population. For those who access energy supplies, human health is threatened by pollution resulting from energy use at household, community, and regional levels. The environmental impacts of many energy-linked emissions—including suspended fine particles and precursors of acid deposition—also contribute to air pollution and degradation of ecosystems. Finally, emissions of anthropogenic greenhouse gases, mostly from the energy sector, are altering the atmosphere in ways that may already be having a discernible influence on the global climate system.[49] The status quo thus perpetuates a dilemma in that the more humans advance their material conditions, the more they risk creating energy induced insecurity.

The demand for energy in China and India could have a serious global effect on energy supplies and transboundary environmental pollution. Forecasts show that between 2000 and 2020, China and India will increase their coal-fired power-generating capacity by at least 220 and 60 gigawatts (GW) respectively.[50] The rapid growth of China's economic productivity over a ten-year period, combined with the population needs of one billion people and socioeconomic shifts from agriculture livelihoods to urban industrial life, had already pushed China's energy capacity to maximum output by 2004. A shift by China to natural gas would benefit the environment. However, that would require major infrastructure changes and also increase pressure on natural gas capacity worldwide. China has instead relied on existing coal-fired power plants to meet severe shortages in electricity production.

By August 2004, China had a 30,000 megawatt electricity shortage. The response was to build additional coal-fired power plants which emit massive amounts of sulfur dioxide into the air causing acid rain and respiratory illnesses. These coal plants account for 75 percent of China's power production capacity. The Chinese government has recognized the scale of their problem, noting that acid rain fell annually on 250 cities in China and caused about $13 billion in economic losses every year. In 2003, some twenty-one tons of sulfur dioxide from coal emissions were discharged. This represented a 12 percent increase from 2002. An additional six million tons was expected to be added to this annual emission in 2005.[51] The World Bank estimates that 400,000 people die every year from air pollution-related illnesses in China. The pollution effects have spread into South Korea and Japan where an estimated 40 percent of their air pollution comes from China and 25 percent of air pollution in Los Angeles, on some days, can be traced to China. A senior Chinese environmental official concludes that by 2020, pollution levels in China could quadruple if energy consumption and automobile use is not moderated.[52]

China's energy policy is environmentally damaging and economically inefficient. To produce the same amount of economic output as Indonesia, China consumes 57 percent more energy. China consumes, as a percentage of relative economic output, 3 times more energy than South Korea, 3.5 times more than the United States, and 8 times more than Japan.[53] China does apply taxes on polluters and has made some efforts to curb pollution. However, its leadership appears convinced that China is not wealthy enough to run a clean energy policy. In July 2004, China ordered emergency shipping of coal on its road and waterways and began building ninety new coal-fired power plants. Meanwhile, large power cuts in cities were reported, street lights were switched off, and factories ordered to stop production or switch to off-peak electricity use hours.[54]

Beyond states, individual materialism and consumption also is causing increases in energy demand with significant human and environmental costs. For example, the use of the SUV-type automobiles grew dramatically in the U.S. during the 1990s. The extreme version, the HUMMER, is highly inefficient—running about 15 miles per gallon of gas. The result was that everyone in the United States, even those who purposefully purchased more fuel-efficient automobiles, paid a higher price for gasoline. While practical and necessary in rough rural or mountain conditions, the SUV and the HUMMER largely became status symbols for urban drivers who had no functional need for such environmentally damaging automobiles. One could now travel to Dublin, Ireland or Beijing, China and see new wealth expressing itself via fuel inefficient cars.

ENVIRONMENTAL DANGERS

There are a number of specific environmental issues that create serious security challenges. Some potentially serious challenges, such as global warming, could have globally devastating effects. Other issues including deforestation, land-use, and water issues can have local impacts, but with broader regional consequences. Energy resource scarcity and safety challenges can cause major instability within states, place large populations at risk, and have present risks of proliferation of dual-use technology applicable for both civilian and military purposes. Consequently, environmental dangers can exacerbate tensions between states already facing traditional security dilemmas while seriously stressing the capacity of governments to meet basic needs of their citizens.

Global Warming

There is broad agreement in the international scientific community that Earth's temperature is elevating because of a combination of natural and human-caused activity. The burning of fossil fuel has significantly increased the amount of carbon dioxide emissions released into Earth's atmosphere, which then traps heat and raises average air temperatures. The danger is that increased air temperatures will lead to a melting of polar ice caps. Human-caused contributions to climate change include activity such as driving cars, using power from coal-powered electricity sources, home heating from natural gas and oil, and large industrial manufacturing. Large-scale deforestation by burning forests to create more agricultural land in underdeveloped countries also contributes to the problem. Some political leaders argue that there is not enough evidence to support the conclusion that human behavior is the primary cause of global warming. However, scientific experts are in agreement on the facts of global warming—as made evident in multiple studies sponsored by the United Nations, national governments, and the private sector.

The United Nations has engaged more than 2,500 of the world's top climate experts, economists, and risk analysts to study global warming. These experts produced a peer reviewed report, which serves as the basis for negotiations over international global warming remedies. According to the UN survey, global warming is already a significant and real problem. Observed evidence of climate changes includes an increase in global average surface temperature of about 1 degree Fahrenheit over the twentieth century; a decrease of snow cover and sea ice extent and the retreat of mountain glaciers in the latter half of the twentieth century; a rise in global average sea level and an increase in ocean water temperatures; a likely increase in average precipitation over the middle and high latitudes of the Northern Hemisphere, and over tropical land areas; and increasing frequency of extreme precipitation events in some regions of the world. Physical and ecological changes already occurring include thawing of permafrost; lengthening of the growing season in middle and high latitudes; poleward and upward shift of plant and animal ranges; decline of some plant and animal species; earlier flowering of trees; earlier emergence of insects; and earlier egg-laying in birds.[55]

Unchecked global warming over an extended period could pose one of the most serious threats to international security that humanity has ever experienced. Even a small rise of about 2 degrees in Earth's temperature could have very significant consequences including further melting of glaciers and polar ice caps, dramatic shifts in agricultural seasons, rain and floods in some areas and desertification in others. The United Nations studies on global warming predict current trends will produce a rise in the atmospheric temperature between 2.5 and 10.4 degrees over the next one hundred years. This, it is estimated, will result in a rise in the sea level between 3.5 and 34.6 inches leading to coastal erosion, flooding during storms, and permanent inundation of seawater; severe stress on many forests, wetlands, alpine regions, and other natural ecosystems; greater threats to human health as mosquitoes and other disease-carrying insects and rodents spread diseases over larger geographical regions; and disruption of agriculture in some parts of the world due to increased temperature, water stress, and sea-level rise in low-lying areas such as Bangladesh or the Mississippi River delta.[56] The Union of Concerned Scientists demonstrates that atmospheric warming in the twentieth century is greater than at any time in the past 400 to 600 years and that seven of the ten warmest years in the twentieth century occurred in the 1990s. The Arctic ice pack lost about 40 percent of its thickness during the past four decades and the global sea level is rising about three times faster over the past 100 years than in the previous 3,000 years.[57] Mountain glaciers around the world have been receding at rates far beyond any normal pattern of ice-melt. With about 75 percent of the world's freshwater stored in glacier ice, this shrinkage has a cumulative effect on river flows and long-term freshwater availability. Africa's highest mountain peak, Mt. Kilimanjaro, is projected at current rates of ice-loss to lose its permanent ice cap by 2020.[58]

Global warming presents a unique environmental security dilemma because the problem is exacerbated by current human behavior. However, the consequences might not be felt for generations. More immediate worst-case scenarios of abrupt climate change do, however, exist. Abrupt global climate changes could result from a shift in a major ocean current and associated winds combined with additional direct effects of ice-melt. The consequences of such environmental shifts could bring about a climate change crisis that emerges not over a century, but over a decade. Current scientific knowledge does not have a baseline for establishing the threshold that would instigate abrupt climate change. How much change, for example, in the flow of ocean currents such as the Gulf Stream might trigger climatic change? The danger is that, once abrupt climate change occurs it could be too late to make effective policy changes.

Donald Kennedy, editor-in-chief of the journal *Science,* asserts that "an environmental scientist concerned with the processes that drive environmental change can say something useful about security."[59] Kennedy describes life at the Ganges-Brahmaputr river delta in Bangladesh which has low elevation and a very dense human population. Ongoing rising sea levels, combined with powerful storm surges caused by global warming, would cause the displacement of tens of millions of people in this region. Already, there has been considerable emigration from the delta to nearby India which exacerbates tensions between native populations and immigrants in areas affected by extreme poverty and overpopulation. Kennedy also notes that a shift in the flow of warm water from the Gulf Stream in the Atlantic would have a major impact on the temperate climates of Europe. An injection of fresh water in the north would impact the salinity of the Atlantic and lead to a significant change in the water temperature or flow of the Gulf Stream. The end result would be a significant decline in fisheries, shortened seasons of agricultural productivity, and an increase in disease—all with associated economic dislocation in Europe. More broadly, Kennedy notes that malaria and other pathogens would spread widely around the world with the increase in numbers and vertical distribution of mosquitoes. A study by the United Nations University projects that by the year 2050, more than two billion people worldwide could be at risk of flood devastation. This number would be twice that which is projected to occur in a period of normal climate change. Just in the period between 1987 and 1997, some 228,000 lives were lost and $136 billion in economic losses were incurred as a result of flooding.[60] Global warming also risks producing an acceleration of the hurricane cycle which normally follows a ten-year period of relative calm and increasingly violent storms followed by additional calm. A typical Caribbean hurricane releases the same destructive power as 100,000 Hiroshima-type nuclear bombs.[61] Meanwhile, the European Environment Agency predicts that Europe is warming faster than the rest of the world and that cold winters could disappear there entirely by the year 2080. European temperatures are expected to rise between 3.6 and 11.3 degrees over the next 100 years.[62]

The United States Department of Defense takes global warming seriously enough to have commissioned a study by two climate change experts, Peter Schwartz (former head of planning at Royal Dutch/Shell Group) and Doug Randall (of the Global Business Network). Schwartz and Randall stressed that they were thinking in worst-case terms to "push the boundaries of current research on climate change so we may better understand the potential implications on United States national security."[63] Schwartz and Randall also stressed that their scenario is plausible, and would have immediate and profound national security implications. Schwartz and Randall accept as a given that significant global warming will occur during the twenty-first century. The changes that they predict could last as long as 100 to 1,000 years once they occur. The end result would be a "significant drop in the human carrying capacity of the Earth's environment."[64]

According to Schwartz and Randall, specific sources of conflict could include food shortages due to decreases in net global agricultural production; decreased availability and quality of fresh water in key regions due to shifted precipitation patterns, causing more frequent floods and droughts; and disrupted access to energy supplies due to extensive sea ice and storminess. The end result would be a new era of global competition between those with resources who seek to build virtual fortresses around their countries. Less fortunate nations would "initiate in struggles for access to food, clean water, or energy. . . . Unlikely alliances could be formed as defense priorities shift and the goal is resources for survival rather than religion, ideology, or national honor."[65] Specific areas of strategic crisis could include an America which turns inward, giving up much of the stability its global presence provides; Europe, hard hit by temperature change, confronting refugee influxes from Africa; China, seriously impacted given its population and food demand; and other areas in Asia such as Bangladesh becoming nearly uninhabitable because of rising sea levels which contaminate inland water supplies. Russia would be particularly vulnerable as its political system increasingly weakens and nearby countries consider invading to gain access to its abundant and untapped natural resources.

The study speculates: Picture Japan eyeing nearby Russian oil and gas reserves to power desalination plants and energy-intensive farming. Envision nuclear-armed Pakistan, India, and China skirmishing at their borders over refugees, access to shared rivers, and arable land. Or Spain and Portugal fighting over fishing rights.[66] The authors conclude that such a scenario would severly damage the world's 'carrying capacity'—the natural resources, social organizations, and economic networks that support the population. . . . Technological progress and market forces, which have long helped boost Earth's carrying capacity, can do little to offset the crisis—it is too widespread and unfolds too fast." Eventually, "an ancient pattern reemerges: the eruption of desperate, all-out wars over food, water, and energy supplies." War itself may "define human life."[67]

Treaties, such as the Kyoto Protocol on global warming, seek to slow the growth in carbon dioxide emissions over time. However, curbing the increase in carbon dioxide emissions inevitably infringes on the right of states to maximize short-term gains from economic growth and development. This is not a minor issue for underdeveloped states already suffering extreme challenges of economic crises and human suffering. Meeting basic human needs in the context of expanding populations in underdeveloped states means providing sanitation, health, employment, and necessities of modern living. This requires the expenditure of energy in societies where clean energy technology does not exist or is too expensive to put in place. Thus the global warming security dilemma places near-term human security for large parts of the world's population in direct conflict with humanity's future. At the same time, much of the problem of global warming is caused by those who enjoy the good life of modern society. The end result of these competing political and economic pressures is that, to date, major efforts to decrease the causal variables affecting global warming have been minimal.

Deforestation and Land Use

Humanity depends on forests and the land for survival, and the depletion of forests and the management of land create a variety of environmental challenges with security implications. Worldwide, some 1.6 billion people rely on forests for their livelihood and 12.4 million acres of tropical forests are destroyed every year.[68] People are directly impacted by deforestation and the process is often a major contributing factor to global warming when forests are burned to make more farmland. The loss of forests simultaneously removes a major means through which carbon dioxide emissions are removed from the air. The loss of forests can lead to desertification and soil erosion, which washes away vital minerals necessary for productive agriculture. The soil can spill out into rivers creating silt and destroying fisheries. This soil runoff and depletion of useable land can lead to population movements away from traditional lifestyles into urban environments contributing to further population pressures in large cities. Deforestation and poor land-management can strain the capacity of states to meet the needs of their populations leading to internal instability or conflict over resources.

The Food and Agricultural Organization (FAO) defines deforestation as the loss of tree cover to below 10 or 20 percent of crown coverage. FAO studies show that most deforestation occurs in the developing world which lost 200 million acres between 1980 and 1995.[69] While some deforestation occurs naturally through fires or other climatic events, the human impact on forests is severe. The primary driver behind deforestation is economic demand. Wealthy people in developed countries use timber for wood materials in construction, while poor people in underdeveloped countries utilize timber provided by forests for living and fuel/heating or for export. Importantly, much of the demand for logging done in underdeveloped countries comes from the developed world and many developed countries have to import their lumber. Thus lumber has become an important means of economic development and trade. While a country like Japan has a stable situation regarding its own forests, it achieves this by consuming 50 percent of all wood that is cut from rainforests. Ethiopia has gone from being 45 percent forested in 1900 to 2.5 percent forested in 2000. Haiti has gone from being mostly forested to a contemporary barren landscape.[70] Overall, 98 percent of Haiti's forests are gone, which leaves no topsoil to hold rains, leading to flooding and the destruction of vital food resources.[71] The specific security implications of deforestation are summarized in a study for the United States Army: reduced carrying capacity of the land; fewer forests as a component of the carbon cycle, resulting in loss of carbon dioxide removal capacity; loss of biodiversity with all of its known and unknown implications; increased flooding and loss of soils with resultant mudslides and waterway siltation; and declining economic benefits from the loss of forests as a renewable resource.[72]

Of 8.7 billion acres of cropland, pastures, and forests worldwide, nearly 2 billion have been degraded over the past fifty years.[73] More than 250 million people and one-third of the Earth's land surface are impacted by resulting desertification.[74] The tropical rainforests of Latin America, especially in Brazil, have received considerable attention since the 1980s when large-scale burning of the rainforests gathered significant international attention. Rainforest destruction from 1995 to 2000 averaged almost two million acres a year— the equivalent to seven football fields a minute. This was a significant increase since the early 1990s. This increase coincided with new plans by the Brazilian government to build expansive road networks, railroads, hydroelectric reservoirs, power lines, and gas lines in a project totaling $40 billion in infrastructure development into the rainforests, which would allow for even further deforestation.[75]

Despite the danger of overdevelopment of the Amazon Rainforest, Brazil has accelerated its exploitation. In 2003, some 9,169 square miles of rainforest disappeared which was a 2 percent increase over the previous year. The near-term economic priorities are driven by Brazil's role as the world's second largest producer of soy and the second largest cattle producer. Between 1997 and 2003, beef exports increased by a factor of five and soy production grew from 32 million tons in 2000 to 52 tons in 2003.[76] A direct security consequence of the dynamics of rainforest depletion is the impact on indigenous peoples. Some tribes in the rainforests have lived for centuries unexposed by the impact of the developed world. They have now been exposed to new diseases. As their habitat has been depleted, many such tribes are dying off. Some six to nine million indigenous people were estimated to inhabit the Brazilian rainforest in 1500 and in 1992 there were less than 200,000.[77]

Mexico lost an average of 2.72 million acres of forests and jungles annually between 1993 and 2000. This deforestation was twice as much as had been officially declared at the time by the Mexican government. Areas including the Yucatan peninsula, Tabasco, Veracruz, and Chiapas were all in critical danger as a result of deforestation. Overall, Mexico had lost 7.8 million pine and fir forests and tropical jungles during this seven-year period. Much of this deforestation resulted from an increase in farming and grazing land cleared by ten to fifteen million poor farmers who have no other means of income.[78] Guillermo Montoya Gomez notes that "these people will starve if they don't cut down more trees, and a comprehensive solution will be complicated and costly."[79]

Some 50 percent of southeast Asia's forests have been destroyed with an annual loss of 1 percent. Throughout east Asia, forest cover is depleting by 1.4 percent annually. Indonesia's 120 million hectares of forests is shrinking at a rate of 1.5 million hectares annually. Since 1985, as much as 30 percent of Indonesia's forest cover has disappeared. In Indonesia, the way trees are felled also has an impact on surrounding forests and future growth. While only 3 percent of the trees are cut, a logging operation in Indonesia generally damages some 49 percent of the trees in a forest area.[80] Indonesia's forests will be reduced by a total of 50 percent by 2030 at current rates of deforestation. The forests of the Philippines, Cambodia, and Malaysia are at risk of disappearing completely by the end of the first decade of the twenty-first century.[81]

Africa also faces serious deforestation challenges. Africa has 30 percent of the world's tropical forest growth, but faces a unique combination of poor governmental attention to the issue, creeping desertification, and human activity. In sub-Saharan Africa cut wood accounts for 52 percent of all energy sources.[82] Mali has been losing about 400,000 acres of tree cover every year resulting from growing demand for timber and fuel wood.[83] This small country of twelve million people uses six million tons of firewood a year—about 1.5 kg per day for every inhabitant of the largest city, Bamako.[84] In Kenya, the combination of population growth, droughts, poor land management, and increasing deforestation has led to accelerated desertification. Kenyan forests now cover only 2.8 percent of total land area.[85] Even without losing any more forests, Benin, Burundi, Cameroon, Côte d'Ivoire, Kenya, and Nigeria could lose more than a third of their primate species within the next several decades. However, this problem is likely to grow substantially worse as West Africa is expected to lose, by the year 2040, 70 percent of its remaining forest. In East Africa the loss is expected to be as high as 95 percent.[86] In Africa, the primary cause of deforestation is direct human use of cut-wood rather than overall economic strategies which destroy forest lands.

As the world warms and numerous habitats are destroyed by human activity, entire ecosystems are placed at risk. By using computer models to estimate the movement of plants, mammals, birds, reptiles, frogs, butterflies, and other invertebrates in response to changes in ecosystems, scientists estimate that in the rich biodiversity regions of the world—about 20 percent of the Earth—some 15 to 37 percent of all species could be driven to extinction by 2050. The impact could eventually drive one million species into extinction—and affect billions of people who rely on complex ecological systems for their survival. The director of UNEP concludes, "If one million species become extinct, it is not just the plant and animal kingdoms and the beauty of the planet that will suffer. . . . Billions of people, especially in the developing world, will suffer too as they rely on nature for such essential goods and services as food, shelter, and medicines."[87]

Water Security

Humans and animals in nature cannot live without water. The combination of water scarcity, degradation, and growing demand therefore makes access to freshwater one of the most significant emerging security issues of the twenty-first century. By the year 2015, the United Nations predicts that 40 percent of the world's population will live in areas where one cannot safely drink the water. Already, 40 percent do not have basic sanitation and one billion people have no access to clean water sources. Even if progress is made in making drinking water more accessible, population growth will likely outstrip improvements. According to a study by UNICEF, some 4,000 children die every day from illnesses caused by lack of clean water.[88] While the world is covered with ocean water, it is salty and undrinkable. As ice caps melt due to global warming, more freshwater will likely accelerate climate change as ice-melt mixes with warm ocean temperatures, thereby affecting the pace of global warming. Too much rain, and resulting flooding, or too little water and expanding desertification are becoming significant trends in heavily populated regions of the world. Agricultural demand currently takes up 70 percent of all water use worldwide while 22 percent of total water use is for industrial activity. People in rich countries use ten times more water than those in underdeveloped countries.[89] Meanwhile, waterways which cross national borders also make downstream or adjacent states vulnerable to the activity of other states. Water can cause conflict over control of water resources, be used as a military tool, be applied as a political tool to gain power, be a target of terrorism, and play a major role in economic development disputes and conflict resolution.[90] It is possible that water will replace oil as the most important strategic natural asset of the twenty-first century.

The United Nations World Water Development Report illustrates the global scale of water security challenges. Water-borne diseases such as diarrheal diseases kill 6,000 people every day. Overall, 1.3 million children under age five die every year from water-borne disease. Over one million people die worldwide from malaria of which about 700,000 are children. By 2015, an additional one billion people will need access to both water supply and sanitation.[91] In a country like Ethiopia, only 20 percent of the population had adequate access to clean water in 2005.[92] Freshwater ecosystems are affected by population and consumption growth which increases water use that impacts entire ecosystems. Infrastructure development such as dams and levees can alter river beds, produce sediment, and change water temperature, thus impacting water quantity and quality, floodplains, delta economies, and fisheries. Land conversion can eliminate major components of aquatic environment which impacts natural flood control and animal habitats. Overharvesting and exploitation of fisheries depletes living resources, which has a negative impact on food production, water supply, water quality, and water quantity. Meanwhile, the release of pollutants to land, air, or water alters the chemistry and ecology of rivers, lakes, and wetlands, thereby damaging the water supply, habitats, water quality, and food production. More than 50 percent of the world's wetlands have been lost since 1900.[93] Every day, two million tons of human waste is disposed of in waterways. Even in the United States, 40 percent of water bodies assessed in 1998 were not fit for world distribution. In Asia, all rivers running through cities are badly polluted. On a global scale, 60 percent of the world's 227 largest rivers are severely fragmented by dams, diversions, and canals.[94]

Water-related disasters that occur in nature, or which will be exacerbated by global climate change, also pose a serious threat to populations. There were some 2,200 water-related disasters between 1990 and 2001. Among these crises, 50 percent were floods, 28 percent water-borne disease outbreaks, 11 percent droughts, 9 percent landslides and avalanche events, and 2 percent famine. Most such disasters occur in Asia (29 percent) and North and South America (20 percent). In 1998 and 1999 a total of 90,000 people died as a result of water-related natural disasters costing $70 billion in 1999. Between 1991 and 2000, droughts accounted for 280,000 deaths. Between 1987 and 1997, some 228,000 lives were lost just in Asia from floods. From 1992 to 2001, developing countries accounted for 20 percent of all water-related disasters, over 50 percent of all disaster fatalities, and people in these countries were thirteen times more likely to die from such disasters than in developed areas of the world.[95] Even highly developed countries are not immune from such disasters, as the United States discovered when hurricanes Katrina, Rita, and Wilma hit in 2005.

A survey of "water hotspots" by the British Broadcasting Corporation shows the diverse nature of the impact of water issues around the world.[96] In Australia, power and irrigation have damaged the two largest rivers and reduced their flows to the sea by 75 percent while providing 40 percent of Australia's farms with water. In India, the sacred Ganges River suffers from depletion, pollution, and is also the source of political conflict between India and Bangladesh. Climate change is reducing the ice melt which feeds the Ganges while deforestation has caused subsoil streams flowing into the river to dry up. India also controls the flow of water into Bangladesh via a hydro-project near their mutual border. India has periodically diverted the river toward Calcutta to stop its port from drying up during hot seasons. This upstream action helps Indian farmers, but denies Bangladeshi farmers water. China suffers from flooding in its south and drought in its north. China has built a massive dam project on the Yangtze River (the Three Gorges Dam) which will be the largest dam of its kind in the world. In its construction, one million people have been uprooted. In 1997, China's Yellow River ran dry for 226 days and between 1991 and 1996, the water table beneath the north China plain fell by an average of 1.5 meters a year.

In Eurasia, the Aral Sea has seen a drop in water level of sixteen meters between 1962 and 1993 as a result of water redistribution programs to grow cotton. This area now has one of the highest infant mortality rates in the world, and anemia and cancers caused by chemicals blowing off the dried sea bed are common. Iraq has lost 90 percent of its wetlands in the southern part of the country. Some 20,000 square kilometers of freshwater were drained by the government leaving only salty, crusted earth behind. Turkey has sought to increase its existing water reserves and to boost its hydroelectric capabilities via a system of twenty-two dams on the Tigris and Euphrates rivers. The filling of these dams has occasionally stopped the flow of water to Iraq and Syria. Israel and its neighbors face the potential for significant competition over water resources. Both Israel and Jordan rely on the River Jordan, though Israel controls it and has cut supplies during times of scarcity. The Sea of Galilee water levels have been declining, which could lead to increased salination of Israel's main reservoir. Israelis in the West Bank use four times as much water as their Palestinian neighbors. In 2002, Israel threatened military action in Lebanon when Lebanon opened a new pumping station taking water from a tributary of the River Jordan.

In Africa, Lake Chad was once a huge lake on the borders of Chad, Niger, Nigeria, and Cameroon. However, it has shrunk in size by 95 percent since the mid-1960s. The region's climate has changed as monsoon rains have been reduced which had previously replenished the lake. Nine million farmers, fishermen, and herders in the region now face water shortages, crop failure, livestock deaths, collapsed fisheries, soil salinity, and increasing poverty. The River Nile may pose the biggest single cause of water conflict in Africa in the coming decades. If populations rise as expected in Egypt, Ethiopia, and Sudan competition for the Nile's waters will be intense. Egypt has already said in 1991 that it was ready to use force to protect its access to the river's flows even though its tributaries run through nine different countries.

In the Western Hemisphere, Mexico City is sinking as the water underneath it has been pumped out. Over the last 500 years the lakes around Mexico City have been drained and the surrounding forests chopped down. As the city grew in size, the water problem magnified. The city is now at serious risk of running out of clean water while an estimated 40 percent of what it does have is lost through leaky pipes over one hundred years old. In North America, much of the freshwater in the United States is underground. One crucial source is the 800-mile Ogallala aquifer that stretches from Texas to South Dakota and supplies water to one-fifth of irrigated land in the United States. The aquifer has been cut off from its original natural sources and is thus being depleted at a rate of twelve billion cubic meters a year. This amounts to a total depletion of a volume equal to the annual flow of eighteen Colorado rivers. Some estimates conclude that the entire aquifer will be dry in as little as twenty-five years.

There is actually little historical evidence that water is a direct cause of war. Historically, water wars have not been strategically effective. There have only been seven cases in which armies were mobilized or shots fired across international borders over water. In these seven cases, disputes did not escalate into warfare.[97] Water conflicts can, however, exacerbate existing tensions. For example, in 2003, Russia built a dike that connected its coast with the Tuzla Island in the Kerch strait near to Ukraine's Crimean Peninsula. Ukraine protested this move as an intrusion on its sovereignty over the island—which Russia said it did not recognize. Ukraine responded by deploying fifty troops to Tuzla and threatened to abandon the agreements with Russia though no actual conflict broke out.[98] While it is true that such conflicts historically do not lead to war, never before has Earth witnessed the kinds of pressures on water supplies that it will confront in the twenty-first century. History, therefore, may not be a useful guide as the world addresses water issues in the decades to come.

A key challenge will be how states will treat shared water resources when confronted with dwindling water supplies. There are many transboundary basins in the world including 59 in Africa; 58 in Asia; 73 in Europe; 61 in Latin America and the Caribbean; 17 in North America; and 1 in Oceania. A total of 141 countries have territory within a transboundary basin and 21 lie entirely within one. The United Nations World Water Development Report notes that, of 1,831 interactions over the last fifty years involving transboundary waterways, only 7 have involved violence (though 507 conflictive events have occurred).[99] Nevertheless, new conditions can create new outcomes and, as William Mitsch notes, "We have had oil wars. . . . That's happened in our lifetime. . . . Water wars are possible."[100]

It is also, however, just as possible that states might see increasing incentives to cooperate and overcome differences to meet their water needs. The real threat relevant to water security might thus not be international conflict, but rather the added burden on state capacity to meet the basic needs of their citizens. The major challenge posed by water security dilemmas might be from instability within states, of which water supply issues might be a major component. With over sixty states facing water stress in the next twenty-five years, it would be a mistake to assume that future instability and conflict might not be affected by this condition.[101] Over a century ago, no one would have considered oil and energy supply scarcity to be a strategic issue, thus highlighting the way new issues can emerge that drive resource-based conflicts including water.

Energy Scarcity and Safety

By summer 2005, the price-per-barrel of oil approached $70.00 and gasoline prices in the United States reached levels that consumers were previously unaccustomed to paying. The immediate problem was not a lack of supply, but rather growing demand relative to the ability to access or refine sufficient energy for industry, society, and transportation. Scarcity or supply disruptions of energy resources such as oil and natural gas places pressure on states to develop oil-containing areas, to burn less-clean sources of energy such as coal, or to seek energy alternatives. Two major security issues are impacted by these trends. First, states that depend on external energy suppliers are vulnerable. Conflicts over the control of energy flows, such as pipelines and shipping lanes, could therefore be a major source of future conflict. Second, the relative safety of energy use creates significant issues for states ranging from the impact on the environment of burning fossil fuels to challenges associated with the more energy-clean use of nuclear energy.

Energy scarcity is a worldwide problem if demand continues to rise and sources of energy become fewer. The International Energy Agency (IEA) estimates that by 2020, global energy demand will increase by 57 percent from levels in the late 1990s with an average annual increase of 2 percent. Demand for both oil and natural gas is expected to increase substantially. The Energy Information Administration predicts the world demand for oil will total almost 118 million barrels per day in 2025.[102] Natural gas and coal demand is rising faster than oil. China and India account for two-thirds of the increased demand. World economic growth is expected to continue and thus energy demand will grow exponentially. Some future projections were built around an assumption that oil and gas prices will remain stable and relatively low. However, the price of oil was over twice the dollar amount in 2005 than the IEA initially projected. Uncertainty has been introduced into global energy markets. As the price of energy goes up with increased demand, it is also possible that states will move toward fuel alternatives. The Energy Information Administration predicts that by 2025, natural gas will meet 24 percent of end-use energy requirements. However, if existing trends remain in place, geothermal and solar energy will provide less than 1 percent of the energy used for space and water heating.

The IEA estimates that the total investment requirement for energy-supply infrastructure worldwide between 2001 and 2030 will be $16 trillion. This expenditure would be necessary to expand supply capacity and to replace existing and future supply facilities that will be exhausted or become obsolete.[103] Electricity is seen as a particularly important area for future investment costing about $10 trillion. Even in countries like the United States, electricity has become a major challenge as outdated electrical power grids have struggled to keep pace with the dramatically accelerated demand. In summer 2003, large areas of the eastern United States and Canada were blacked out when integrated power networks failed because tree limbs fell on some wires. The energy situation is far worse in the developing world where China is expected to have to spend $2.3 trillion to meet its growing energy needs. Worldwide, most of the projected investments in energy infrastructure are needed just to maintain current levels of demand and do not account for growing future demand. According to the IEA, 51 percent of investment in energy will be needed to replace or maintain existing and future production capacity. The remaining 49 percent will be needed to meet the rising demand of natural gas at 2.4 percent annually; oil at 1.6 percent annually; coal at 1.4 percent annually; and electricity at 2.4 percent annual growth.[104] China, Russia, India, Indonesia, and Brazil will account for one-third of future global electricity investment.

States that factor environmental concerns into their energy policies could have an important positive impact on the worldwide demand for energy investment and extraction. If, however, the environmental costs of the burning of fossil fuels are not substantially addressed by governments, or if alternative energy sources are not fully utilized, then the overall costs of major climate change for the world's security could be insurmountable. As populations grow and demand the basic necessities of life, more energy will be needed. States that cannot afford substantial investments into clean energy sources will likely continue to exploit resources, doing considerable environmental damage over time. The immediate demand for energy and its impact on populations in the underdeveloped world is often overlooked by societies seeking to secure access to cheap gasoline to drive their automobiles. For example, the *World Energy Outlook 2002* shows that 1.6 billion people had no access to electricity and 2.4 billion depended on basic wood or dung sources for cooking and heating, which accelerates air pollution problems. Even with substantial investment in energy sources over the next thirty years, 1.4 billion people will still live day-to-day with no electricity.[105] This means no electricity for making clean and drinkable water, no electricity for hospitals, and no electricity for schools. Currently, four out of five people without electricity live in rural areas of the developing world—primarily in sub-Saharan Africa and south and southeast Asia. By 2030, it is expected that large segments of this population will have moved into massive third-world megacities creating enormous strains on current urban capacity to provide for basic energy needs, health and sanitation, education, and other social requisites for human development.

The growth of China's economy coupled with the movement of agrarian peasants into cities and a new generation of wealth is having an especially significant impact on global energy demand. As China emphasizes coal-burning for energy, its contribution to global warming will rise. China can sustain its rapid economic growth by mining more coal. However, China will still face major oil shortages of 5.9 to 8.8 million barrels per day by 2015 according to the United States Department of Energy.[106] As urban environmental pressures mount, public attitudes in China are also likely to create pressures for cleaner energy sources combined with increasing demand in industry and transportation sectors of the Chinese economy. If China were to move rapidly toward a substitution strategy moving away from coal and toward oil, combined with increasing use of petroleum fuel for automobiles, the impact on global energy supply prices could be significant. In a worst case, China's demand for energy could prompt new alliances over pipeline flows from the Middle East and central Asia, purchases of energy production facilities from Russia, or even military conflict in areas such as the South China Sea. At a minimum, China's growing energy demand will increase pressure for further energy exploration and likely raise prices for those countries whose economies are currently benefiting from low-cost energy supplies.

Nuclear Energy

Nuclear power is one of the cleanest and cheapest sources of energy—and also potentially the most dangerous. Nuclear power generating plants account for 20 percent of the world's energy. Some countries like France rely on them for as much as 75 percent of their energy supply. Nuclear power plants release low levels of waste during normal operations and emissions are under strict control by states around the world. In small amounts, radiation exposure is not harmful to human beings—though long-term exposure can have some genetic impact. Nuclear accidents have been rare. However, in circumstances where accidents have occurred, human exposure to radiation has had dangerous consequences. Humans can be exposed to radiation from nuclear power source accidents including from rain washing materials out of the air, external radiation directly emanating from a radioactive cloud, external doses from radioactive materials deposited on the ground, and internal exposure from eating and drinking radioactive materials in food and water.[107]

The International Atomic Energy Agency (IAEA) notes that most environmental impacts from radiation have resulted from nuclear weapons tests. These tests have propelled a variety of radionuclides including hydrogen-3 and plutonium-241 into the upper atmosphere which then fall on the Earth's surface. Some 500 above-ground nuclear explosions were conducted up until 1963 and a number of others were conducted in the 1980s and 1990s. The IAEA concludes that the global collective dose of radiation from weapon tests fallout is now about 30,000 man Sv annually.[108] The Cold War legacy of nuclear weapons testing and storage is one of the most serious environmental hazards confronting the world today. Even a wealthy country like the United States has not been able to determine effectively what to do with its nuclear waste storage and how to manage the environmental impact of weapons manufacturing and storage facilities. However, the most serious challenge is in the former Soviet Union, where it is still not entirely understood where the nuclear hotspots are. Loosely stored nuclear warheads waiting for decommission, decaying nuclear submarines, and large areas of uninhabitable land dot the Russian landscape. In 1957, a nuclear accident in Mayak released seventy to eighty tons of radioactive materials into the air. Siberia's two main rivers, the Ob and the Yenisei, are radioactively contaminated. Once privileged Russian nuclear scientists often go without pay and, as such, some are available to the highest foreign bidder for employment. In the Kola Peninsula, there are 29,040 fuel elements, nine reactor cores, and 21,067 cubic meters of solid-fuel nuclear waste.[109]

Russia has an acute experience with the dangers of nuclear energy. There are eleven nuclear sites in the area of the former Soviet Union and in April 1986, one of them went very wrong at Chernobyl. While putting the poorly designed plant through a test, workers failed to communicate with each other. In the process they created a power surge that set off explosions in the nuclear core of one of the reactors. High levels of radioactivity were released over ten days. This radiation fell not only around the Soviet Union but also in northern and southern Europe, Canada, Japan, and the United States. In some areas near the reactor, and other local hotspots where radiation fell due to weather patterns, radioactive cesium will be present for 300 years. The spread of radioactivity was stemmed by the brave efforts of emergency responders—thirty-one of whom died from direct exposure. They responded by placing a cap on top of the burning reactor core.

More than 100,000 persons within a thirty-mile radius around the accident site at Chernobyl were evacuated and they received significant radiation doses to their body and thyroid glands. So-called "liquidators" included 600,000 workers and military personnel who were involved in emergency actions during the accident and subsequent clean-up lasting several years. About 400 people received very high exposure to radiation during the accident itself. About 270,000 people continue to live in areas of the former Soviet Union that were contaminated with radiocesium and require protection measures. Outside the former Soviet Union, radioactive materials including iodine and caesium spread through the northern hemisphere. Health and agricultural impact outside the former Soviet Union has been minimal—though there are areas in Scotland where radioactivity still required careful monitoring of livestock fifteen years later. Around the area of the accident, soil and agriculture continue to be affected by radioactivity. High rates of thyroid cancers and lingering psychological effects persist.

The problem at Chernobyl was actually never resolved as the fire in the reactor was capped but not permanently extinguished. The "sarcophagus" which encases the reactor was only meant to be a temporary solution and it is increasingly at risk for corrosion and leakage. Around the plant there are 800 sites of buried equipment contaminated with radioactivity all of which are sources of groundwater contamination. Some estimates suggest that as many as 3.5 million people, one-third of whom are children, have suffered illness as a result of this accident. Overall, the radiation leak was 500 times greater than that released by the atomic bomb on Hiroshima at the end of World War II.[110] The level of radioactive contamination of the land is 23 percent in Belarus, 5 percent in Ukraine, and 1.5 percent of total land in Russia.[111]

The IAEA concludes that the overall impact of Chernobyl was actually less serious than was initially feared would be the case. While about 1,800 children developed thyroid cancer from overexposure to radioactive isotopes, this is a treatable disease and rarely is fatal. However, this was also the largest group of cancer known to have occurred from a single incident in history.[112] The IAEA concludes that "with this exception, there is no scientific evidence of increases in overall cancer incidence or mortality or in nonmalignant disorders that could be related to radiation exposure."[113] The IAEA concluded that there was "no evidence of a major public health impact attributable to radiation exposure 14 years after the accident."[114] Yet at the same time at least 8,000—and in some estimates as many as 15,000—people died as a result of exposure to radiation over time.[115] Meanwhile about 4.5 million people continue to receive government relief as a direct result of displacement from the incident which strains governments in Ukraine and Belarus.

Even in the highly advanced country of Japan, a major nuclear accident occurred in 1999 at a plant northeast of Tokyo. Worker error led to a major radiation leak exposing 600 people to radiation and dislocating about 320,000. The United States experienced a nuclear accident at Three Mile Island in Pennsylvania in 1979. By 2005, the United States had 103 operating plants that were aging, had few inspections, and was spending less money on maintenance. The Davis-Besse plant near Cleveland, Ohio, has been found to have been operating with cracks in the infrastructure around the nuclear reactor core. This plant has had to be shut down for extended periods of time. The U.S. Department of Energy recovers on average three unwanted, high-risk radiological sources every week in the United States. Four sources of strontium-90 were recovered inside Houston in 2004 on the day the city was hosting Super Bowl XXXVIII. A general international lack of awareness of the nature of the radiological challenge is summarized by one Russian national who had a radiation dump discovered near his garage saying: "I'm from Moldova and I drink Moldovan wine. . . . It cleans everything. Radiation doesn't hurt me."[116]

Even small amounts of radiation used in medical laboratories or university research institutes can pose a threat if they are used as "radioactive dispersal devices." A radiological dispersal devise (RDD) is "any device, including any weapon or equipment, other than a nuclear explosive devise, specifically designed to employ radioactive material by disseminating it to cause destruction, damage, or injury by means of the radiation produced by the decay of such material."[117] The spread of radioactive isotopes in the environment could make an area of major economic activity uninhabitable for many decades or create extremely costly cleanup needs. The pure volume of radioactive material held by governments and in the private sector makes the control over such material very hard to secure. Even a technologically advanced country like the United States has serious problems in this area. Between 1998 and 2003, there were an estimated 1,300 disappearances of radioactive materials in the United States. Most of this material was recovered, but in reality, the United States does not know how much low-grade radioactive materials exist in private use on its territory. Some 114 American universities that possess radioactive plutonium-239 have tried (unsuccessfully) to return it to the U.S. government, but the U.S. Department of Energy has not had enough storage space. In March 1998, a North Carolina hospital discovered that nineteen sealed sources of radiological material including highly dispersible cesium-137 had gone missing from a locked safe. In March 1999, an industrial radiography camera with iridium-192 was stolen from a private Florida home and two universities found that doors where this same material was stored had been found left unlocked.[118]

SUMMARY

The environment and energy are extraordinarily important challenges that have expanded significantly the debate over the meaning of security. The most significant threats will likely affect the capacity of states to meet the basic needs of their peoples, which risks the spread of instability within and among states. Skeptics of the role the environment historically plays in conflict have considerable evidence to support that conclusion. Moreover, it is also just as possible that environmental and energy scarcities will produce cooperation rather than conflict. However, even the best-case scenario projections for future environmental and energy dynamics expose a future for Earth and its carrying capacity for which experience provides little previous guidance. The complex relationship between the environment, energy, and security is moving the world into an uncertain future for which there is no precedent in human experience.

NOTES

1. Richard A. Matthew, "Introduction," in *Contested Grounds: Security and Conflict in the New Environmental Politics*, ed. Daniel Duedney and Richard A. Matthew (Albany, N.Y.: SUNY Press, 1999), 13.

2. Thomas Homer-Dixon, "Global Environmental Change and International Security," in *Building a New Global Order*, ed. David Dewitt et al. (Oxford: Oxford University Press, 1994), 185–228.

3. Homer-Dixon, "Global Environmental Change," 191.

4. Homer-Dixon, "Global Environmental Change," 214.

5. Richard Ullman, "Redefining Security," *International Security* 8, no. 1 (1983): 129–53.

6. Homer-Dixon, "Global Environmental Change," 216.

7. Thomas Homer-Dixon and Jessica Blitt, eds., *Ecoviolence: Links among Environment, Population, and Security* (Lanham, Md.: Rowman and Littlefield, 1998), 6.

8. Homer-Dixon and Blitt, *Ecoviolence*, 223–28.

9. Peter H. Gleick, "Water and Conflict: Fresh Water Resources and International Security," *International Security* 18, no. 1 (Summer 1993): 79–112.

10. Gleick, "Water and Conflict," 87.

11. Gleick, "Water and Conflict," 95.

12. Gleick, "Water and Conflict," 104.

13. Miriam R. Lowi, "Bridging the Divide: Transboundary Resource Disputes and the Case of West Bank Water," *International Security* 18, no. 1 (Summer 1993): 113–15.

14. Lowi, "Bridging the Divide," 113–15.

15. Lowi, "Bridging the Divide," 113–38.

16. Robert C. North, "Toward a Framework for the Analysis of Scarcity and Conflict," *International Studies Quarterly*, no. 21 (December 1977): 569–91.

17. Michel Frederick, "A Realist's Conceptual Definition of Environmental Security," in *Contested Grounds: Security and Conflict in the New Environmental Politics*, ed. Daniel Duedney and Richard A. Matthew (Albany, N.Y.: SUNY Press, 1999), 100.

18. Frederick, "A Realist's Conceptual Definition," 101–4.

19. Muir Papers, University of the Pacific, Stockton, California; also see Stephen R. Fox, *The American Conservation Movement: John Muir and His Legacy* (Madison: University of Wisconsin Press, 1986).

20. "Address on the Sierra Forest Reservation," *The Sierra Club Bulletin,* no. 7 (1896): 276.

21. Rachel Carson, *Silent Spring* (Boston: Houghton Mifflin, 1962).

22. Oran R. Young, *International Governance* (Ithaca, N.Y.: Cornell University Press, 1994), 19–26.

23. Marc Levy, "Is the Environment a National Security Issue?" *International Security* 20, no. 2 (1995): 35–62.

24. Julian Simon, *The Ultimate Resource* (Princeton, N.J.: Princeton University Press, 1987).

25. Simon Dalby, *Environmental Security* (Minneapolis: University of Minnesota Press, 2002).

26. Dalby, *Environmental Security,* 157.

27. Dalby, *Environmental Security,* 167.

28. Dalby, *Environmental Security,* 167.

29. Dalby, *Environmental Security,* 172.

30. John Barnett, *The Meaning of Environmental Security* (London: Zed Books, 2001), 2–3.

31. Barnett, *Meaning of Environmental Security,* 14.

32. Barnett, *Meaning of Environmental Security,* 22.

33. Barnett, *Meaning of Environmental Security,* 108.

34. Barnett, *Meaning of Environmental Security,* 122.

35. Ronnie Lipschutz, *Global Civil Society and Global Environmental Governance: The Politics of Nature from Place to Planet* (Albany, N.Y.: SUNY Press, 1996).

36. Lipschutz, *Global Civil Society,* 51.

37. President Jimmy Carter, Address to the Nation, April 18, 1977.

38. Donald J. Goldstein, "Energy as a Security Issue," in *Energy as a Security Issue,* ed. Donald J. Goldstein (Washington, D.C.: National Defense University Press, 1981), 7.

39. Goldstein, "Energy as a Security Issue," 16.

40. Goldstein, "Energy as a Security Issue," 19.

41. Howard Bucknell III, *Energy and the National Defense* (Lexington: University of Kentucky Press, 1981), 103.

42. Bucknell III, *Energy and the National Defense,* 126.

43. Michael Klare, *Resource Wars* (New York: Metropolitan Books, 2001), 6.

44. Klare, *Resource Wars,* 7.

45. Klare, *Resource Wars,* 21–22.

46. Klare, *Resource Wars,* 69.

47. See http://www.eia.doe.gov/emeu/security/Oil/index.html (accessed Fall 2004).

48. See www.eia.doe.gov/emeu/security (accessed Fall 2004).

49. Jose Goldemberg, "Energy and Sustainable Development," in *World's Apart:*

Globalization and the Environment, ed. James Gustave Speth (Washington, D.C.: Island Press, 2003), 57–58.

50. Martha Harris, "Energy and Security," in *Grave New World: Security Challenges in the 21st Century,* ed. Michael E. Brown (Washington, D.C.: Georgetown University Press, 2003), 167–68.

51. "Booming China's Acid Rain 'Out of Control,'" *Reuters,* November 30, 2004.

52. Jim Yardley, "China's Next Big Boom Could Be the Foul Air," *New York Times,* October 30, 2005.

53. "China's Dependence on Coal for Energy Causing Pollution at Home and Abroad," *AFP,* July 28, 2004.

54. Louisa Lim, "China Tackles Energy Shortages," *BBC News,* July 29, 2004.

55. Union of Concerned Scientists, "Global Warming," at www.ucsusa.org/global_warming/accessed (accessed Fall 2004).

56. Union of Concerned Scientists, "Global Warming."

57. Union of Concerned Scientists, "Global Warming."

58. Ed Cropley, "Melting Glaciers Threaten World Water Supply," *Reuters,* November 17, 2004.

59. Donald Kennedy, comments at seminar "Environmental Change and Conflict Liability," held at Stanford University, Center for International Security and Cooperation, May 2002.

60. Tim Radford, "Flood Risk to 2 bn by 2050, Says Study," *The Guardian,* June 14, 2004, at www.guardian.co.uk (accessed Spring 2004).

61. Tim Radford, "Destructive Power of 100,000 A-bombs," *The Guardian,* August 16, 2004, at www.guardian.co.uk (accessed Summer 2004).

62. Anna Mudeva, "European Winters Could Disappear by 2080," *Reuters,* August 18, 2004.

63. As summarized by David Stipp, "Climate Change a National Security Threat," *Fortune,* January 26, 2004. The original study is at www.gbn.com (accessed December 2005).

64. Stipp, "Climate Change a National Security Threat."

65. Stipp, "Climate Change a National Security Threat."

66. Stipp, "Climate Change a National Security Threat."

67. The original reporting of this study was by David Stipp, "Climate Change a National Security Threat," *Fortune,* January 26, 2004.

68. UN News Center, "UN-Backed Congress Calls for New Global Political Commitment to Save Forests," September 29, 2003, at www.un.org (accessed Fall 2004).

69. World Resources Institute, "Deforestation: The Global Assault Continues," at www.wri.org/wr-98–99/deforest.htm (accessed Fall 2004).

70. Col. W. Chris King, *Understanding International Environmental Security: A Strategic Military Perspective* (Atlanta, Ga.: Army Environmental Policy Institute, 2000), 51–52.

71. Amy Bracken, "Deforestation Exacerbates Haiti Floods," *Associated Press,* September 23, 2004.

72. King, *Understanding International Environmental Security.*

73. "Backgrounder," International Food Policy Research Institute, at www.ifpri.org (accessed Fall 2004).

74. Anthony Boadle, "U.N. Seeks Donors to Fight Loss of Fertile Soil," *Reuters*, August 27, 2003.

75. Smithsonian Institution, "Smithsonian Researchers Show Amazonian Deforestation Accelerating," January 15, 2002, at www.sciencedaily.com/releases/2002/01/020115075118.htm (accessed Spring 2004).

76. Andrew Downie, "Amazon Destruction Rising Fast," *Christian Science Monitor*, April 22, 2004.

77. Catherine Caufield, *In the Rainforest* (Chicago: University of Chicago Press, 1984).

78. Lisa J. Adams, "Mexico in Danger of Losing Forests," *Associated Press*, December 5, 2001.

79. Gretchen Peters, "No Quick Solution to Deforestation in Lush Chiapas," *Christian Science Monitor*, January 14, 2002.

80. Gerals Urquhart, Walter Chomentowski, Davike Skole, and Chris Barber, "Tropical Deforestation," *NASA Earth Observatory*, at www.earthobservatory.nasa.gov (accessed Fall 2004).

81. Brad Glosserman, "ASIA: Environmental Security Risks," *Japan Times*, November 26, 2002.

82. Yvonne Agyei, "Deforestation in Sub-Saharan Africa," *African Technology Forum* 8, no. 1 (1998).

83. United Nations Office for the Coordination of Humanitarian Affairs, "Mali: Government Imposes Six-Month Ban on Tree Felling," August 18, 2004, at www.irin-news.org (accessed Fall 2004).

84. United Nations Office for the Coordination of Humanitarian Affairs, "Mali: Government Imposes Six-Month Ban."

85. United Nations Office for the Coordination of Humanitarian Affairs, "Kenya: Desertification Threatening Millions, Government Warns," July 2, 2002, at www.irin-news.org (accessed Fall 2004).

86. "Studies Suggest Extinctions Continue Long after Deforestation," CNN, October 12, 1999.

87. Alex Kirby, "Climate Risk 'To Million Species,'" *BBC News*, January 7, 2004.

88. UNICEF, August 2004, at www.unicef.org (accessed Fall 2004).

89. Alex Kirby, "Why World's Taps Are Running Dry," *BBC News,* at http://news.bbc.co.uk/2/hi/science/nature/2943946.stm (accessed Fall 2004).

90. Peter Gleick, "Water Conflict Chronology—Introduction," August 2003, at www.worldwater.org/conflit (accessed Fall 2004).

91. United Nations World Water Development Report, at www.unesco.org/water/wwap/facts_figures (accessed Fall 2004).

92. UNICEF, "State of the World's Children: 2005," at www.unicef.org (accessed Fall 2004).

93. United Nations World Water Development Report.

94. United Nations World Water Development Report.

95. United Nations World Water Development Report.

96. "World Water Crisis," at www.news.bbc.co.uk (accessed Fall 2004).

97. AVISO, "Water and Human Security," no. 3 (June 1999): 2.

98. International Institute of Strategic Studies, *Strategic Survey 2003/2004: An Evaluation and Forecast of World Affairs* (Oxford: Oxford University Press, 2004), 127.

99. United Nations World Water Development Report.

100. Quoted in Patrick McLoughlin, "Scientists Say Risk of Water Wars Rising," *Reuters*, August 20, 2004.

101. Green Cross International, "National Sovereignty and International Watercourses," March 2000.

102. Energy Information Administration, *Annual Energy Outlook 2004*, at www.eia.doe.gov (accessed Fall 2004).

103. International Energy Agency, *World Energy Outlook 2002*, at www.worldenergyoutlook.com (accessed Fall 2004).

104. International Energy Agency, *World Energy Outlook 2002*.

105. International Energy Agency, *World Energy Outlook 2002*.

106. I. Iain McCreary et al., *China's Energy: A Forecast to 2015* (Los Alamos, N.M.: U.S. Department of Energy Office of Energy Intelligence, 1999).

107. International Atomic Energy Agency, *Radiation, People, and the Environment*, at www.iaea.org (accessed Fall 2004).

108. International Atomic Energy Agency, *Radiation, People, and the Environment*.

109. "Analysis: The Soviet Nuclear Legacy," *BBC News*, June 5, 2000.

110. "Chernobyl's Grim Legacy," *BBC News*, April 26, 2000.

111. "Millions of Chernobyl Victims Still Suffering," *BBC News*, February 7, 2002.

112. "Chernobyl's Cancer World Record," *BBC News*, at http://news.bbc.co.uk/2/hi/health/1615299.stm (accessed Fall 2004).

113. "Chernobyl 'Not So Deadly,'" *BBC News*, June 13, 2000.

114. "Chernobyl 'Not So Deadly.'"

115. "Millions of Chernobyl Victims Still Suffering."

116. C. J. Chivers, "Moscow's Nuclear Past Is Breeding Perils Today," *New York Times*, August 10, 2004.

117. James L. Ford, "Radiological Dispersal Devices: Assessing the Transnational Threat," *Strategic Forum*, no. 136 (March 1998): 1–5.

118. John Soloman, "Radioactive Materials Missing in U.S.," *Associated Press*, November 11, 2003.

SUGGESTED READING

Simon Dalby, *Environmental Security* (Minneapolis: University of Minnesota Press, 2002).

Theresa Manley Degeest and Dennis Clark Parages, *Ecological Security: An Environmental Perspective on Globalization* (Lanham, Md.: Rowman and Littlefield, 2003).

Paul F. Diehl and Nils Petter Gleditsch, eds., *Environmental Conflict* (Boulder, Colo.: Westview Press, 2000).

Peter H. Gleick, *The World's Water 2004–2005: The Biennial Report on Freshwater Resources* (Washington, D.C.: Island Press, 2004).

Peter M. Haas, Robert O. Keohane, and Marc Levy, eds., *Institutions for the Earth* (Cambridge, Ma.: MIT Press, 1993).

Thomas Homer-Dixon, *Environment, Scarcity, and Violence* (Princeton, N.J.: Princeton University Press, 2001).

Jan Kalicki and David L. Goldwyn, eds., *Energy and Security: Toward a New Foreign Policy Strategy* (Baltimore: Johns Hopkins University Press, 2005).

Michael Klare, *Resource Wars: The New Landscape of Global Conflict* (New York: Owl Books, 2002).

Paul Roberts, *The End of Oil on the Edge of a Perilous New World* (New York: Houghton Mifflin, 2004).

Michael Williams, *Deforesting the Earth: From Prehistory to Global Crisis* (Chicago: University of Chicago Press, 2002).

Chapter Ten

Meeting the Challenges
of Power and Peace

Mastering the art of writing in Karachi, Pakistan. *Source*: UN Photo by John Issac.

Meeting the challenges of power and peace surveyed in this book requires applying the full range of conceptual frameworks for thinking about global security. The traditions of realism which focus on power and the traditions of idealism which focus on peace each have prominent roles to play. The application and testing of conceptual frameworks helps distinguish between what will, and will not, work in organizing power in the pursuit of peace. The cases in this book show the extent to which security has become a global phenomenon. Some of the threats confronting humanity are truly overwhelming. However, a careful examination of security challenges shows that the more which is known about particular security threats, the more likely they can be resolved or averted. This chapter reviews the relationship between evolving conceptual frameworks and global security. The conclusion stresses the role of education as a strategic asset in moving the world toward a condition in which the pursuit of power and peace can be one and the same.

APPLYING GLOBAL SECURITY CONCEPTS

Realists often criticize idealist schools as being naive toward the inherent dangers in the international system. Meanwhile, idealists tend to criticize the realist schools as perpetuating self-fulfilling prophecies that preclude more positive outcomes of cooperation in favor of lasting peace. This book is neutral on the value of each general approach and instead offers the general conclusion that each has a role to play. Some frameworks do have greater applicability than others depending on the issue area. However, understanding each approach in the context of particular issues, and testing conceptual frameworks with empirical evidence can lead to stronger theories and more effective policy. Of course, what defines a successful security outcome is highly contingent on whom, or what, is being secured. Thus, students and practitioners have to make choices. These decisions will more likely increase security if existing assumptions are challenged with a range of conceptual choices and creative policy options available in the quest for power and the search for peace.

The Quest for Power

The end of the Cold War and the proliferation of new security challenges initially made realism seem outdated. Nonetheless, as this book shows, the relative distribution of power in the international system remains the fundamental constant that defines international security outcomes. The meaning of power and application of power are changing as a result of globalization—but, as realists posit, power remains a central starting point to understanding international security. The globalization of security also confirms the realist focus on anarchy in the international system. The global diffusion of power makes the international system highly unpredictable and heightens the sense of uncertainty that decision-makers confront when shaping policies. The realist focus on the nation-state also remains valid—though with some significant qualifications. The state remains the primary barrier that delineates the international system from domestic politics and is a key line of defense against international threats. However, the capacity for nation-states to meet security challenges with traditional tools of power is increasingly challenged by the nature of new threats. It is a paradox that the state is, at the same time, both challenged and strengthened in the twenty-first century.

Realism appears to have its highest explanatory value when applied to relationships among the world's great powers. At the dawn of the twenty-first century, the global security system was framed by American political, economic, and military primacy. However, the distribution of power within the various major regions of the world shows that America's dominance confronts significant constraints. In particular, the nuclear capabilities of Russia and China, as well as the role of Europe, provide some important constraints on the exercise of American power. In this sense, the classical function of deterrence and balance of power appears alive and well. While power might fluctuate in the international system, direct war between the major countries of the world appears unlikely. Additionally, deterrence appears to help contain regional conflicts including between India and Pakistan, China and Taiwan, and on the Korean peninsula. Defensive strategies also appear to still have an important role to play. For example, despite the official rationales for invading Iraq, the policy of containing its weapons of mass destruction programs through UN weapons inspections, international sanctions, and selected military power in the 1990s had actually worked. When America chose a strategy of preemption and invaded Iraq, no weapons or related programs were found. Nonetheless, realist scholarship has also historically allowed for the role that perception and misperception can play in heightening the security dilemma and this point is more applicable in conditions when bad information is guiding decision-making. Alternatively, offensive realism also explains why states might feel compelled to conduct strategies that prompt them to advance their quest for power with military force. Also, realism has been adapted to account for the role that soft power can play in defining balancing strategies for nation-states and other international actors.

Realism also can provide an important framework for understanding sources of international cooperation. The survival of international institutions such as NATO after the Cold War has been presented as evidence by some scholars that realist understanding of alliances existing solely as a response to an external threat is limited. While NATO did survive, by 2005 the effectiveness of its survival was in significant question. Other forms of alliance behavior remain consistent with realist explanations. Even if not organized around state-to-state relationships, alliances ultimately reflect approaches by international actors to cooperate over how to organize power. Alliances can occur as formalized institutions or as coalitions-of-the-willing among states. Alliances can also include networks of relationships among non-state actors. Either way, these are alliances organized around resolving particular security problems. Realism provides important foundations for understanding this kind of cooperation among like-minded countries or groups of people. Basic elements of realism also help to explain the continued role that concert arrangements and strategic partnerships play among global or regional powers. While classical deterrence might have new limitations, dissuasion provides a useful alternative by raising the costs of asymmetrical aggression.

Realism can explain asymmetric tactics and the strategic rationale behind them. Terrorism, for example, is a tactic employed in a broader strategic goal. One does not win wars against tactics—wars are won by taking battles to the strategic center of gravity of an enemy. New approaches to understanding the strategic logic behind asymmetrical threats can help to inform decision-makers on how to defeat these barbaric tactics. Realist warnings over potential negative impacts of interdependence and potential clashes of civilizations resulting from globalization also show how globalization can lead to conflict. Realism has also focused on the key role of relative power—and in particular the economic foundations of power. Additionally, realism allows for optimism regarding international cooperation. If states and the key actors in the system place a high value on cooperation and applying power toward peace, there is nothing inherent in realism that precludes such outcomes. Realism does, however, provide a strong dose of skepticism from which to challenge other approaches toward the search for peace.

The Search for Peace

History reflects a continuing desire among the Earth's peoples to live in peace. Of course, history is also written around devastating wars and conflicts that shatter such noble goals. However, there is no reason that the international system must always reflect anarchy, competition, conflict, and war. While idealist traditions embodied in classical collective security such as the League of Nations faltered, modern applications are available to those who wish to begin their inquiries into global security with the proposition that peace is possible. The diffusion of power in the twenty-first century creates a more level playing field on which individuals who wish to prioritize peace can organize and unite across borders influencing the agenda of global security. Modern idealism is, perhaps, more potent now than at any time in history. This conclusion is ironic given the nature of the severe security challenges that confront humanity. Humankind has, nevertheless, shown considerable resilience, adaptability, and optimism. It is in humanity's interests to find mechanisms to resolve the proliferating security challenges and there is no reason that people across borders cannot marshal the networks of power to serve the search for peace.

There is no guarantee that efforts to promote peace in the international system will not be violent. Moral causes continue to justify war as a primary tool for international change as was the case in Kosovo in 1999. Intervention in the name of ideals raises the dilemma of what is "moral" in the search for peace and who defines which values and principles are to be spread in the name of security. Short of war and intervention, diplomacy and economic incentives advance peaceful change. The globalization of security might even place a higher priority on such tools than the use of military power. Diplomatic and economic isolation were successful at fostering internal change in South Africa in the 1980s. This isolation contributed to the fall of the oppressive minority white government which ruled over the majority black population. This domestic political transformation resulted in the decision by the new South African government to abandon its nuclear weapons programs. Diplomatic and economic isolation contributed to Libya's decision in 2003 to abandon its nuclear ambitions. Thus the historical record shows that the peaceful evolution towards democracy can be an effective tool for managing security threats such as nuclear proliferation. There is therefore no inherent reason why such approaches cannot apply to countries like Iran and North Korea—particularly if effectively calibrated with a complementary application of military power to make diplomatic and economic carrots and sticks credible.

Among the modern conceptual tools in the search for peace, neoliberal institutionalism has been dominant since the end of the Cold War. The primary evidence to support neoliberal approaches to international security is the proliferation of international institutions that reflect cooperative security. The role of international institutions like the United Nations, NATO, and the European Union was challenged by various crises as in the Balkans and Rwanda during the 1990s. Moreover, internal debates over its future direction had, by 2005, put significant constraints on the role that the EU might play in global politics. Nonetheless, international institutions promoting cooperative security have had an important role to play by fostering transparency and information sharing that can increase security. While not always adhered to, information sharing by institutions can help state decision-makers adjust policies to reflect new realities. The more states learn about the global impact of human security and environmental security threats, for example, the more likely they may be to work together to find common solutions. The conditions of global security place a high value on good information and in this context international institutions might have an increasingly important role to play in the twenty-first century.

The globalization of economic interdependence also places considerable importance on the role of commercial liberalism. The belief that commercial interaction stimulates cooperation is deeply embedded in the idea that globalization creates mutual gains. Globalization accelerates free trade and economic interdependence. However, globalization also provides a significant voice to those who oppose its effects or see commercial liberalism as a form of structural dominance benefiting the world's wealthy. Evidence suggests that, despite such criticisms, most underdeveloped countries do not oppose globalization but rather seek to enter its processes and make gains from access to global trading markets. The biggest obstacle to the benefits of commercial liberalism could come from developed countries that create barriers to trade from underdeveloped markets. Embedded within the networks of global trade are both benefits and risks. The proliferation of technology can work to enhance the lives of billions of people worldwide. However, the networks of global trade also can serve as the means through which new forms of power can be utilized for dangerous purposes. Just as trade is the engine that drives globalization, it can also be the means through which new forms of power competition occurs and through which security threats are channeled.

The belief that democracy produces peace is a priority for many Western countries. Democracy is important for advancing the cause of human security because the system requires governments to be responsive to human needs. There is also strong evidence that shows modern democracies are not inclined to fight with each other. Indeed, democracies are more likely to place a high value on trust because of their ability to negotiate in a climate of transparency. There are, however, some dilemmas that the approach confronts. First, it is not clear how the democratic peace theory translates into an era where asymmetrical threats are common. The freedoms that democracy protects can be taken advantage of by terrorists and others who would do harm to a country. Second, as states respond to external and internal threats such as terrorism, there is a danger that democratic freedoms could be sacrificed in the name of security. Third, if the democratic peace theory is accurate, then the question arises: Is war an appropriate means of spreading the democratic peace? Fourth, some of the world's most brutal dictators emerged from constitutionally legitimate democratic processes. Finally, some groups use democratic processes to expand knowledge and help societies meet new security challenges. However, interest groups can also hinder responses to new challenges and make it more difficult for states to plan effectively for long-term security challenges.

A number of new approaches to international security seek to expose structural and practical components of the quest for power and the search for peace. Constructivism offers social explanations of why and how states formulate the policies that they advocate and how state activity both shapes and is simultaneously shaped by the international system. In this view anarchy, states, and other cornerstones of the international security system are manifestations of a reality that is conditioned upon human experience. This approach implies that there is considerable room in the international system for the power of ideas to shape the international security environment. The evolution of a transnational civil society of activists and networks of professionals that reach beyond state borders also challenges the lead role of states and international institutions in agenda-setting. Meanwhile, pacifists and peace movements provide a moral alternative to violence. Pacifism does have significant limitations, but it could prove far more powerful an asymmetric tactic than violence. Eric Weiner writes: "Pictures of unarmed Palestinians lying down before bulldozers about to raze their homes or marching up to the gates of Jewish settlements in the West Bank and Gaza—again unarmed and completely peacefully—would be powerful images that could do more to advance the Palestinian cause than 100 suicide bombings."[1]

Postmodernism along with feminism and gender analysis provide dramatic conceptual challenges to traditional thinking about international security. These approaches are important because they challenge the meaning and sources of "power" and "security" and seek to expose how these concepts are reinforced by social interactions. The postmodern framework provides an important perspective for understanding dramatic advancements in technology and communications. From the feminist and gender perspective, new ways of thinking about power relationships can expose inequalities and biases in both theories and policymaking. Other more revolutionary theories, such as Marxism, no longer hold the appeal that they did for many observers during the Cold War. However, the analysis of economic disparity as a source of conflict can explain sources of some conflict. Some of these newer frameworks for security analysis are often abstract and lack empirical application—particularly constructivism and postmodernism. These approaches therefore often fail to translate into the realm of policymaking and risk self-isolation from central debates over global security. For these, and all conceptual frameworks, it will be an important challenge to ensure that that those who work in theory and practice can communicate effectively so that each can benefit from the expertise and experience that both have.

FROM THEORY TO PRACTICE:
EDUCATION AS A STRATEGIC ASSET

The most important tool needed to begin addressing the various threats of the twenty-first century is education. Education can defeat ignorance, which breeds fear, and thus helps to place various threats in perspective while facilitating effective problem solving. For example, before September 11, 2001, terrorism experts inside and outside government persistently warned of the al Qaeda threat to the United States. However, these warnings were not relayed effectively to decision-makers or the public. Before September 11, Americans were highly vulnerable to terrorism but not worried about it. Americans were considerably safer after September 11, but their level of fear was higher. Surveys released by the National Mental Health Association in January 2004 showed that 49 percent of Americans were "worried," 41 percent were "afraid," 8 percent were emotionally upset for no apparent reason, and 7 percent had sleep problems.[2] By a 2:1 margin, Americans fear terrorism more than natural disasters. Yet statistically, any one individual is more likely to be hit by lightning than to be affected directly by a terrorist incident. Fear is, nevertheless, a real emotion and can significantly drive policy outcomes—thus also illustrating a need for thinking of education as a security priority. Exposure to facts can raise awareness of security problems which is the essential first step toward resolving them.

Understanding Threats

The case of environmental security and global warming shows the critical role that facts, knowledge, and education play as tools for both identifying and responding to global security challenges. For example, the facts show that average temperatures in Alaska, western Canada, and eastern Russia increased by as much as seven degrees between 1954 and 2004. About half of the Arctic Sea ice is projected to melt by the end of the twenty-first century.[3] The year 2004 was the fourth hottest on record and between 1990 and 2004, the ten hottest years, on average, were recorded. In some cases, exposing the economic costs of security challenges will heighten a sense of self-interest in change. In 2004, for example, hurricanes in the Caribbean and the United States did over $43 billion in damage and the first ten months of the year cost the insurance industry over $35 billion—up from $16 billion in 2003. Total economic losses, including for people without insurance, was likely to be over $90 billion.[4] In 2005, one single hurricane—Katrina—did an estimated $200 billion worth of damage to the city of New Orleans and the surrounding Gulf Coast of the United States. With global warming, the hurricane season in the Atlantic Ocean is expected to lengthen and intensify.

Conversely, when contemplating dramatic cuts in greenhouse gas emissions that cause global warming, the economic impact on modern economies also has to be considered. The United States estimates that the Kyoto Treaty to reduce carbon dioxide emissions would cost it nearly $400 billion and five million jobs.[5] Nonetheless, investments in education and retraining could redirect these jobs into areas of the economy stressing competitive skills in information technologies or into the development of alternative energy sources. Fortunately for the developed world, such educational investments are possible. In the lesser developed countries that seek to raise the basic standard of living beyond the $1–2 average daily earnings, such alternatives simply do not exist. While many developing countries would be happy to contribute to more environmentally friendly energy consumption patterns, they point out that they are being asked to pay a high price to not develop their economies in the same way that the current wealthy industrial nations did. If current owners of wealth had the right to damage the environment en route to their riches, some argue, why should that not be the case with India or China? To offset the opportunity cost of prioritizing the environment over traditional paths to development, many lesser developed countries also posit that they need offsetting financial aid.

New forms of information gathering and 24–7 mass media coverage can shine light on important international security issues. But consumers of information also have to be careful to scrutinize sources. Governments—even democracies—will purposefully manipulate information if it appears to suit their interests. In 2002, the chief of staff to the White House Council on Environment Quality (which establishes American policy on environmental issues) altered the wording of formal scientific findings done by the U.S. government on global warming. This official, Phillip Cooney, inserted phrases such as "significant and fundamental" before the word "uncertainties" in order to raise doubt about official scientific findings. Mr. Cooney inserted the word "extremely" to the sentence: "The attribution of the causes of biological and ecological changes to climate change or variability is extremely difficult." Part of the study that illustrated how global warming would affect water access and flooding included a paragraph that showed projected glacier and snow pack melt. The official entirely crossed that section out. The same official who made these changes had, before joining government, been the "climate team leader" at the American Petroleum Institute where he led the effort to fight against governmental limits on carbon dioxide emissions. The White House official who altered the documents had no scientific training.[6] When this story broke, Mr. Cooney announced a "long-planned" retirement from government—and within several days took up a position working for Exxon.

Investment in education that stresses science and technology is critical to achieving a balance between environmental and energy security pressures.

Investing in research and the development of energy sources that burn cleaner, while finding ways to sift excess carbon dioxide out of the atmosphere, can also be an important form of slowing global warming. New forms of transportation will also contribute to a balance between the environment and energy consumption. The United States invested $8 billion into climate change research between 2001 and 2004. However, technology alone will not solve the problem of global climate change. Hard political and economic choices also require leadership that educates as to the nature of the problem and the reasons for associated sacrifice. As the head of NASA's Goddard Institute for Space Studies, James E. Hanson, said, "As the evidence gathers, you would hope they would be flexible," referring to the United States government. "You can't wait another decade" to cut emissions of carbon dioxide, according to Hanson.[7] Eventually, the demands of international economic competition could force the United States and other countries to adjust energy consumption behavior. As businesses in Europe and elsewhere become more environmentally friendly, they can gain competitive advantages—also costing the United States economic power. For example, as gasoline prices skyrocketed in 2005, sales of large, U.S.-made automobiles dropped by 24 percent for General Motors in September 2005, relative to September 2004, and by 20 percent for Ford Motor Company during that same period. For Japanese automakers, which generally produce small and fuel-efficient cars, sales increased 10 to 12 percent during that same time period. The Japanese company Honda had a 25 percent increase in sales of its gasoline-electric hybrid Civic model and sales of the hybrid Toyota Prius almost doubled.[8]

As this global warming example shows, when security is placed within a global context, a range of priorities emerges that can be very different from those stressed when states conceive of security in uniquely national terms. Approximately 8,000 Africans die every day from AIDS and globally ten million children die every year from preventable and curable diseases. These facts rarely make the front pages of the world's major newspapers or appear on *CNN*, *MSNBC*, or *FOXNEWS*. Terrorism, which has prompted seemingly endless media attention, on average kills several hundred people a year worldwide. If one were to rank threats in terms of the capacity to affect the lives of tens of millions of people, first order priorities are the risk of a war between India and Pakistan, conflict in Asia, transnational disease and worst-case environmental scenarios. Terrorism does, of course, require very high-level priority given the deadly mix of religious fanaticism, weapons of mass destruction, and the proven willingness of terrorists to conduct extreme and barbaric attacks against civilian populations.

As terrorism with weapons of mass destruction is a significant concern, facts also help to make judgments as to how to address the problem with effective policy. For example, the United States spent more money every three days in Iraq during 2004 than it had in the previous three years combined to secure its own 361 seaports. These ports are the primary means through which a terrorist group might get a nuclear weapon into the United States.[9] America had, by 2006, committed $300 billion to Iraq, a relatively prosperous country sitting on one of the world's largest oil reserves. Yet the United States could have solved the problem of insecure nuclear weapons in the former Soviet Union with an expenditure of $30 billion spread out over ten years.[10] Meanwhile, the United States has moved forward to deploy national missile defenses. A fully functional missile defense shield, should one ever work, could eventually cost $250 billion. Yet national missile defenses will do nothing to stop nuclear proliferation from the former Soviet Union and nothing to stop terrorists from infiltrating America's ports with a nuclear bomb.

Beyond the concern over terrorists with nuclear weapons, there remains a growing demand for states to attain nuclear status. In the next several decades there may be strong incentives to get nuclear deterrents in Taiwain, South Korea, Japan, Brazil, Argentina, Iran, and Saudi Arabia. Meanwhile, the stability of nuclear owner Pakistan was in significant question by 2005. There is, of course, no predetermined reason why humankind must aspire to keep nuclear weapons. Why, for example, must a country like France have nuclear weapons other than prestige? If South Africa, Belarus, Ukraine, Kazakhstan, and Libya could abandon their desire to have nuclear weapons, France could also. If the United States can, according to the former general who headed its strategic nuclear forces, eliminate its nuclear weapons and still deter and defeat any enemy in the world with conventional power, why should it keep its nuclear weapons? Of course, there is a powerful and persuasive counterargument—that the technology cannot be eliminated and nuclear deterrence prevents war.

If abandoning nuclear weapons is not realistic, there is a middle ground available that would increase global security. For example, states that currently possess nuclear weapons could de-alert their arsenals from hair-trigger status to prevent accidental launches.[11] There is no reason why nuclear powers could not agree to remove warheads from missiles, keeping them verifiably secured near a missile. Through on-site verification and satellite surveillance, compliance with this approach to arms control would increase security and retain basic deterrence. Meanwhile, states like India and Pakistan are going to have to learn to live with the bomb and make nuclear deterrence more effective—while avoiding unnecessarily expensive and wasteful arms races. Small steps, such as an agreement in late 2004 between India and Pakistan to develop a hotline for direct communication in a crisis could facilitate further confidence-building measures.[12] India and Pakistan might agree that they each benefit from deterrence, enhance early warning systems and other tools to prevent accidental nuclear war, and limit the growth in weapons. From there, diplomacy might be engaged to address the root causes of their conflict.

Education and Action for Global Security

Education is perhaps the most important strategic tool to foster long-term solutions to the many global security threats. More educated younger adults are more likely to delay having children, avoid dangerous sexual practices that spread HIV/AIDS, and develop the tools necessary to find local solutions to their own problems. The underdeveloped world, however, confronts significant difficulties in providing the most basic aspects of education. In India, for example, on any given day about 25 percent of teachers are absent from school. Daily teacher absenteeism is 27 percent in Uganda, 17 percent in Zambia, and 16 percent in Bangladesh. In a developed country like the United States, daily teacher absenteeism is 5–6 percent. The problem is especially challenging for a large country like India which contains 34 percent of the world's illiterate population. Among the reasons that many teachers in India do not report for work are the facilities—of which over 50 percent have a leaking roof, 89 percent lack functional toilets, and 50 percent have no water supply. In addition to teaching children, some schools are used as cattle sheds, police camps, teacher residences, or for drying cow dung cakes.[13]

The problem of education in the underdeveloped world goes further than merely investing in school infrastructure. For example, by creating more educational opportunities for training health care workers and creating monetary incentives to stay in their country of origin to practice medicine, underdeveloped countries can begin to conquer their own human security challenges. There was, by 2005, a shortage of an estimated four million healthcare workers in the underdeveloped world. This shortage was not for a lack of ability. There were more Malawian doctors, for example, working in Manchester, England, than there were actually working in Malawi. Of 600 doctors trained in Zambia, only fifty had stayed in that country. In Uganda, there is only one nurse for every 11,000 people and in Haiti, only one per 10,000. In Africa, in order to even begin to grapple with the HIV/AIDS crisis, an additional one million new health workers are needed.[14] Educating people to provide such services, combined with incentives to apply those skills in their local communities, are examples of key strategic investments with relatively low cost and high return.

By 2005, some 125 million children in the world did not go to school every day. The United Nations estimates that 1 billion children are effectively denied a childhood. Many of these children are forced into labor, slavery, and prostitution.[15] In Pakistan, for example, 11 million girls are denied basic education while the government spends six times more on military purchases than on primary schools. There are already creative proposals available to address such challenges. In 2004, the Global Campaign for Education advocated a Global Action Plan to assure access to primary school for every child in the world by 2015 with a projected cost of $8 billion a year. This would be complemented by coordinated debt relief to poor countries, increased aid for basic education, changes in International Monetary Fund policies to protect education spending during economic crises, increased investment in education, and changes in national policies by developing countries.[16] Aside from the economic gains to be made by advancing commercial liberalism, such an investment could also be essential to winning the hearts and minds necessary for undermining asymmetric threats. By 2005, the United States had increased its overall spending on defense, homeland security, and combating terrorism by $160 billion in two years. By 2005, the United States had committed over $300 billion to its invasion and occupation of Iraq. Some cost estimates suggest U.S. expenses in Iraq would total $600 billion by 2010. One can only imagine what an investment of a relatively minor $8 billion a year for global education could do for America's declining international image. It would cost a combined $110 billion over ten years to secure all the nuclear weapons material in the former Soviet Union and to provide primary educational services for all of the children in the world. This is one-third what the United States spent in just the first three years of its occupation of Iraq.

Already, low-cost investments in human and environmental security are showing benefits. Global health trends have improved with the proliferation of more advanced medical care. In 1950, 25 percent of infants in underdeveloped countries died. By the mid-1990s, that rate was 6 percent. In 1974, only 5 percent of the world's infants received vaccinations, by the mid-1990s, this number rose to 90 percent. In 1996, 2.5 million fewer children died than in 1990. Each year, two million deaths are prevented by measles vaccinations alone.[17] The combined impacts of population growth and poverty have also been addressed by general improvements in international women's rights. Since the United Nations sponsored an international conference on women's issues in 1994, 151 poor countries surveyed by the UN Population Fund have implemented laws or put policies into action which recognize reproductive rights. Now, 61 percent of couples worldwide use modern forms of contraception. This is an increase of 55 percent in ten years.[18]

These examples show that relatively inexpensive educational efforts and programmatic investments can yield significant improvements in human security. On the other hand, in some key issue areas, low-cost opportunities to forestall current and pending crises are also being ignored. With nearly two million people dying each year from tuberculosis worldwide, the World Health Organization has set targets of a 50 percent reduction in infection rates by 2015. This would cost a total of $37 billion to achieve. This averages to expenditure of about $3.7 billion each year between 2005 and 2015. However, by 2005, the donor countries were only spending a combined $1 billion a year, leaving a $2.5 billion gap in required funding for programs to eliminate this preventable and curable disease which takes a particularly brutal toll on children.[19]

Meanwhile, new actors in international politics might form the basis for an emerging transnational civil society that advances human security priorities. In May 2005, a network of 132 American cities was formed by their respective mayors representing twenty-nine million U.S. citizens in thirty-five states. The mayors agreed that they would strive to meet emissions requirements under the Kyoto Protocol on global warming even though the United States as a country had rejected the treaty.[20] Local city governments also began shaping a transnational alliance by signing the "Urban Environmental Accords" in June 2005. Meeting in San Francisco, the mayors of Zurich, Istanbul, Melbourne, Seattle, and dozens of other cities agreed to establish principles that would reduce carbon dioxide emissions. These accords also commit participating cities to expand public transportation and to achieve access for all citizens to safe drinking water by 2015. The recommendations would also commit the signatories to increase the use of renewable energy to provide 10 percent of peak electric demand by 2012.[21] While these transnational urban accords are not legally binding, they reflect local leadership that is not waiting for national governments to resolve challenges to human and environmental security.

Education and National Power

In this era of global security, states that cultivate a citizenry that can work effectively with people across borders are likely to gain significant strategic advantages. International communication and travel breaks down traditional national security barriers so that ideas can flow across borders freely. Yet just as the Internet can be a door opener, communities can become isolated from other networks if only like-minded people are talking to each other. A new communications divide could emerge over the Internet with an English pool, Spanish-speaking pool, Chinese, Arabic, etc. Such communication barriers could bring about a virtual isolation of civilizations and reduce the potential benefits of global communication.[22] Societies that have the capacity to integrate within and break through such barriers will likely have significant advantages in the twenty-first century. Moreover, language skills combined with sociological understanding of other cultures are becoming critical tools of national security. For example, being able to work with and read Arabic websites which might be used for terrorist communication is essential if new threats are to be confronted.

A country like the United States would benefit dramatically from a major investment in language programs at the primary, secondary, and university level—with a particular emphasis on Arabic, Spanish, and Chinese. Three years after September 11, 2001, the United States still had thousands of intercepted documents from possible terrorist sources waiting to be translated. The Central Intelligence Agency, however, had turned away many qualified Arab linguists who were patriotic American citizens but had relatives overseas. Their foreign relatives thus were making full background checks difficult. The Department of Defense was forced under existing U.S. law to fire homosexual linguists and translators. Overall, the American intelligence community had, nearly four years after September 11, lagged far behind goals established by the Congress to expand expertise in Arabic, Chinese, Farsi, and Pashtu.[23] This difficulty in recruiting talented agents for domestic intelligence is a critical problem for counter-terrorism defenses—as Britain discovered tragically during July 2005. In major attacks on the London transport system, "homegrown" British citizens engaged in suicide bombings to express sympathy with foreign terrorist movements. Penetrating into the organization of such groups will thus be a critical mission for future counter-terrorist operations. In the United Kingdom, the job requirements, updated in 2004, for an MI5 (domestic intelligence) surveillance officer were: be able to blend in, average height, build, and appearance, be able to remain alert during periods of inactivity, and be flexible and able to cope with frequent disruption. An MI5 linguist's requirements included: mother tongue knowledge or honors degree equivalent in required language, British by birth or naturalization with close links to the UK, and good hearing. The MI5 would face a significant challenge in that only 4 percent of its staff was black or Asian.[24]

Interdisciplinary education, integrated into international security policy mechanisms can provide unique opportunities to enhance national security. Expertise in physics, biology, geology, geography, medicine, communications, language, math, and information technology are all areas where applied skills are essential for national security. For example, mathematics and information technology skills can be used for intelligence activity such as codebreaking and sifting through the massive volumes of security data. By linking data such as names and emails from suspected or captured terrorists, their communications might be traced to a particular location. This can help to expose, infiltrate, or disrupt a terrorist network. Abstract mathematical modeling also can help counter-terrorist organizations better understand how best to attack terrorist networks and to disrupt their communications. Mathematical models can even help to anticipate how, where, and when terrorist groups might attack. At Carnegie Mellon University, laboratory researchers have built simulations of Hamas and al Qaeda by placing publicly available information about these organizations into a database. The data is then searched for patterns and relationships between individuals which helps to identify both known and unknown leadership nodes within a terrorist organization.[25]

Beyond technical skills, creative, unconventional thinking is a vital national security asset. In early 2002, the U.S. National Security Adviser, Condoleezza Rice, noted that no one could have imagined people taking airplanes and using them as missiles against buildings. Yet imagining just this kind of challenge was at the very nature of her job description. Reflecting the shift from the Cold War era to the post-9/11 era, the Bush Administration was well staffed with some of the most experienced foreign and national security policy experts in America. Yet, they were also experts for a Cold War world which no longer existed and therefore had to relearn on the job. Dr. Rice's previous government experience was as an expert on the Soviet military—an institution that in 2001 no longer existed. The opposition Democrats had done no better in articulating a new form of twenty-first century leadership. A new generation of creative thinkers working beyond partisan politics is necessary so that asymmetrical challenges and other nonconventional threats can be met with workable policy solutions. The ability of states to train their citizens to work effectively with advanced technology, but also to think "outside the box" will be an important measure of national security in the twenty-first century. Often maligned for promoting cultural and political conformity, China is increasingly applying strategic approaches to education that encourage initiative. As the journalist Tom Friedman has shown, in 1998, Microsoft gave IQ tests to 2,000 of China's leading engineers and scientists and opted to hire 20 of them. By 2005, Microsoft had expanded to have 200 full-time Chinese researchers employed. Friedman quotes the Chinese vice-minister of education as saying that promoting "creative thinking and entrepreneurship are the exact issues we are putting attention to today."[26]

Despite the renewed focus on foreign policy in the United States since the September 11, 2001 attacks and the 2003 invasion of Iraq, there remains a significant lack of public attention to important details regarding America's place in the world. For example, a survey of foreign policy attitudes just before the 2004 election showed that the majority of President Bush's supporters incorrectly believed that he favored including labor and environmental standards in trade agreements (84 percent), and the United States being part of the Comprehensive Test Ban Treaty (69 percent), the International Criminal Court (66 percent), the treaty banning land mines (72 percent), and the Kyoto Treaty on global warming (51 percent). These were policies more attributable to Bush's opponent, Sen. John Kerry. Among Bush voters, 41 percent believed that the president planned to do more research until capabilities were proven before deploying missile defense—a program he had already begun deploying with no evidence of proven capabilities.[27]

The United States faces significant challenges to its primacy in international education—which is a key foundation of its global power. As other states invest strategically in education, they can level the playing field of global security. Federal testing guidelines intended to increase American school quality often have the impact of giving teachers incentives to "teach to the test" rather than cultivating creative problem-solving. Facing steep budget cuts and lack of funding, American public schools have often had to consider (and implement) elimination of programs in the arts and sports. Yet the creative and performing arts and sport activities cultivate creative thinking, leadership, and teamwork skills. In the crucial area of science and technology America has declined significantly. The percentage of American jobs requiring a Ph.D. in science and technology that are filled by foreign workers rose from 24 percent to 38 percent between 1990 and 2000. Due to new opportunities provided by globalization, many of these workers are finding better career opportunities in their native countries, leaving a vacuum that American education is not prepared to fill. American high school seniors rank below their equivalent age students in seventeen other countries in math and science, and last among sixteen countries tested for physics competency. Only 26 percent of high school graduates in 2003 scored well enough on college entrance exams to pass an entry-level university science course. The United States also lacks qualified science teachers. Among high school teachers that teach a science class, 28 percent do not have a special training in the sciences. In physical sciences, 60 percent of teachers do not have training in one or another particular area of sciences that they teach.[28]

Fewer international students are coming to study in America. In 2003–2004, there was a decline of 5 percent among undergraduate foreign students in the United States. This was the first decline in total enrollments among foreign students in the United States since 1971. The United States continues to attract a large portion of its students from Asia, though those numbers were also in decline. Even more problematic was a steep decline in students from the Islamic world, which is where the United States has most needed to influence hearts and minds in its war against terrorism. In 2002–2003, the United States suffered a decline of 10 percent and in 2003–2004 a decline of 9 percent among students from the Middle East.[29]

Foreign students brought $13 billion a year into the American economy by 2004. Yet, foreign students have been increasingly avoiding the United States because of real or perceived immigration-visa difficulties, a perception that foreign students are not welcome in the United States, and because of aggressive recruitment from universities in other countries. As Joseph S. Nye of Harvard University notes, the United States is not producing enough scientists and engineers to meet its domestic needs. This gap is filled by foreign students remaining and working in American industries after they graduate. But also, those students and graduates eventually return home to their countries and carry with them American ideals, values, and have positive stories to tell about their American experiences.[30] Similar problems exist with attracting top scholars, scientists, and other experts to take up residences in American universities. This decline is also manifested in high school foreign student exchanges, which have seen a sharp decline in students coming to America for extended stays. In this case the reason appears to be a lack of ability or willingness among local schools and host families to pay the costs combined with a general decline in American funding for such programs.[31]

CRISIS MANAGEMENT IN THE TWENTY-FIRST CENTURY

To manage the security challenges of the twenty-first century, states are going to have to balance investments in traditional defense with more comprehensive strategic concepts. Increasingly, states will require highly mobile and precise military forces combined with large concentrations of military and professional civilian personnel for deployment in peace operations and nation-building. Troops are going to have to be equipped and trained to conduct combat and noncombat operations in circumstances where they are attacked through asymmetrical means ranging from small arms and roadside bombs to nuclear, chemical, and biological weapons. Militaries that have not been dramatically transformed risk growing irrelevant in that technical advances or asymmetrical threats such as terrorism cannot be easily defeated with conventional military power.[32] Additionally, states are going to have to plan for complex emergencies. Some natural events, like the December 2004 tsunami in south Asia, can be unpredictable, catastrophic, and have serious security implications. Other crises are far more predictable. For example, eventually the American policy of containment of North Korea might lead to a Soviet-style collapse there. What then is the operations plan for preventing chaos from emerging in the context of a state collapse where nuclear weapons are present? What are the new shocks to the international system that have serious security implications that might be averted, or lessened in their severity, if action is taken today? These are the kinds of questions that responsible decision-makers will be required to ask of their strategic planners in the decades ahead.

Waging Wars and Winning the Peace

Modern warfighting is likely to involve a range of tactical means toward defeating an enemy. Nonetheless, the meaning of "war" also has taken on a new dimension as the tactics of warfare will increasingly rely less on conventional military power and more on technological advantages at one level, and asymmetrical attacks at another. Some states will increasingly look for ways to combine both conventional and asymmetrical tactics as the battlefield of modern warfare transforms into the battlespace of modern society. For countries like the United States there might be a temptation to focus on technological advantages in warfare that will allow it to engage enemies at a great distance with precision weaponry and few troops. The dilemma in such an approach is that there is little evidence to suggest that advanced technology will be decisive in modern wars. Even the most technologically advanced country likely will still need well-trained and hardened "boots on the ground." However, regular armies will increasingly be needed not only for ground combat, but for postwar public security and nation-building operations.

Major military establishments like that of the United States will take time, perhaps a generation, to alter concepts and capabilities. As an example, in 1989, strategic planners in the U.S. military wrote about the emerging threat of terrorism and anti-American insurgency warfare that would define future military engagement. These planners warned that the military had to adapt and that its heavy investment in advanced technology would face serious limitations in the battlefield against terrorist and insurgent fighters. Dubbed "Fourth Generation Warfare" these planners noted that, while the United States spends $500 million on a stealth bomber airplane, a "terrorist stealth bomber" would be a car that looks like every other car—but that has a bomb in it. Despite the fact that this kind of attack was responsible for most American deaths in Iraq, the United States continued with plans to invest more than $120 billion by 2015 in digitally linked vehicles, weapons, and unmanned aircraft that are all based on conventional warfighting concepts.[33]

The U.S. Army gave its soldiers in Iraq a "revised" field manual for fighting insurgents in November 2004—though it had actually not been updated in more than ten years. An army lieutenant colonel who spent a year in Iraq fighting against insurgents concluded, "If you know your enemy and if you know yourself, you'll never lose. . . . We know about half of what we should about the enemy, and we don't know ourselves. . . . We can't figure out what kind of Army we want to be."[34] The military analysts writing in 1989 concluded, "Mass, of men or fire power, will no longer be an overwhelming factor. . . . In fact, mass may become a disadvantage, as it will be easy to target. . . . Small highly maneuverable, agile forces will tend to dominate."[35] In some cases it seems that the military so disliked the idea of having to wage combat against insurgents, particularly as a result of the Vietnam experience, that it instead opted to avoid preparation for that kind of conflict. Moreover, some aspects of this resistance to change could have been budget driven. Defeating insurgencies must be done politically—meaning more money for diplomacy and economic strategies—not high-tech bomber planes.

Getting into a military conflict and defeating an enemy can be accomplished with a reasonable amount of conventional force applied by modern militaries. The more difficult challenge for states facing complex security threats is how to sustain the peace after military intervention. If the peace cannot be won after a military intervention, then the chances are that waging war in the first place was not worth it. As Carl Bildt, a diplomat with considerable experience in dealing with such contingencies, concluded, there are seven key lessons to apply in the context of state-collapse: (1) it is imperative to establish a secure environment very fast; (2) the central challenge is not reconstruction, but state-building; (3) to build a state, you need to know what state to build; (4) there must be an early focus on the preconditions for long-term economic growth; (5) there has to be a benevolent regional environment; (6) the greater the international support, the easier the process; and (7) nation-building takes a longer time, and requires more resources, than most initially believe.[36]

In such postintervention peace support operations, militaries are engaged mainly in supporting nonmilitary missions. This shift can create an additional dilemma if a military becomes overburdened in missions beyond warfighting. A military can lose its capacity to fight and win wars if these core missions are diluted. As retired American 4-star general Anthony Zinni writes, "We have to come to grips with the issue of an appropriate ethos for our service members. . . . Are they still warriors requiring values much like those of their uniformed forefathers, or have technology and changing social attitudes made that outdated? It is hard to imagine that the coming age of cyberwarriors and remote control battle has removed the need for a warrior culture."[37] Moreover, chains of command also might find it necessary to reward risk takers and mavericks who innovate in the battlefield and thus gain promotion not by simply saying yes to powerful commanders, but rather by challenging existing assumptions. Of course, language and cultural training would help too.

The military can make important contributions addressing a range of modern security challenges from deterrence to assisting with the consequences of environmental catastrophe. However, many of the security challenges of the twenty-first century are best handled by civilian means, civilian-police means, or a combination of civilian-police-military means. Nonetheless, it is tempting to invest in and use the resource that one has, thus increased pressure is put on the military to react to new kinds of security contingencies. In fall 2005,

U.S. President George Bush suggested that there might be a significant domestic role for the army in the event of an avian flu pandemic in the United States. There are two problems in this scenario, however. First, just because the military is available, does not mean it is the best resource; and second, the military's overuse in nontraditional security missions could dilute its overall effectiveness. The idea of using the military in this kind of domestic role was described by the director of the National Center for Disaster Preparedness at Columbia University, Dr. Irwin Redlener, as an "extraordinarily Draconian measure" that would not be necessary if the right resources were invested in a sound public health system and a capacity for rapid vaccine production. Dr. Redlener concluded that the translation of this kind of application of military power was "martial law in the United States."[38] The need for well-trained multinational police forces which can deploy to regional crises locations, provide immediate public security, and train local personnel for long-term security missions is especially urgent. The most serious planning in this regard has emerged in the European Union. In 1997, the European countries assumed responsibility for the rebuilding of the Albanian police force after the state collapsed there. In 2004, the European Union announced plans to create a 3,000 person gendarmerie force for global deployment including police from France, Italy, Spain, Portugal, and the Netherlands. The plan is to have a core of 800 to 900 members available for rapid deployment within thirty days and a reserve of 2,300 reinforcements on call.

Squaring the Circle: Unilateralism versus Multilateralism

Postwar peace operations and nation-building are likely to be increasingly necessary to ensure that human security problems do not spread and create added instability. As it is, no single country in the world is in a position to police the map of global security alone. Such crises will require states to organize early-response mechanisms with well-organized, well-trained teams in integrated command structures which are able to address civilian, police, and military challenges. Heavy demands will require enhanced capacity for securing humanitarian relief, demilitarization programs and small-arms disarmament programs for refugee camps and safe-havens, protection for internally displaced peoples, provision of public safety in refugee camps, provision of staff and monitors for elections, and monitoring of human rights in states that are rebuilding or building their governmental structures.[39] It will likely be necessary to conduct such operations simultaneously in multiple geographic locations around the world. These kinds of challenges cannot be handled alone and will inevitably have to be organized multilaterally, and with clear command and control, logistical support, and reinforcements. Such military operations also must be trained to act in concert with nongovernmental organizations and have the cultural and language skills necessary to work with, train, and support local officials. All of these challenges share one common trait—that they cannot be easily achieved with unilateral state action. Nevertheless, for the very powerful countries in the world, the temptation to avoid the hard work of building alliances and coalitions might take a backseat to the speedier and seemingly easier path of unilateral military action during crises. While unilateralism is a strategic choice available to any country, policymakers must also be prepared to integrate a hard sense of realism as to what is, and is not, possible when undertaking what one analyst refers to as "strategic adventures."[40]

The 2003 American invasion and postwar effort in Iraq illustrates a particularly significant security challenge regarding military intervention in crisis situations. The United States launched a preemptive war against Iraq with a coalition of the willing, though ultimately Washington provided 90 percent of the military power, with most of the rest provided by Britain. The United States appeared to have found that, in terms of military action, it was easier to fight alone, without the political and operational constraints and inefficiencies allies can create. The United States had the ability to conduct a military invasion without first obtaining legitimacy in the eyes of the international community via a UN authorization of force. In fall 2002, the UN Security Council authorized a resolution that allowed for punishment if Iraq did not comply with various UN resolutions. However, in the eyes of much of the world, by not gaining a second resolution explicitly authorizing force, the United States and its allies had acted without the legitimacy of the international community. This approach worked well enough for the United States in terms of the limited objective of removing the government of Saddam Hussein. Having done that, the United States also inherited responsibility for Iraq's future. The next several years would be spent struggling with the tragic burden of lives and treasure being lost—exacerbated by a lack of support from the international community.

How states will accommodate the tension between the short-term efficiency of acting unilaterally, versus the need for allies to win the peace and share burdens is a critical puzzle. States cannot wait forever for international organizations like the United Nations to agree to take action in a crisis. States can also ill-afford to act without the legitimacy that an institution like the United Nations provides. The United Nations has tried to generate thinking among its members with suggested guidelines for intervention in crises including defining security to include wars, failing states, weapons of mass destruction, but also to include poverty, transnational disease, and environmental disasters. It also recommended that the Security Council be enlarged from fifteen to twenty-four members and be given more flexibility to authorize international intervention in crises. Recommended criteria for authorizing UN-sponsored intervention would include identifying a clear threat, making the purpose of intervention clear, using military power as a last resort, adopting proportionate means relative to the task at hand, and providing a full assessment in advance of potential consequences of action.[41]

GLOBAL SECURITY: ONE STEP FORWARD— TWO STEPS BACK?

At the moment when international society is only beginning to grapple with the implications of the Internet and advanced communications, it is increasingly expanding the dimensions of strategic engagement into new spheres of technology. For example, the United States has moved forward with plans to test a Common Aero Vehicle (CAV), a hypersonic glider with a global range that can carry 1,000 pounds of munitions or sensors. Such munitions could include penetrating conventional warheads, small smart bombs, or other precision munitions. With a velocity of mach 10–15, the CAV would be able to maneuver so as to avoid flying directly over sensitive locations while having an ability to strike within ninety minutes anywhere on the planet.[42] This program moved forward with no serious public discussion of the moral or ethical implications of such a capacity, how it might be used, whether it could be deployed inside the United States against domestic targets, or the risks of this technology proliferating once developed. In 1945, technology yielded the revolutionary breakthrough of the atomic bomb—a device very few in public would have imagined at the time, but with extraordinary consequences. The possibilities for future technological advancement appear to be limited only by the extent of the imagination and the limits of science and technology. Humankind has the opportunity, though with increasingly less time, to assess in advance the extent to which it wants to make its dreams for the future reality—or to ensure that new realities are constructed in ways that produce peace, and not less security.

States are going to have to place increasing priority on managing asymmetrical threats—particularly international terrorism. Terrorism could become less of a threat over time. Several historical terrorist organizations have abandoned violence and sought political legitimacy, including the main elements of the Irish Republican Army, the Palestine Liberation Organization, and the Kurdish Workers Party. In June 2005, the Basque separatist movement in Spain—ETA—announced that it was no longer going to target Spanish politicians. Meanwhile, Spain indicated that it might enter a dialogue with ETA if it were to lay down its arms completely. States that face asymmetrical threats might evaluate their own policies in light of the new threats that they face. A state can ill-afford to make concessions to terrorists. Once that is done, only more terrorism will be encouraged. It is, however, reasonable to conclude that the terrorists who attacked the United States do not simply hate Americans for their freedoms. Much of the animosity in the world toward the United States exists because America is seen as being selective about the freedoms that it advocates.

The former top al Qaeda expert in the Central Intelligence Agency concludes that al Qaeda and its supporters hate America not for what it is, but rather because of its policies. These policies were thought to include unquestioned support for Israel, America's presence on the Arabian peninsula, and support for authoritarian governments which are pro-U.S. but which oppress their Muslim populations.[43] The United States will have to engage political and economic means as the key to winning the war on terrorism. However, because the enemy is absolutist, these tools must be employed not to directly tame a group like al Qaeda, but rather to outflank it. Therefore, central to winning the war on terrorism is the ability to "think outside the box"—by mobilizing the intellectual infrastructure of society.[44] Three years after America was attacked, it had yet to develop a grand strategy for winning the war in which it was now engaged. An analyst from within the U.S. Defense Department concluded that it may be misleading to call the "global war on terrorism" (GWOT) a "war" because the role of the military in it is unclear, and "to the extent that the GWOT is directed at the phenomenon of terrorism, as opposed to flesh-and-blood terrorist organizations, it sets itself up for strategic failure."[45]

Because terrorists cannot always be found and identified, defensive measures are necessary so that modern technology, such as an airplane, is no longer vulnerable for use against civilian populations. The simplest technological adaptation regarding airline security was put in place right after September 11, 2001—lock the doors to the airplane cockpit. Anticipating the next challenge is essential, and thus it is important that airlines are, for example, investing in missile defense for their planes given the proliferation of antiaircraft missile technology. One such system would work by placing a canoe-shaped pod underneath an airliner toward the back of the plane. This system would function without any action needing to be taken by the pilot or crew. Sensors would scan in ultraviolet range in all directions for heat sources from threats. A processor would then receive signals from the sensors, and determine whether or not the threat is real. If a threat is determined, the missile would be tracked and a laser then fired to jam the guidance system of a threatening missile.[46] Innovations in shipping container inspections also offer significant technological promise for increasing security. For example, as Stephen Flynn and Lawrence Wein demonstrate, in Hong Kong and Singapore technology is used to photograph the inside of a box while screening for radioactive mate-

rial, while gamma-ray images of the contents, including identifying thick lead materials that might hide radiation, are created as loading trucks move toward ships at 10 miles per hour—all at a cost of $7.00 per container. In order to successfully dissuade a terrorist, for example, from exporting dirty bomb material, inspectors would need to analyze on average 20 to 30 percent of imagery collected. While such technology might increase the chance of detection of radioactive material, it would also serve to create a forensic database to track back material to a source in the event of detection or any successful attack.[47]

No society is ever likely to achieve a situation of perfect security. Some basic things should, however, be done right. Canada, for example, manages to lose or have stolen 25,000 passports every year. In spite of allocating, in 2001, $7.7 billion over five years for counterterrorism, basic information about missing or stolen passports still was not being transmitted to Canadian border control officers three years later.[48] The American government has increased spending on biological defenses by eighteen times, up to $7.6 billion for 2004, and yet the United States remains almost completely unprepared to manage a large-scale biological terrorism event.[49] Conversely, the New York City Police Department has made innovative strategic and tactical investments which make New York as secure a city as it can be. Police in New York have trained for crisis scenarios ranging from having to board cruise ships in the harbor to conducting rescue missions in Midtown theaters. The city has also begun a pilot program developed in collaboration with the Lawrence Livermore National Laboratory to test the air across the city for biological agents constantly for over one hundred different bacteria and viruses. Until this program is fully functional, the city relies on what thirty other major American cities use, a system called *Biowatch* which uses air monitors to search for about fifteen different bacteria or viruses. This system is limited because it does not provide instant detection. Rather, this system provides filters, which must be collected each day and then tested in labs. New York City has also prepared a citywide plan for getting antibiotics or vaccines to every resident in the event of a widespread biological attack. Local police officers have also obtained federal top-secret security clearances so that they can engage in information-sharing regarding particular threats.[50]

Every emerging global security challenge addressed in this book has some form of solution readily available for decision-makers who choose to act. Developed states, for example, have the power and the resources to substantially alter the dynamic of everyday life for citizens in the underdeveloped world. However, before such actions are taken, a broader understanding of mutual security interests will likely have to take hold in the developed world. A rather simple, pragmatic, and effective approach offered by the United Kingdom in June 2005 illustrates how states can reconcile near- and long-term strategic responses to global security challenges. Britain called for a doubling of European aid to Africa—up to $80 billion by 2010, an end to restrictive trade subsidies that penalize Africa, and 100 percent debt relief. While Britain took the lead on this process, the first response of the American president George W. Bush was that the plan "doesn't fit our budgetary process."[51] Developed states also have the information that they need to curb the major causes of global warming—but they must make the key choice to act. Finding means to sustain access to freshwater and cleaner means of burning energy are going to be more difficult. In these cases, humankind must adapt, innovate, or risk a very dark future. But some problems require minimal sacrifice to achieve solutions. In December 2005, the United Nations launched its largest annual appeal to raise $4.7 billion for programming to help victims of war, famine, and natural disasters in twenty-six countries during 2006. While this was the largest humanitarian aid drive in the history of the United Nations, a senior U.N. official noted, "We are asking exactly the amount of 48 hours of military spending in this world, or we're asking for the equivalent of two cups of coffee per rich person."[52] The world caught but a glimpse of what could go severely wrong on September 11, 2001. The challenge to the citizens of the world is to begin working to ensure that September 11 was the beginning of the end of these security threats, the last shot of a dying age.

CONCLUSION

People who live in the more secure parts of the world will have more opportunities than others to shape the international security environment for the positive, and it is likely to be from there that much of the initiative and resources for change will come. Perhaps being fortunate enough to live in secure conditions creates a special obligation to heed the call of international or national public service. Whether it is in the military, as a diplomat, as an intelligence analyst, a peacecorps volunteer, a customs worker, firefighter, policeman, teacher, or politician, public and community service is a key place to begin making an individual contribution to increasing global security. International organizations, nongovernmental organizations, universities, research institutes, sciences, laboratories, doctors, nurses, information systems managers, linguists, community groups, or even just one person with a pen and paper—each has the power to engage in the search for peace in this new era. The globalization of security allows opportunities for every individual to prove to those who would use the networks of global power for evil that they will be outdone by someone advancing the search for peace.

NOTES

1. Eric Weiner, "Palestinians Need a Gandhi, Not a New Arafat," *Los Angeles Times*, November 10, 2004.

2. National Mental Health Association, "Public Perceptions on the Mental Health Effects of Terrorism," January 2004, at www.nmha.org/newsroom/surveys.cfm (accessed Spring 2005).

3. "Arctic Climate Impact Assessment," November 2004, at www.amap.no/acia (accessed Spring 2005).

4. "2004 Was Fourth-Warmest Year on Record," *Associated Press*, December 15, 2004; and "Press Release: Global Temperature in 2004 Fourth Warmest," World Meteorological Association, no. 718 (December 15, 2004).

5. "Climate Report Leaves U.S. Policy Unchanged," *Associated Press*, November 10, 2004.

6. Andrew C. Revkin, "Official Played Down Emissions' Links to Global Warming," *New York Times*, June 8, 2005.

7. Juliet Eilperin, "Climate Talks Bring Bush's Policy to Fore," *Washington Post*, December 5, 2004.

8. Sholnn Freeman, "Truck and SUV Sales Plunge as Gas Prices Rise," *Washington Post*, October 4, 2005.

9. Stephen Flynn, "The Neglected Homefront," *Foreign Affairs* 83, no. 5 (September/October 2004): 20–33.

10. Walter Pincus, "Panel Urges $30 billion to Secure Russian Nuclear Arms," *Washington Post*, January 11, 2001.

11. Robert D. Green, *Fast Track to Zero Nuclear Weapons* (Cambridge, Mass.: Middle Powers Initiative, 1999).

12. "Pakistan and India to Start Nuclear Hotline, No Deal on Missile Tests," *AFP*, December 15, 2004.

13. Diana Coulter, "India's Troubling Truants: Teachers," *Christian Science Monitor*, December 20, 2004.

14. Joint Learning Institute, "Human Resources for Health: Overcoming the Crisis," at www.globalhealthtrust.org/ (accessed Spring 2005).

15. "The State of the World's Children: 2005," at www.unicef.org (accessed Spring 2005).

16. "Global Campaign Will Put Every Child in School," Global Education Campaign, Press Release, at www.campaignforeducation.org (accessed Fall 2004).

17. Available at www.who.int/archives/who50/en/prevention.htm (accessed Summer 2005).

18. Beth Gardiner, "U.N. Reports Progress on Health, Poverty," *Associated Press*, September 15, 2004.

19. See special issue of the *Journal of the American Medical Association*, "Tuberculosis," *JAMA* 293, no. 22 (June 2005): 2693–820.

20. Eli Sanders, "Rebuffing Bush, 132 Mayors Embrace Kyoto Rules," *New York Times*, May 14, 2005.

21. Justin M. Norton, "Mayors Sign 'Urban Environmental Accords,'" *Associated Press*, June 6, 2005.

22. James C. Bennett, "Networking Nation-States: The Coming Info-National Order," *The National Interest*, no. 74 (Winter 2003/2004): 17–30.

23. Douglas Jehl, "C.I.A. Is Reviewing Its Security Policy for Translators," *New York Times*, June 8, 2005.

24. "MI5 Expands to Meet Terror Threat," *BBC News*, March 5, 2004.

25. Matt Crenson, "Mathematicians Offer Help in Terror Fight," *Associated Press*, October 10, 2004.

26. Thomas L. Friedman, "From Gunpowder to the Next Big Bang," *New York Times*, November 4, 2005.

27. Steven Kull, "Public Perceptions of the Foreign Policy Positions of the Presidential Candidates," *The PIPA/Knowledge Networks Poll: The American Public on International Issues*, September 29, 2004, 2.

28. William C. Symonds, "America's Failure in Science Education," *Business Week Online*, March 15, 2004, at www.businessweek.com (accessed Summer 2004).

29. Institute of International Education, "Open Doors 2004: International Students in the U.S.," at www.opendoors.iienetwork.org (accessed Fall 2004).

30. Joseph S. Nye Jr., "You Can't Get Here From There," *New York Times*, November 29, 2004.

31. David B. Caruso, "Few Exchange Students in U.S. Schools," *Associated Press*, November 26, 2004.

32. Rob De Wijk, "The Limits of Military Power," *The Washington Quarterly* 25, no. 1 (2001): 75–92.

33. Stephen J. Hedges, "Critics: Pentagon in Blinders," *The Chicago Tribune*, June 6, 2005.

34. Hedges, "Critics: Pentagon in Blinders."

35. Hedges, "Critics: Pentagon in Blinders."

36. Carl Bildt, "Analysis: State-Building Lessons," *BBC News*, January 18, 2004.

37. Anthony C. Zinni, "A Military for the 21st Century: Lessons from the Recent Past," *INSS Strategic Forum*, no. 181 (July 2001): 6.

38. "Bush Military Bird Flu Role Slammed," CNN, October 5, 2005.

39. Michael Dziedzic, "Protection for Humanitarian Relief Operations," *INSS Strategic Forum*, no. 168 (December 1999): 1–5.

40. Anthony H. Cordesman, *Transnational Threats: The Emerging Strategic Lessons from the US Intervention in Iraq* (Washington, D.C.: Center for Strategic and International Studies: 2003), iv.

41. Paul Reynolds, "UN Plan Demands More Intervention," *BBC News*, November 29, 2004.

42. Simon P. Worden and Randall R. Correll, "Responsive Space and Strategic Information," *Defense Horizons*, no. 40, Center for Technology and National Security Policy (April 2004): 7.

43. Michael Scheuer, *Imperial Hubris: Why the West Is Losing the War on Terror* (London: Brassey's, 2004).

44. Jonathan Stevenson, "Counter-terrorism: Containment and Beyond," *Adelphi Paper*, no. 367, International Institute of Strategic Studies (2004).

45. Jeffrey Record, *Bounding the Global War on Terrorism* (Carlisle, Pa.: US Army War College, 2003), 2.

46. Philip Shenon, "Missile Defense for Airliners Is Possible Soon, Makers Say," *New York Times*, March 26, 2004.

47. Stephen E. Flynn and Lawrence M. Wein, "Think Inside the Box," *New York Times*, November 29, 2005.

48. "Canada Anti-Terror Plans 'Flawed,'" *BBC News*, March 30, 2004.

49. John Mintz and Joby Warrick, "U.S. Unprepared Despite Progress, Experts Say," *Washington Post*, November 8, 2004.

50. William K. Rashbaum and Judith Miller, "New York Police Take Broad Steps in Facing Terror," *New York Times*, February 15, 2004.

51. "UK Pushing for African Debt Plan," BBC, June 3, 2005.

52. "UN Launches Biggest Annual Appeal," *BBC News*, December 1, 2005.

SUGGESTED READING

Matthew Brzezinski, *Fortress America: On the Frontlines of Homeland Security—An Inside Look at the Coming Surveillance State* (New York: Bantam, 2004).

Kurt Campbell, Robert J. Einhorn, and Mitchell Reiss, *The Nuclear Tipping Point: Why States Reconsider Their Nuclear Choices* (Washington, D.C.: Brookings, 2004).

Stephen Flynn, *America the Vulnerable: How Our Government Is Failing to Protect Us from Terrorism* (New York: Harper Collins, 2004).

Thomas X. Hammes, *The Sling and the Stone: On War in the 21st Century* (Osceola, Wis.: Zenith Press, 2004).

G. John Ikenberry, *After Victory: Institutions, Strategic Restraint, and Rebuilding of Order after Major Wars* (Princeton, N.J.: Princeton University Press, 2000).

Kaz Mazurek, Margaret A. Winzer, and Czezlaw Majorek, *Education in a Global Society: A Comparative Perspective* (New York: Allyn and Bacon, 1999).

Joseph S. Nye, *The Paradox of American Power: Why the World's Only Superpower Can't Go It Alone* (Oxford: Oxford University Press, 2002).

Clyde Prestowitz, *Three Billion New Capitalists: The Great Shift of Wealth and Power to the East* (New York: Basic Books, 2005).

Scott D. Sagan and Kenneth N. Waltz, *The Spread of Nuclear Weapons: A Debate Renewed*, 2nd ed. (New York: W. W. Norton, 2002).

Fareed Zakaria, *The Future of Freedom: Illiberal Democracy at Home and Abroad* (New York: W. W. Norton, 2004).

Index

About the Author

Sean Kay is associate professor of politics and government at Ohio Wesleyan University, where he is chair of the international studies program and the Libuse L. Reed Professor. He specializes in international security, globalization, international organization, and American foreign policy. Dr. Kay is a Mershon Associate at the Mershon Center for International Security Studies at the Ohio State University and also a non-resident fellow in foreign and defense policy at the Eisenhower Institute in Washington, D.C. He was previously a visiting assistant professor in the government department at Dartmouth College and assistant professor at Rhodes College.

Kay received his Ph.D. from the University of Massachusetts at Amherst in international relations. Before joining academe, he was a visiting research fellow at the Institute for National Strategic Studies in the U.S. Department of Defense, where he also served as an adviser to the U.S. Department of State on NATO enlargement. He worked previously for the NATO Parliamentary Assembly in Brussels, Belgium.

Kay lectures frequently in the United States and Europe on global security trends and their strategic implications. He is the author of numerous articles, book chapters, and opinion pieces in major newspapers on international security issues. His previous books include *NATO and the Future of European Security* (Rowman & Littlefield) and the coedited volumes *NATO after Fifty Years* and *Limiting Institutions? The Challenge of Eurasian Security Governance.*